Resource Management in Real-Time Systems and Networks

Resource Management in Real-Time Systems and Networks

C. Siva Ram Murthy and G. Manimaran

The MIT Press
Cambridge, Massachusetts
London, England

This book was set in Times Roman by Windfall Software using ZzTEX.

Printed and bound in the United States of America.

Library of Congress Cataloging-in-Publication Data

Murthy, C. Siva Ram.
  Resource management in real-time systems and networks / C. Siva Ram Murthy and G. Manimaran.
    p.   cm.
  Includes bibliographical references and index.
  ISBN 0-262-13376-8 (hc.: alk. paper)
  1. Real-time programming. 2. Computer networks. I. Manimaran, G. II. Title.

QA76.54. M87   2001
005.2′73—dc21

00-056866

To my wife, Sharada,
my son, Chandrasekhar,
and my daughter, Sarita.

C. Siva Ram Murthy

Contents

Preface

Real-time computing and communication are enabling technologies for many current and future application areas. A list of these areas includes process control, agile manufacturing, avionics, air traffic control, multimedia, telecommunications (the information superhighway), medicine (e.g., telemedicine and intensive-care monitoring), and defense (e.g., command, control, and communications). In particular, most computer systems that handle safety-critical applications and many embedded computer systems are real-time systems. Further, real-time technology is becoming increasingly pervasive; that is, more and more of the world's infrastructure depends on it. Future real-time systems are expected to support an increasingly broader spectrum of applications ranging from multimedia applications, which have soft real-time constraints, to avionics and process control, which have both hard and soft real-time constraints.

Many future real-time systems are expected to be highly dynamic. These systems operate for long periods in fault-prone nondeterministic environments under timing constraints. They need to be robust while delivering high real-time performance. Thus there is a need for adaptive high-performance real-time systems that *dynamically* address real-time constraints and provide both a priori acceptable system-level performance guarantees and graceful degradation in the presence of failures and timing constraints. Parallel and distributed systems (high-performance systems) are natural candidates for satisfying such requirements because of their potential for high performance and reliability. Such high-performance real-time systems demand efficient techniques for resource management.

Most multimedia systems are distributed in nature and predominantly group-oriented. A distributed multimedia system is an integrated computing, communication, and information system. Multimedia applications are computing and data intensive and require performance guarantees in terms of end-to-end delay and end-to-end throughput, so they require high performance in terms of processing power and transmission speed. Therefore, efficient use of computing and network resources is very important. Achieving this goal requires coordination among computing and communication subsystems. The major functions of the computing subsystem are to schedule tasks to meet their deadline requirements and to ensure graceful degradation in the presence of overloads. The major functions of the communication subsystem are to (1) negotiate, control, and manage service contracts of the clients and (2) reserve, allocate, and release network resources according to the negotiated values. This demands efficient techniques for resource management in distributed multimedia systems to provide end-to-end Quality of Service (QoS) guarantees to the multimedia applications. Group-oriented multimedia applications demand efficient support for multicasting.

Objectives

The objective of this book is to introduce readers to the concepts and state-of-the-art research developments in the area of resource management in parallel and distributed real-time systems and networks. Unlike other textbooks on real-time systems, this book covers the entire spectrum of issues in resource management ranging from task scheduling, fault tolerance, and resource reclaiming (in multiprocessor real-time systems) to task scheduling and object-based task scheduling (in distributed real-time systems), to message scheduling, QoS routing, dependable communication, multicast communication, and medium access protocols (in real-time networks).

The unique feature of this book is that it gives algorithmic treatment to all the issues addressed, highlights the intuition behind each of the algorithms presented, explains most of the algorithms with the help of illustrative examples, and discusses the performance of algorithms along some important dimensions. A key feature of the book is that it takes into account the practical requirements of real-time applications and emphasizes the need for interaction between computing and communication subsystems, wherever applicable, together with fault tolerance requirements to meet the level of performance desired by the complete integrated system. Though input/output management is also an important issue, it is not discussed here, as it involves addressing issues such as storage representation and retrieval, which can be found elsewhere.

The book devotes a chapter to scheduling of object-based tasks in distributed real-time systems. This is becoming an issue of growing importance because of the development of reusable software components using object-based technology to conquer the complexity of large and complex real-time software. Two chapters present case studies of real-world problems.

To realize these goals, the entire book is divided into four parts: resource management in parallel (multiprocessor) real-time systems, resource management in distributed real-time systems, resource management in real-time networks, and case studies.

Scope

Part I: Resource Management in Multiprocessor Real-Time Systems

• Chapter 2 introduces the basic results of real-time task scheduling in uniprocessor and multiprocessor systems and discusses different scheduling paradigms, along with some well-known algorithms under each of these paradigms.

• Chapter 3 presents a model for dynamic scheduling of tasks, motivates the need for resource reclaiming, and discusses several well-known resource reclaiming algorithms.

• Chapter 4 introduces the basic concepts of fault tolerance in real-time systems and discusses different fault-tolerant scheduling approaches as well as some well-known algorithms under each of these approaches.

Part II: Resource Management in Distributed Real-Time Systems

• Chapter 5 introduces a generic architecture for resource management in distributed real-time systems that encompasses three components: (1) local scheduling, (2) global scheduling, and (3) message scheduling. Further, it discusses the components of global scheduling—transfer policy, selection policy, information policy, and location policy—in detail for several well-known algorithms.

• Chapter 6 introduces the object-based task model, programming model, and concurrency model and presents algorithms for scheduling object-based tasks in distributed real-time systems. It also discusses the dynamic path-based paradigm and its scheduling issues for object-based real-time tasks.

Part III: Resource Management in Real-Time Networks

• Chapter 7 introduces a resource management architecture for real-time networks that deals with issues such as real-time channel establishment, routing, call admission control, rate control, scheduling, and switching and discusses all these issues in detail (except for routing).

• Chapter 8 introduces the QoS routing problem in wide area networks and discusses several route selection approaches used for establishing real-time channels. It also discusses dependable real-time channels.

• Chapter 9 introduces the fundamentals of group communication, such as types of groups, and discusses the issues involved in multicasting, namely, group addressing, multicast routing, and traffic control in real-time networks. Both constrained and unconstrained versions of static and dynamic multicast routing algorithms are discussed. The chapter also presents multicasting protocols in the Internet and asynchronous transfer mode networks.

• Chapter 10 deals with resource management in multiple access networks, addressing controlled access and contention-based channel access protocols. It discusses both probabilistic and deterministic guarantee protocols as well as guarantee-based protocols in switched multiple access networks.

Part IV: Case Studies

To reinforce the fundamental concepts presented in the three previous parts of the book, two case studies, distributed air defense system (chapter 11) and air traffic control system (chapter 12), are presented. These chapters describe complete solutions to these distributed real-time problems using the concepts presented earlier.

Target Audience

This book is intended as a textbook for senior undergraduate and graduate-level courses on real-time systems for computer science or computer engineering students. The first, second, and third parts of the book can constitute a portion of an advanced-level course on operating systems, distributed computing, and computer networks, respectively. In addition, chapters 4 and 8 can be used as part of a course on fault-tolerant computing. Students who intend to work in the area of real-time computing should read all of parts I and II; those who intend to work in the area of real-time communication should read all of part III and attempt all the exercises.

In addition, the book will be valuable to professionals in the field and researchers in other areas who want an introduction to current research frontiers in real-time computing and networking. The book is descriptive and adopts an algorithmic approach throughout. It assumes that readers have some familiarity with data structures and algorithms, operating systems, and computer networks.

Acknowledgments

We would like to thank the following students, who have contributed mightily to this project: R. Sriram, Samphel Norden, M. Shashidhar, Anand Manikutty, I. Santoshkumar, Machiraju Vijay, K. Mahesh, Indranil Gupta, Anita Mittal, S. Balaji, G. Mohan, and Aaron Striegel. We would like to give special thanks to Professors V. Rajaraman, Arun Somani, Krithi Ramamritham, C. M. Krishna, and Parameshwaran Ramanathan for their encouragement throughout this endeavor. Thanks are also due to the Ministry of Human Resource Development, New Delhi, which provided funds to prepare this book for publication. We would also like to acknowledge the support of the Indian Institute of Technology, Madras, and Iowa State University. Last but not least we are thankful to Douglas Sery, computer science acquisitions editor, and his colleagues at MIT Press for their excellent work in producing this book.

1 Introduction

1.1 Real-Time Systems

The consistent decrease in the cost of hardware has led to the employment of computers in many applications. As a consequence, the complexity of modern computer systems has increased proportionally, and more effort is needed to maintain the dependability of these computer systems. Systems in which the complexity exists in the dimension of time are called *real-time systems,* defined as those systems in which the correctness of the system depends not only on the logical result of computation, but also on the time at which the results are produced [4]. Examples of current real-time systems range from very simple microcontrollers in embedded systems to highly sophisticated and complex systems such as air traffic control and avionics.

A real-time system usually has a mission to achieve. A typical real-time system consists of a *controlling system,* a *controlled system,* and the *environment,* as shown in figure 1.1. The controlling system is a computer that acquires information about the environment through input devices (sensors), performs certain computations on the data, and activates the actuators through some controls. Because a mismatch between the state of the environment as perceived by the controlling system and the actual state of the environment can lead to disastrous results, periodic monitoring of the environment as well as timely processing of the sensed information is necessary. Thus, *time* is the most precious resource to manage in real-time systems.

Consider a mission of reaching an intended destination safely by car. Here, the controlling system is the human driver, the controlled system is the car, the operating environment is the road conditions and other cars on the road, the sensors are the eyes and ears of the driver, and the actuators are the wheels, engine, and brakes of the car. The various means through which the actuators can be controlled are the accelerator, steering wheel, and brake pedal. Supposing the controlling system is a computer instead of a human driver, the sensors are cameras, infrared receiver, and laser telemeter.

1.1.1 Real-Time Tasks

Computations occurring in a real-time system that have timing constraints are called *real-time tasks.* The computer should execute the real-time tasks so that each task will meet its timeliness requirement. In other words, a real-time task should finish its execution before a certain time, called the *deadline.*

A real-time application usually consists of a set of cooperating tasks activated at regular intervals and/or on particular events. A task typically senses the state of the system, performs certain computations, and if necessary sends commands to change the state of the system. Tasks in a real-time system are of two types, *periodic tasks* and *aperiodic tasks* [6].

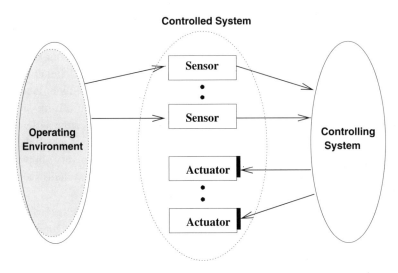

Figure 1.1
A typical real-time system

1.1.1.1   Periodic Tasks   Periodic tasks are time-driven and recur at regular intervals called the *period*. Characteristics of a periodic task such as its period and worst-case computation time are known a priori. Most sensory processing in real-time applications is periodic. For example, the temperature monitor of a nuclear reactor must monitor the temperature periodically and be able to detect any changes such that coolant can be circulated if the temperature exceeds a threshold. Some periodic tasks exist from the point of system initialization. The temperature monitor of a nuclear reactor is an example of such a permanent periodic task, occurring from the moment the reactor goes online. Others may come into existence dynamically. The computation in radars that monitors a particular flight begins when the aircraft enters an air traffic control region and ends when the aircraft leaves the region; it is an example of a dynamically created periodic task.

1.1.1.2   Aperiodic Tasks   Aperiodic tasks are event-driven and activated only when certain events occur. Characteristics of aperiodic tasks such as ready time, worst-case computation time, and deadline are known only when the task arrives. Aperiodic tasks with known minimum interarrival times are known as *sporadic tasks*. Most of the dynamic processing requirement in real-time applications is aperiodic. For example, in an aircraft control system, the controllers activate various tasks depending on what appears on their monitors; such tasks are therefore aperiodic. Similarly, in an industrial control system, the robot that monitors and controls various processes may have to perform path planning dynamically, which results in activation of aperiodic tasks. Another system with aperiodic tasks is one that monitors the condition of several patients in an intensive care unit of a hospital, which signals actions that have to be taken as soon as the condition of a patient changes.

1.1.1.3 Other Task Requirements In addition to timing constraints, tasks in a real-time application can also have other requirements common to the tasks in traditional non-real-time applications [6]. A task may require access to certain resources other than the processor, such as input/output (I/O) devices, communication buffers, data structures, and files. Systems can offer access to a resource either in *shared mode* or in *exclusive mode*. In shared mode, more than one task is allowed to access a particular resource, whereas in exclusive mode, at most one task can access that resource at any point of time. A *resource constraint* exists between two tasks if both require the same resource and access to that resource is exclusive. Tasks can impose *precedence constraints* on other tasks, meaning that the results of some tasks are required before other tasks can start their execution. Another requirement, that tasks be *fault-tolerant,* is important in that it enables the continued operation of the system even in the presence of faults.

1.2 Multidimensional View of Real-Time Systems

The full definition of a real-time system takes on various subtleties depending on the following system dimensions [9]: (1) the granularity of deadline and laxity of the tasks, (2) the strictness of deadlines, (3) the reliability requirements of the system, (4) the size of the system and degree of interaction among components, and (5) the characteristics of the environment in which the system operates.

1.2.1 Granularity of Deadline and Laxity of Tasks

If the time between a task's activation and its deadline is short, then the deadline is *tight* (i.e., the granularity of the deadline is small). This implies that the system reaction time has to be short and that the scheduling algorithm that has to be executed must be fast and very simple. Tight time constraints may arise even when the deadline for a task is far away from its activation time (i.e., the granularity of deadline is large) when the task requires a large amount of computation. In other words, even large granularity deadlines can be tight when the *laxity* (deadline minus computation time minus current time) of a task is small. In many real-time systems, tight timing constraints predominate, and consequently designers focus on developing very fast and simple techniques for reacting to this type of activation.

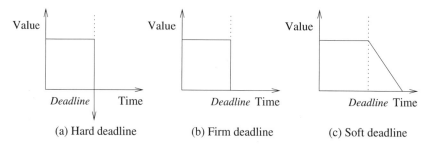

Figure 1.2
Different types of deadlines

1.2.2   Strictness of Deadlines

Real-time systems are broadly classified into three categories based on the nature of the deadlines they face: (1) *hard* real-time systems, in which the consequences of not executing a task before its deadline may be catastrophic; (2) *firm* real-time systems, in which the result produced by a task ceases to be useful as soon as the deadline expires, but the consequences of not meeting the deadline are not very severe; and (3) *soft* real-time systems, in which the utility of results produced by a task decreases over time after the deadline expires [6]. Figure 1.2 depicts the relationship between value and time for different types of deadlines. Examples of hard real-time systems are those involved in avionic control and nuclear plant control. Online transaction processing applications, such as airline reservation and banking are examples of firm real-time systems, and telephone switching systems and multimedia applications are examples of soft real-time systems.

1.2.3   Reliability Requirements

Many real-time systems operate under stringent reliability requirements. That is, they involve hard real-time tasks, and the failure to meet the deadlines of those tasks may result in catastrophic consequences. An off-line analysis is usually conducted for such systems to ensure that they meet their deadlines. Such an analysis should be able to guarantee that all critical tasks always meet their deadline (a 100% guarantee), subject to certain workload and failure assumptions. Designers and developers of some types of real-time systems may not know all the characteristics of all critical tasks a priori and hence cannot perform off-line analysis; thus they cannot guarantee that all hard deadlines will be met. For such systems, an on-line schedulability analysis must be performed.

1.2.4 Size of System and Degree of Coordination

Real-time systems vary considerably in size and complexity. In most current real-time systems, the entire system code is loaded into memory, or if there are well-defined phases, each phase is loaded just prior to the beginning of the phase. In many applications, subsystems are highly independent of each other, and cooperation among tasks is limited. The ability to load entire subsystems' code into memory and to limit task interactions simplifies many aspects of building and analyzing real-time systems. For the next generation of real-time systems, however, which are expected to be large and complex, having completely memory-resident code and highly independent tasks may not always be practical. Consequently, increased system size and task coordination give rise to many problems that must be addressed and complicate the notion of predictability, which is defined later.

1.2.5 Environment

The environment in which a real-time system is to operate plays an important role in the design of the system. Many environments are well defined and deterministic. These environments give rise to small, *static real-time systems* in which all deadlines can be guaranteed a priori, since the characteristics of tasks are known a priori.

The approaches taken in relatively small, static systems, however, do not scale to larger, much more complicated, and less controllable environments. Many future-generation applications will be large, complex, distributed, and dynamic; contain many types of timing constraints; need to operate in fault-prone highly nondeterministic environments; and evolve over a long system lifetime. Systems that handle such applications are called *dynamic real-time systems.*

1.2.6 Predictability

The characteristics of the environment decide whether a real-time system is static or dynamic. Depending on the dimensions discussed in the previous sections, many different system designs are possible. However, one common denominator that is expected from a real-time system regardless of variations in design is *predictability* [9]. The behavior of a real-time system must be predictable, which means, in this context, that given certain assumptions about workload and failures, it should be possible to show at the time of design that all the timing constraints of the application will be met. The notion of predictability has a somewhat different meaning and involves somewhat different criteria depending on whether a system is static or dynamic.

The concept of predictability is tied closely to the idea of reliability, discussed in section 1.2.3. For static systems, since the characteristics of periodic tasks are known a priori, guarantees can be given, at design time, that all their timing constraints will be satisfied [6]. Static systems therefore have predictability at the time of design; one can accurately predict their reliability before the system becomes operational. The same guarantees cannot be given for dynamic real-time systems, however, since the characteristics of all tasks are not necessarily known a priori. Consequently, one cannot predict at design time which tasks will meet their timing constraints and which will not. Dynamic systems therefore have very little, if any, predictability at the design stage.

In dynamic systems, the necessary deadline guarantees can be given only at run time, using an on-line schedulability analysis. Such a schedulability analysis determines whether or not the constraints of a given task can be satisfied without jeopardizing the deadline guarantees provided to other tasks. If they can, then the task is admitted into the system [6]. (If the constraints cannot be satisfied, the task is rejected [6], and the system may invoke some recovery action.) Predictability in the case of a dynamic real-time system means that once a task is admitted into the system, its deadline guarantee is never violated as long as the assumptions under which the task was admitted hold.

It is important to note that deadline guarantees are possible only if task characteristics are known. It is difficult to obtain exact information on task characteristics for dynamic real-time systems, so for the purposes of schedulability analysis, worst-case values are assumed or derived from extensive simulations, testing, and other means. These values may not be "true" worst-case values, and the actual values may exceed them on some rare occasions. Such an event is called *specification violation* [2]. Real-time systems should monitor such events and take recovery actions when they occur.

In conclusion, it is not really possible to guarantee the real-time performance of a system because we cannot guarantee that the hardware will not fail and the software is bug free or that the operating conditions will not violate the specified design limits [7]. True system "predictability" is therefore never a realistic possibility. One can hope only to minimize the probability of failure in the system one builds. The relevant question is, of course, how to build systems in such a way that we can have as much confidence as possible that they meet specifications at acceptable costs. In real-time system design, one should attempt to allocate resources judiciously to make certain that the system can satisfy any critical timing constraints with the available resources, assuming that the hardware and software function correctly and the environment does not stress the system beyond what it is designed to handle. The fact that, with a nonzero probability, the hardware and software may not function correctly or the operating conditions imposed by the environment may exceed the design limits does not give the designer license to increase the odds of failure by not allocating resources carefully to meet the critical timing constraints. It is certainly not possible to guarantee anything outside human control, but one should control those things to the full degree that one can [7].

1.2.7 Common Misconceptions about Real-Time Systems

There have been some common misconceptions about real-time systems. Here we discuss some of the important ones [7, 8].

Real-time computing is equivalent to fast computing. The objective of fast computing is to minimize average response time of a given set of tasks. The objective of real-time computing, in contrast, is to meet the individual timing requirements of each of the tasks involved. Rather than speed (which is a relative concept), the most important property that a real-time system should have is predictability. Though fast computing is certainly helpful in meeting stringent timing constraints, it does not in itself guarantee predictability. Factors other than fast hardware or algorithms—such as processor architecture, implementation language, and environment—determine predictability. To negate the claim that real-time computing is equivalent to fast computing, the following question can be asked. Given a set of stringent real-time requirements and an implementation using the fastest hardware and software possible, can one show that the specified timing behavior is indeed being achieved for all required tasks? As we have seen above, testing is not the answer, because it cannot offer performance guarantees. Therefore, predictability, not speed, is the foremost goal in real-time system design.

Real-time programming is assembly coding, priority interrupt programming, and writing device drivers. To meet stringent timing constraints, current practice in real-time computing relies heavily on machine-level optimization techniques. These techniques are labor intensive and sometimes introduce additional timing assumptions on which the correctness of an implementation depends. The reliance on clever hand coding and difficult-to-trace timing assumptions is a major source of bugs in real-time programming. A primary objective in real-time systems research is in fact to automate, by exploiting optimizing techniques and scheduling theory, the synthesis of highly efficient code and customized schedulers through timing specifications. On the other hand, although assembly language programming and writing device drivers are aspects of real-time computing, they do not constitute open scientific problems except in their automation.

Real-time systems operate in a static environment. Depending on the operating mode, a real-time system may have to satisfy different sets of timing constraints at different times. For example, the takeoff, flying at high altitude, and landing are the three different phases of a flight mission. In a flight control system, these phases are activated dynamically, and the set of tasks corresponding to each of these phases is different. Also, many applications, such as industrial process control, air traffic control, and life support systems, operate in nondeterministic environments, which often results in activation of aperiodic tasks and thereby demands for dynamic real-time systems. For example, in an industrial control system, the robot that monitors and controls various processes may encounter obstacles or may have to pass through a dark region as a result of the nondeterministic nature of the environment, resulting in activation of a set of tasks to deal with these situations.

The problems in real-time system design have all been solved in other areas of computer science. Although real-time system design should certainly try to exploit the problem solving techniques developed in more established research areas, real-time systems present unique problems that have not been solved in any other area. For example, performance analysis in computer science has been mostly concerned with assessing the average values of performance parameters, whereas an important consideration in real-time system design is whether timing constraints can be met. Queueing models and randomized algorithms traditionally make use of convenient stochastic assumptions that are justified in many areas. Analytical results based on these assumptions may be quite useless, however, for many real-time applications. Similarly, the combinatorial scheduling in operations research deals mostly with one-shot tasks—that is, each task needs to be scheduled only once—whereas in real-time systems, tasks are periodic, aperiodic, or both, and these tasks may have synchronization and resource constraints that are quite different or not found in conventional task scheduling. The general synthesis problem of arbitrary timing behavior certainly requires new techniques not found in other areas.

1.3   Computing Systems and Communication Networks

A controlling system is a computer, which could be a uniprocessor, a multiprocessor, or a distributed system. A controlling system may also have some associated resources. As its name implies, a *uniprocessor system* has only one processor for executing tasks. In a *multiprocessor system,* multiple processors communicate either through a shared memory (referred to as a *shared memory multiprocessor*) or through message passing (called a *distributed memory multiprocessor*). In a shared memory multiprocessor, the processors are connected to a set of memory modules via an interconnection network such as shared bus, crossbar, or multistage networks (figure 1.3(a)). The processors communicate by writing into and reading from the shared memory. In shared memory multiprocessors, the

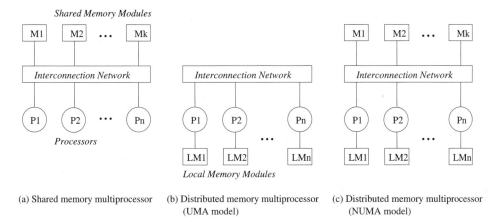

(a) Shared memory multiprocessor   (b) Distributed memory multiprocessor   (c) Distributed memory multiprocessor
                                     (UMA model)   (NUMA model)

Figure 1.3
Multiprocessor systems

time it takes to access any memory location is approximately the same, since only shared memory is present, so this type of multiprocessor is also called a uniform memory access (UMA) multiprocessor. In a distributed memory multiprocessor, each processor has its own local memory and is usually connected to the others using an interconnection network such as hypercube, mesh, or their variants (figure 1.3(b)). The processors communicate by explicitly sending messages from one to another. A third type of multiprocessor has both shared memory and local memory, and the processors are connected to a set of memory modules (shared memory) through an interconnection network such as shared bus or crossbar (figure 1.3(c)). This type is called a nonuniform memory access (NUMA) multiprocessor. In NUMA, the time taken to access a memory location varies widely depending on whether the location is in local memory or in shared memory—thus, the name NUMA.

A *distributed system* has multiple nodes connected either through a multihop (point-to-point) network or through a multiple access network. Each node can be a uniprocessor, shared memory multiprocessor, or distributed memory multiprocessor. The nodes communicate by sending messages from one node to another. In a *multihop network* (figure 1.4(a)) a message may pass through multiple intermediate nodes before reaching the destination node. The presence of multiple disjoint paths between nodes in multihop networks makes them robust to link and node failures. Also, because it is possible to support simultaneous transmission of messages on different links, these networks provide a higher total through-put [3]. Internet is a well-known example of a multihop network. In a *multiple access*

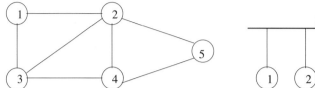
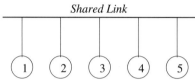

(a) Multihop network with 5 nodes   (b) Multiple access bus network with 5 nodes

Figure 1.4
Types of networks

network (figure 1.4(b)), all the nodes share a single link for communication. This means that at any given time, only one node can transmit. Multiple access networks can tolerate node failures but may not tolerate link failures. Ethernet is a well-known example of a multiple access network.

1.4   Issues in Real-Time Systems

Designing a real-time system requires dealing with a number of issues. Some of the most important are (1) resource management, (2) architecture, and (3) software. Resource management issues deal with scheduling, resource reclaiming, fault-tolerance, and communication. Architecture issues involve processor architecture, network architecture, and I/O architecture. Software issues encompass specification and verification of real-time systems, programming languages, and databases. Each type of issue is briefly discussed below. As its title indicates, this book focuses on resource management issues.

1.4.1   Resource Management Issues

1.4.1.1   Task Scheduling   Meeting task deadlines is of great importance in real-time systems, because failure to meet task deadlines may result in severe consequences, possibly loss of human life. Scheduling of tasks involves the allocation of processors (including resources) and time to tasks in such a way that certain performance requirements are met [4]. The scheduling algorithms have to satisfy not only the timing constraints of tasks, but also the resource constraints and/or precedence constraints among tasks, if any. Similarly, providing predictable intertask communication is also of great significance in real-time systems, because unpredictable delays in the delivery of messages can affect the completion time of tasks participating in the message communication.

property	preemptive	non-preemptive
Schedulability	High	Low
Processor utilization	High	Low
Context switch overheads	High	Low
Blocking for resource	Yes	No
Latency to new tasks	Low	High
Understandability	Difficult	Better
Software testing	Difficult	Easier

Figure 1.5
Comparison of preemptive and non-preemptive scheduling

Preemptive versus Non-preemptive Scheduling   Task scheduling can be either preemptive or non-preemptive. In *non-preemptive scheduling,* once a task starts executing on a processor, it finishes; that is, no other task can use the processor between the start and finish times of the task. In *preemptive scheduling,* on the other hand, a task that has started executing on a processor need not finish on the same start. Another task (which might have higher priority) can preempt it, and the interrupted task can be resumed later. Preemptive scheduling offers better schedulability than its non-preemptive counterpart, but because of the context switches involved, preemptive scheduling is associated with higher overheads than non-preemptive scheduling. Figure 1.5 compares these two scheduling approaches.

Task-Scheduling Paradigms   Several task-scheduling paradigms emerge, depending on (1) whether a system performs schedulability analysis, (2) if it does, whether it is done statically or dynamically, and (3) whether the result of the analysis itself produces a schedule according to which tasks are dispatched at run time. Based on this, the following classes of scheduling algorithms have been identified [4]:

• *Static table-driven approaches.* These perform static schedulability analysis, and the system uses the resulting schedule, usually stored in the form of a table, to decide *when* a task must begin its execution.

• *Static priority-driven preemptive approaches.* These perform static schedulability analysis but no explicit schedule is constructed. At run time, tasks are executed in highest-priority-first order.

• *Dynamic planning-based approaches.* Unlike in the previous two approaches, schedulability of a task is checked at run time, that is, a dynamically arriving task is accepted for execution if it is found to be schedulable. Once scheduled, a task is *guaranteed* to meet its performance requirements. The schedulability analysis results in a schedule that is used to decide when a task can begin its execution.

• *Dynamic best-effort approaches.* Here, no schedulability check is done. The system tries to do its best to meet requirements (deadlines) of tasks. Any task may be aborted during its execution, since the system gives no guarantee for its completion.

Performance Metrics   Classical task-scheduling theory typically employs metrics such as minimizing schedule length and the sum of completion times. Traditional (non-real-time tasks) load-balancing algorithms in a distributed system attempt to maximize throughput and fairness and minimize response time. In real-time systems, these metrics have secondary importance, since they do not directly address the fact that individual tasks have deadlines. The most important performance metric in real-time systems is the *schedulability* of tasks, defined as the system's ability to schedule real-time tasks before their deadlines.

In static scheduling, the performance requirement is that every task in the system meet its deadline. In dynamic scheduling, however, the system may be unable to meet the deadlines of all tasks because it lacks knowledge about future task arrivals. Therefore, the metric used in a dynamic real-time system is the *guarantee ratio* [5], defined as the percentage of the total number of tasks that have arrived in the system for which deadlines are met. Any dynamic real-time task-scheduling algorithm has improving the guarantee ratio as its objective.

1.4.1.2   Resource Reclaiming   *Resource reclaiming* [5] is a run time issue, and it refers to the problem of employing resources (processor times and resource times) left unused by a task when

• it executes at less than its worst-case computation time. The actual execution of a task can require less time than its worst-case computation time because of data-dependent loops and conditional statements in the task code and because of architectural features of the system, such as cache hits and branch predictions.

• it is deleted from the current schedule. Tasks are deleted when extra tasks are initially scheduled to account for fault tolerance; that is, in a fault-tolerant schedule, when the primary version of a task completes execution successfully, the backup versions need not be executed.

When a task is deleted or executes more quickly than the time allotted, the resource-reclaiming mechanism informs the scheduler of the amount of time reclaimed so that the scheduler can incorporate this time when scheduling new tasks. Thus, the more time reclaimed, the better is schedulability.

1.4.1.3 Fault Tolerance Fault tolerance is informally defined as a system's ability to deliver the expected service even in the presence of faults. A common misconception about real-time computing is that fault tolerance is orthogonal to real-time requirements [6]. It is often assumed that a system's dependability requirements can be addressed independent of its timing constraints. This assumption, however, does not consider the distinguishing characteristic of real-time systems: the timeliness of correct results. In other words, a real-time system may fail to function correctly either because of errors in its hardware, software, or both, or because it fails to respond in time to meet the timing requirements its environment imposes. Hence, a real-time system can be viewed as one that must deliver the expected service in a timely manner even in the presence of faults. This makes fault tolerance an inherent requirement of any real-time system.

The basic principle of fault-tolerant design is *redundancy*. Redundancy, however, costs both money and time. Therefore, the design of a fault-tolerant system should be optimized by trading off the amount of redundancy built into it against the desired level of fault tolerance.

1.4.1.4 Real-Time Communication The term *real-time communication* is used to describe any kind of communication in which the messages involved have timing constraints [1]. Real-time messages are broadly classified into two categories: periodic and aperiodic. *Periodic messages* are generated in communicating periodic tasks. The periodicity of the message stream spaces the arrival times of periodic messages. If a periodic message encounters a delay that is longer than its period, it is considered to be lost in transmission. Periodic messages are often used for sending sensory data. The intertask communication between periodic tasks is also periodic. *Aperiodic messages* are generated in communicating aperiodic tasks. As opposed to the deterministic nature of periodic messages, the arrival pattern of aperiodic messages is stochastic in nature. The characteristics of aperiodic messages, like those of aperiodic tasks, are known only when they arrive. Each aperiodic message has an end-to-end deadline before which it must reach its intended destination. If it fails to reach its destination prior to this deadline, it is considered to be lost.

A distributed real-time system guarantees the timely availability of computational results only if the underlying network supports timely delivery of messages. That is, if the time at which a message is sent and the length of the message are known, it should be possible to predict the time at which the message will be delivered at the destination.

Such a requirement can be satisfied only if the network ensures predictable communication delays [1]. Thus, to ensure the safety of a real-time application implemented on a distributed real-time system, the tasks (as well as the messages) must be properly scheduled on the nodes (as well as on the communication channels) of the distributed system so that their timing constraints and other requirements are satisfied.

As mentioned earlier, the network in a real-time system can be multihop or multiple access. The fundamental difference between message scheduling in multihop networks and multiple access networks is that a node in a multihop network can choose a link among many links to which it is connected to route (schedule) messages, whereas in a multiple access network, multiple nodes contend for a single link.

1.4.2 Architectural Issues

Many real-time systems can be viewed as a three-stage pipe: data acquisition, data processing, and output to actuators and/or displays [7]. A real-time system architecture must be designed in such a way that all the three components provide predictability. For the first and last components, the architecture must provide extensive I/O capabilities while providing fast and reliable computations and communications for the second component. Thus, the design of a real-time architecture involves issues at three levels: the computing subsystem, the communication subsystem, and the I/O subsystem.

1.4.2.1 Computing Subsystem   At the level of the computing subsystem, each processor must provide predictability in executing real-time tasks, handling interrupts, and interacting with the environment. One might try to accomplish this by making operations like instruction execution, memory access, and context switching more predictable. Real-time systems seldom use virtual memory to do this, because page faults cause unpredictable delays in accessing memories. Similarly, designers of real-time systems also try to avoid the use of caches because uncertainty of cache hit/miss causes unpredictable memory access delays. In fact, the superscalar feature (execution of multiple instructions at a time), data pipelines, and branch prediction strategies commonly available in today's off-the-shelf microprocessors make it very difficult to achieve predictability at the level of the computing subsystem [6]. In the presence of such uncertainties, one has to take the worst-case situation (for memory access and branch prediction, etc.) while deciding the worst-case computation time of tasks.

1.4.2.2 Communication Subsystem   At the level of the communication subsystem, internode communication and fault tolerance are the two main issues that make it difficult to achieve predictability. These issues are unavoidable, because the high performance and high reliability of distributed systems make them attractive for real-time applications. Irrespective of its exact topology, a network should support scalability, ease of implementation, and reliability. The low-level function of the network subsystem involves packet processing, routing, error control, flow control, support for meeting message deadlines, timer management, and housekeeping. Since support of these issues impedes the execution of application tasks, nodes in a distributed system usually have a custom-designed processor for handling these activities, often referred to as the *network processor,* whose main function is to execute operations necessary to deliver messages from a source task to its intended recipient(s) in a timely manner [6]. To achieve reliable delivery of messages, the network processor may have to select primary and alternate routes. The network processor must also have support for multiple levels of interrupts to manage messages with different priority levels. Additionally, it must implement buffer management policies that maximize utilization of buffer space but guarantee the availability of buffers to the highest-priority messages.

1.4.2.3 Input/Output Subsystem   The I/O subsystem in a real-time system is also a very important component. A real-time system can process data no faster than it can acquire data from the input devices such as sensors and operators. Because of the timing and reliability requirements associated with the real-time I/O devices, the solutions proposed for accessing data from and sending data to devices associated with non-real-time systems, such as magnetic disks and tapes, are inapplicable to real-time I/O devices [6]. Real-time I/O devices are usually distributed and managed by relatively simple and reliable controllers. In some systems, the I/O devices are clustered together, and a controller is assigned to manage access to the devices in each cluster. Moreover, to improve both accessibility and performance, there must be multiple paths to these I/O devices [6].

1.4.2.4 Desirable Architectural Features   Any architectural design for a real-time system should ideally adopt a synergistic approach in which the theory, the operating system, and the hardware are all developed with the single goal of achieving real-time constraints in a cost-effective and integrated fashion. The following are some of the desirable features that a real-time architecture should support [7]:

• *Fast and reliable communication.* Hardware support for routing, handling priority levels, buffer management, and timer management is important.

• *Error handling.* It is essential to have hardware support for speedy error detection, reconfiguration, and recovery. This includes self-checking circuitry, voters, system monitors, and so on.

• *Scheduling algorithms.* To support real-time scheduling algorithms, architectures may need to support fast preemptability, sufficient number of priority levels, efficient support for data structures like priority queues, and sophisticated communication and I/O scheduling, among other features.

• *Real-time operating systems.* Real-time operating systems will benefit the system if the underlying hardware provides support for real-time protocols; multiple contexts; real-time memory management, including caching and garbage collection; interrupt handling; clock synchronization; and so on.

• *Real-time language features.* Special-purpose architectures designed to support real-time programming languages more explicitly and efficiently can provide immense benefits to real-time systems. For instance, language constructs implemented in hardware aid in accurately estimating worst-case execution time of tasks.

1.4.3   Software Issues

1.4.3.1   Requirements, Specification, and Verification   The demands placed on a real-time system arise from the needs of the application and are often called *requirements.* Determining the precise requirements placed on a system is very important and can be accomplished only with very good knowledge and experience of the application. Large systems often fail because of errors in defining requirements.

Requirements are often divided into two classes: *functional requirements,* which define the operations of the system and their effects, and *nonfunctional requirements,* such as timing properties. Since both logical correctness and timeliness are important in real-time systems, their functional and nonfunctional requirements must be precisely defined and together used to construct their specifications.

A *specification* is a mathematical statement of the properties a system must exhibit. A specification should be abstract, so that (1) it can be checked for conformity with the requirement and (2) its properties can be examined independently of the way in which it will be implemented, that is, as a program executing on a particular system. This means that a specification should not enforce any decisions about the structure of the software, the programming language to be used, or the kind of system on which the program will be executed: These are implementation decisions.

The fundamental challenge in the specification and verification of real-time systems is how to incorporate the timing constraints [7]. Methods must be devised for including timing constraints in specifications and for establishing that a particular system satisfies such specifications. The usual approaches for specifying computing system behavior entail enumerating events or actions in which the system participates and describing orders in which they can occur. It is not well understood how to extend such approaches for real-time constraints, nor is it well understood how to extend programming notations to allow the programmer to specify computations that are constrained by real time.

1.4.3.2 Real-Time Languages   As the complexity of real-time systems increases, high demand will be placed upon the programming abstractions provided by languages. The following are some of the desirable features a real-time language should support [7]:

• *Management of time.* (1) The language constructs should support the expression of timing constraints. (2) The programming environment should provide the programmer with the primitives to control and keep track of the resource utilizations; this includes the ability to develop programs with predictable performance in terms of time. (3) Language constructs should support the use of scheduling algorithms.

• *Schedulability analysis.* With proper support for the management of time, it may be possible to perform schedulability checks at compile time.

• *Reusable real-time software modules.* Software reusability is becoming an important issue because of the complexity associated with large software. Since future real-time systems are expected to be very complex, it is desirable if the language provides support for development of reusable real-time software modules.

• *Distributed programming and fault tolerance.* The problem of predicting the timing behavior of real-time programs in distributed systems is growing in importance as the number of distributed real-time applications increases.

A few formal languages capable of dealing with timing constraints have been developed. These languages have been used to specify and verify small-scale real-time systems. There is, however, a serious need for better understanding of the fundamental problems in the area and their scalability. Such an understanding will lead to better specification languages that can be used for building large real-time systems [7].

1.4.3.3 Real-Time Databases   Many real-time applications require database systems that support stringent timing constraints to help these applications manage large volumes of data and information sharing among tasks. Applying existing database technology to real-time systems presents a number of difficulties, however, the chief one being that conventional database architectures are not designed to provide the performance levels (such as response time guarantees) real-time systems require [6]. Most conventional database systems are disk based and use transaction logging and two-phase locking protocols to ensure transaction atomicity and serializability. These characteristics preserve data integrity, but they also result in relatively slow and unpredictable response times. In a real-time database system, important issues include transaction scheduling to meet deadlines, explicit semantics for specifying timing and other constraints, and checking the database system's ability to meet transaction deadlines during application initialization.

1.5   Summary

• Real-time systems are defined as those systems in which the system's correctness depends not only on the logical result of computation, but also on the time at which the results are produced.

• A typical real-time system consists of a controlling system, a controlled system, and the environment. The controlling system is a computer, which could be a uniprocessor, multiprocessor, or a distributed system.

• Real-time systems are broadly classified into three categories based on the nature of the deadlines involved: hard real-time systems, firm real-time systems, and soft real-time systems.

• Tasks in a real-time system are of two types, periodic tasks and aperiodic tasks. Periodic tasks are time-driven, whereas aperiodic tasks are event-driven.

• The notion of predictability is very important in real-time systems. However, there is no single clear definition for predictability, and its meaning depends on the application.

• There have been some common misconceptions about real-time systems: (1) Real-time computing is equivalent to fast computing. (2) Real-time programming is assembly programming and writing device drivers. (3) Real-time systems operate in a static environment. (4) The problems in real-time system design have all been solved in other areas of computer science.

• Some of the most important issues in the design of real-time systems are scheduling, resource reclaiming, fault tolerance, communication, architectural issues, system specification and verification, programming languages, and databases.

References

[1] C. M. Aras, J. F. Kurose, D. S. Reeves, and H. Schulzrinne. "Real-time communication in packet-switched networks." *Proc. IEEE,* vol. 82, no. 1, pp. 122–139, Jan. 1994.

[2] S. Chodrow, F. Jahanian, and M. Donner. "Run-time monitoring of real-time systems." In *Proc. Real-Time Systems Symp.,* pp. 74–83, 1991.

[3] D. D. Kandlur, K. G. Shin, and D. Ferrari. "Real-time communication in multihop networks." *IEEE Trans. Parallel and Distributed Systems,* vol. 5, no. 10, pp. 1044–1056, Oct. 1994.

[4] K. Ramamritham and J. A. Stankovic. "Scheduling algorithms and operating systems support for real-time systems." *Proc. IEEE,* vol. 82, no. 1, pp. 55–67, Jan. 1994.

[5] C. Shen, K. Ramamritham, and J. A. Stankovic. "Resource reclaiming in multiprocessor real-time systems." *IEEE Trans. Parallel and Distributed Systems,* vol. 4, no. 4, pp. 382–397, Apr. 1993.

[6] K. G. Shin and P. Ramanathan. "Real-time computing: A new discipline of computer science and engineering." *Proc. IEEE,* vol. 82, no. 1, pp. 6–24, Jan. 1994.

[7] J. A. Stankovic. "Real-time computing systems: The next generation." Technical report, Dept. of Computer and Information Science, Univ. of Massachusetts, Amherst, 1988.

[8] J. A. Stankovic. "Misconceptions about real-time computing." *IEEE Computer,* vol. 21, no. 10, pp. 10–19, Oct. 1988.

[9] J. A. Stankovic and K. Ramamritham. "What is predictability for real-time systems?" *Real-Time Systems,* no. 2, pp. 247–254, 1990.

[10] J. A. Stankovic. "Strategic directions in real-time and embedded systems." *ACM Computing Surveys,* vol. 28, no. 4, pp. 751–763, Dec. 1996.

[11] H. Zhang. "Service disciplines for guaranteed performance service in packet-switching networks." *Proc. IEEE,* vol. 83, no. 10, pp. 1374–1396, Oct. 1995.

2 Task Scheduling in Multiprocessor Real-Time Systems

Overview

Task scheduling is an important component of resource management in uniprocessor and multiprocessor real-time systems. In this chapter, we discuss the scheduling problem in such systems in detail, addressing both static and dynamic scheduling. First, we present a summary of task scheduling results for these systems, then we describe some known algorithms, with illustrative examples, under each of the scheduling paradigms discussed in the previous chapter.

2.1 Introduction

Multiprocessors have emerged as a powerful computing means for real-time applications such as avionic control and nuclear plant control because of their capability for high performance and reliability. The central problem in multiprocessor scheduling is to determine when and on which processor a given task executes. This can be done either statically or dynamically. Static algorithms determine a priori the assignment of tasks to processors and the time at which the tasks start execution. They are often used to schedule periodic tasks with hard deadlines. The main advantage of this approach is that if a feasible schedule[1] is found, one can be sure that all deadlines will be guaranteed. However, this approach is not applicable to aperiodic tasks, whose characteristics are not known a priori. Scheduling such tasks in a multiprocessor real-time system requires dynamic scheduling algorithms. In dynamic scheduling [27, 33], when new tasks arrive, the scheduler dynamically determines the feasibility of scheduling these new tasks without jeopardizing the guarantees that have been provided for the previously scheduled tasks. Chapter 3 discusses a model for dynamic scheduling of tasks.

A static scheduling algorithm is said to be optimal if, for any set of tasks, it always produces a schedule that satisfies the constraints of the tasks whenever any other algorithm can do so [36]. A dynamic scheduling algorithm is said to be optimal if it always produces a feasible schedule whenever a static scheduling algorithm with complete prior knowledge of all the possible tasks can do so [36]. An important performance metric for any dynamic scheduling algorithm is the *guarantee ratio,* which is the ratio of the total number of tasks guaranteed to the number of tasks that have arrived in the system. An optimal dynamic scheduling algorithm maximizes the guarantee ratio.

It is very important to understand the computational complexity of algorithms so as to decide if a particular algorithm is suitable for a particular type of problem under practical

---

1. A feasible schedule is one in which the constraints of all the component tasks are met.

conditions. Researchers and designers need to bear in mind in particular the following observations concerning algorithms [43]:

- Understanding the boundary between polynomial and NP-complete[2] problems can provide insights into developing useful heuristics.

- Understanding the algorithms that achieve some of the polynomial results can again provide a basis for developing heuristics.

- Understanding the fundamental limitations of on-line (dynamic) algorithms will help designers avoid scheduling anomalies and misconceptions.

2.2   A Summary of Task-Scheduling Results for Multiprocessor Systems

In this section, we discuss some important results pertaining to preemptive, non-preemptive, and parallelizing task scheduling.

2.2.1   Preemptive Scheduling of Tasks

Though in most cases the scheduling problem is easier to handle if tasks are preemptable, in certain situations preemption offers no advantage. The following are classical results pertaining to preemptive task scheduling in multiprocessor systems.

Result 1:   For any instance of the multiprocessing problem with P identical processors, preemption allowed, and minimizing the weighted sum of completion times, there exists a schedule with no preemption for which the value of the sum of completion times is as small as that for any schedule with a finite number of preemptions [29].

That is, for a given metric, there may be no advantage due to preemption. However, the problem of finding such a schedule with or without preemption is NP-hard. Note that if the metric is a simple sum of completion times, the shortest-processing-time-first greedy algorithm, which takes polynomial time, solves the problem. In this case also preemption offers no advantage. Since for practical reasons, it is better to reduce the number of preemptions, a designer would not use a preemptive algorithm when preemption is known to offer no advantage for a given problem.

Result 2:   The multiprocessing problem of scheduling on P processors with task preemption allowed and with minimization of the number of late tasks is NP-hard [21].

This result indicates that one of the most common forms of real-time multiprocessing scheduling—that is, the minimization of number of late tasks—requires heuristics.

---

2. NP-complete and NP-hard problems are those for which it is believed that no polynomial time solution exists.

processors	resources	ordering	comp. time	complexity	reference
2	0	arbitrary	unit	polynomial	[8]
2	0	independent	arbitrary	NP-complete	[11]
2	0	arbitrary	1 or 2 units	NP-complete	[11]
2	1	forest	unit	NP-complete	[11]
3	1	independent	unit	NP-complete	[11]
N	0	forest	unit	polynomial	[14]
N	0	arbitrary	unit	NP-complete	[45]

Figure 2.1
Summary of basic multiprocessor (non-preemptive) static scheduling theorems assuming a single deadline for all tasks

In dynamic scheduling, performance bounds and overload analysis are important issues [43]. Assume *sporadic tasks* (aperiodic tasks with known minimum interarrival time) with preemption permitted. Also assume that if a task meets its deadline, then a value equal to its execution time is obtained; otherwise, no value is obtained. The system has two processors and operates in both normal and overload conditions. The following result holds.

Result 3:   No on-line scheduling algorithm can guarantee a cumulative value greater than one half for the dual-processor case [3].

The above result states that, for two processors, the maximum cumulative value that an algorithm can obtain is one half of that a clairvoyant scheduler can obtain.[3] For a general case, it is proven that no dynamic scheduling algorithm can guarantee a cumulative value greater than one fourth of the value a clairvoyant scheduler can obtain.

2.2.2   Non-Preemptive Scheduling of Tasks

Non-preemptive scheduling is computationally more difficult than preemptive scheduling. Many non-preemptive scheduling problems have been shown to be NP-complete, implying that heuristics must be used to solve such problems. NP-completeness mainly results from nonuniform task computation time and resource requirements. Figure 2.1 summarizes basic multiprocessor scheduling theorems for static scheduling without preemption [43].

The next question is whether any dynamic algorithm is optimal in general. The answer is no. The following is the applicable result.

Result 4:   For two or more processors, no deadline-scheduling algorithm can be optimal without complete a priori knowledge of deadlines, computation times, and task ready times [31].

---

3. A clairvoyant scheduler is one that has complete knowledge of the future requests.

This result implies that none of the classical scheduling algorithms that require such knowledge can be optimal if used on-line. These negative results motivated the heuristic approaches for solving the scheduling problem. Many heuristic scheduling algorithms have been proposed to dynamically schedule a set of tasks with computation times, deadlines, and resource requirements. In general, these heuristics use a non-preemptive model.

2.2.3 Parallelizable Task Scheduling

Meeting deadlines and achieving high resource utilization are the two main goals of task scheduling in real-time systems. As mentioned above, both preemptive and non-preemptive algorithms are available in the literature to achieve such goals. A preemptive algorithm always has a higher schedulability than its non-preemptive version. However, a preemptive algorithm must obtain its higher schedulability at the cost of higher scheduling overhead due to preemption. *Parallelizable* task scheduling is an intermediate solution that tries to meet the conflicting requirements of high schedulability and low overhead. When the laxity of tasks is tight, task parallelization has also been shown to be an effective way to improve the system's schedulability [27].

Most known scheduling algorithms consider each task to be executable on a single processor only, which results in tasks' missing their deadlines when their computation time requirements exceed their deadlines. In the parallelizable task model, each real-time task is characterized by its deadline and worst-case computation time on p processors, where p is the degree of parallelization of the task. In this model, a task can be parallelized and the component tasks (known as *split tasks*) can be executed concurrently on multiple processors. The scheduling algorithms for the parallelizable tasks attempt to exploit the parallelism in tasks as a means to improve schedulability. The scheduling algorithm determines the degree of parallelization of a task. In a variation of the parallelizable task model, the scheduler does not determine the degree of parallelization of a task; rather, it is specified as part of the requirements of the task itself. This scheduling model is known as *partitionable* multiprocessor scheduling [2, 4].

Parallelizable real-time task scheduling has wide applicability in problems such as robot arm dynamics and image processing. For example, the robot arm dynamics problem involves modules for two computations: the dynamics and the solution of a linear system of equations, both of which exhibit a high degree of parallelism and have real-time constraints [49]. Similarly, a typical real-time image-processing application involves pixel-level operations such as convolution that can be carried out in parallel on different portions of the image, and operations within a task such as matching, grouping, and splitting of objects can also be conducted in parallel.

Many researchers have studied the parallelizable task-scheduling problem and shown it to be NP-complete. Many, assuming sublinear task speedups due to interprocessor communication overhead, have proposed approximation algorithms [4, 18] for the problem. A heuristic algorithm for precedence-constrained tasks with linear speedup assumption is reported in [46]. In real-time systems tasks have additional constraints, namely, ready times and deadlines. This makes the real-time scheduling problem harder than non-real-time scheduling. In [24], with linear-speedup assumption, an optimal pseudo-polynomial time algorithm is proposed to schedule imprecise computational tasks in real-time systems. This solution is for static scheduling and cannot be applied to the dynamic case. In [2], algorithms for scheduling real-time tasks on a partitionable hypercube multiprocessor are proposed. In [28], a parallelizable task-scheduling algorithm for dynamically scheduling independent real-time tasks on multiprocessors is proposed. Most importantly, none of these algorithms considers resource constraints among tasks, which is a practical requirement in any complex real-time system. The algorithm proposed in [27] is a dynamic-scheduling algorithm that considers resource constraints among tasks and exploits parallelism in the tasks to meet their deadlines, thereby improving the guarantee ratio.

2.2.4   Multiprocessing Anomalies

When dealing with dynamic scheduling, it becomes necessary to be aware of several anomalies, called Richard's anomalies, so that they can be avoided. Assume that a set of tasks is optimally schedulable on a multiprocessor with some priority order, a fixed number of processors, fixed computation times, and precedence constraints.

Result 5:   For the stated problem, changing the priority list, increasing the number of processors, reducing the computation times, or weakening the precedence constraints can increase the schedule length [12].

This result implies that if tasks have deadlines, then the accompanying increase in the schedule length due to the anomaly can result in the missing of task deadlines for which guarantees were given before. This counterintuitive result is attributable to the nature of timing constraints and multiprocessing. Suppose a task finishes before its worst-case finish time. A simple solution to avoid the run time anomaly is to keep the processor idle until the worst-case finish time of the task. But this is very inefficient in terms of processor and resource utilization and results in poor schedulability, motivating the need for reclaiming algorithms to dynamically reclaim resources from tasks under such circumstances and avert a run time anomaly. Chapter 3 deals with the issue of resource reclaiming in multiprocessor real-time systems.

A specific case of result 5 is that run time anomalies may occur when a task's actual computation time differs from its worst-case computation time in a non-preemptive multiprocessor schedule with resource constraints. These anomalies may cause some already .guaranteed tasks to miss their deadlines. It can easily be shown that the run-time anomalies cannot occur in a multiprocessor schedule when the tasks are sequential and independent, that is, when tasks have no resource or precedence constraints. Informally, this is because the completion of a task earlier than scheduled cannot postpone the start time of other tasks, since they are sequential and independent. However, this is not true for a schedule having parallelized tasks, as given in result 6. Section 2.4 discusses some solutions to overcome the run-time anomaly when dealing with parallelizable tasks.

Result 6: Run-time anomaly may occur in a multiprocessor schedule with parallelized tasks when the actual computation time of a task is less than its worst-case computation time, even when the tasks are independent [28].

2.2.5   Scheduling Tasks with Precedence Constraints

The dependencies between the tasks in a task set T are specified by their precedence constraints; they are given by partial order relation $\prec$ over T. $T_i \prec T_j$ if the execution of T_j cannot begin until the task T_i completes execution. T_j is a *successor* of T_i if $T_i \prec T_j$. For a schedule to be valid, the precedence constraints among tasks must be satisfied in addition to the timing constraints or other constraints, if any. The tasks in a set are said to be *independent* if the partial order relation $\prec$ is empty, that is, the tasks can be executed in any order.

For uniprocessor systems, most scheduling problems that consider precedence constraints among tasks can be solved in polynomial time. It was shown in [19] that scheduling non-preemptable tasks with deadlines and arbitrary precedence constraints can be solved by the *latest-deadline-first* algorithm in $O(n^2)$ time, where n is the number of tasks. This algorithm schedules tasks one at a time, from last to first; each time, the task with least deadline is chosen among those whose successor tasks (as per the precedence relation) have already been scheduled. In [5] it was proved that, for this scheduling problem, a preemptive schedule exists if and only if a non-preemptive schedule exists. Since non-preemptive schedules are always preferred, as noted above, preemptive scheduling need not be used for this case. In [5] it was also shown that earliest-deadline-first scheduling (described later) can be used to schedule preemptable tasks with arbitrary ready times and precedence constraints. The main idea behind this algorithm is to modify the ready times and deadlines of tasks such that they comply with the tasks' precedence constraints. Therefore, the precedence constraints need not be considered explicitly. A feasible schedule on a uniprocessor system exists for a set T of tasks with given ready times and deadlines if and only if there exists a feasible schedule of T with modified ready times and deadlines. The ready time and deadline modifications are described below.

The given deadline of a task in this scheduling problem may be later than that of its successors. Rather than working with the given deadlines, it is convenient to use modified deadlines that are consistent with the precedence constraints and are computed as follows. The modified deadline d_i of a task T_i that has no successor is equal to its given deadline d_i'. Let A_j be the set of all the successors of T_j. The modified deadline d_j of T_j is $\min\{d_j', \min_{T_k \in A_j}\{d_k\}\}$.

Similarly, the given ready time of a task in this scheduling problem may be earlier than that of its predecessors. The ready times of tasks are modified as follows. The modified ready time r_i of a task T_i that has no predecessors is equal to its ready time r_i'. Let B_j be the set of all the predecessors of T_j. The modified ready time of r_j of T_j is $\max\{r_j', \max_{T_k \in B_j}\{r_k\}\}$.

2.3 Priority-Driven Preemptive Scheduling Approach

In the priority-driven preemptive scheduling approach, each task is assigned a priority related to the timing constraints associated with the task. This priority assignment can be either static or dynamic. This priority assignment policy has the advantage, for periodic tasks, of imposing schedulability bounds on processor utilization by the tasks. This scheduling approach is adopted mostly for scheduling in uniprocessor systems. In the rest of this section, we discuss some important uniprocessor scheduling algorithms.

The priority-driven scheduler is usually preemptive. A priority-driven preemptive scheduler always executes the highest-priority task first. While the scheduler is executing a task, if a new task arrives whose priority is higher than the currently executing task or the priority of a waiting task becomes greater than that of the current task, the new highest-priority task preempts the current task, which is interrupted.

2.3.1 Scheduling Independent Periodic Tasks

2.3.1.1 Static Priority Policy
Many efficient algorithms have been developed for scheduling periodic tasks. For uniprocessor systems, Liu and Layland [23] developed a rate-monotonic scheduling (RMS) scheme to determine the schedulability of a set of independent periodic tasks. They showed this scheme to be optimal among fixed-priority scheduling schemes and to require a preemptive scheduler. All tasks are assigned a priority according to their period: the shorter the task's period, the higher its priority. The

RMS algorithm has two parts: the first decides whether a given set of independent tasks is schedulable under the RMS policy; the second assigns static priorities to the tasks based on their periods. The RMS algorithm can schedule a set of n tasks on a uniprocessor system if the following bound on processor utilization is satisfied:

$$\sum_{i=1}^{n} c_i/p_i \leq n(2^{1/n} - 1), \tag{2.1}$$

where c_i and p_i are worst-case computation time and period of the task T_i, respectively. The term $n(2^{1/n} - 1)$ approaches $\ln 2$, that is, about 0.69, as n goes to infinity. Thus, if a task set has a processor utilization of less than 69%, the RMS algorithm is guaranteed to schedule it. However, the above schedulability test is a sufficient but not a necessary condition, which means that there are some task sets that are schedulable using the RMS algorithm that fail the schedulability test. If the periods of the tasks are integer multiples of each other (known as *simple periodic tasks*), the utilization bound can reach 1, which is the theoretical maximum. That is, the schedulability test for scheduling a set of n simple periodic tasks is $\sum_{i=1}^{n} c_i/p_i \leq 1$.

Necessary and Sufficient Condition—Exact Analysis: Under static priority assignment, a schedulability test that is both necessary and sufficient has been found in [22]. Let there be n tasks ordered in decreasing priority. Consider any task T_i. The workload over $[0, t]$ (for arbitrary $t > 0$) due to all tasks of equal or higher priority than T_i is given by

$$W_i(t) = \sum_{j=1}^{i} c_j \lceil \frac{t}{p_j} \rceil. \tag{2.2}$$

The term $\lceil \frac{t}{p_j} \rceil$ represents the number of times task T_j arrives in time t, and therefore $c_j \lceil \frac{t}{p_j} \rceil$ represents its computational demand in time t.

Suppose that task T_i completes its execution exactly at time t. This means that the total cumulative demand from the i tasks up to time t, $W_i(t)$, is exactly equal to t, that is, $W_i(t) = t$. A method for finding the completion time of task T_i, that is, the time at which $W_i(t) = t$, is known as *completion time test* [7] and is shown in figure 2.2.

A task T_i is schedulable if $W_i(t) \leq d_i$, where $W_i(t) = t$. An entire task set is schedulable if this condition holds for all the tasks in the set. Greater processor utilization than in equation (2.1) can be obtained through exact analysis.

2.3.1.2   Dynamic Priority Policies   Also, for uniprocessor systems, an earliest-deadline-first (EDF) algorithm has been proposed [23] that is an optimal dynamic-priority scheme. Like the RMS algorithm, it also uses a preemptive scheduler. EDF assigns the highest priority to the task having the least deadline, where the deadline of a periodic task

$$
\begin{array}{|l|}
\hline
\text{Set } t_0 = \sum_{j=1}^{i} c_j \\[2mm]
t_1 = W_i(t_0) \\
t_2 = W_i(t_1) \\
t_3 = W_i(t_2) \\
\quad \vdots \\
t_k = W_i(t_{k-1}) \\
\text{Stop when } W_i(t_k) = t_k \\
\hline
\end{array}
$$

Figure 2.2
Completion time test: Finding minimum t, where $W_i(t) = t$

is the end of its period. The schedulability test for scheduling a set of n periodic tasks using the EDF algorithm is given by

$$
\sum_{i=1}^{n} c_i/p_i \leq 1. \tag{2.3}
$$

That is, the processor utilization can increase to as much as 1, even when the task periods are not multiples of the smallest period. This condition is both sufficient and necessary.

For uniprocessor systems, the least-laxity-first (LLF) algorithm offers another optimal dynamic priority scheme. It makes the same assumptions as the EDF algorithm, assigning the task with the least laxity the highest priority, where laxity of a task T_i is $(d_i - \overline{c_i} - t)$, where t denotes the current time and d_i and $\overline{c_i}$ denote the deadline and remaining computation time ($\overline{c_i}$ decreases as t progresses) of task T_i, respectively. The smaller the laxity, the higher the task's urgency and hence the higher the assigned priority, and specifically, when the laxity of a task becomes negative, it cannot be completed before its deadline.

In LLF policy, a task whose laxity has decreased below that of the currently executing task preempts the current task. An executing task has constant laxity, whereas those of the tasks not currently executing are in flux. For a given task set, LLF scheduling might result in more preemptions than EDF scheduling as the laxity of the tasks shifts. A problem arises with LLF when two tasks have similar laxities. One task runs for a short while and then gets preempted by the other as its laxity changes, and vice-versa, leading to many context switches in each of the tasks. This can result in *thrashing:* The processor spends more time performing context switches than useful work.

2.3.1.3   Comparison of Static and Dynamic Priority Policies   Many of the scheduling algorithms designed for periodic tasks are based on fixed priority assignment schemes,

task	comp. time	period
T_1	2	6
T_2	2	8
T_3	3	12

(a) An example of real-time task set

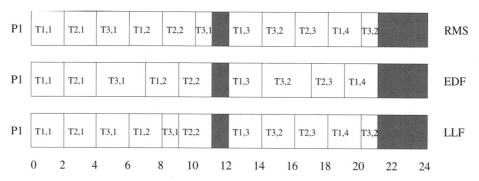

(b) Schedules produced by RMS, EDF, and LLF algorithms

Figure 2.3
A task set and its schedules (RMS, EDF, LLF)

which have the advantage of very small scheduling overheads, because the only requirement at run time is to preempt a lower-priority task with a newly arriving higher-priority
task using the prioritized interrupt mechanism. These schemes are highly inflexible, however, because changing of a task's priority assignment, in a situation where dynamic
priority assignment is required, is difficult. In contrast to static priorities, the dynamic priority of a task changes when a new task with an earlier deadline arrives, which makes
dynamic priority schemes more expensive than static schemes in terms of run time
overheads.

Figure 2.3(b) shows the schedules produced by RMS, EDF, and LLF algorithms for the
example task set given in figure 2.3(a). Note that as predicted above, the LLF schedule has
more preemptions than the EDF schedule.

2.3.1.4 Extending to Multiprocessors The development of appropriate scheduling algorithms for multiprocessor systems is problematic, not only because the uniprocessor
algorithms are not directly applicable, but also because some of the apparently correct
methods are counterintuitive. Mok and Dertouzos [30] have shown that the optimal algorithms for uniprocessor systems are not optimal for the case of multiprocessors. Consider,

for example, scheduling of three periodic tasks, T_1, T_2, and T_3, on two processors. Let c_i and p_i denote the computation time and period of task T_i, respectively. Let c_1, c_2, and c_3 be 25, 25, and 80, respectively, and p_1, p_2, and p_3 be 50, 50, and 100, respectively. If the RMS or EDF algorithm is used, T_1 and T_2 will have the highest priority and will run on the two processors in parallel for their required 25 units, leaving T_3 with 80 units of computation to execute in 75 available units. Using the RMS or EDF algorithm, T_3 will thus miss its deadline, even though the average processor utilization is only 65%. However, an allocation that schedules T_1 and T_2 on one processor and T_3 on the other processor meets the deadlines of all the tasks. Thus, for multiprocessor systems, neither RMS, nor EDF, nor LLF is optimal.

The above example shows that judicious allocation of tasks can significantly affect schedulability. For scheduling periodic tasks on multiprocessor systems, many researchers have adopted a partitioning approach in which the periodic task set is partitioned among the minimum number of processors required such that each partition of the periodic tasks can be scheduled on a single processor according to an RMS or EDF priority scheme. For most variations of the scheduling problem, finding an optimal solution is difficult and computationally intractable. Therefore approximate algorithms have been proposed with associated optimality bounds.

2.3.2 Scheduling Communicating Tasks

The above results are applicable only to independent tasks. Tasks do interact, however, through resources that cannot be shared simultaneously. For example, a task may be writing to a block in memory. Until this operation is completed, no other task can access that block, either for reading or for writing. That is, different tasks' access to a sharable resource must be mutually excluded. A task that is currently holding a sharable resource is said to be in the *critical section* associated with the resource. Synchronization primitives such as semaphores, locks, monitors, and Ada Rendezvous are used to regulate different tasks' entry into the critical section.

2.3.2.1 Priority Inversion Problem Direct applications of these synchronization mechanisms may lead to an indefinite period of *priority inversion,* which occurs when a low-priority task prevents a high-priority task from executing [39, 40]. The following example illustrates the priority inversion problem.

Let T_1, T_2, and T_3 be three periodic tasks in decreasing order of priority. Let T_1 and T_3 share a resource. Consider the following scenario:

- T_3 obtains a lock on the semaphore S and enters its critical section to use a shared resource.

- T_1 becomes ready to run and preempts T_3. Then T_1 tries to enter its critical section by first trying to lock S. But T_3 has already locked S, and hence T_1 is blocked.

- T_2 becomes ready to run. Since only T_2 and T_3 are ready to run, T_2 preempts T_3 while T_3 is in its critical section.

Ideally, in such a scenario, one would prefer that the highest-priority task (T_1) be blocked no longer than the time required for T_3 to complete its critical section. However, the duration of blocking is, in fact, unpredictable, because T_3 can be preempted by the medium-priority task T_2. As a result, the highest-priority task T_1 will be blocked until T_2 and any other pending tasks of intermediate priority are completed. Thus, the duration of priority inversion becomes a function of task computation times and is not bounded by the duration of critical sections.

2.3.2.2 Priority Inheritance and Priority Ceiling Protocols *Priority inheritance protocol* [39] solves the problem of priority inversion. Under this protocol, if a lower-priority task T_L blocks a higher-priority task T_H because T_L is currently executing the critical section needed by T_H, T_L temporarily inherits the priority of T_H. When blocking ceases (i.e., T_L exits the critical section), T_L resumes its original priority. Unfortunately, though it appears on first glance to be a perfect solution, priority inheritance may lead to *deadlock*.

Consider, for example, two tasks T_1 and T_2 with T_2 having higher priority than T_1. Let CS_1 and CS_2 be two critical sections. The first table in figure 2.4 shows the sequence of operations the tasks perform on the critical sections, and the second table shows the execution scenario of these tasks that results in deadlock.

Another protocol, called *priority ceiling protocol* [39], solves the priority inversion problem and also overcomes the deadlock problem. It is a variant of priority inheritance protocol and works as follows:

- For each semaphore, a *priority ceiling* is defined whose value is the highest priority of all the tasks that may lock it.

- When a task T_i attempts to execute one of its critical sections, it will be suspended unless its priority is higher than the priority ceiling of all semaphores currently locked by tasks other than T_i.

- If task T_i is unable to enter its critical section for this reason, the task that holds the lock on the semaphore with the highest priority ceiling is said to be blocking T_i and hence inherits the priority of T_i.

- As long as a task T_i is not attempting to enter one of its critical sections, it will preempt every task that has a lower priority.

task	operation sequence on critical section			
T_1	$Lock(CS_2)$	$Lock(CS_1)$	$Unlock(CS_1)$	$Unlock(CS_2)$
T_2	$Lock(CS_1)$	$Lock(CS_2)$	$Unlock(CS_2)$	$Unlock(CS_1)$

time	task	action
t_0	T_1	starts execution
t_1	T_1	locks CS_2
t_2	T_2	activated and preempts T_1 due to its higher priority
t_3	T_2	locks CS_1
t_4	T_2	attempts to lock CS_2, but is blocked because T_1 has a lock on it
t_5	T_1	inherits the priority of T_2 and starts executing
t_6	T_1	attempts to lock CS_1, but is blocked because T_2 has a lock on it
$\geq t_7$	–	both the tasks cannot proceed (deadlocked)

Figure 2.4
Priority inheritance protocol resulting in deadlock

The priority ceiling protocol is identical to the priority inheritance protocol, except that a task T_i can now be blocked from entering a critical section if any other task is currently holding a semaphore whose priority ceiling is greater than or equal to the priority of task T_i.

In the above example, the priority ceiling for both CS_1 and CS_2 is the priority of T_2. From time t_0 to t_2, the operations are the same as before. At time t_3, T_2 attempts to lock CS_1, but is blocked since CS_2 (which has been locked by T_1) has a priority ceiling equal to the priority of T_2. Thus T_1 inherits the priority of T_2 and proceeds to completion, thereby preventing the deadlock situation.

2.3.2.3 Real-World Example for Priority Inversion Problem

An interesting example of the priority inversion problem occurred during the Pathfinder mission to Mars (July 4, 1997). The problem scenario and the solution to the problem are discussed below. (This is an edited version of the email message from Mike Jones ⟨mbj@microsoft.com⟩ to the research community, dated December 5, 1997.)

What Happened on Mars? VxWorks, a real-time embedded systems kernel, was the operating system used in the Mars Pathfinder mission. VxWorks provides preemptive priority scheduling of threads. Tasks on the Pathfinder spacecraft were executed as threads with priorities that were assigned in the usual manner, reflecting the relative urgency of the tasks.

Pathfinder contained an "information bus," which can be thought of as a shared memory area used for passing information between different components of the spacecraft. A bus management task ran frequently, with high priority given to moving certain kinds of data in and out of the information bus. Access to the bus was synchronized with mutual exclusion locks (mutexes).

The meteorological data-gathering task ran as an infrequent, low-priority thread and used the information bus to publish its data. When publishing its data, it would acquire a mutex, do writes to the bus, and release the mutex. If an interrupt caused the information bus thread to be scheduled while this mutex was held, and if the information bus thread then attempted to acquire this same mutex in order to retrieve published data, this would cause it to block on the mutex, waiting until the meteorological thread released the mutex before it could continue. The spacecraft also contained a communications task that ran with medium priority.

Most of the time this combination worked fine. However, very infrequently it was possible for an interrupt to occur that caused the (medium-priority) communications task to be scheduled during the short interval while the (high-priority) information bus thread was blocked waiting for the (low-priority) meteorological data thread. In this case, the long-running communications task, having higher priority than the meteorological task, would prevent it from running, consequently preventing the blocked information bus task from running. After some time had passed, a watchdog timer would go off, notice that the data bus task had not been executed for some time, conclude that something had gone drastically wrong, and initiate a total system reset. This scenario is a classic case of priority inversion.

How Was This Debugged? VxWorks can be run in a mode where it records a total trace of all interesting system events, including context switches, uses of synchronization objects, and interrupts. After the failure, Jet Propulsion Lab (JPL) engineers spent many hours running the system on the exact spacecraft replica in their lab with tracing turned on, attempting to replicate the precise conditions under which they believed that the reset occurred. Finally, the reset was reproduced in the replica. Analysis of the trace revealed the priority inversion.

How Was This Problem Corrected? When created, a VxWorks mutex object accepts a boolean parameter that indicates whether priority inheritance should be performed by the mutex. The mutex in question had been initialized with the parameter off (FALSE); had it been on (TRUE), the low-priority meteorological thread would have inherited the priority of the high-priority data bus thread blocked on it while it held the mutex, causing it to be scheduled with higher priority than the medium-priority communications task, thus preventing the priority inversion. The problem was fixed by changing the mutex in question (and two other variables that could have caused the same problem) from FALSE to TRUE. After this correction, no further system resets occurred.

2.3.3 Scheduling Periodic Tasks Together with Sporadic Tasks

Most real-time systems involve both periodic and aperiodic tasks. In [31], it has been shown that EDF remains optimal when both periodic and aperiodic tasks must be scheduled, assuming the aperiodic tasks are sporadic. The EDF algorithm, although optimal, suffers from unpredictability when transient overload occurs; that is, it does not miss task deadlines in strictly increasing order of the value that would be obtained by meeting the tasks' deadlines. On the other hand, the RMS algorithm can be adapted to schedule aperiodic tasks. The simplest approach is to create a periodic task (periodic server), with a certain computation time and period, whose purpose is to service one or more aperiodic tasks each time it is invoked. Aperiodic tasks are executed only when the periodic server is scheduled. The problem with this approach is that there may be no aperiodic task to execute at any particular time the server is scheduled, or there might be too many aperiodic tasks in any given instance when the server is scheduled because of the bursty nature of aperiodic tasks. In either case, the time alloted to the server is being used ineffectively. To overcome this problem, a number of bandwidth-preserving algorithms have been proposed; a few are discussed below.

2.3.3.1 Priority Exchange Algorithm In the priority exchange algorithm, a periodic task (server) is created to serve aperiodic tasks. When the server period starts, the server runs only if there are any outstanding aperiodic tasks. If no aperiodic task exists, the high-priority server exchanges its priority with a lower-priority periodic task, decreasing the server's priority but maintaining its computation time. As a consequence, the aperiodic tasks get low preference for execution, leading to deadlines being missed unpredictably under overload. The computation time allowance for the server is replenished at the start of its period.

2.3.3.2 Deferrable Server In the deferrable server algorithm, a periodic task known as a deferrable server is created to serve aperiodic tasks. When the server is invoked but no aperiodic tasks are outstanding, the server does not execute but defers its assigned time slot. When an aperiodic task arrives, the server is invoked to execute aperiodic tasks and maintains its priority. Unlike in the priority exchange policy, the server's time is preserved at its initial priority. In this algorithm, under overload, deadlines are missed predictably. The computation time allowance for the server is replenished at the start of its period.

2.3.3.3 Sporadic Server The sporadic server algorithm combines the advantages of both the priority exchange algorithm (serving more aperiodic tasks) and the deferrable server algorithm (maintaining the priority of the server) by varying the points at which the computation time of the server is replenished, rather than merely replenishing at the start of each server period. In other words, any spare capacity (i.e., that not being used by periodic tasks) is available for an aperiodic task on its arrival. In this algorithm, as in deferrable server, deadlines are missed predictably under overload.

2.4   Static Table-Driven Scheduling Approach

Static table-driven scheduling is motivated by the idea that the resources needed to meet the deadlines of safety-critical tasks should be preallocated so that each individual task can meet its deadline even under the worst-case conditions. This is mainly applied to periodic tasks, though sporadic tasks can also be scheduled using static table-driven algorithms by converting them into periodic tasks. For a set of periodic tasks, a feasible schedule exists if and only if all the task instances are feasible in the schedule for a time duration equal to the least common multiple (LCM) of the task periods (also known as the *planning cycle*) [20].

2.4.1   Scheduling Parallelizable Periodic Tasks

In this section, we discuss a non-preemptive parallelizable task-scheduling algorithm [28] that combines the advantages of higher schedulability and lower scheduling overhead offered by the preemptive and non-preemptive task scheduling models, respectively. This algorithm involves checking the schedulability of periodic tasks (if necessary, by paralleliz-ing them) off-line and scheduling of the schedulable periodic tasks at run time together with dynamically arriving aperiodic tasks.

The schedulability check algorithm is basically a non-preemptive EDF algorithm, except that it considers running a parallel version of a task when the task's deadline cannot be met. It chooses the degree of parallelization of a task instance in such a way that the task just meets its deadline, and this value (degree) cannot be changed during the scheduling of subsequent tasks. The run time scheduling is also a non-preemptive version of an EDF algorithm, only it does allow for reduction in the degree of parallelization for tasks due to reclaiming. The novelty of this approach is that it does not store the entire schedule up to the LCM. Instead, it stores only the degree of parallelization of tasks' instances for which this degree is greater than 1. To avoid the run time anomaly that may occur when a task's actual computation time is less than its worst-case computation time, an efficient run time mechanism is also presented.

2.4.2   Example for Run-Time Anomaly

Figure 2.6 is an example postrun schedule for run time anomaly for the periodic task set, schedulable based on the worst-case computation times, given in figure 2.5(a), assuming the actual computation time of $T(4, 1)$ is 2 as against its worst-case computation time of 3. Here c_i^j is the worst-case computation time of T_i when run on j processors in parallel. The notation $T(i, j)$ in the schedule denotes the jth instance of T_i. Because of the early

tasks (T_i)	T_1	T_2	T_3	T_4	T_5
c_i^1	4	3	4	3	10
c_i^2	3	3	3	2	5
periods (p_i)	4	4	6	6	12

(a) An example for parallelizable periodic tasks

$T(i, j)$	$T_{1,1}$	$T_{2,1}$	$T_{3,1}$	$T_{4,1}$	$T_{5,1}$	$T_{1,2}$	$T_{2,2}$	$T_{3,2}$	$T_{4,2}$	$T_{1,3}$	$T_{2,3}$
r_i	0	0	0	0	0	4	4	6	6	8	8
d_i	4	4	6	6	12	8	8	12	12	12	12

(b) Periodic task instances up to the planning cycle

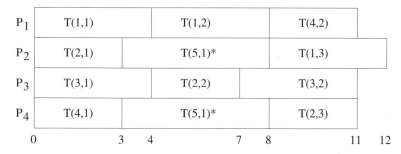

(c) Feasible pre-run schedule with task $T(5, 1)$ parallelized

Figure 2.5
Periodic task schedule

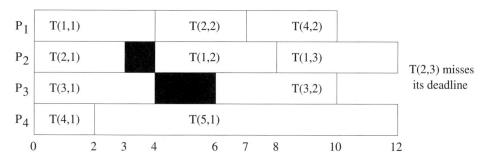

Figure 2.6
Infeasible postrun schedule with actual computation time of $T(4, 1) = 2$

completion (at time 2) of $T(4, 1)$, $T(5, 1)$, which was parallelized on two processors during the schedulability check, can now be scheduled without parallelizing it. This results in the creation of *holes* of length 1 and 2 in the schedule for processors P_2 and P_3 at time units 3 and 4, respectively. This leads to impossibility of scheduling the task set at run time, as the deadline of $T(2, 3)$ (whose computation times are 4 and 3 on one and two processors, respectively, and deadline is 12) cannot be met.

2.4.3   Solutions to Run-Time Anomaly

This section shows that the run time anomaly can be avoided by maintaining certain information during schedulability check that the run time scheduler will use. The following are a couple of the approaches [28]:

1. Keep the degree of parallelization for each periodic task at run time equal to its degree of parallelization determined during the schedulability check; that is, all the instances of a periodic task will have the same degree of parallelization.

2. Keep the degree of parallelization for each periodic task instance at run time equal to its degree of parallelization determined during the schedulability check.

Approach 1 is better in terms of storage requirements, because we need only to keep the degree of parallelization of every periodic task, and is poorer in terms of schedulability, because all the instances of a periodic task are forced to use the same degree of parallelization, which might create holes in the schedule. Approach 2 has exactly the opposite strengths and weaknesses, because it keeps information on all the tasks' instances whose degree of parallelization is greater than 1 and allows different instances to have different degrees of parallelization, resulting in better processor utilization. Since the schedulability of task sets is more important than the storage space, we feel that approach 2 is better than the first overall. Therefore, we consider approach 2 for further investigation.

2.4.4   Implementation Issues of Approach 2

In many of today's real-time systems, memory constraints are still a bottleneck and therefore need to be accounted for [34]. Since parallelizable task scheduling combines the benefits of both the static table-driven and dynamic scheduling approaches, the storage efficiency of this approach is compared with that of the static table-driven approach. In the static table-driven approach the start time and finish time for each task instance is stored in the form of a table (of length equal to the planning cycle). On the other hand, approach 2 stores the instance IDs and their corresponding degrees of parallelization up to the planning cycle for instances of tasks whose degree of parallelization is greater than 1. The size of start and finish times are x-bits, which is $\lceil \log \{ \text{LCM(task periods)} \} \rceil$, whereas the number of bits required for storing instance ID is $\lceil \log \{ \frac{2^x}{p_1} \} \rceil$ bits, where p_1 is the smallest period.

The number of bits required for storing the degree of parallelization is log ρ, which is at most log m when $\rho = m$, where ρ and m are maximum degree of task parallelization and number of processors, respectively. So approach 2 has lower storage requirements than the static table-driven approach. The *storage overhead* for implementing approach 2 is defined as follows:

$$\% \text{ of Storage Requirement (SR)} = \frac{\text{storage requirement for approach 2}}{\text{storage requirement for table-driven approach}} * 100.$$

In summary, the approach proposed in [28] is compared with the EDF approach in terms of schedulability and with a static table-driven approach in terms of storage efficiency. The simulation study concludes that parallelizable task scheduling always offers higher schedulability than that of the EDF algorithm for a wide variety of task parameters and incurs less than 3.6% of the storage overhead of the static table-driven approach, even under heavy task loads.

2.5 Dynamic Planning-Based Scheduling Approach

Dynamic planning combines the flexibility of dynamic scheduling with the predictability offered by schedulability checking. When a task arrives, the system attempts to guarantee the task by constructing a plan for its execution without violating the guarantees of the previously scheduled tasks. The schedulability check for a task takes into account the worst-case computation time, timing and precedence constraints, and the resource and fault-tolerant requirements of the task. Once a task passes the schedulability check (and is admitted into the system) and the assumptions about its characteristics hold, it will meet its deadline. Thus, predictability is checked for each task on arrival. If the schedulability check for a task fails, the task is not feasible and a *timing fault* is forecast. If this possibility is known sufficiently ahead of the deadline, there may be time to take alternate actions.

2.5.1 Timing of Planning

As the number of tasks increases, so does the cost of planning, and less time is available for planning, which will make planning-based algorithms perform poorly under overloads. So when a system overload is anticipated, use of a method that controls the overhead is essential. Thus, it is important to decide *when* to plan the execution of a newly arriving task. There are two simple approaches [36]:

1. *Scheduling at arrival time,* in which the schedulability check is performed on task arrival, and all tasks that have not yet executed are considered during the schedulability check so that their guarantees are not violated.

2. *Scheduling at dispatch time,* in which the schedulability check is postponed until a task is chosen for execution. This can be done very easily for non-preemptive task execution as it involves checking if the task will finish before its deadline as projected from the current time.

The first approach provides sufficient lead time for considering alternate (recovery) actions, whereas the second approach is flexible, has less overhead, and announces task rejection very late. Both approaches avoid resource wastages as they do not commit a task to the schedule unless it is feasible. Therefore, there is a trade-off between (strictness of) guarantee and flexibility. Instead of performing the schedulability check at either of the extremes involved in these two approaches, it may be advantageous to do it somewhere in between, at a most opportune time (known as the *punctual point*). Doing so will minimize the number of tasks considered for scheduling (or rescheduling)[4] without rescheduling the tasks that have no effect on the scheduling of the new task, resulting in reduced scheduling overhead.

The choice of punctual point must take into account the laxities of tasks. The larger the mean laxity and the higher the load, the more tasks are ready to run. The punctual point is the minimum laxity value before which the task becomes ineligible for schedulability check. In other words, a task's schedulability check is postponed until its laxity becomes the punctual point. The choice of punctual point should also take into account the semantics of the application (how much lead time the application requires for performing a recovery action). Thus, scheduling using punctual point reduces scheduling overheads compared to scheduling at arrival and is also better than scheduling at dispatch time in terms of allowing the application to take alternate actions.

2.5.2   Practical Considerations

Dynamic planning-based scheduling involves three main activities: schedulability checking, schedule construction, and dispatching (task execution). In a multiprocessor system, the scheduler performs (schedulability checking and) schedule construction, which is independent of dispatching, thus allowing the two to run in parallel. One of the crucial issues in dynamic scheduling is the cost (overheads) of scheduling: The more time spent on scheduling, the less time is left for task execution. Planning-based schedulers typically use non-preemptive schedules [36]. Dispatching a task should ensure that there is no run time anomaly. The issue of dispatching a task as early as possible without leading to any run time anomalies is known as the *resource reclaiming problem*. Resource reclaiming is addressed in the next chapter, in which a dynamic scheduling model

---

4. Tasks already scheduled may have to be rescheduled to accommodate new tasks.

is discussed and the trade-offs between scheduling cost and performance are also studied.

2.5.3 Task Model and Definitions

In the context of this chapter, a dynamic scheduling algorithm has complete knowledge about the currently active set of tasks but not about any new tasks that may arrive while scheduling the current set. Tasks are aperiodic, and each task T_i is characterized by its arrival time (a_i), ready time (r_i), worst-case computation time (c_i), and deadline (d_i). Each task might need some resources for its execution. There are two types of accesses to a resource: shared and exclusive. Resource conflict exists between two tasks T_i and T_j if both require the same resource and one of the accesses is exclusive. The following definitions are necessary to describe the scheduling algorithms:

2.5.3.1 Terminology

Definition 1:   The earliest available time (EAT_k^s, EAT_k^e) is the earliest time when resource R_k becomes available for shared (or exclusive, respectively) usage [33].

Definition 2:   Let P be the set of processors and R_i be the set of resources requested by task T_i. The *earliest start time* of a task T_i, denoted as $EST(T_i)$, is the earliest time when its execution can be started, defined as

$$EST(T_i) = \max(r_i, \min_{j \in P}(\text{avail time}(j)), \max_{k \in R_i}(EAT_k^u)),$$

where avail time(j) denotes the earliest time at which the processor P_j becomes available for executing a task and the third term denotes the maximum among the earliest available times of the resources requested by task T_i, in which $u = s$ for shared mode and $u = e$ for exclusive mode.

Definition 3:   A task T_i is feasible in a schedule if its timing constraint and resource requirements are met in the schedule, that is, if $EST(T_i) + c_i \leq d_i$. A schedule for a set of tasks is said to be a feasible schedule if all the tasks are feasible in the schedule.

Definition 4:   A partial schedule is a feasible schedule for a subset of tasks. A partial schedule is said to be *strongly feasible* if *all* the schedules obtained by extending the current schedule by any one of the remaining tasks within a window, called the *feasibility check window*, of size K are also feasible [33].

2.5.4 Myopic Scheduling Algorithm

As discussed in section 2.2.2, heuristics algorithms are used for dynamic scheduling of tasks. In [48], it was shown for uniprocessor systems that a simple heuristic that accounts

Myopic Scheduling(K)
begin
    1. Tasks (in the task queue) are ordered in nondecreasing order of deadline.
    2. Start with an empty partial schedule.
    3. Determine whether the current schedule is *strongly feasible* (strong feasibility is determined
        with respect to the first K tasks in the task queue, called the feasibility check window).
    4. **If** (strongly feasible)
        (a) Compute heuristic function H for each task, where $H_i = d_i + W * EST(T_i)$.
        (b) Extend the schedule with the task having the best (smallest) H value.
    5. **else**
        (a) Backtrack to the previous search level.
        (b) Extend the schedule with the task having next-best H value.
    6. **Repeat** steps (3–5) **until** a termination condition is met.
end.

Figure 2.7
Myopic algorithm

for resource requirements significantly outperforms heuristics, such as scheduling based on EDF, that ignore resource requirements. For multiprocessor systems with resource-constrained tasks, a heuristic search algorithm, called the myopic scheduling algorithm, was proposed in [33], and it was shown that an integrated heuristic that is a function of deadline and earliest start time of a task performs better than simple heuristics such as the EDF, LLF, and minimum-processing-time-first.

The myopic scheduling algorithm is a non-preemptive heuristic search algorithm for scheduling real-time tasks with resource constraints (figure 2.7). A vertex in the search tree represents a partial schedule. The schedule from a vertex is extended only if the vertex is strongly feasible. If the current vertex is strongly feasible, the algorithm computes a heuristic function for each task within the feasibility window and then extends the schedule by a task having the least heuristic value. The heuristic function for a task T_k is $H_k = d_k + W * EST(T_k)$, an integrated heuristic that captures the deadline and resource requirements of task T_k, where W is a constant which is an input parameter. If the current vertex is not strongly feasible, the algorithm backtracks to the previous search point and from there on extends the schedule using the task having the next minimum heuristic value. The larger the size of the feasibility check window, the higher the scheduling cost and more the look-ahead nature.

The termination conditions are that (1) a complete feasible schedule has been found, (2) the maximum number of backtracks or H function evaluations has been reached, or (3) no more backtracking is possible. The time complexity of the myopic scheduling algorithm for scheduling n tasks is $O(Kn)$. The value of K is usually much smaller than n for practical purposes. The myopic scheduling algorithm is implemented in the Spring kernel [42].

2.5.5   A Variant of Myopic Algorithm (ParMyopic) for Parallelizable Tasks

Here we present a variation of the myopic scheduling algorithm proposed in [27] (henceforth referred to as *ParMyopic*), which exploits parallelism in tasks to meet their deadlines. In addition to the task model used in the myopic algorithm, the following assumptions are made about the parallelizable task model:

- The worst-case computation time (c_i^j) of a task T_i is the upper bound on the computation time for each of the processors, when the task is run on j processors in parallel, where $1 \leq j \leq m$.

- When a task is parallelized, all its parallel subtasks (also called *split tasks*) have to start at the same time in the schedule, to synchronize their executions.

- Tasks are non-preemptable, that is, once a task or a split task starts executing, it finishes.

- For each task T_i, the worst-case computation time for any j and k, with $j < k$, satisfies $j * c_i^j \leq k * c_i^k$. This is called the *sublinear speedup assumption,* and the sublinearity is due to the overheads associated with communication and synchronization among the split tasks of a task.

The ParMyopic scheduling algorithm is similar to the myopic algorithm, except in that it parallelizes a task whenever its deadline cannot be met, and has the same scheduling cost. It chooses the degree of parallelization (i.e., the number of split tasks) of a task in such a way that the task's deadline is just met. It selects the processor(s) and the resource(s) that have the minimum earliest *available time* for scheduling a task. The scheduling cost of the ParMyopic algorithm is made equal to that of the myopic algorithm by performing a feasibility check for only $\overline{K}$ tasks, where $\overline{K} \leq K$, as compared to K in the myopic algorithm. The value of $\overline{K}$ depends on the number of tasks parallelized and their degrees of parallelization; that is, feasibility is checked until the sum of the degrees of parallelization of these tasks reaches K. In other words, in the ParMyopic algorithm, the number of tasks checked for feasibility is less than or equal to the size of the feasibility check window (K). In the worst case, if none of the tasks needs to be parallelized, the ParMyopic algorithm behaves like the myopic algorithm, in which case $\overline{K} = K$. The algorithm backtracks only when a task's deadline cannot be met using any degree of parallelization up to *max-split*, as defined in figure 2.8, which shows the ParMyopic algorithm for scheduling a set of currently active tasks.

Parallelizable Task Scheduling$(K, \textit{max-split})$ /* K: size of feasibility check window,
   $\textit{max-split}$: maximum degree of parallelization of a task; both are input parameters. */

begin

1. Order the tasks (in the task queue) in nondecreasing order of their deadlines and then start
   with an empty partial schedule.

2. Determine whether the current vertex (schedule) is strongly feasible by performing feasibility
   check for K or less than K tasks in the feasibility check window as given below:

   - Let $\overline{K}$ be the count of the number of tasks for which feasibility check has been done.
   - Let T_i be the $(\overline{K} + 1)$-th task in the current task queue.
   - Let $\textit{num-split}$ be the maximum degree of parallelization permitted for the current task T_i.
   - Let $cost$ be the sum of degree of parallelization over all the $\overline{K}$ tasks for which feasibility
     check has been done so far.

   (a) $\textit{num-split} = \textit{max-split}; \quad \overline{K} = 0; \quad cost = 0; \quad feasible = \text{TRUE}.$

   (b) **While** ($feasible$ is TRUE) **do**

      i. **If** $(K - cost < \textit{num-split})$ $\textit{num-split} = K - cost.$

      ii. Compute $EST(T_i)$ for task T_i.

      iii. Find the smallest j such that $EST(T_i) + c_i^j \le d_i$, where $1 \le j \le \textit{num-split}.$

      iv. **If** (such j exists) $\overline{K} = \overline{K} + 1; cost = cost + j.$

      v. **else if** ($\textit{num-split} < \textit{max-split}$) break.

      vi. **else** $feasible = \text{FALSE}.$

3. **If** ($feasible$ is TRUE)

   (a) Compute the heuristic function (H) for the first $\overline{K}$ tasks, where $H_k = d_k + W * EST(T_k)$
      for task T_k.

   (b) Extend the schedule by the task having the best (smallest) H value.

4. **else**

   (a) Backtrack to the previous search level.

   (b) Extend the schedule by the task having the next-best H value.

5. Move the feasibility check window by one task.

6. **Repeat** steps (2–5) **until** termination condition is met.

end.

Figure 2.8
ParMyopic algorithm. From G. Manimaran and C. Siva Ram Murthy [27], in *IEEE Trans. Parallel and Distributed Systems* 9 (3). © IEEE, 1998.

2.5.6   Example for Myopic and ParMyopic Algorithms

Figure 2.9(b) is a feasible schedule produced by the ParMyopic scheduling algorithm for the task set given in figure 2.9(a) with four processors and one resource having two instances. The arrival time (a_i) of all the tasks in figure 2.9(a) is 0. For this, the input values for K, W, number of backtracks, and *max-split* are taken as 4, 1, 1, and 2, respectively. Figures 2.10(a) and (b) show the search tree constructed by the myopic scheduling algorithm for the task set given in figure 2.9(a). The myopic algorithm is unable to produce a feasible schedule for this task set, whereas the ParMyopic algorithm is able to do so. The search tree constructed by the ParMyopic algorithm is given in figures 2.10(a) and (c). In Figure 2.9(b), the tasks T_{11} and T_{13} are parallelized and scheduled on processors P_2 and P_4, and P_1 and P_3, respectively.

In figures 2.10(a)–(c), each node of the search tree is represented by two boxes: the left box shows the earliest available time of processors for executing a new task, and the right box has two entries (separated by a comma) that correspond to earliest available time of resource instances, with one entry per resource instance. In each entry, the value within (without) parentheses indicates the available time of that particular resource instance in exclusive (shared) mode. For example, an entry such as 0(30),34(34) indicates that the first instance of the resource is available for shared mode at time 0 and for exclusive mode at time 30, and the second instance of the resource is available for shared and exclusive modes at time 34. The forward arcs correspond to extending the schedule, whereas the backward arcs correspond to backtracking. The label $T_a(b)$ on a forward arc denotes that the task T_a is scheduled on processor P_b. For example, $T_{13}(3, 1)$ denotes that the task T_{13} is parallelized and scheduled on processors P_3 and P_1.

To illustrate the working of the myopic algorithm, consider the first vertex of figure 2.10(b). At that point, tasks T_{10}, T_{11}, T_{12}, and T_{13} are in the feasibility check window. $EST(T_{10}) = \max(17, 21, 0) = 21$, and hence T_{10} is feasible. Similarly, the other three tasks are also feasible. Therefore, the current schedule is strongly feasible. The heuristic values for these four tasks are 58, 61, 61, and 64, respectively. The best (the smallest heuristic value) task is T_{10}, and the schedule is extended by scheduling it on P_3. The new vertex thus obtained is not strongly feasible because T_{11} is not feasible, hence the algorithm backtracks to the previous vertex and extends the schedule from there using the next-best task T_{11}.

For ParMyopic scheduling algorithm, consider the vertex after scheduling T_{10} in figure 2.10(c). The size of feasibility check window will be 3, since only three tasks are to be scheduled. Out of these three, only T_{11} (with *split* = 2) and T_{12} are checked for feasibility, since feasibility checking of T_{13} exceeds K. $EST(T_{11}) = \max(19, 29, 30) = 30$, and hence $H_{11} = 70$, whereas $H_{12} = 64$, since $EST(T_{12}) = \max(21, 24, 0) = 24$. Therefore, the schedule is extended by scheduling T_{12} on P_1. Now among T_{11} and T_{13}, T_{11} has the lower

task	ready time	comp. time		deadline	resource
T_i	r_i	c_i^1	c_i^2	d_i	requirement
1	0	11	6	13	share
2	0	10	6	14	share
3	0	10	6	15	
4	0	15	8	18	
5	4	8	5	22	
6	7	11	6	26	
7	10	13	7	28	
8	12	14	8	34	
9	14	12	7	36	share
10	17	9	5	37	exclusive
11	19	13	7	40	exclusive
12	21	9	5	40	
13	23	14	8	41	

(a) An example of real-time task set

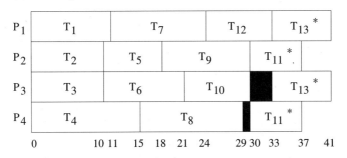

(b) Feasible schedule produced by ParMyopic algorithm

Figure 2.9
A task set and its schedule. From G. Manimaran and C. Siva Ram Murthy [27], in *IEEE Trans. Parallel and Distributed Systems* 9 (3). © IEEE, 1998.

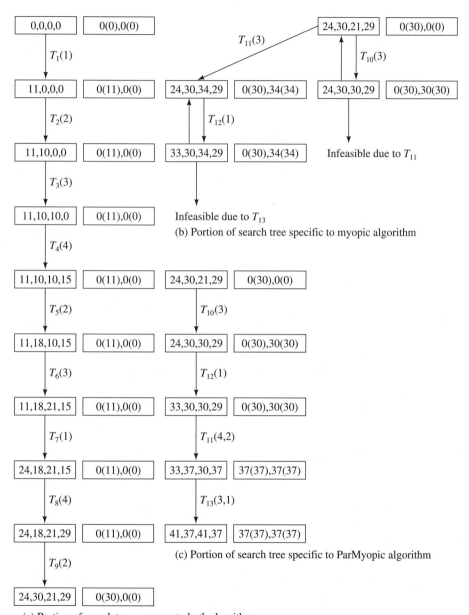

(a) Portion of search tree common to both algorithms

Figure 2.10
Search trees of the myopic and ParMyopic algorithms. From G. Manimaran and C. Siva Ram Murthy [27], in *IEEE Trans. Parallel and Distributed Systems* 9 (3). © IEEE, 1998.

parameter	explanation
MIN_C	minimum computation time of tasks, taken as 30
MAX_C	maximum computation time of tasks, taken as 60
R	laxity parameter denotes the tightness of the deadline
UseP	probability that a task uses a resource
ShareP	probability that a task uses a resource in shared mode, taken as 0.5
K	size of feasibility check window
W	weightage given to $EST(T_i)$ for H calculation
num-btrk	number of backtracks permitted in the search
num-proc	number of processors considered for simulation
num-res	number of resource types considered for simulation
max-split	maximum degree of parallelization of a task

Figure 2.11
Simulation parameters. From G. Manimaran and C. Siva Ram Murthy [27], in *IEEE Trans. Parallel and Distributed Systems* 9 (3). © IEEE, 1998.

H value ($H_{11} = 70$ as compared to $H_{13} = 71$). Therefore, the schedule is extended by T_{11} by parallelizing it and scheduling its split tasks on P_2 and P_4. Finally, T_{13} is scheduled. Note that all the tasks are feasible in the schedule.

2.5.7 Simulation Studies of Myopic and ParMyopic Algorithms

The effectiveness of task parallelization in meeting a task's deadline has been studied in [27] for the ParMyopic scheduling algorithm to see whether all tasks in a given task set are schedulable before their deadlines. The metric used was schedulability of task sets, called the *success ratio,* defined as the ratio of the number of task sets found schedulable (by a scheduling algorithm) to the number of task sets considered for scheduling. Figure 2.11 gives the parameters used in the simulation studies.

For simulation, schedulable task sets are generated using the following approach:

1. Tasks (of a task set) are generated to form a schedule until the schedule length is *schedule length,* which is an input parameter, with no idle time in the processors, as described in [33]. The computation time c_i^1 of a task T_i is chosen randomly between *MIN_C* and *MAX_C*.

2. The deadline of a task T_i is randomly chosen in the range from *SC* to $(1 + R) * SC$, where *SC* is the *shortest completion time* of the task set generated in the previous step.

3. The resource requirements of a task are generated based on the input parameters *UseP* and *ShareP*.

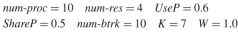

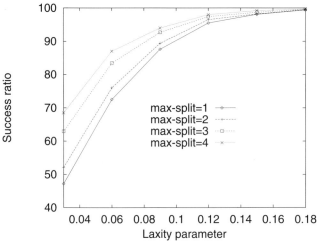

Figure 2.12
Effect of laxity parameter. From G. Manimaran and C. Siva Ram Murthy [27], in *IEEE Trans. Parallel and Distributed Systems* 9 (3). © IEEE, 1998.

4. The computation time c_i^j of a task T_i when executed on j processors, $j \geq 2$, is equal to $\lfloor c_i^{j-1} * (j - 1)/j \rfloor + 1$. For example, when $c_i^1 = 12$, the computation times c_i^2, c_i^3, and c_i^4 are 7, 5, and 4, respectively.

Each point in the performance curves (figures 2.12–2.16) is the average of five simulation runs each with 200 task sets. Each task set contains 175 to 200 tasks because the *schedule length* is fixed at 800 during the task set generation. For all the simulation runs, the number of instances of every resource is taken as two.

Figures 2.12–2.16 represent the success ratio by varying R, W, $UseP$, $num\text{-}btrk$, and K, respectively. When *max-split* is 1, the task is considered to be nonparallelizable, and the ParMyopic algorithm behaves like the myopic algorithm. Note that the scheduling costs for different values of *max-split* are held equal, by making the number of tasks checked for feasibility $(\overline{K})$ a variable, as discussed earlier; that is, when *max-split* $= 1$, $\overline{K} = K$, and $\overline{K} \leq K$ for *max-split* > 1. From figures 2.12–2.16, it is interesting to note that an increase in the degree of parallelization increases the success ratio for the speedup function used.

2.5.7.1 Effect of Laxity Parameter Figure 2.12 shows the effect on success ratio of the laxity parameter (R), which helps in investigating the sensitivity of task parallelization

num-proc = 10   *num-res* = 4   *UseP* = 0.6
ShareP = 0.5   *R* = 0.09   *K* = 7   *num-btrk* = 10

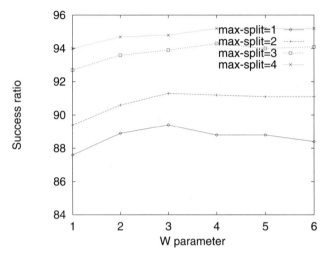

Figure 2.13
Effect of *W* parameter. From G. Manimaran and C. Siva Ram Murthy [27], in *IEEE Trans. Parallel and Distributed Systems* 9 (3). © IEEE, 1998.

to varying laxities. From figure 2.12, it is clear that lower values of *max-split* are more sensitive to change in *R* than higher values of *max-split*. For example, the success ratio offered by *max-split* = 1 varies from 47.2% to 99.4% as compared to the variation in success ratio (68.5%–99.7%) offered by *max-split* = 4, because tasks require a higher degree of parallelization (in order to meet their deadlines) when their laxities (deadlines) are tight, but the same tasks with looser laxities rarely need parallelization, since their deadlines can be met without parallelizing them. This shows that task parallelization is more effective for tasks having tighter laxities.

2.5.7.2 Effect of *W* Parameter   The sensitivity of the integrated heuristic to various degrees of task parallelization is studied in figure 2.13. The effect of *W* for different values of *max-split* offers a similar trend, as the success ratio increases initially with increasing *W* and saturates for larger values of *W*. Increasing *W* beyond 6.0 would decrease the success ratio (which is not shown in the figure), because when *W* is very large, the integrated heuristic behaves like a simple heuristic, which takes care of only the availability of processors and resources, ignoring the task's deadline. Similarly, when *W* = 0, the success ratio would be very poor, as the integrated heuristic reduces to EDF, which is also a simple heuristic.

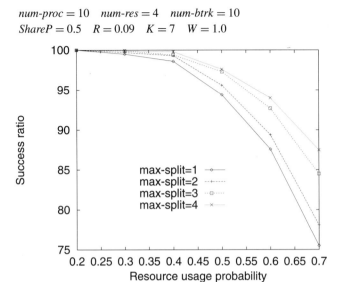

num-proc = 10   *num-res* = 4   *num-btrk* = 10
ShareP = 0.5   *R* = 0.09   *K* = 7   *W* = 1.0

Figure 2.14
Effect of resource usage probability. From G. Manimaran and C. Siva Ram Murthy [27], in *IEEE Trans. Parallel and Distributed Systems* 9 (3). © IEEE, 1998.

2.5.7.3 Effect of Resource Usage   Figure 2.14 shows the effect of resource usage on success ratio by fixing *R*, *K*, *num-btrk*, and *ShareP* values as 0.09, 7, 10, and 0.5, respectively. From figure 2.14, we observe that the success ratio decreases with increasing *UseP* because resource conflicts among tasks increase, causing the value of EST(T_i) to be decided by the availability of required resources rather than by the availability of processors and ready time of the task T_i. For lower values of resource usage (*UseP*), the difference between the success ratio offered by *max-split* = 4 and *max-split* = 1 is less compared to the difference in the success ratio at higher values of *UseP*. This shows that task parallelization is more effective when the resource constraints among tasks are high. When *UseP* is fixed and *ShareP* is varied (not shown), the success ratio increases with increasing *ShareP*.

2.5.7.4 Effect of Number of Backtracks   Figure 2.15 plots the impact of number of backtracks on the success ratio for various values of *max-split*. From the plots, it is interesting to note that the success ratio does not improve significantly with increasing values of *num-btrk*, for all values of *max-split*. This clearly motivates the need for finding techniques that increase the success ratio without increasing scheduling cost by fixing the number of backtracks. The exploitation of parallelism in a task used in the ParMyopic algorithm

$num\text{-}proc = 10 \quad num\text{-}res = 4 \quad UseP = 0.6$
$ShareP = 0.5 \quad R = 0.09 \quad K = 7 \quad W = 1.0$

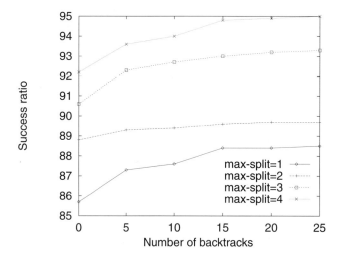

Figure 2.15
Effect of number of backtracks. From G. Manimaran and C. Siva Ram Murthy [27], in *IEEE Trans. Parallel and Distributed Systems* 9 (3). © IEEE, 1998.

is one such technique, as demonstrated by the simulation results for different values of *max-split*.

2.5.7.5   Effect of Size of the Feasibility Check Window   Figure 2.16 shows the effect of varying the size of feasibility check window (K) on success ratio for different values of *max-split*. Note that for larger values of K, the algorithm has a more look-ahead nature, and the number of H function evaluations in a feasibility window is more, which also means an increase in scheduling cost. Increasing K increases the success ratio for all values of *max-split*. This effect is greater for lower values of *max-split*; that is, larger values of *max-split* are less sensitive to changes in K, indicating that more task sets can be feasibly scheduled, for the same scheduling cost, by allowing task parallelization than by nonparallelizable task scheduling.

2.5.7.6   Summary of Simulation Studies

• Increasing the size of the feasibility check window (K) increases the success ratio for all values of *max-split*.

• Task parallelization is more effective when tasks have tighter laxities and when resource constraints among tasks are high.

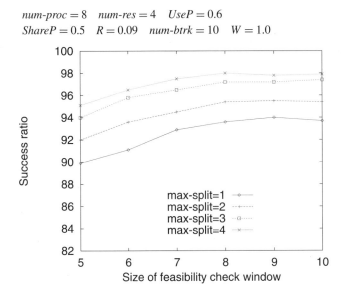

Figure 2.16
Effect of size of feasibility check window. From G. Manimaran and C. Siva Ram Murthy [27], in *IEEE Trans. Parallel and Distributed Systems* 9 (3). © IEEE, 1998.

• The sensitivity of *W* for different values of task parallelization offers a similar trend.

• The number of backtracks has a less significant impact on the success ratio compared to that of the other parameters. This clearly indicates the need to spend scheduling cost on task parallelization rather than on backtracking.

2.6 Dynamic Best-Effort Scheduling Approach

In dynamic best-effort scheduling, no schedulability check is performed while admitting a new task into the system. In some sense, every task that has arrived in the system is admitted, and the scheduler tries its level best to guarantee the execution of these new tasks. Therefore, a best-effort scheduler cannot ensure the predictability of every task's execution. In this approach, tasks are assigned priorities based on RMS, EDF, or LLF policies, and task execution occurs in priority order. The arrival of a high-priority task preempts a currently executing low-priority task. A task is executed, possibly with preemption, until it completes its execution before its deadline or its deadline has arrived, whichever happens first. The EDF and LLF algorithms have optimal behavior as long as no overloads occur, but performance degradation can occur under system overloads, which is the major disadvantage of the dynamic best-effort approach. But since dynamic algorithms must perform well under varying loading conditions, the task selected by the algorithm for execution or rejection has to be chosen very carefully. In practice, this requires that confidence in the system be gained through extensive simulation, recoding the tasks, and adjusting the priorities.

If tasks have values associated with them, during overloads, those with lower values should be discarded to improve the overall performance of the system. There are several ways to achieve this. Tasks of lower importance can be removed one at a time and in strict order from lowest to highest importance. This incurs higher overhead compared to a scheme that chooses any lower-valued task, but neither method takes into account, in deciding which tasks to abandon, how much time can be gained by discarding a particular task. Discarding tasks in lowest-value-density-first (LVDF) order does, however, take a task's computation time into consideration in making this decision [33]. The LVDF policy considers the value and worst-case computation time of a task, defined as value of the task and divided by worst-case computation time, signifying value per unit time, in determining what tasks to execute and which to discard.

There is no optimal algorithm for on-line scheduling of tasks to maximize the total task value. Therefore, attention has turned to competitiveness analysis, a worst-case-bound method, which provides good insight into the design of best-effort scheduling algorithms. To evaluate a particular on-line scheduling algorithm, the algorithm's worst-case performance is compared with that of all possible competing algorithms, including the clairvoyant algorithm. The results of such analysis can be useful in handling overloads effectively. In [3], the relationship between the amount of overloading permitted and the bound is also quantified.

2.6.1   Competitiveness Analysis of Best-Effort Approaches

Assume tasks are aperiodic (no a priori knowledge about tasks), independent, and preemptable without penalty. In a multiprocessor system, a preempted task can be resumed on any processor. The *competitive factor,* B_A, of an on-line scheduling algorithm, A, is defined as

$$\frac{V_A(S)}{V_{CA}(S)} \geq B_A, \quad \text{for all } S, \tag{2.4}$$

where $V_A(S)$ is the total value obtained by algorithm A, $V_{CA}(S)$ is the total value obtained by the clairvoyant algorithm, and $B_A \in [0, 1]$ because $\forall S\ V_A(S) \leq V_{CA}(S)$. The *upper bound,* B, is defined as $B \geq B_A, \forall A$. A bound is tight if it can be reached.

Suppose a task has a value equal to its computation time on successful completion and 0 otherwise. It is known that no dynamic scheduling algorithm can guarantee a cumulative value greater than 0.25 of the value obtained by a clairvoyant algorithm (general case of result 3). This result can be extended to cases in which tasks have different value densities. Let γ be the ratio of the highest and lowest value densities of tasks. The upper bound of the competitive factor for the on-line scheduling is $1/(\gamma + 1 + 2\sqrt{\gamma})$. As a special case, if γ is 1, the upper bound is 0.25, which is the same result mentioned above. With two processors, the upper bound is 0.5 (result 3) and is tight when all the tasks have the same value density and zero laxity. Thus, in the worst case, for the dual-processor case, the upper bound is twice the value obtained from two separate uniprocessor systems. These results open up scope for employing multiprocessor systems with dynamic best-effort approaches in some real-time systems without sacrificing predictability.

2.6.2   Practical Considerations

Dynamic best-effort approaches require implementation mechanisms similar to those found in priority-based non-real-time systems, the primary difference being the way the two approaches assign priorities. In dynamic best-effort approaches, two queues are maintained: a ready queue and a wait queue. The ready queue is sorted based on priority order. Tasks waiting for a nonprocessor resource are queued in the wait queue. When a task releases a resource or completes its execution, one or more tasks may move from the wait queue to the ready queue. Such a move or the arrival of a high-priority task may preempt the currently running task because of the change in the relative priorities of tasks. Thus, the task priorities must be recomputed each time a new task enters the ready queue, and the ready queue should be reordered based on the new priorities. Dispatching involves preemption and context switching, with the possibility of placing the preempted task, according to its priority, back into the ready queue for future resumption [36].

2.7   Integrated Scheduling of Hard and Quality of Service–Degradable Tasks

Real-time systems have tasks with varying deadline requirements: hard, firm, and soft, as discussed in section 1.2.2. Multimedia information is increasingly being used as input in hard real-time systems. For example, in attack helicopters such as the Comanche, audio and video sensors support monitoring and sophisticated control of the helicopter [16]. This requires flexible and dynamic scheduling of the hard real-time and multimedia (soft deadline) tasks. Because of the wide range of applications having tasks of both the hard- and soft-deadline category, it is natural to look at the possibility of a common platform that supports both hard and soft real-time tasks. Scheduling algorithms for supporting multimedia in conjunction with traditional non-real-time applications can be found in [15, 17, 32].

2.7.1   Multimedia Server Approach

In [16], a dynamic planning-based algorithm was proposed for scheduling of multimedia streams[5] and hard real-time tasks using a multimedia server approach. A *multimedia server* is a periodic task that is dynamically created and scheduled along with hard real-time tasks. Multiple multimedia streams are multiplexed into multimedia server instances to reduce the cost of scheduling the multimedia streams, since the cost of scheduling each multimedia stream instance as a hard real-time task would be too high. Two approaches, proportional allocation and individual allocation, have been proposed for allocating multimedia streams to server instances. In the proportional-allocation approach, each multimedia task instance is proportionally allocated to multiple server instances. In the individual-allocation approach, each multimedia task instance is individually assigned to a server instance between the task's ready time and its deadline. If no such server instance exists, then a new server instance with a period equal to that of the multimedia stream is created dynamically. All server instances whose start times[6] are before the latest deadline of the hard real-time task in the currently active task set are scheduled along with the hard real-time tasks using the myopic algorithm. If the task set is not schedulable, then the system resorts to quality of service (QoS) degradation by reducing the computation time of each of the server instances. However, in [16], no limit was fixed regarding the amount by which the stream computation time could be decreased. How to quantify the resulting QoS of the degraded streams was left as an open problem. Moreover, the study did not deal with how to specify and guarantee the minimum quality requirement for multimedia streams.

2.7.2   Integrated Task-Scheduling Algorithms

In [1], algorithms for integrated scheduling of hard and QoS-degradable tasks have been proposed. These algorithms quantify QoS degradation by characterizing the multimedia streams using the (m, k)-firm guarantee model [37], a task model that provides scheduling flexibility by compromising on result quality to meet task deadlines. In the (m, k)-firm guarantee model, a periodic task may be given an (m, k)-firm guarantee, which means that task performance is considered acceptable as long as at least m tasks in a window of k consecutive task instances meet their deadlines. A periodic task with an (m, k)-firm guarantee experiences dynamic failure if fewer than m task instances in a window of k task instances meet their deadlines. The m and k parameters capture the minimum quality requirement of the multimedia streams. In [1], multimedia streams are mapped onto server instances using the individual-allocation algorithm, since the proportional-allocation

---

5. Streams are periodic tasks.

6. A server's start time is equal to the beginning of its period.

algorithm has high context switch overhead [16]. Some of these multimedia tasks would be characterized as optional by the (m, k) parameters of the stream. Hence a server instance will have a *mandatory* computation time equal to the sum of the computation times of the mandatory instances of the streams multiplexed onto it and a *total* computation time equal to the sum of computation times of all the stream instances multiplexed onto it. Four scheduling algorithms have been proposed that essentially differ in the policy used for degrading the QoS of multimedia streams to improve schedulability.

2.7.2.1 Scheduling Algorithm   In integrated task scheduling, the scheduler performs the following steps when a new task arrives:

1. **If** the task is a multimedia stream, multiplex the instances of the stream whose start times are before the latest deadline of the hard real-time tasks in the task set onto the existing server instances, if possible, **else** create new server instances. Insert these server instances whose start times are before the latest deadline of the hard real-time task into the task set.

2. **Else if** the task is a hard real-time task

(a) **If** the deadline of the new task is less than that of the existing hard real-time tasks, then insert the new task into the task set.

(b) **Else** insert all the server instances whose start times are before the deadline of the incoming task into the task set, along with the incoming task.

3. Schedule the tasks in the task set using one of the four integrated task-scheduling algorithms (presented later).

4. **If** *feasible* is TRUE admit the new task **else** reject it.

The algorithm will guarantee the minimum quality of all the admitted streams even if doing so requires rejection of a newly arrived hard real-time task.

Two types of algorithms have been proposed: In type 1 algorithms, a newly arrived task is either accepted or rejected based on the result of a single scheduling attempt. No rescheduling of tasks takes place. In type 2 algorithms, if the first scheduling attempt fails, the task set (including the new task) is iteratively rescheduled with QoS degradation until either a feasible schedule is produced or a specified maximum number of iterations is reached. The algorithms use preliminary admission tests that check the schedulability of tasks before actually running the scheduling algorithm to increase their efficiency.

2.7.2.2 Type 1 Algorithms   Two extreme cases are possible in which no rescheduling is required. The algorithms corresponding to these two cases are as follows:

1. *Maximum-quality algorithm.* In this algorithm, the optional portion of all the tasks in the task set is treated as mandatory. A preliminary *maximum-quality admission test* checks

the feasibility of tasks without any quality degradation. If the task set including a new task fails the admission test, then the new task is rejected without running the scheduling algorithm. Otherwise, the newly arrived task is scheduled using the myopic algorithm and admitted if the resulting task set can be feasibly scheduled and rejected if it cannot. Though the quality for the tasks is maximal, the schedulability of tasks is low.

2. *Minimum-quality algorithm.* In this algorithm, the optional portion of all the tasks in the task set is skipped completely (even if the resources are idle). A preliminary *minimum-quality admission test* checks whether a new task can be guaranteed while meeting the minimum quality requirement of all the tasks in the task set. If the task set including the new task fails the admission test, then the new task is rejected without running the scheduling algorithm. Otherwise, the newly arrived task is scheduled using the myopic algorithm and admitted if the resulting task set can be feasibly scheduled and rejected if it cannot. Though the quality of the tasks is minimal, the schedulability is high.

2.7.2.3   Type 2 Algorithms   Two type 2 algorithms result depending on whether rescheduling is done once or more than once:

1. *0/1 degradation algorithm.* In this algorithm, a new task is rejected if the resulting task set when the new task is included fails the minimum-quality admission test; otherwise the maximum-quality admission test is performed. If the task set passes the maximum-quality admission test, the tasks in the task set are scheduled, treating the optional portion of all the tasks as mandatory, using the myopic algorithm. If the task set is not schedulable or if the task set fails the maximum-quality admission test, then the optional portions of all the tasks in the task set are skipped totally, and the task set is rescheduled using the myopic algorithm. The new task is admitted or rejected depending on whether scheduling succeeds or fails. This is called a 0/1 degradation algorithm, since we provide either maximum or minimum quality for the multimedia streams.

2. *Multilevel degradation algorithm.* In this algorithm, the QoS of the tasks is degraded iteratively, so as to give maximum possible quality while meeting the deadlines of tasks. When a new task arrives, it is rejected if the resulting task set when the new task is included fails the minimum-quality admission test; otherwise the maximum-quality admission test is performed. If the task set fails the maximum-quality admission test, the computation time of the optional portion of the tasks in the task set is reduced to the point that the maximum-quality admission test succeeds, and the task set is scheduled using the myopic algorithm. If the task set is not schedulable, it is rescheduled iteratively by reducing the computation time of the optional portion of the tasks, using the divide-and-conquer approach, until *maximum* − 1 iterations have been performed or scheduling succeeds, whichever is earlier. If the task set is still not schedulable after *maximum* − 1 iterations,

then (in the last iteration) the optional portion of all the tasks is skipped totally and the task set is rescheduled. The new task is accepted or rejected depending on whether the task set is schedulable.

Simulation Results: In simulation studies, two metrics, success ratio (measure of schedulability) and quality of multimedia streams, were used to evaluate the algorithms' performance. It was observed that the QoS degradation algorithms always have higher schedulability than the maximum-quality algorithm (no QoS degradation). An increase in the percentage of multimedia stream load in the system or a lowering of the minimum QoS requirement of streams increases schedulability without compromising much on quality. An increase in the laxity of hard real-time tasks increases both schedulability and quality. It was also observed that the multilevel degradation algorithm offers the best performance on both metrics. Even a small degradation in the quality of multimedia streams can significantly improve schedulability of both hard real-time tasks and multimedia streams.

2.8   Real-Time Scheduling with Feedback Control

Despite the significant body of research on the four paradigms of real-time scheduling, most known scheduling algorithms, such as RMS, EDF, and Spring (Myopic) scheduling, are of open-loop type. *Open-loop* refers to the fact that once schedules are created in these algorithms, they are not adjusted based on continuous feedback [44]. Although open-loop scheduling algorithms can perform well in static or dynamic systems in which the workload (tasks) can be accurately modeled, they perform poorly in unpredictable dynamic systems where the workload cannot be accurately modeled [25, 44]. For example, EDF scheduling results in rapid degradation in performance under overload situations, whereas dynamic planning-based algorithms, such as the Spring scheduling algorithm, underutilize system resources, as they schedule tasks based on worst-case workload parameters (e.g., worst-case computation time of tasks), even though they employ resource reclaiming (discussed in chapter 3).

Unfortunately, many real-world systems are dynamic, and their workloads are unpredictable. It is usually expensive to build a *resource-sufficient* system to prevent all transient overloads caused by changes in the environment and/or faults in the system. Thus it is impossible to meet every task deadline. The objective of scheduling in such systems is to meet as many deadlines as possible, with a provision for guaranteeing the deadlines (or handling the deadline misses) of all hard real-time tasks.

In an uncertain environment, there is always a difference between what is desired and what a system can offer. If this difference is not fed back into the scheduling scheme, its

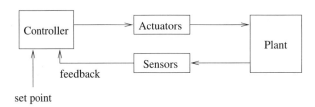

Figure 2.17
General structure of a feedback control system

performance will be unsatisfactory. Thus, a scheduling scheme can offer a better performance in an uncertain environment only if it has a method to adapt its functioning based
on observed data.

Feedback strategies are the focus of the control systems area. This area is highly mature
and thus can offer significant insights into differing feedback strategies [6, 9]. One of the
lessons control theory offers is that feedback, if intelligently used, can provide significant
dividends in guarding against uncertainty. In recent years, interest in applying feedback
control theory to real-time task scheduling has been growing [25, 44].

Figure 2.17 shows a typical feedback control system, consisting of a controller, a plant
to be controlled, sensors, and actuators. The system defines the following quantities:

• *Controlled variable.* The quantity that is measured and controlled.

• *Set point.* The constant that represents the correct value of the controlled variable.

• *Error.* The difference between the current value of the controlled variable and the set
point.

• *Manipulated variable.* The quantity that the controller varies to affect the value of the
controlled variable.

A typical feedback control system works as follows:

1. The system periodically monitors (through sensors) and compares the controlled variable to the set point to determine the error.

2. The controller computes the required control, using the control function of the system,
based on the error.

3. The actuators change the value of the manipulated variable to control the system.

To apply feedback control techniques in real-time scheduling, the various quantities—
such as the controlled variable, manipulated variable, set point, error, control function,
and actuation mechanisms—need to be identified and the feedback loop set up based on

these selections. The choice of controlled variable depends on system goal. Task *miss ratio,* defined as the percentage of scheduled (admitted) tasks that miss their deadlines, is a choice for the controlled variable. System utilization is a choice for the manipulated variable, as the miss ratio and rejection (guarantee) ratio depend on this. Other possible choices for the manipulated variable are the periods/deadlines of tasks, in applications that have the flexibility to adjust these task parameters [38].

Note that in a dynamic scheduling environment, there are two performance metrics: task rejection ratio and task miss ratio. The former depends on the schedulability check of the scheduling algorithm, and the latter depends on the actual computation times of the tasks in comparison to the computation times based on which they were scheduled. If the actual computation time of a task is greater, then the task misses its deadline. One would think that the miss ratio could be maintained at zero by scheduling tasks based on a very conservative estimation of computation times. But this would increase the rejection ratio of the system, making the system underutilized. Thus the computation time of tasks introduces a trade-off between rejection ratio and miss ratio. The objective of a scheduling algorithm is to reduce the rejection ratio by maintaining a constant miss ratio (equal to the set point).

A feedback control–based scheduling system usually starts with a schedule based on the nominal assumptions of the arriving tasks (expected computation time and deadline). The system then monitors the actual performance of the schedule, compares it to the system requirements, and computes the differences. The system then invokes control functions to assess the impact of these differences and apply a correction mechanism to keep the system within an acceptable range of performance. Under feedback control–based scheduling, the following questions, which are among the key areas of current research, need to be answered:

1. What are the right choices of the system parameters and the control functions for building a stable, high-performance predictable scheduler?

2. How should a feedback control scheduling system be modeled?

3. How should uncertainty be quantified?

2.9   Summary

• The problem of multiprocessor scheduling is to determine when and on which processor a given task executes. This can be done either statically or dynamically.

• The RMS algorithm assigns static priorities to tasks based on their periods, and the EDF and LLF algorithms assign dynamic priorities to tasks based on their deadlines and laxities, respectively. For a uniprocessor system, RMS is an optimal fixed priority scheduling scheme, and EDF and LLF are optimal dynamic priority scheduling schemes.

• Priority inversion is a situation in which a low-priority task prevents a high-priority task from executing. This can occur among tasks that access sharable resources. Priority inheritance and priority ceiling are two well-known protocols that prevent priority inversion.

• Non-preemptive scheduling is computationally more difficult than preemptive scheduling. Many non-preemptive scheduling problems have been shown to be NP-complete, implying that heuristics must be used for such problems.

• Parallelizable task scheduling is an intermediate solution that tries to reconcile the conflicting demands of higher schedulability and lower scheduling overhead offered by preemptive and non-preemptive scheduling, respectively.

• When dealing with dynamic scheduling, it becomes necessary to be aware of several anomalies so that they can be avoided.

• Dynamic planning combines the flexibility of dynamic scheduling with the predictability offered by schedulability checking.

• As multimedia information is being increasingly used in hard real-time systems, integrated scheduling of hard-deadline and multimedia (soft-deadline) tasks is becoming a problem of growing interest.

• Open loop scheduling algorithms perform poorly in unpredictable environments. Feedback control-based scheduling algorithms offer better performance in such environments.

Exercises

1. What are the motivations for dynamic scheduling of real-time tasks?

2. What is predictability in the context of static and dynamic scheduling algorithms?

3. In a real-time system, memory is a bottleneck, and the periods of tasks are relatively prime. Which scheduling approach is best suited for this system? Why?

4. What are the motivations for parallelizable task scheduling?

5. Construct a periodic task set (with computation times and periods) that can be feasibly scheduled by the EDF but not by the RMS algorithm.

6. Show that run-time anomaly occurs for the periodic task set in figure 2.18 when the actual computation of first instance of T_3 is 3.

7. In the myopic algorithm, does the feasibility check window make sense when the tasks are independent and the task queue is ordered based on deadlines?

task	comp. time		period
T_i	c_i^1	c_i^2	p_i
T_1	3	2	4
T_2	3	2	4
T_3	4	2	8

Figure 2.18
Exercise 2.6 task set (run-time anomaly)

task	ready time	comp. time	deadline	resource usage
T_1	0	6	10	shared
T_2	0	8	14	shared
T_3	0	5	17	exclusive
T_4	0	7	18	

Figure 2.19
Exercise 2.8 task set (Myopic schedule)

task	ready	comp. time		deadline	resource
T_i	time (r_i)	c_i^1	c_i^2	d_i	usage
T_1	0	6	4	10	
T_2	1	7	4	13	shared
T_3	0	3	2	16	exclusive
T_4	2	7	4	17	
T_5	3	9	5	19	

Figure 2.20
Exercise 2.9 task set (Myopic and ParMyopic schedule)

8. Construct schedules for the task set in figure 2.19 using MIN-D, MIN-S, MIN-L, MIN-S + MIN-D, MIN-S + MIN-L, and MIN-D + EST() heuristics, where MIN-D, MIN-S, MIN-L, and EST() denote minimum deadline first, minimum processing time first, minimum laxity first, and earliest start time, respectively. Assume the size of feasibility check window to be 2 and the number of processors to be 2.

9. Construct schedules for the task set in figure 2.20 using the myopic and ParMyopic algorithms. Assume the size of feasibility window to be 3, the W parameter to be 1, and the number of processors to be 2. What is the number of backtracks required for obtaining a feasible schedule for both the algorithms?

References

[1] M. Anita, G. Manimaran, and C. Siva Ram Murthy. "Integrated dynamic scheduling of hard and QoS degradable real-time tasks in multiprocessor systems." In *Proc. IEEE Intl. Conf. on Real-Time Systems and Applications,* Hiroshima, Japan, 1998.

[2] D. Babbar and P. Krueger. "On-line hard real-time scheduling of parallel tasks on partitionable multiprocessors." In *Proc. Intl. Conf. on Parallel Processing,* vol. 2, pp. 29–38, 1994.

[3] S. Baruah, G. Koren, D. Mao, B. Mishra, A. R. L. Rosier, D. E. Shasha, and F. Wang. "On the competitiveness of on-line real-time task scheduling." *Real-Time Systems,* vol. 4, no. 2, 1992.

[4] K. P. Belkhale and P. Banerjee. "Approximate algorithms for the partitionable independent task scheduling problem." In *Proc. IEEE Intl. Conf. on Parallel Processing,* vol. 1, pp. 72–75, 1990.

[5] J. Blazewicz. "Scheduling dependent tasks with different arrival times to meet deadlines." In *Modelling and Performance Evaluation Computer Systems* (E. Gelenbe, ed.), North-Holland, Amsterdam, 1976.

[6] S. P. Boyd and C. H. Barratt. *Linear Controller Design: Limits of Performance.* Prentice Hall, Englewood Cliffs, New Jersey, 1991.

[7] A. Burns. "Scheduling hard real-time systems: A review." *Software Engg. Journal,* vol. 6, no. 3, pp. 116–128, May 1991.

[8] E. G. Coffman and R. Graham. "Optimal scheduling for two-processor systems." *Acta Informatica,* no. 1, pp. 200–213, 1972.

[9] M. A. Dahleh and I. J. Diaz-Bobillo. *Control of Uncertain Systems: A Linear Programming Approach.* Prentice Hall, Englewood Cliffs, New Jersey, 1995.

[10] M. L. Dertouzos and A. K. Mok. "Multiprocessor on-line scheduling of hard real-time tasks." *IEEE Trans. Software Engg.,* vol. 15, no. 12, pp. 1497–1506, Dec. 1989.

[11] R. Garey and D. Johnson. "Complexity bounds for multiprocessor scheduling with resource constraints." *SIAM J. Computing,* vol. 4, no. 3, pp. 187–200, 1975.

[12] R. Graham. "Bounds on the performance of scheduling algorithms." In *Computer and Job Shop Scheduling Theory* (E. G. Coffman, ed.), John Wiley and Sons, pp. 165–227, 1976.

[13] K. S. Hong and J. Y-T. Leung. "On-line scheduling of real-time tasks." *IEEE Trans. Computers,* vol. 41, no. 10, pp. 1326–1331, Oct. 1992.

[14] T. C. Hu. "Parallel scheduling and assembly line problems." *Operations Research,* vol. 9, pp. 841–848, Nov. 1961.

[15] M. B. Jones, D. Rosu, and M-C. Rosu. "CPU reservations and time constraints: Efficient, predictable scheduling of independent activities." In *Proc. ACM Symp. on Operating Systems Principles,* Oct. 1997.

[16] H. Kaneko, J. A. Stankovic, S. Sen, and K. Ramamritham. "Integrated scheduling of multimedia and hard real-time tasks." In *Proc. IEEE Real-Time Systems Symp.,* pp. 206–217, 1996.

[17] K. Kong, M. Kim, H. Lee, and J. Lee. "A rate regulating scheme for scheduling multimedia tasks." *IEICE Trans. Information and Systems,* vol. E80-D, no. 12, pp. 1166–1175, Dec. 1997.

[18] R. Krishnamoorthy and E. Ma. "An approximate algorithm for scheduling tasks on varying partition sizes in partitionable multiprocessor systems." *IEEE Trans. Computers,* vol. 41, no. 12, pp. 1572–1579, Dec. 1992.

[19] E. L. Lawler. "Optimal scheduling of a single machine subject to precedence constraints." *Management Science,* vol. 19, 1973.

[20] E. L. Lawler and C. U. Martel. "Scheduling periodically occurring tasks on multiprocessors." *Information Processing Letters,* vol. 12, no. 1, pp. 9–12, Feb. 1981.

[21] E. L. Lawler. "Recent results in the theory of machine scheduling." In *Mathematical Programming: The State of the Art* (Bachen et al., ed.), Springer-Verlag, pp. 202–233, 1983.

[22] J. P. Lehiczky, L. Sha, and Y. Ding. "The rate monotonic scheduling algorithm—Exact characterization and average-case behaviour." In *Proc. IEEE Real-Time Systems Symp.*, Dec. 1989.

[23] C. Liu and J. Layland. "Scheduling algorithms for multiprogramming in a hard real-time environment." *Journal of ACM,* vol. 20, no. 1, pp. 45–61, Jan. 1973.

[24] J. W. S. Liu, K. J. Lin, W. K. Shih, A. C. Yu, J. Y. Chung, and W. Zhao. "Algorithms for scheduling imprecise computations." *IEEE Computer,* vol. 24, no. 5, pp. 58–68, May 1991.

[25] C. Lu, J. A. Stankovic, G. Tao, and S. H. Son. "Design and evaluation of feedback control EDF scheduling algorithm." In *Proc. Real-Time Systems Symp.*, 1999.

[26] G. Manimaran, C. Siva Ram Murthy, Machiraju Vijay, and K. Ramamritham. "New algorithms for resource reclaiming from precedence constrained tasks in multiprocessor real-time systems." *Journal of Parallel and Distributed Computing,* vol. 44, no. 2, pp. 123–132, Aug. 1997.

[27] G. Manimaran and C. Siva Ram Murthy. "An efficient dynamic scheduling algorithm for multiprocessor real-time systems." *IEEE Trans. Parallel and Distributed Systems,* vol. 9, no. 3, pp. 312–319, Mar. 1998.

[28] G. Manimaran, C. Siva Ram Murthy, and K. Ramamritham. "A new approach for scheduling of parallelizable tasks in real-time multiprocessor systems." *Real-Time Systems,* vol. 15, pp. 39–60, July 1998.

[29] R. McNaughton. "Scheduling with deadlines and loss functions." *Management Science,* vol. 6, no. 1, pp. 1–12, 1959.

[30] A. K. Mok and M. L. Dertouzos. "Multiprocessor scheduling in a hard real-time environment." In *Proc. Texas Conf. on Comput. Systems,* 1978.

[31] A. K. Mok. "Fundamental design problems of distributed systems for the hard real-time environment." Ph.D. diss., Dept. of Electrical Engineering and Computer Science, Massachusetts Institute of Technology, Cambridge, MA, May 1983.

[32] J. Neih and M. S. Lam. "The design, implementation and evaluation of SMART: A scheduler for multimedia applications." In *Proc. ACM Symp. on Operating Systems Principles,* Oct. 1997.

[33] K. Ramamritham, J. A. Stankovic, and P.-F. Shiah. "Efficient scheduling algorithms for real-time multiprocessor systems." *IEEE Trans. Parallel and Distributed Systems,* vol. 1, no. 2, pp. 184–194, Apr. 1990.

[34] K. Ramamritham and J. A. Stankovic. "Scheduling algorithms and operating systems support for real-time systems." *Proc. IEEE,* vol. 82, no. 1, pp. 55–67, Jan. 1994.

[35] K. Ramamritham. "Allocation and scheduling of precedence-related periodic tasks." *IEEE Trans. Parallel and Distributed Systems,* vol. 6, no. 4, pp. 412–420, Apr. 1995.

[36] K. Ramamritham. "Dynamic priority scheduling." In *Real-Time Systems—Specification, Verification, and Analysis* (M. Joseph, ed.), pp. 66–96, Prentice Hall (International Series in Computer Science), London, 1996.

[37] P. Ramanathan. "Graceful degradation in real-time control applications using (m, k)-firm guarantee." In *Proc. IEEE Fault-Tolerant Computing Symp.*, pp. 132–141, Seattle, 1997.

[38] D. Seto et al. "On task schedulability in real-time control systems." In *Proc. IEEE Real-Time Systems Symp.*, 1996.

[39] L. Sha, R. Rajkumar, and J. P. Lehoczky. "Priority inheritance protocols: An approach to real-time synchronization." *IEEE Trans. Computers,* vol. 39, no. 9, pp. 1175–1185, Sept. 1990.

[40] L. Sha, R. Rajkumar, and S. S. Sathaye. "Generalized rate-monotonic scheduling theory: A framework for developing real-time systems." *Proc. IEEE,* vol. 82, no. 1, pp. 68–82, Jan. 1994.

[41] C. Shen, K. Ramamritham, and J. A. Stankovic. "Resource reclaiming in multiprocessor real-time systems." *IEEE Trans. Parallel and Distributed Systems,* vol. 4, no. 4, pp. 382–397, Apr. 1993.

[42] J. A. Stankovic and K. Ramamritham. "The Spring Kernel: A new paradigm for real-time operating systems." *ACM Operating Systems Review,* vol. 23, no. 3, pp. 54–71, July 1989.

[43] J. A. Stankovic. "Implications of classical scheduling results for real-time systems." *IEEE Computer,* vol. 28, no. 6, pp. 16–25, June 1995.

[44] J. A. Stankovic, C. Lu, S. H. Son, and G. Tao. "The case for feedback control real-time scheduling." In *Proc. EuroMicro Conf. on Real-Time Systems,* 1999.

[45] J. D. Ullman. "Polynomial complete scheduling problems." *ACM Symp. Operating Systems Principles,* pp. 96–101, 1973.

[46] Q. Wang and K. H. Cheng. "A heuristic of scheduling parallel tasks and its analysis." *SIAM J. Computing,* vol. 21, no. 2, pp. 281–294, Apr. 1992.

[47] J. Xu and D. L. Parnas. "Scheduling processes with release times, deadlines, precedence, and exclusion relations." *IEEE Trans. Software Engg.,* vol. 16, no. 3, pp. 360–369, Mar. 1990.

[48] W. Zhao, K. Ramamritham, and J. A. Stankovic. "Scheduling tasks with resource requirements in hard real-time systems." *IEEE Trans. Software Engg.,* vol. 13, no. 5, pp. 564–577, May 1987.

[49] A. Y. Zomaya. "Parallel processing for real-time simulation: A case study." *IEEE Parallel & Distributed Technology,* pp. 49–56, June 1996.

3 Resource Reclaiming in Multiprocessor Real-Time Systems

Overview

In the previous chapter, we highlighted that the dynamic scheduling of tasks in a multiprocessor real-time system involves the scheduling of dynamically arriving real-time tasks onto the processors and reclaiming resources at run time to utilize system resources efficiently. In this chapter, we discuss the resource reclaiming problem in detail, considering the following: (1) a model for dynamic scheduling of tasks that accommodates resource reclaiming, (2) motivations for resource reclaiming, (3) properties of resource-reclaiming algorithms, (4) some of the known resource reclaiming algorithms, (5) experimental issues in comparing different reclaiming algorithms, and (6) a comparative study of these algorithms.

3.1   Scheduler Model

In dynamic scheduling, when a new set of tasks arrives at the system, the scheduler dynamically determines the feasibility of scheduling these new tasks without jeopardizing the guarantees that have been provided for the previously scheduled tasks. Thus, for predictable executions, schedulability must be analyzed before a task begins executing. For schedulability analysis, tasks' worst-case computation times must be taken into account. A feasible schedule is generated if the timing, resource, and precedence constraints of all the tasks in the new set can be satisfied, that is, if the schedulability analysis is successful. If a feasible schedule cannot be found, the new set of tasks is rejected, and the previous schedule remains intact. Such planning allows admission control and results in a reservation-based system. Tasks are dispatched according to the feasible schedule generated in the schedulability analysis. This type of scheduling approach is called dynamic planning-based scheduling [10]. Spring kernel [9] is an example of dynamic planning-based scheduling.

Dynamic scheduling can be either distributed or centralized. In a *distributed* dynamic scheduling scheme, tasks arrive independently at each processor (node), and the local scheduler at the processor determines whether it can satisfy the constraints of the incoming task. The task is accepted if its constraints can be satisfied; otherwise the local scheduler tries to find another processor that can accept the task.

In a *centralized* scheme, all the tasks arrive at a central processor, the scheduler, from which they are distributed to other processors in the system (*application processors*), which in turn dispatch the tasks for execution; that is, the system has two phases, namely, the *scheduling phase* and the *dispatching phase*. The scheduler and the application processors communicate through *dispatch queues*. Each application processor P_i has its own dispatch queue $DQ[i]$. This organization, shown in figure 3.1, ensures that the application

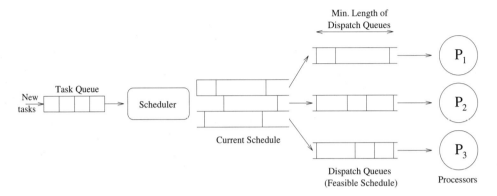

Figure 3.1
Parallel execution of scheduler and processors. From [7]. © 1997 by Academic Press.

processors will find some tasks in the dispatch queues when they finish the execution of their current tasks. The scheduler will be running in parallel with the application processors by scheduling the newly arriving tasks and periodically updating the dispatch queues. The scheduler must ensure that the dispatch queues are always filled to their minimum capacity (if there are tasks left with it) for this parallel operation. What this minimum capacity is depends on the worst-case time the scheduler requires to reschedule its already scheduled tasks upon the arrival of a new task [12]. The scheduler arrives at a feasible schedule taking the worst-case computation times, deadlines, and constraints of the tasks into account.

In a centralized dynamic scheduling scheme with resource reclaiming, there is an additional phase, called the *resource reclaiming phase,* apart from the standard scheduling and dispatching phases. The scheduling is done by the scheduler, dispatching is done by the application processors, and the resource reclaiming can be done either locally at the application processors or centrally at the scheduler. In the former case, an application processor invokes a reclaimer immediately after the completion of its currently executing task. On the other hand, if the resource reclaimer runs on the central processor, the central processor sends new schedules to the application processors whose feasible schedules have been modified as resources have been reclaimed. In a dynamic real-time system, predictability is one of the most important issues, meaning that once the scheduler admits a task into the system, the task's guaranteed execution should never be violated by the scheduler, dispatcher, or reclaimer.

Figure 3.2 demonstrates the entire parallel operation of the scheduler and the processors. The cut-off time in the algorithm depicted in the figure is to ensure this parallel operation and is directly related to the minimum length of the dispatch queues. Further, the scheduler must be aware of the amount of time reclaimed by the reclaiming algorithm so that it can

1. **For** all processors P_i, $1 \le i \le m$, where m is the number of application processors
    1.1 Take the first task T_f from $DQ[i]$.
    1.2 **If** T_f can be executed, start execution.
    1.3 **While** $DQ[i]$ is not empty **do**
        1.3.1 **If** there is a task under execution on P_i,
            1.3.1.1 Wait for its completion.
            1.3.1.2 Invoke resource reclaiming.
(a) Execution of the tasks on processors

1. **While** (true) **do**
    1.1 **Repeat**
        1.1.1 Whenever a new task arrives,
        1.1.2 Perform the schedulability check.
        1.1.3 Form a feasible schedule taking into account the constraints.
    1.2 **until** cut-off-time.
    1.3 Update the dispatch queues.
    1.4 Compute new cut-off-time.
(b) Scheduler

Figure 3.2
Parallel operation of the processors and the scheduler. From [7]. © 1997 by Academic Press.

schedule the new tasks correctly and effectively. A protocol for achieving this is suggested in [12]. Therefore, to achieve better performance, any dynamic scheduling scheme should have a scheduler with associated resource reclaiming.

A centralized scheduling scheme is more appropriate for shared memory multiprocessor systems. A distributed scheduling scheme is more appropriate for distributed memory multiprocessors and distributed systems.[1] In this chapter, we consider only the centralized scheduling scheme. The distributed scheduling scheme is considered in chapter 5.

3.2 Motivations for Resource Reclaiming

Resource reclaiming [12] refers to the problem of utilizing resources left unused by a task when

1. it executes at less than its worst-case computation time, because of data-dependent loops and conditional statements in the task code or architectural features of the system, such as cache hits and branch predictions, or both.

---

1. A distributed system having multiprocessors as nodes can have both centralized and distributed scheduling schemes.

2. it is deleted from the current schedule, because the primary version of a task completes execution successfully and there is no need for the temporally redundant backup version, initially scheduled to account for fault tolerance, to be executed.

3. it is dropped to make room for more critical tasks.

Resource reclaiming can be used to adapt dynamically to these unpredictable situations. The goal of resource reclaiming is to improve the system's resource utilization and thereby improve its schedulability. If the system does not reclaim unused resources, tasks are executed strictly based on their scheduled start times according to the feasible schedule, which leaves the resources unused, thereby reducing the system's schedulability.

3.3   Properties of Resource Reclaiming Algorithms

Any resource reclaiming algorithm should possess the following four important properties [12]:

1. *Correctness.* A resource reclaiming algorithm must maintain the feasibility of guaranteed tasks; that is, any possible run-time anomalies, situations in which some of the guaranteed tasks miss their deadlines, must be avoided.

2. *Inexpensiveness.* The overhead cost of resource reclaiming should be very low compared to tasks' computation times, since a resource reclaiming algorithm may be invoked very frequently.

3. *Bounded complexity.* The complexity of a resource reclaiming algorithm should be independent of the number of tasks in the schedule so that its cost can be incorporated into the worst-case computation time of a task. A reclaiming algorithm is said to have *bounded complexity* if its complexity is in terms of number of processors rather than in terms of number of tasks.

4. *Effectiveness.* The effectiveness of a resource reclaiming algorithm aims at improving its *guarantee ratio,* defined as the ratio of number of tasks guaranteed to meet their deadlines to the number of tasks that have arrived. The larger the amount of resources the algorithm reclaims, the higher will be the guarantee ratio (or the better will be the performance of the system). A resource reclaiming algorithm is effective only when the system's performance is better when the algorithm is employed than when no resource reclaiming is used.

The correctness property ensures that there are no run time anomalies, and bounded complexity requirements necessitate running the resource reclaiming algorithm through the application processors rather than the scheduler. The requirement of inexpensiveness together with the requirement of effectiveness demands that the cost (execution time) of a reclaiming algorithm not offset the gain obtained (in time) through reclaiming.

3.4 Task Model

We first define the task model used in this chapter and then make some definitions necessary to explain the working of reclaiming algorithms discussed in the next section. Each task T_i in the model has the following attributes:

1. *Ready time.* The ready time r_i of a task T_i is the earliest time before which T_i cannot start its execution.

2. *Deadline.* The deadline d_i of a task T_i is the latest time by which T_i must finish its execution.

3. *Worst-case computation time.* The worst-case computation time c_i is the upper bound on the computation time of T_i, when all the overheads of scheduling and resource reclaiming are included.

4. *Actual computation time.* The actual computation time c_i' of a task T_i is the actual time taken by the task during execution. By definition, the actual computation time of any task is always less than or equal to its worst-case computation time, that is, $c_i' \leq c_i$.

5. *Resource constraints.* A task requires various resources, such as data structures, variables, and communication buffers, for its execution. Every task can have two types of accesses to a resource: (a) exclusive access, in which case, no other task can use the resource with it, or (b) shared access, in which case it can share the resource with another task. (The other task must also be able to share the resource.) We say that a resource conflict exists between two tasks T_i and T_j (denoted as $T_i \odot T_j$) if at least one of these tasks requires the resource in exclusive mode.

6. *Precedence constraints.* If there is a precedence relation from task T_j to task T_i (denoted $T_j \prec T_i$), then T_j has to finish its execution before the beginning of T_i.

In addition, we assume the following:

• At any instant, at most one task can be executed on a given processor. Tasks are not preemptable.

• Once assigned, tasks cannot migrate from one processor to another; that is, if the scheduler assigns a processor P_i to a task T_i, then T_i has to be executed on P_i. (We relax this assumption later, in section 3.7.2.)

• The dispatch queues are placed in a memory shared by all the processors (shared memory multiprocessor model).

3.4.1 Terminology

Definition 1: The scheduler fixes a *feasible schedule* (also known as *prerun schedule*) S, taking into account the timing, resource, and precedence constraints of all the tasks. The feasible schedule uses the worst-case computation time of a task for scheduling it and ensures that the deadlines of all the tasks in S are met.

Definition 2: Starting from a feasible schedule, a *postrun schedule* S' is the layout of the tasks in the same order as they are executed at run time, by the application processors, with respect to their actual computation times.

Definition 3: The notations st_i and ft_i denote the *scheduled start* and *finish times* of the task T_i in the feasible schedule S, whereas st_i' and ft_i' denote the *actual start and finish times* of the task T_i when it executes, as depicted in the postrun schedule S'.

Definition 4: Given a postrun schedule S', a task T_i starts *on time* if $st_i' \leq st_i$. A postrun schedule S' is *correct* if $\forall i, 1 \leq i \leq n, ft_i' \leq d_i$, where n is the number of tasks in the postrun schedule. If all the tasks start on time, then the postrun schedule will be correct [12].

3.5 Resource Reclaiming Algorithms

In a dynamic real-time environment, predictability and efficiency are of major concern for the resource reclaiming algorithms. As discussed earlier, predictability means an absence of run-time anomalies and efficiency demands that the guarantee ratio obtained when resources are reclaimed be better than that when no reclaiming is used. Two extreme approaches provide the lower and upper bounds on the cost, in terms of time, of reclaiming resources:

1. Dispatching tasks according to the scheduled start times. This implies no resource reclaiming, and the resource reclaiming cost in this case is equal to 0.

2. Total rescheduling of the rest of the tasks in the schedule whenever reclaiming is done. This approach can be used only if the cost of this rescheduling is less than the time reclaimed.

The general problem of optimal scheduling of dynamically arriving non-preemptive tasks on a multiprocessor system is NP-complete [2]. Therefore, any practical dynamic scheduling algorithm used in a real-time system must be approximate or heuristic. Clearly, a useful resource reclaiming algorithm should have a complexity less than total rescheduling while being just as effective. Two classes of resource reclaiming have been identified in [12]: (1) algorithms with passing and (2) algorithms without passing.

Definition 5: A task T_i *passes* another task T_j if $st_i' < st_j'$, but $ft_j < st_i$. Thus *passing* occurs when a task T_i starts execution before another task T_j that is scheduled to finish execution before T_i was originally scheduled to start.

A resource reclaiming algorithm that allows passing has a higher time complexity than its nonpassing counterpart, because passing implies altering the ordering of tasks imposed by the feasible schedule, which involves searching for suitable tasks (in the schedule) that can efficiently use the reclaimed time. Any searching will have a complexity of $O(\log n)$, where n is the number of tasks, which implies that reclaiming algorithms that allow *passing* cannot satisfy the bounded complexity requirement [12]. However, we will discuss an algorithm in section 3.7 that permits restricted passing and still satisfies the bounded complexity requirement.

In what follows, we will discuss some reclaiming algorithms that have been proposed for tasks having different characteristics. First, we present a greedy algorithm that can reclaim resources from independent tasks, and we show a situation that results in run time anomaly when the greedy algorithm is applied to tasks that are not independent, that is, tasks that have resource and/or precedence constraints among themselves. Then, we describe basic and early-start algorithms proposed in [12] for resource-constrained tasks, and finally restriction vector (RV)–based algorithms proposed in [7] for tasks having resource and precedence constraints. The reclaiming algorithms discussed in this chapter assume a centralized scheduler model in which the central processor carries out scheduling and the application processors perform dispatching, execution of tasks, and resource reclaiming, as explained in section 3.1.

3.5.1 Resource Reclaiming from Independent Tasks

Resource reclaiming is straightforward in a uniprocessor schedule because there is only one task executing at any moment on the processor. Resource reclaiming is also straightforward in a multiprocessor system with independent tasks. The resource reclaiming in such a system can be greedy in nature, referred to as *work-conserving* or *bandwidth-preserving* resource reclaiming, which means that the resource reclaiming never leaves a processor idle if there is a dispatchable task. The prerun schedule in figure 3.4(a) corresponds to the task set given in figure 3.3 (and also in figure 3.8) and is assumed to be produced by a dynamic planning-based scheduling algorithm, such as the myopic algorithm [9] used in the Spring kernel. The ready times of tasks in figure 3.3 are assumed to be 0. Figure 3.4(b) shows the postrun schedule without resource reclaiming. Figure 3.4(c) shows the postrun schedule produced by the work-conserving reclaiming algorithm. This schedule is obtained by (1) taking the actual computation times of tasks (column 4 of figure 3.3) and (2) ignoring the resource and precedence constraints among the tasks. From

task	deadline	worst case comp. time	actual comp. time	resource requirement (r)
T_1	100	50	25	
T_2	250	175	75	
T_3	350	75	50	
T_4	500	100	100	share
T_5	600	150	100	
T_6	150	150	125	
T_7	200	50	50	exclusive
T_8	300	75	75	
T_9	600	100	100	exclusive
T_{10}	50	50	50	
T_{11}	300	100	50	
T_{12}	450	150	100	share
T_{13}	575	100	100	

Figure 3.3
Real-time tasks. From [7]. © 1997 by Academic Press.

figure 3.4(c), for example, task T_2 starts its execution 25 units earlier than in figure 3.4(b) because task T_1 finishes 25 units earlier and the work-conserving reclaiming algorithm reclaims that time. Also, note that resource reclaiming has reduced the overall completion time of the task set from 550 to 350, which in turn may improve the system's guarantee ratio.

3.5.2   Run Time Anomaly

The previous section showed that resource reclaiming is fairly straightforward in a multiprocessor system when tasks are independent. However, the potential parallelism provided by a multiprocessor and potential resource or precedence constraints among tasks make resource reclaiming in a multiprocessor system with resource- or precedence-constrained tasks more complicated. When the actual computation time of a task differs from its worst-case computation time in a non-preemptive multiprocessor schedule with resource constraints, run-time anomalies may occur [4] if a work-conserving reclaiming scheme is used. These anomalies may cause some of the already guaranteed tasks to miss their deadlines. In particular, one cannot simply implement a work-conserving scheme without verifying that the task deadlines will not be missed.

Figure 3.5 offers an example of a run time anomaly that may occur when a work-conserving algorithm is used. Suppose there are four tasks, T_1, T_2, T_3, and T_4, with

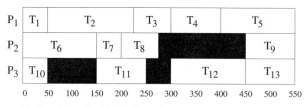

(a) Feasible schedule in dispatch queues

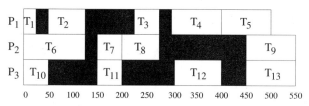

(b) Postrun schedule without resource reclaiming

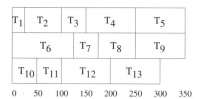

(c) Postrun schedule with work-conserving algorithm for independent tasks

Figure 3.4
Feasible and postrun schedules for real-time tasks in figure 3.3

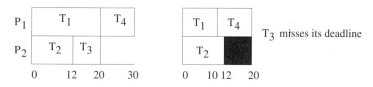

Figure 3.5
Run time anomaly under work-conserving algorithm

parameters ready time, worst-case computation time, and deadline, respectively, as given in parentheses: $T_i = (a_i, c_i, d_i)$; $T_1 = (0, 20, 22)$, $T_2 = (0, 12, 25)$, $T_3 = (10, 8, 26)$, $T_4 = (8, 10, 30)$. Also, let T_3 and T_4 be the only tasks that have resource conflicts. The first schedule in figure 3.5 is a prerun schedule in which all the four tasks are feasibly scheduled. Let the actual computation time of T_1 be 10. In the second schedule of figure 3.5, the postrun schedule, task T_4 is dispatched at time 10 because task T_1 finishes early. Since T_3 and T_4 have resource conflicts, this results in T_3 being blocked till time 20, which is the completion time of T_4, and T_3 misses its deadline, even though it was feasibly scheduled in the prerun schedule. It is left as an exercise to the reader to show that the postrun schedule produced by the work-conserving algorithm for the tasks in figure 3.3 with resource requirements leads to run time anomaly.

For static systems (off-line scheduling) with tasks having precedence constraints, Manacher [6] proposed an algorithm to avoid run time anomalies by imposing extra precedence constraints among tasks to preserve the order in which they can run. Manacher's algorithm does not deal with resource constraints among tasks and does not satisfy the bounded complexity requirement. The algorithm's primary purpose is to ensure the feasibility of the original schedule in a static system in the event that tasks execute at less than their worst-case computation times, rather than to reclaim resources dynamically.

3.6   Resource Reclaiming from Resource-Constrained Tasks

In [12], Shen et al. proposed two algorithms, *Basic* and *Early start,* for reclaiming resources from resource-constrained tasks in multiprocessor real-time systems. These two algorithms use a conservative approach to guarantee that the resource reclaiming never leads to a run time anomaly. The time complexities of Basic and Early start algorithms are $O(m)$ and $O(m^2)$, respectively, where m is the number of application processors in the system, and hence the algorithms satisfy the bounded complexity requirement.

To implement these reclaiming algorithms efficiently, the scheduler maintains a master queue, MQ_s, that maintains the list of all the tasks scheduled in the system, sorted in nondecreasing order of scheduled start times. Thus, MQ_s imposes a *total ordering* on the guaranteed tasks. The reclaimer consults MQ_s to shift the already scheduled tasks for earlier completion as resources become available through reclaiming. Clearly, the reclaimer must modify the MQ_s if reclaiming changes the sorted order of the tasks. Also, each application processor maintains its own dispatch queue in nondecreasing order of task start times. The implementation details of these algorithms are discussed in [12].

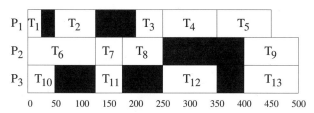

(a) Postrun schedule with Basic reclaiming for tasks with resource constraints

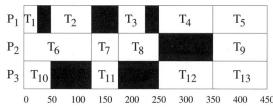

(b) Postrun schedule with Early start for tasks with resource constraints

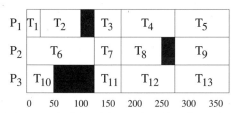

(c) Postrun schedule with RV algorithm for tasks with resource and precedence constraints

Figure 3.6
Postrun schedules for real-time tasks in figure 3.3. From [7]. © 1997 by Academic Press.

3.6.1 Basic Reclaiming

Basic algorithm essentially looks for *simultaneous holes* (i.e., periods during which all the system's application processors are idle) and makes subsequent tasks in the schedule on all the processors start their execution that much earlier, subject to their ready times.

Figure 3.6(a) shows the postrun schedule produced by the Basic algorithm for the prerun schedule in figure 3.4(a). Note that in figure 3.4(b) (in which no reclaiming is used), simultaneous holes occur between times 125 and 150 and between times 275 and 300, which means that tasks with scheduled start times between 150 and 275 can start their execution 25 units earlier. Similarly, tasks whose start times are on or after

300 units can start their execution 50 $(= 25 + 25)$ units earlier. Hence, the completion times of the last tasks in all the processors are reduced by 50 units, as shown in figure 3.6(a).

3.6.2   Early Start Algorithm

The Early start algorithm reclaims resources under the condition that if two tasks do not overlap in the prerun schedule, they should not overlap in the postrun schedule. The Early start algorithm has the following definitions:

Definition 6: $T_{<i} = \{T_j : ft_j < st_i\}$; $T_{>i} = \{T_j : st_j > ft_i\}$; $T_{\simeq i} = \{T_j : T_j \notin T_{<i}, T_j \notin T_{>i}\}$. Thus, $T_{<i}$ denotes the set of tasks that are scheduled in S to finish before T_i starts, $T_{>i}$ denotes the set of tasks that are scheduled to start after T_i finishes, and $T_{\simeq i}$ denotes the set of tasks that overlap with T_i in S.

Definition 7: $T_{<i}(j) = \{T_k : T_k \in T_{<i}$ and T_k is assigned to processor $P_j\}$. From this it follows that, for any task T_i, $T_{<i} = \bigcup_{j=1}^{m} T_{<i}(j)$.

The tasks of $T_{<i}(j)$ are ordered according to their scheduled start times in the feasible schedule. Similarly, $T_{\simeq i}(j)$ and $T_{>i}(j)$ are also defined. More formally, the Early start algorithm allows the tasks in $T_{\simeq i}$ to execute concurrently on different processors and also ensures that they do not overlap in execution with the tasks in either $T_{<i}$ or $T_{>i}$.

The check $st_i > ft_j$, that is, whether the next task (say T_i) to be dispatched on an idle processor (P_k) overlaps with another task (say T_j) that is either running or to be dispatched on another processor P_m ($P_m \neq P_k$) can be conducted in constant time. This check has to be repeated for at most $(m - 1)$ other processors to determine whether T_i can overlap with all such T_js. Since there are at most m idle application processors in the system and each of them doing the above check causes the rest of the processors to wait, the overall time complexity of the Early start algorithm is $O(m^2)$.

Referring to the postrun schedule in figure 3.6(a), notice that T_9 could have started 50 units earlier, that is, at time 350, because $T_9 \in T_{\simeq 5}$ and $T_9 \in T_{\simeq 13}$. Similarly, T_{13} could also have started 50 units earlier. The Early start algorithm [12] allows these earlier starts for tasks that are scheduled overlappingly. Figure 3.6(b) gives the postrun schedule using the Early start algorithm for the prerun schedule presented in figure 3.4(a).

It has been shown through simulation, in [12], that the Basic and Early start reclaiming algorithms together with the myopic scheduling algorithm [9] are inexpensive—that is, they are better than no reclaiming—and that the Early start algorithm is more effective than the Basic algorithm for a wide range of task and system parameters. Both of these algorithms are implemented in the Spring kernel.

3.7   Resource Reclaiming from Resource- and Precedence-Constrained Tasks

In [7], the resource reclaiming algorithms proposed in [12] have been extended to a task model in which precedence constraints also exist among tasks. Two resource reclaiming algorithms have been proposed for this extended task model based on the notion of *restriction vectors* (RVs). Interestingly, the RV data structure captures any type of constraints in a unified way. It has been shown that the RV data structure captures resource and precedence constraints [7], fault-tolerant constraints [8], and parallelizing constraints [8] among tasks. The RV algorithms are correct, satisfy the bounded complexity requirement, and permit restricted passing.

The first RV algorithm reclaims resources under the constraint that once a task is scheduled on a processor, it must execute on the same processor. The second RV algorithm, known as *RV migration* or *RV with dispatch queue swapping,* migrates tasks from one processor to another in an attempt to increase the guarantee ratio. We first define some data structures that we will use to describe the RV algorithms:

Definition 8:   Each task T_i has an associated m-component vector, $RV_i[1 \ldots m]$, called the *restriction vector,* where m is the number of application processors. $RV_i[j]$ for a task T_i contains the *last task* in $T_{<i}(j)$ that must be completed before the execution of T_i begins.

$$RV_i[j] = \begin{cases} T_k & \text{if } \text{Proc}(i) = j, \text{ where } T_k \in T_{<i}(j) \text{ and } \not\exists T_l \text{ such that } st_l > st_k, \\ & \text{where } T_l \in T_{<i}(j), \text{ and Proc}(i) \text{ denotes the processor on which task } T_i \\ & \text{is scheduled,} \\ T_m & \text{if } \text{Proc}(i) \neq j, \text{ where } T_m \in T_{<i}(j) \text{ and } (T_m \prec T_i \text{ or } T_m \odot T_i), \text{ and} \\ & \not\exists T_l \text{ such that } st_l > st_m, \text{ where } T_l \in T_{<i}(j) \text{ and } (T_l \prec T_i \text{ or } T_l \odot T_i), \\ \text{``}-\text{''} & \text{if no such task exists.} \end{cases}$$

Definition 9:   A *completion bit matrix* (*CBM*) is an $n \times m$ boolean matrix indicating whether a task has completed execution, where n is the number of tasks in the feasible schedule:

$$CBM[i,j] = \begin{cases} 0 & \text{iff } T_i \text{ scheduled to execute on } P_j \text{ has not yet completed its execution,} \\ 1 & \text{otherwise.} \end{cases}$$

All the elements of *CBM* are initialized to 0. The scheduler periodically updates the dispatch queues (*DQ*s), which contain the feasible schedule, as described in Section 3.1. Each *DQ* can be maintained as a linked list with the first element pointing to the first task ready for execution in it.

RV Algorithm()
begin
    Whenever a task T_i finishes execution on processor P_j
        1. Set $CBM[i, j]$ to 1.
        2. **For** all idle processors P_k
            2.1 Let T_f be the first task in $DQ[k]$.
            2.2 **For** all the components of the RV_f, check CBM to see if
                the tasks in RV_f have finished execution.
            2.3 **If** all of them have finished execution
                2.3.1 Start the execution of T_f on P_k.
                2.3.2 Remove T_f from DQ_k.
end.

Figure 3.7
RV algorithm. From [7]. © 1997 by Academic Press.

3.7.1 RV Algorithm

The RV algorithm expects the scheduler to compute the restriction vectors for each of the tasks in the feasible schedule before updating the dispatch queues (step 1.3 of figure 3.2). For computing the restriction vector $RV_i(j)$ of a task T_i on processor P_j, the scheduler checks at most k (known as the *RV-check constant*) tasks, in nonincreasing order of scheduled start times, in $T_{<i}(j)$ to see whether any of these k tasks have a resource or precedence conflict with T_i. The first task (say T_m), in order, that exerts a constraint on T_i becomes the restriction; that is, $RV_i(j) = T_m$. If none of the k tasks has a conflict with T_i, then the kth task (say T_n), in order, becomes the restriction; that is, $RV_i(j) = T_n$.

The RV algorithm [7], shown in figure 3.7, says the following: start executing a task T_i only if the processor on which T_i is scheduled is idle and all the tasks in its restriction vector have finished their execution.

3.7.1.1 Example for RV Algorithm   Figure 3.8 shows the precedence relations among tasks (task graph) given in figure 3.3. A directed arc between two tasks in this figure indicates the precedence relation between them. This figure also shows the resource requirements of a resource r. Tasks T_7 and T_9 need exclusive accesses to the resource r, whereas tasks T_4 and T_{12} can share the resource r.

Figure 3.9 shows the RVs for the tasks given in figure 3.3, with associated task graph given in figure 3.8, assuming $k = 2$. For example, $RV_3 = [T_2, T_6, -]$, indicating that T_2 and T_6 have to finish their execution on processors P_1 and P_2, respectively, before T_3 starts its execution. $RV_3[1] = T_2$ indicates that T_2 is the immediate predecessor of task T_3 on processor P_1 and $RV_3[2] = T_6$ indicates that T_6 is the last task in $T_{<3}(2)$ that has precedence

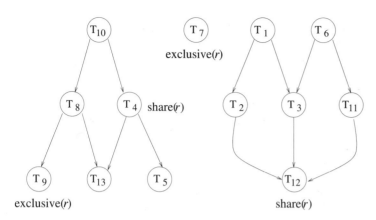

Figure 3.8
Precedence and resource constraints of tasks given in figure 3.3. From [7]. © 1997 by Academic Press.

task	RV	task	RV
T_1	$[-,-,-]$	T_8	$[-,T_7,T_{10}]$
T_2	$[T_1,-,-]$	T_9	$[T_4,T_8,T_{12}]$
T_3	$[T_2,T_6,-]$	T_{10}	$[-,-,-]$
T_4	$[T_3,T_7,T_{10}]$	T_{11}	$[-,T_6,T_{10}]$
T_5	$[T_4,T_7,T_{10}]$	T_{12}	$[T_3,T_7,T_{11}]$
T_6	$[-,-,-]$	T_{13}	$[T_4,T_8,T_{12}]$
T_7	$[-,T_6,-]$		

Figure 3.9
RVs for real-time tasks in figure 3.3. From [7]. © 1997 by Academic Press.

conflict with T_3. $RV_3[3] = $ " $-$ " indicates that there is no direct restriction on T_3 from any task on processor P_3. Similarly, $RV_9 = [T_4, T_8, T_{12}]$, because T_9 has resource conflicts with T_4 and T_{12} and exerts a precedence constraint on T_8. Though tasks T_5 and T_7 have no resource or precedence constraints, $RV_5[2] = T_7$ because of the k parameter. Thus RVs take both the precedence constraints and resource conflicts into account.

The postrun schedules given in figure 3.6 are correct, since every task in these schedules finishes before its deadline. In figure 3.6(b), T_3 could have started at time 125 because neither T_7 nor T_{11} has any resource or precedence conflicts with T_3. The Early start algorithm does not reclaim this resource, since $T_3 \notin T_{\simeq 7}$. The RVs defined in the previous section offer a better picture of the resource and precedence constraints from the reclaiming point of view. From the restriction vector of T_3 (RV_3), there clearly are no constraints or conflicts between T_3 and T_7. $RV_3[2] = T_6$, which indicates that T_3 is restricted only by

T_6 and not by any task after T_6 on P_2. Therefore, the execution of T_3 can overlap with T_7, and the RV algorithm exploits this. The postrun schedule with the RV algorithm (Figure 3.6(c)) shows that it reclaims more resources than the Early start algorithm for the tasks in figure 3.3, even with precedence constraints.

3.7.1.2   Complexity of the RV Algorithm   The Basic and Early start reclaiming algorithms have resource reclaiming complexities of $O(m)$ and $O(m^2)$, respectively. Step 2.2 in the RV algorithm of figure 3.7 takes $O(m)$ time since all m components of the restriction vector have to be checked to find out whether the corresponding tasks have finished executing. There can be at most m idle processors, and hence the time complexity of the algorithm is $m * O(m)$, which is $O(m^2)$. Hence, the RV algorithm satisfies the bounded complexity requirement and has the same time complexity as the Early start algorithm.

3.7.1.3   Proof of Correctness

Lemma: Given a feasible real-time multiprocessor schedule S, if $\exists T_i$ such that T_i does not start on time in a postrun schedule, then passing should have occurred [12].

Proof: Since T_i does not start on time, $st_i' > st_i$. Assume the contrary, that is, assume no passing occurred. Then the tasks in $T_{<i}$ must have been dispatched before T_i started and the tasks in $T_{>i}$ must have been dispatched after T_i finished execution. By the definition of a feasible schedule, the tasks in $T_{\simeq i}$ overlap with task T_i in S, which means that they have no resource or precedence conflicts with T_i; therefore, no matter in what order these tasks were dispatched with respect to the dispatching time of T_i, they would not have delayed the dispatching time of T_i. This contradicts the premise that T_i did not start on time.   □

Theorem: Given a feasible multiprocessor schedule with resource and precedence constraints, the postrun schedule produced by the RV algorithm is correct.

Proof: To prove this we need to show that RV algorithm does not lead to any run time anomalies.

By the above lemma, if there is a task T_i on processor P_k that does not start on time, then passing must have occurred. Consider a schedule in which T_i and T_j are scheduled on P_k and P_j, respectively, with $st_j \geq ft_i$. Assume that T_i missed its deadline in the postrun schedule because T_j has passed T_i. We consider two cases.

Case 1: T_i and T_j have resource or precedence conflicts.

If there is a precedence or a resource conflict, then $RV_j[k] = T_i$, or T_i is transitively included in the restriction vector of T_j, and hence the RV algorithm does not permit this passing.

Case 2: T_i and T_j have no conflicts between them.

In this case, T_i need not wait for the completion of T_j. They can overlap in execution and hence T_i can still start on time.

Since all the tasks start on time, there will be no run time anomalies.

It may be noted that the RV algorithm allows passing in a restricted way. A task T_i is allowed to pass all those tasks in $T_{<i}$ that have no precedence or resource conflicts with it. The above theorem proves that this passing does not lead to run time anomalies.

3.7.2   RV Algorithm with Task Migration

Another algorithm, known as RV migration [7], when run on a processor P_i, attempts, if P_i cannot start its first task immediately, to swap P_i's dispatch queue with the dispatch queue of some other processor whose first nonexecuting task can be started immediately. This means that a task that was scheduled on a processor in the prerun schedule might get executed on some other processor at run time because dispatch queues have been swapped. For this, a shared memory model is assumed in which the dispatch queues are global and one processor has access to the tasks in the dispatch queues of all the processors.

In the RV algorithm, DQ_i is always assigned to processor P_i. In this section, DQ_i represents a pointer to the dispatch queue that is *currently* assigned to processor P_i. The assignment of dispatch queues to processors varies dynamically during the algorithm's execution. At any point of execution, only one DQ will be assigned to any processor, and no DQ will be assigned to more than one processor. The following mechanism is used for migrating tasks from one processor to another. When a task T_i completes execution on processor P_i, P_i examines the RV of the first task in DQ_i to see if it can be executed immediately. If it cannot, P_i examines the dispatch queues of $\overline{k}$ other processors to see if the first task in any of them can be executed immediately. If P_i finds that such a dispatch queue exists, say DQ_j ($i \neq j$), then P_i *swaps* pointers DQ_i and DQ_j, so that the dispatch queues now associated with P_i and P_j will be reversed. Then P_i starts the execution of the first task in its new dispatch queue.

The value of $\overline{k}$, which is the number of dispatch queues that must be checked to find an executable task, determines both the algorithm's efficiency and its complexity. The cost of migration might prove excessive, specifically when a task should be memory resident and moving a task from one processor to another implies loading it onto another's processor memory, which would take typically more time than the potential gain from resource reclaiming.

Figure 3.10 demonstrates dispatch queue swapping. A feasible schedule of 12 tasks on three processors is given in figure 3.10(b), and figure 3.10(a) shows the relevant precedence

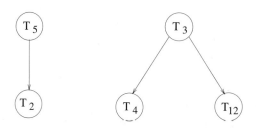

(a) Precedence relations

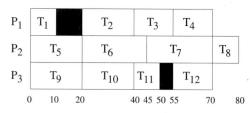

(b) Feasible schedule and postrun schedule with RV algorithm

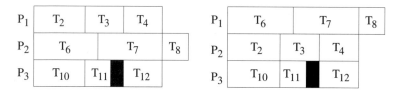

Dispatch queues
(c) When T_1 finishes execution   (d) After swapping DQ_1 and DQ_2

(e) Postrun schedule with task migration (dispatch queue swapping)

Figure 3.10
RV algorithm with task migration

relations. We assume that the RV algorithm gives the same postrun schedule as the feasible schedule given in figure 3.10(b) (i.e., no task has finished executing before its worst-case computation time). When T_1 finishes execution, P_1 checks DQ_1 to find that T_2 is the first task ready for execution. But T_2 cannot be executed immediately because $RV_2[2] = T_5$, and T_5 has not yet finished its execution on P_2. In the RV algorithm with task migration, P_1 checks DQ_2 and finds that the first task in DQ_2 (i.e., T_6) can immediately be dispatched on P_1. Hence P_1 swaps DQ_1 and DQ_2. Figure 3.10(d) shows the dispatch queues as seen by P_1 and P_2 after this swapping. With the new dispatch queues, P_1 starts executing T_6. Later, when T_5 finishes execution on P_2, P_2 finds T_2 as the first task in its dispatch queue, which can readily be dispatched. The postrun schedule using RV algorithm with task migration is given in Figure 3.10(e). The following condition must hold if the dispatch queues are to be swapped in such a way as to avoid run time anomalies.

Condition: If P_i wants to swap the dispatch queues DQ_i and DQ_j without incurring run time anomalies, the start time of the first task in DQ_i should be greater than or equal to the expected finish time of the currently executing task on P_j.

In the example of figure 3.10, P_1 can swap the dispatch queues DQ_1 and DQ_2 because the start time of T_2 is equal to the expected finish time of T_5. Further, when T_{11} finishes executing on P_3, T_{12} cannot be executed immediately because it has a precedence conflict with T_3. P_3 now checks the other dispatch queues, namely, DQ_1 and DQ_2. The first task in DQ_1 is T_8, and since the start time of T_{12} is less than the expected finish time of T_7, DQ_3 and DQ_1 cannot be swapped. (If they were swapped, T_{12} could not start on time on P_1, and this might lead to a run time anomaly.) Further, DQ_2 and DQ_3 also cannot be swapped, since T_4 also has a precedence conflict with T_3.

The condition discussed above ensures that there are no run time anomalies, since it guarantees that every task starts on time even after the dispatch queues are swapped. The proof of this algorithm's correctness follows from this fact and the correctness of the RV algorithm. The complexity of this algorithm is $O(\bar{k}m^2)$, since each processor will check at most $\bar{k}$ dispatch queues, as opposed to only one dispatch queue in the original RV algorithm.

3.8   Experimental Evaluation of Resource Reclaiming Algorithms

Evaluating the performance of the resource reclaiming algorithms and studying the trade-off between system overhead costs and run time savings (both due to resource reclaiming) requires that the worst-case computation (cost) of the algorithm under evaluation be known. The relative performance of different reclaiming algorithms can be evaluated in two ways:

1. Adding the cost of the most complex algorithm (i.e., the algorithm with the highest cost) to the worst-case computation of every task while evaluating any algorithm. This makes a high-cost algorithm see a small hole and an algorithm with less cost see a large hole. Note that some holes may already be present in the prerun schedule and may get expanded, and new holes may also get created as tasks finish early.

This evaluation scheme is explained by the following example: Let the worst-case and actual computation times of a task T_i be 10 and 8, respectively, and let another task T_j, scheduled on the same processor, have a scheduled start time that is the same as the scheduled finish time of T_i. Let the worst-case computation time of the Basic, Early start, RV, and RV migration algorithms be 1, 2, 2, and 3, respectively. Then the overall worst-case computation time of task T_i, evaluating all these algorithms, will be 13 ($10 + 3$). When T_i finishes after executing for 8 units, the Basic, Early start, RV, and RV migration algorithms will see a reclaimable hole size as $4(13 - (8 + 1))$, $3(13 - (8 + 2))$, $3(13 - (8 + 2))$, and $2(13 - (8 + 3))$, respectively.

2. Invoke an algorithm at run time depending on the size of a hole. This approach is adaptive in nature; that is, depending on the size of a hole, one can choose a reclaiming algorithm selectively. Note that for running RV algorithms, the scheduler is expected to build the RVs for all the tasks in the feasible schedule. Hence, this cost has to be considered (in the worst-case computation time of tasks) if an RV algorithm is chosen adaptively.

3.8.1 Simulation Studies

The simulation studies presented here are taken from [7], which used the first approach discussed above for evaluation, that is, adding the algorithm cost (AC) to the worst-case computation time of the tasks, chosen uniformly between *wcc-min* (a task's minimum worst-case computation time) and *wcc-max* (its maximum worst-case computation time). AC includes the scheduling cost (SC) and the reclaiming cost (RC). The SC for the RV algorithms includes the overhead costs incurred in computing RVs. In the case of the RV algorithm with task migration, RC is a function of number of migration attempts. To study the pure effects of reclaiming algorithms and compare their effectiveness in reclaiming resources, the simulation studies do not include the scheduling cost. Hence AC is taken to be equal to the value of RC. However, the extra costs incurred in computing the RVs is included in the case of RV algorithms. Figure 3.11 gives the simulation parameters.

3.8.2 Effect of Precedence and Resource Constraints

Figure 3.12 shows the effect of varying the resource and precedence constraints among the tasks, keeping the *num-procs*, *wcc-min*, and *wcc-max* fixed (at 4, 25, and 50, respectively). The parameter P_p, the *precedence and resource constraint probability,* is varied

parameter	explanation
wcc-min	task's minimum worst-case computation time
wcc-max	task's maximum worst-case computation time
task graph density (P_p)	probability that the new task will have precedence and resource constraints with the already existing tasks, ranges from 0.0 to 1.0, a value of 0.0 indicates independent tasks
aw-ratio	ratio between actual computation time and worst-case computation time, ranges from 60% to 90%
num-procs	number of processors used during simulation
RV-comp-cost	cost incurred in the computation of RVs, taken as 1 for 4, 5, and 6 processors, and 2 for 12, 14, and 16 processors
mig-attempts	number of dispatch queues checked by the RV algorithm with task migration (defined as $\overline{k}$ in section 3.7.2), taken as 1
task arrival rate	arrival rate of tasks, ranges from 0.4 to 0.9
$RC_{no\ reclaiming}$	0
RC_{Basic}	1
$RC_{Earlystart}$	*num-procs* $* RC_{Basic}$
$RC_{RV\ algorithm}$	$RC_{Earlystart} + RV\text{-}comp\text{-}cost$
$RC_{RV\ migration}$	$RC_{RV\ algorithm} + f(\textit{mig-attempts}, RC_{Earlystart})$, taken as 6, 7, and 8 for 4, 5, and 6 processors, respectively, and 15, 17, and 19 for 12, 14, and 16 processors, respectively

Figure 3.11
Simulation parameters. From [7]. © 1997 by Academic Press.

from 0.3 to 0.9. A higher value of P_p indicates that the newly arrived tasks will have more conflicts with the already arrived tasks. Further, a higher value of P_p also indicates that any given task will have a larger number of precedence and resource conflicts with the immediately preceding tasks (on other processors) in the feasible schedule. On the other hand, a smaller value of P_p indicates that new tasks will have fewer constraints (be more independent). No reclaiming, Basic reclaiming, and Early start algorithms give horizontal lines for this variation, because precedence relations have no effect on these algorithms. In the RV algorithm, as the tasks have more constraints, they are more restricted from starting earlier, and hence the guarantee ratio decreases. It is also clear from the graph that as P_p

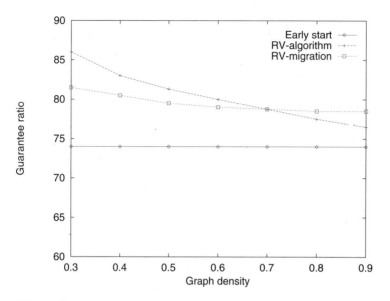

Figure 3.12
Effect of precedence and resource constraints (*num-procs* $= 4$, *wcc-min* $= 25$, *wcc-max* $= 50$). From [7]. © 1997
by Academic Press.

approaches its maximum value of 1.0, the RV algorithm tends to behave like the Early start
algorithm.

3.8.3   Effect of Worst-Case Computation Time

As the worst-case computation time of a task decreases, the ratio of resource reclaiming cost to worst-case computation time increases. Since RC is a part of worst-case
computation time, it will not be feasible to perform reclaiming if the worst-case computation time decreases beyond a certain limit. An experimental study was conducted
to get an estimate of these limits for the various resource reclaiming algorithms. Figure 3.13 plots the graphs. *num-procs* was fixed at 4, *wcc-min* was varied from 20 to
34 units of time, and the worst-case computation time of a task was uniformly distributed between *wcc-min* and *wcc-max* before adding the RC, where *wcc-max* was
taken to be twice *wcc-min*. When *wcc-min* $= 20$, the ratio of RC to worst-case computation time will range between 10% and 20% (using $RC_{Early\ start}$, given in figure 3.11).
Hence, the overhead associated with reclaiming will be 10% to 20%. When *wcc-min* $= 34$,
this overhead will be only 6% to 12%. From the graphs, it is clear that the RV algorithm performs no better than no reclaiming and the Early start algorithm when *wcc-
min* $= 20$, since at this point the reclaiming costs overtake the improvement in performance

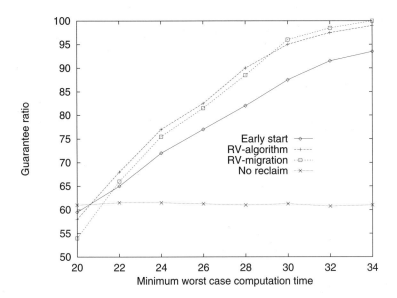

Figure 3.13
Effect of worst-case computation time (*num-procs* = 4, graph density = 0.8, *wcc-max* = 2 × *wcc-min*). From [7].
© 1997 by Academic Press.

obtained through reclaiming. Thus it pays to use RV algorithm only when *wcc-min* ≥ 22 units.

3.8.4   Effect of Actual to Worst-Case Computation Time Ratio

Figure 3.14 shows the effect of varying the actual to worst-case computation time ratio, keeping *num-procs*, *wcc-min*, and P_p fixed at 4, 25, and 0.8, respectively. For smaller values of *aw-ratio* (≤ 0.65), the guarantee ratio is 100% in both the Early start and the RV algorithms. As the *aw-ratio* increases, the guarantee ratio decreases. The RV algorithm (without task migration) gives better results than the Early start algorithm, even if the amount of reclaimable computation time through the RV algorithm is less than that through Early start, because the RV algorithm is more effective in fully utilizing the reclaimable time, whereas Early start makes only a partial utilization, as discussed in section 3.7.1.

3.8.5   Effect of Number of Processors

Figure 3.15 shows the effect of varying the number of processors on the performance of various algorithms. The effect varying the task load has on the guarantee ratio was studied for 12, 14, and 16 processors. All three graphs exhibit the same behavior in

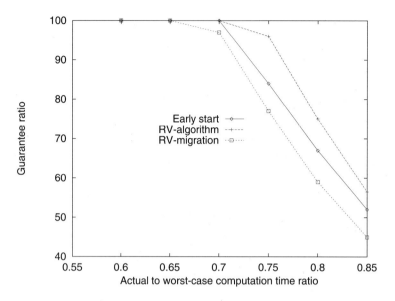

Figure 3.14
Effect of actual to worst-case computation ratio (*num-procs* = 4, graph density = 0.8, *wcc-min* = 25, *wcc-max* = 50). From [7]. © 1997 by Academic Press.

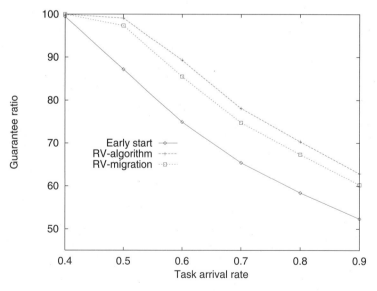

(a) (*num-procs* = 12   graph density = 0.8   *wcc-min* = 50   *wcc-max* = 100)

Figure 3.15
Effect of number of processors (12, 14, and 16). From [7]. © 1997 by Academic Press.

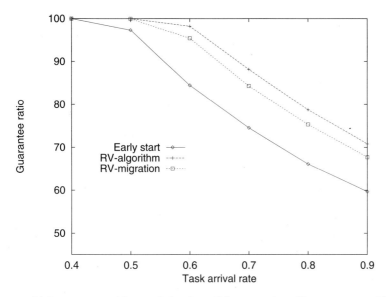

(b) (*num-procs* = 14   graph density = 0.8   *wcc-min* = 50   *wcc-max* = 100)

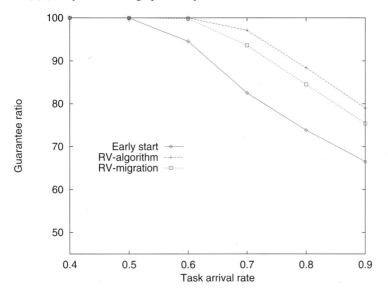

(c) (*num-procs* = 16   graph density = 0.8   *wcc-min* = 50   *wcc-max* = 100)

Figure 3.15 *(continued)*

the sense that the guarantee ratio decreases as the task load increases. It can also be seen across panels of figure 3.15, that for a fixed task load, as the number of processors increases, the guarantee ratio increases, because there are more processors available for dispatching new tasks. The graphs clearly indicate the superiority of RV algorithms.

3.8.6 Effect of Task Migration

The RC in the case of RV algorithm with task migration depends on the number of migration attempts (*mig-attempts*). Graphs were plotted to study how the additional costs as the number of migration attempts increases influence the guarantee ratio offered by the RV migration algorithm. From the graph shown in figure 3.12, the RV migration algorithm is effective when P_p is greater than 0.7. When precedence relations constrain the tasks to a greater degree, the RV algorithm gives a poorer performance compared to the RV migration algorithm, since the former checks only its own dispatch queue, and it is more likely that the first task in its dispatch queue cannot be immediately executed because of the higher value of P_p. For smaller values of minimum worst-case computation times (20), the ratio of RC to *wcc-min* is as high as 35%. Hence, the guarantee ratios offered by the RV algorithms increase as the average worst-case computation time of a task increases (figure 3.13). From the graph in figure 3.14, the RV migration algorithm offers a poorer guarantee ratio than the other two, because it generates a greater overhead cost than the other two. The amount of reclaimable computation time is less in the case of RV migration algorithm than with the others, and hence the guarantee ratio it offers is less. From figure 3.15, the guarantee ratio with the RV migration algorithm is between the guarantee ratios offered by the Early start and RV algorithms.

3.9 Summary

• Resource reclaiming refers to the problem of utilizing resources left unused by a task when it executes at less than its worst-case computation time or when a task is deleted from the current schedule. Resource reclaiming can be used to adapt dynamically to these unpredictable situations to improve system performance.

• A real-time system with resource reclaiming has three phases: scheduling, dispatching, and reclaiming. The system overhead incurred in scheduling, dispatching, and resource reclaiming should not introduce uncertainty into the system.

• A resource reclaiming algorithm should satisfy the requirements of correctness, inexpensiveness, bounded complexity, and effectiveness. The correctness requirement ensures that resource reclaiming results in no run time anomalies, wherein some of the guaranteed tasks miss their deadlines. The effectiveness of a resource reclaiming algorithm aims at improving the algorithm's guarantee ratio, defined as the ratio of number of tasks guaranteed to the number of tasks that have arrived. Effectiveness also means that the guarantee ratio obtained when a reclaiming algorithm is used should be more than that when no reclaiming is used.

• The work-conserving reclaiming algorithm works correctly and efficiently in a multiprocessor real-time system with independent tasks. But it may lead to run time anomalies when used to reclaim resources from tasks having resource or precedence constraints.

• Basic and Early start algorithms work correctly for resource-constrained tasks, and of the two, Early start is more effective than the Basic algorithm. Restriction vector–based algorithms work correctly with resource- and precedence-constrained tasks and are more effective than the Early start.

• The use of progressively more complex algorithms in an attempt to reclaim more resources will incur progressively higher overhead that at some point will nullify the advantages obtained. Experimental studies show that the RV algorithm with task migration is one such algorithm, beyond which it will not pay to use more sophisticated algorithms to reclaim more resources.

Exercises

1. What is the predictability of a real-time system?

2. What is a run time anomaly? When does it occur?

3. What causes the actual computation time of a task to be less than its worst-case computation time?

4. What mandatory and optional properties is a resource reclaiming algorithm required to satisfy?

5. A multiprocessor system has two resources, R1 and R2.

(a) Can a run time anomaly occur in the following situations when the work-conserving algorithm is used?

i. All the resource accesses are in shared mode.

ii. All the resource accesses are in exclusive mode.

iii. Some accesses are in shared mode and the others are in exclusive mode.

(b) All accesses to resource R1 are in shared mode, and those tasks that use R1 are scheduled on a set, say S1, of processors. All accesses to resource R2 are in exclusive mode, and those tasks that use R2 are scheduled on another set, say S2, of processors. Sets

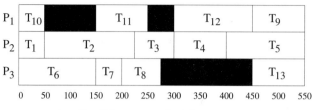

Feasible prerun schedule

Figure 3.16
Exercise 3.10 prerun schedule

S1 and S2 are disjoint. For what cardinalities of sets S1 and S2 will run time anomaly never occur if the work-conserving algorithm is used?

6. In a multiprocessor system with m (application) processors, suppose the ratio of actual to worst-case computation times of all the tasks scheduled on n processors, where $n < m$, is 1.0. Under this situation, (a) Does the Basic algorithm ever reclaim? (b) When does it never reclaim? Assume that all tasks have ready times of 0.

7. Consider a multiprocessor system with m (application) processors having independent tasks. What percentage of time do different resource reclaiming algorithms reclaim in the following cases, assuming the ratio of actual to worst-case computation times of tasks to be 0.5? Assume that the cost of the algorithms is equal.

(a) When the scheduled start time, in the prerun schedule, of every task is equal to its ready time.

(b) When the ready time of every task is 0.

8. Under what conditions do the following equalities hold (assuming the cost of the algorithms is equal)?

(a) RV algorithm = Early start

(b) Early start = Basic algorithm

(c) RV algorithm = Early start = Basic algorithm = Work-conserving algorithm

(*Hint:* Set the system parameters appropriately.)

9. Under what situations is no reclaiming better than reclaiming?

10. Figure 3.16 shows the prerun schedule of tasks given in figure 3.3, whose precedence relations are shown in figure 3.8.

(a) Assume that there are no precedence conflicts among tasks. Show that a run time anomaly occurs when the work-conserving algorithm is used.

(b) Assume that the work-conserving algorithm satisfies the precedence constraints among tasks. Can a run time anomaly occur when the work-conserving algorithm is used? Justify your answer by showing the postrun schedule.

(c) Show the postrun schedule produced by Basic, Early start, and RV algorithms.

11. For any given prerun schedule satisfying precedence constraints among tasks, do Basic and Early start algorithms produce a valid postrun schedule? Justify your answer.

12. In parallelizable task scheduling (e.g., ParMyopic, described in the previous chapter), a task can be parallelized, and the component tasks can be executed concurrently on multiple processors. When a task is parallelized, all its parallel subtasks have to start at the same time. Devise a method to construct RVs in the presence of parallelized tasks in the feasible schedule.

13. What makes it difficult to estimate the worst-case computation time of tasks?

14. What happens when the actual computation time of a task exceeds its worst-case computation time? Suggest a mechanism to overcome this problem.

References

[1] M. L. Dertouzos and A. K. Mok. "Multiprocessor on-line scheduling of hard real-time tasks." *IEEE Trans. Software Engg.,* vol. 15, no. 12, pp. 1497–1506, Dec. 1989.

[2] M. R. Garey and D. S. Johnson. *Computers and Intractability: A Guide to the Theory of NP-Completeness.* W.H. Freeman Company, San Francisco, 1979.

[3] S. Ghosh, R. Melhem, and D. Mossé. "Fault-tolerance through scheduling of aperiodic tasks in hard real-time multiprocessor systems." *IEEE Trans. Parallel and Distributed Systems,* vol. 8, no. 3, pp. 272–284, Mar. 1997.

[4] R. L. Graham. "Bounds on multiprocessing timing anomalies." *SIAM J. Appl. Math.,* vol. 17, no. 2, pp. 416–429, Mar. 1969.

[5] K. S. Hong and J. Y-T. Leung. "On-line scheduling of real-time tasks." *IEEE Trans. Computers,* vol. 41, no. 10, pp. 1326–1331, Oct. 1992.

[6] G. K. Manacher. "Production and stabilization of real-time task schedules." *Journal of ACM,* vol. 14, no. 3, pp. 439–465, July 1967.

[7] G. Manimaran, C. Siva Ram Murthy, Machiraju Vijay, and K. Ramamritham. "New algorithms for resource reclaiming from precedence constrained tasks in multiprocessor real-time systems." *Journal of Parallel and Distributed Computing,* vol. 44, no. 2, pp. 123–132, Aug. 1997.

[8] G. Manimaran and C. Siva Ram Murthy. "A new scheduling approach supporting different fault-tolerant techniques for real-time multiprocessor systems." *Journal of Microprocessors and Microsystems,* vol. 21, no. 3, pp. 163–173, Dec. 1997.

[9] K. Ramamritham, J. A. Stankovic, and P.-F. Shiah. "Efficient scheduling algorithms for real-time multiprocessor systems." *IEEE Trans. Parallel and Distributed Systems,* vol. 1, no. 2, pp. 184–194, Apr. 1990.

[10] K. Ramamritham and J. A. Stankovic. "Scheduling algorithms and operating systems support for real-time systems." *Proc. IEEE,* vol. 82, no. 1, pp. 55–67, Jan. 1994.

[11] K. Ramamritham. "Allocation and scheduling of precedence-related periodic tasks." *IEEE Trans. Parallel and Distributed Systems,* vol. 6, no. 4, pp. 412–420, Apr. 1995.

[12] C. Shen, K. Ramamritham and J. A. Stankovic. "Resource reclaiming in multiprocessor real-time systems." *IEEE Trans. Parallel and Distributed Systems,* vol. 4, no. 4, pp. 382–397, Apr. 1993.

[13] K. G. Shin and P. Ramanathan. "Real-time computing: A new discipline of computer science and engineering." *Proc. IEEE,* vol. 82, no. 1, pp. 6–24, Jan. 1994.

[14] J. A. Stankovic and K. Ramamritham. "The spring kernel: A new paradigm for real-time operating systems." *ACM Operating Systems Review,* vol. 23, no. 3, pp. 54–71, July 1989.

[15] D. B. Stewart and P. K. Khosla. "Mechanisms for detecting and handling timing errors." *Communications of the ACM,* vol. 40, no. 1, pp. 87–93, Jan. 1997.

[16] H. Streich. "Task pair-scheduling: An approach for dynamic real-time systems." *Intl. Journal of Mini & Microcomputers,* vol. 17, no. 2, pp. 77–83, Jan. 1995.

[17] J. Xu and D. L. Parnas. "Scheduling processes with release times, deadlines, precedence, and exclusion relations." *IEEE Trans. Software Engg.,* vol. 16, no. 3, pp. 360–369, Mar. 1990.

4 Fault-Tolerant Task Scheduling in Multiprocessor Real-Time Systems

Overview

In chapters 2 and 3, we discussed the scheduling of tasks and resource reclaiming in multi-processor real-time systems, respectively. In this chapter we specifically address the issue of scheduling tasks with fault-tolerant requirements. We first discuss the importance of fault tolerance in real-time systems and classify faults according to type. Then we present the various techniques employed for fault-tolerant scheduling of tasks in multiprocessor real-time systems. Finally, we present several scheduling algorithms, with illustrative examples, each employing a different fault-tolerant technique.

4.1 Introduction

Greater reliance on computers in a variety of real-time applications has made the consequences of failure and down time more severe. In critical applications, such as flight control, medical life support, process control, telecommunication switching, and on-line transaction processing systems, failure of computing resources can cost lives and/or money. Fault tolerance is informally defined as a system's ability to deliver the expected service even in the presence of faults. A common misconception about real-time computing is that fault tolerance is orthogonal to real-time requirements. It is often assumed that a system's dependability requirements can be addressed independent of its timing constraints. This assumption, however, does not consider the distinguishing characteristic of real-time systems: the *timeliness* of correct results. In other words, a real-time system may fail to function correctly either because of errors in its hardware and/or software or because it does not respond in time to meet the timing requirements its environment imposes. Hence a real-time system can be viewed as one that must deliver the expected service in a timely manner even in the presence of faults. This makes fault tolerance an inherent requirement of any real-time system [21].

4.1.1 Classification of Real-Time Systems by Fault Tolerance

Real-time systems are often classified as soft or hard on the basis of their dependability requirements. Hard real-time systems can sometimes be classified based on their failure modes: (1) *fail-safe systems,* in which one or more safe states can be identified that can be accessed in case of a system failure, and (2) *fail-operational systems,* in which such safe states cannot be identified [6]. The railway signaling system is an example of a fail-safe system in which, on detection of a failure, all trains can be stopped to avoid severe consequences. A flight control system is an example of a fail-operational system, as the system must deliver minimal level of service even in the case of failure in order to avoid catastrophe, because unlike trains, airplanes in flight cannot simply be stopped while the system failure is rectified.

4.1.2   Expressing Fault Tolerance

Dependability is a qualitative system attribute that is quantified through specific measures that express the system's ability to tolerate failures. The two primary measures of dependability are reliability and availability [23]. *Reliability* is the probability of a system's surviving (potentially despite faults) over an interval of time. For instance, the performance requirement might be stated as a 0.999999 reliability for a 10-hour mission. In other words, the probability of failure during the mission may be at most 10^{-6}. Hard real-time systems, such as flight control and process control systems, in which a failure could mean loss of life, demand high reliability. *Availability* is the probability of a system's being operational at any given instant. A 0.999999 availability, for example, means that a system is not operational at most one hour in every million hours. It is important to note that a system with high availability may in fact fail. However, failure frequency and recovery time should be small enough to achieve the desired availability. Soft real-time systems, such as telephone-switching and airline reservation systems, require high availability.

4.1.3   Fault Hypothesis

Any real-time system has finite processing power. If we intend to guarantee by design that the system can satisfy the given temporal requirements of all critical real-time tasks, then we have to postulate a set of assumptions about the behavior of the environment. The load hypothesis and fault hypothesis are two of these assumptions. The *load hypothesis* defines the peak load that is assumed to be generated by the environment, and the *fault hypothesis* defines the types and frequency of faults that a fault-tolerant system must be capable of handling. If a specified fault scenario develops, a fault-tolerant system must still provide a specified level of service. If more faults are generated than what is specified in the fault hypothesis, then sometimes the performance of the system must *degrade gracefully;* that is, the system must not suddenly collapse as the number of the faults increases, but should instead continue to execute part of the workload. The worst-case scenario that a fault-tolerant real-time system must be capable of handling is at peak load with the maximum number of faults.

The load hypothesis and fault hypothesis for a particular system must properly capture the behavior of the environment in which the system operates. The concept of *assumption coverage* defines the probability that the load hypothesis and fault hypothesis—and all other assumptions made about the behavior of the environment—are in agreement with reality.

4.2 Fault Classifications

A *fault* is a deviation in hardware or software from its intended function. Faults can arise during all stages of a computer system's evolution—specification, design, development, manufacturing, and installation—and throughout its operational life. Testing is used to remove most faults before system deployment. Faults not removed prior to deployment can reduce the system's dependability. Faults occurring during system operation can be classified based on (1) the duration of the fault, (2) the output behavior of the fault, and (3) correlation with other faults.

When a fault causes an incorrect change in system state, an *error* occurs. The time between fault occurrence and the first appearance of an error is called *fault latency*. Even if a fault remains localized, multiple errors can originate from one fault and propagate throughout the system. If necessary mechanisms are present to detect a propagating error, the time required to detect such an error is called *error latency*. When these fault tolerance mechanisms detect an error, they may initiate several actions to handle the fault and contain its errors. *Recovery* occurs if these actions are successful. Otherwise, the system malfunctions, and eventually *failure* occurs.

Error recovery is the process by which the system attempts to recover from the effects of an error. It takes two forms: *forward error recovery* and *backward error recovery*. In forward error recovery, the error is masked without any computations having to be redone, whereas in backward error recovery, the system is rolled back to a state before the error is believed to have occurred and the subsequent computations are carried out again.

4.2.1 Classification by Fault Duration

There are three categories of faults in terms of duration: permanent, intermittent, and transient. *Permanent faults* are caused by irreversible failures within a component due to damage, fatigue, or improper manufacturing. Once a permanent fault has occurred, the faulty component can be restored only by replacement, or, if possible, repair. *Transient faults,* on the other hand, are triggered by environmental disturbances such as electromagnetic interference, radiation, or voltage fluctuations. These events usually have short duration, and the system can afterwards return to the normal operating state without causing any lasting damage. For example, if there is a burst of electromagnetic radiation and the memory is not properly shielded, the contents of the memory can be altered without the memory chips themselves suffering any structural damage. When the memory is rewritten, the fault will disappear. Transient faults are more frequent than permanent faults, although this depends on the system's operating environment. *Intermittent faults,* which tend to oscillate between periods of erroneous activity and dormancy, may also surface during system operation. These faults are introduced due to imperfections in the requirements specifications, detailed design, implementation of design, and other phases leading up to operation of the system. They can also be caused, for example, by loose wires. Intermittent faults manifest themselves only under heavy or unusual workloads and eventually lead to system failures.

4.2.2 Classification by Output Behavior

A fault may also be characterized in terms of the output it generates, namely, malicious and nonmalicious. Whenever a fault can cause a unit to behave arbitrarily, *malicious* or *Byzantine failure* is said to happen. An example of such a fault would be a sensor sending conflicting outputs to different processors. Stuck-at faults, on the other hand, are *nonmalicious*. An output line that stays afloat rather than stuck at 0 or 1 is considered to be malicious, because it is difficult to conclude consistently whether the output is 0 or 1. Failures corresponding to an inconsistent output state (i.e., malicious fault) are much harder to detect than nonmalicious faults. A unit is said to be *fail-stop* if it responds to up to a certain maximum number of failures by simply stopping, rather than producing incorrect output. A fail-stop unit typically has many processors running the same tasks and comparing the outputs. If the outputs do not agree, the whole unit turns itself off. As mentioned earlier, a system is said to be *fail-safe* if one or more safe states can be identified that can be accessed in case of a system failure to avoid catastrophe.

4.2.3 Independent and Correlated Faults

Faults in system components may be independent of one another or correlated. A fault is said to be *independent* if it does not directly or indirectly cause another fault. Faults are said to be *correlated* if they are related in some way, possibly through physical or electrical coupling of units. Correlated faults are more difficult to detect than independent faults.

4.3 Fault Tolerance in Real-Time Systems

A good fault-tolerant system design requires a careful study of system design, possible faults, the causes of these faults, and the system's response to the faults. Planning to avoid faults, known as *fault avoidance,* is one important strategy for building fault tolerance into a system. A second important strategy is to design the system to tolerate faults that occur while the system is in operation.

The most basic principle of fault-tolerant design is *redundancy.* We first discuss the various redundancy approaches and then present several techniques that use these redundancy approaches to achieve fault tolerance.

4.3.1 Redundancy

There are four basic approaches for achieving redundancy:

• *Hardware redundancy.* The system is provided with far more hardware than it would need if all the units were perfectly reliable.

• *Software redundancy.* The system is provided with different software versions of tasks so that when one version of a task fails under certain inputs, the other versions can be used.

• *Temporal (time) redundancy.* A computation or communication action is repeated in the domain of time. That is, a task (or message) can be rerun (or retransmitted) if necessary and still meet its deadline. This is a backward error recovery scheme.

• *Information redundancy.* Through a specific encoding technique, source data are encoded incorporating some redundancy to enable the detection and correction of errors introduced into the encoded data.

Temporal redundancy is typically employed to detect and possibly tolerate the occurrence of transient faults. Information redundancy is often used to protect state information and to protect the delivery of messages (for instance, in cyclic redundancy checks). Hardware (software) redundancy is generally used if permanent hardware (software) faults have to be tolerated. Hardware redundancy in particular can be further classified as either active or passive.

• *Active redundancy* (also known as hot standby) refers to a redundancy organization that activates all redundant physical resources simultaneously. Active redundancy requires that the replicated subsystems visit the same states at about the same time.

• *Passive redundancy* (also known as cold standby) refers to a redundancy organization that activates redundant physical resources only after the corresponding primary resource has failed. It is implicitly assumed that the primary resource contains error detection mechanisms to detect errors in its internal states before it delivers an output. *Rollback recovery* is an example of passive redundancy using time redundancy. *Exception handling* is another type of passive redundancy in which, when a processor detects an exception during an execution of a task, control is transferred to the exception handler, which terminates the computation after rolling forward or rolling back the computation of the task.

4.3.2 The Space-Time Trade-Off

Redundancy costs both money and time. Therefore, the design of a fault-tolerant system should represent the optimum trade-off between the amount of redundancy used and the desired level of fault tolerance. The design methodology for fault-tolerant systems has

often been characterized as involving the trade-off between *time* and *space* redundancy
[21]. Non-real-time systems treat time as a cheap resource, and most fault-tolerant techniques for such systems concentrate on space optimization. On the other hand, in real-time
systems, since time is a more crucial resource, the tendency is to trade space for time. However, trading space for time also has a potential limit, since spatial redundancy introduces
additional overhead (in time) for managing the redundancy. Thus, a system's timeliness and
fault tolerance requirements seem to pull each other in opposite directions. For example,
frequent error checks and complex recovery routines will enhance fault tolerance but may
increase the chance of tasks' missing their deadlines. Therefore, alternative approaches
must be considered to deal with this problem. For example, the *quality* of the computation
(result) can become a third dimension of the problem. Quality of computation introduces
the principle of graceful degradation, by which a system continues to meet the deadlines
of tasks, but with a reduced quality of produced results.

4.3.3   Fault-Tolerant Techniques in Real-Time Systems

In the rest of this section, we will discuss different techniques employed for tolerating hardware and software failures in multiprocessor real-time systems. Four different techniques
have evolved for fault-tolerant scheduling of real-time tasks:

- N-modular redundancy
- N-version programming
- Recovery blocks
- Imprecise computations

4.3.3.1   N-Modular Redundancy   N-modular redundancy (NMR) is a forward error
recovery scheme. In an NMR approach, N multiple identical processors concurrently
execute the same task and the results produced by these processors are voted on by another
processor. This voter processor compares the other processors' outputs to determine the
correct output using, for example, majority vote. The value of N is usually odd, and the
typical value used is 3, referred to as triple modular redundancy (TMR). In a TMR system,
it is assumed that at most one processor can fail. In general, in the NMR approach, the value
of N required to design a system to tolerate m processor failures is taken to be $2m + 1$. The
voter in the NMR approach is assumed to be reliable, possibly by redundancy. NMR is a
general technique that can tolerate most of the hardware faults in a minority of the hardware
modules (or processors) by masking the faults in these modules.

4.3.3.2   N-Version Programming   N-version programming (NVP) [1] is also a forward
error recovery scheme, and it can tolerate software faults as well as hardware faults. It is

based on the principle of *design diversity;* that is, a task is coded by different teams of programmers, in multiple versions. Diversity can be introduced by employing different algorithms for obtaining the same solution or by choosing different programming languages for coding the same task. A voter receives the outputs from these versions and determines which is correct. NVP can therefore tolerate software faults that affect a minority of the versions but not correlated faults.

Deciding the number of versions required to ensure acceptable levels of software reliability is an important design consideration in NVP. Figure 4.1(a) shows a TMR approach combined with NVP.

4.3.3.3 Recovery Blocks Recovery block (RB) [19] is a backward error recovery scheme that uses multiple alternates to perform the same function. One module (task) is primary; the others are secondary. The primary task executes first. When the primary task completes execution, an *acceptance test* checks its outcome. If the output is not acceptable, a secondary task executes after undoing the effects of the primary task (i.e., rolling back to the state at which primary was invoked), and so on, until either an acceptable output is obtained, the alternates are exhausted, or the deadline of the task is missed. The acceptance tests are usually *sanity checks;* these consist of making sure that the output is within a certain acceptable range or that the output does not change at more than the allowed maximum rate. Selecting the range for the acceptance test is crucial. If the allowed ranges are too small, the acceptance tests may label correct outputs as bad. If they are too large, the probability that incorrect outputs will be accepted will be higher. The RB scheme can tolerate software faults because the alternates are usually implemented with different approaches. RB differs from NVP in executing the versions of a task serially, as opposed to the concurrent execution of versions in the NVP. Figure 4.1(b) shows the RB approach.

4.3.3.4 Imprecise Computations One way to avoid timing faults during transient overloads and to introduce fault tolerance by graceful degradation is the use of the imprecise computation (IC) technique [10]. The IC model provides scheduling flexibility by trading off result quality to meet task deadlines. In this approach, a task is divided into a mandatory part and an optional part. The mandatory part must be completed before the task's deadline for an acceptable quality of result. The optional part, which can be skipped, if necessary, to conserve system resources, refines the result. A task is said to have produced a *precise* result if it has executed both its mandatory and its optional parts before its deadline; otherwise it is said to have produced an *imprecise* (i.e., approximate) result (when it executes the mandatory part alone). Figure 4.1(c) shows the IC approach.

There are two types of imprecise computational tasks, namely, monotone tasks and 0/1 constraint tasks. A task is *monotone* if the quality of its intermediate result does not

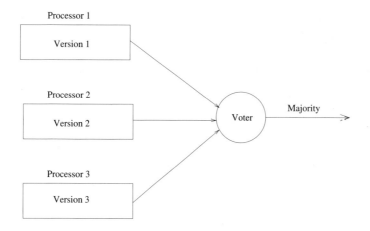

(a) N-version programming - Triple modular redundancy

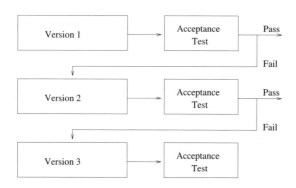

(b) Recovery block

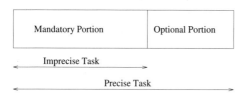

(c) Imprecise computation

Figure 4.1
Fault-tolerant scheduling techniques

decrease as it executes longer. An imprecise task with *0/1 constraint* requires that the optional part of the task be either fully executed or not at all. In some applications, one may prefer timely imprecise results to late precise results, such as in image processing and tracking. It is often better to have frames of fuzzy images or estimates of target locations in time than perfect images or accurate location data too late. For example, in a tracking and control system, a transient fault may cause tracking computation to terminate prematurely and produce an approximate result. No recovery action is needed if the result still allows the system to keep track of its targets. Similarly, as long as the approximate result a control law computation produces is sufficiently accurate for the controlled system to remain stable, the fault that causes the computation to terminate prematurely can be tolerated.

4.4   Fault-Tolerant Scheduling Algorithms for Multiprocessor Real-Time Systems

In this section, we discuss some recent developments in fault-tolerant scheduling in real-time multiprocessor systems. Insofar as scheduling is concerned, the NMR and NVP are the same.

Scheduling in a multiprocessor system involves determining when and on which processor a given task executes. This can be done either statically or dynamically. Static algorithms determine a priori the assignment of tasks to processors and the time at which the various tasks start execution and are often used to schedule periodic tasks with hard deadlines. Such algorithms use a static *table-driven approach,* discussed in chapter 2, to store the resulting schedules. Their main advantage is that, if a solution is found, all deadlines will be guaranteed. However, the static approach is not applicable to aperiodic tasks, whose characteristics are not known a priori. Scheduling aperiodic tasks in a multiprocessor real-time system requires dynamic scheduling algorithms. In dynamic scheduling, it is not possible to obtain an optimal schedule if the arrival times of tasks are not known a priori. In safety-critical applications, tasks may have hard deadlines even if they are aperiodic. Moreover, they may have fault tolerance requirements to operate despite failures in the system. The question is then how to guarantee the deadlines, with fault tolerance requirements, of such tasks in the absence of an optimal dynamic scheduling algorithm. There are three approaches to deal with this problem, depending on the nature of application:

1. *Dynamic planning-based approach.* In this approach, when a new task arrives in the system with a specified fault tolerance requirement, the scheduler dynamically determines the feasibility of scheduling the new task without jeopardizing the guarantees that have been provided for the previously scheduled tasks. If a feasible schedule cannot be found satisfying the fault-tolerant requirement, the new task is rejected, and the previous schedule

remains intact. This type of planning allows the system to take appropriate actions following the rejection of the task.

2. *Static overallocation of resources.* This approach ensures that the system has enough resources to schedule all the tasks with their fault-tolerant requirements even at the peak load. Fault tolerance is achieved by scheduling redundant copies of each task. For this approach, the minimum number of processors required to meet the peak load needs to be determined, by taking into account the system load and the characteristics of arriving tasks. In this approach, the worst-case combination of task arrivals must be known a priori, and hence it is static in nature.

3. *Fault tolerance based on resource availability.* In this approach, fault tolerance (FT) is applied unequivocally only to the most critical tasks; for the rest of the tasks, FT is applied subject to the availability of resources at the time the tasks are executed. Moreover, redundant copies for a less critical task are scheduled so as to affect neither the schedulability of more critical tasks (with FT) nor that of less critical tasks (without FT). This approach relies on either a dynamic planning-based approach or a static resource overallocation approach for scheduling more critical tasks (with FT) and less critical tasks depending on the presence or absence of a priori knowledge about the tasks.

Applications such as automatic flight control and medical support systems require dynamic scheduling with fault-tolerant requirements. In a flight control system, for example, controllers often activate tasks depending on what appears on their monitor. If a dynamic planning-based approach is employed in such a system, when an airplane running on autopilot experiences wind turbulence, and the additional task generated due to disturbance cannot be executed while providing fault tolerance, then the pilot has the option of taking over manual control of some or all functions of the airplane's navigational system.

Another example is a system that monitors the condition of several patients in the intensive care unit of a hospital. Certain actions must be taken as soon as the condition of a patient changes. For example, if a patient's heart rate decreases below a certain threshold, a corrective action must be taken, such as injecting a drug in the patient's IV, within a certain hard deadline. The life criticality of such an application demands that the desired action be performed even in the presence of faults, and such a system should ensure that the task is executed within its deadline even if a fault occurs in one of the processors. For such an application, when a dynamic planning-based scheduling approach is employed, if the system cannot monitor one more patient in critical condition, because of the additional tasks being generated, a recovery action such as dispatching a nurse to monitor the patient can be implemented. We now discuss some of the scheduling algorithms under each of the above three approaches.

4.5   Real-Time Task Scheduling with Recovery Block Fault Tolerance

In an RB scheme, when the number of (retry) blocks is two, it is called primary-backup (PB) approach in the scheduling context. Here, we discuss two dynamic planning-based algorithms, namely, a backup overloading algorithm with deallocation [3] and a distance myopic algorithm [14], for scheduling of real-time tasks with PB-based fault tolerance requirements. The backup overloading algorithm assumes tasks to be independent, whereas the distance myopic algorithm allows resource constraints among tasks. The objective of these algorithms is to improve the system's guarantee ratio while satisfying all task requirements (including the fault tolerance requirements). Both algorithms to be discussed here use the following system model.

4.5.1   System Model

1. Tasks are aperiodic. Every task T_i has the following attributes: *arrival time* (a_i), *ready time* (r_i), *worst-case computation time* (c_i), and *deadline* (d_i).

2. Each task T_i has two versions, namely, the *primary copy* and the *backup copy*. The worst-case computation time of a primary copy may be longer than that of its backup. The other attributes and resource requirements of both the copies are identical.

3. Each task can encounter at most one failure due to either processor failure or software failure; that is, if the primary fails, its backup always succeeds.

4. Tasks are non-preemptable; that is, when a task starts execution on a processor, it finishes.

5. Tasks are not parallelizable, which means that a task can be executed on only one processor. This necessitates that the sum of worst-case computation times of primary and backup copies of a task should be less than or equal to $(d_i - r_i)$ so that both the copies of the task are schedulable within this interval.

6. The system has multiple identical processors connected through a shared medium.

7. Faults can be transient or permanent and are independent; that is, correlated failures are not considered.

8. A fault-detection mechanism such as acceptance tests is present to detect processor and software failures.

4.5.1.1   Terminology

Definition 1: $st(T_i)$ is the scheduled start time of task T_i, which satisfies $r_i \leq st(T_i) \leq d_i - c_i$. $ft(T_i)$ is the scheduled finish time of task T_i, which satisfies $r_i + c_i \leq ft(T_i) \leq d_i$.

Definition 2: $proc(T_i)$ is the processor to which task T_i is scheduled. Any processor to which task T_i should not get scheduled is denoted as *exclude proc(T_i)*.

Definition 3: $st(Pr_i)$ is the scheduled start time and $ft(Pr_i)$ is the scheduled finish time of the primary copy of a task T_i. Similarly, $st(Bk_i)$ and $ft(Bk_i)$ denote the same for the backup copy of T_i.

Definition 4:   The primary and backup copies of a task T_i are said to be mutually exclusive in time, denoted as *time exclusion(T_i)*, if $st(Bk_i) \geq ft(Pr_i)$.

Definition 5:   The primary and backup copies of a task T_i are said to be mutually exclusive in space, denoted as *space exclusion(T_i)*, if $proc(Pr_i) \neq proc(Bk_i)$.

Definition 6:   A task is said to be feasible in a fault-tolerant schedule if it satisfies the following conditions:

$$r_i \leq st(Pr_i) < ft(Pr_i) \leq st(Bk_i) < ft(Bk_i) \leq d_i.$$

Primary and backup copies of a task should be mutually exclusive in space and time in the schedule. Space exclusion is necessary to tolerate permanent processor failures. Time exclusion is needed because both copies of a task must satisfy the timing constraints, and it is assumed that the backup is executed only after the failure in its primary is detected. Failure is detected, through an acceptance test or some other means, only at the completion of every primary copy. The time exclusion between the primary and backup copies of a task can be relaxed if the backup is allowed to execute in parallel [5] (or overlap) with its primary.

4.5.2   The Backup Overloading Algorithm

Here, we discuss the algorithm proposed by Ghosh, Melhem, and Mossé (which we call the GMM algorithm) in [3] for fault-tolerant scheduling of dynamic real-time tasks. It uses *backup overloading* and *backup deallocation* strategies. Backup overloading allows the backup copies of different tasks to overlap in time on the same processor. Backup deallocation strategies reclaim the time allocated to a backup copy in the case of fault-free operation of its primary. The condition under which backups can be overloaded is stated as follows: If Pr_i and Pr_j are scheduled on two different processors, then their backups Bk_i and Bk_j can overlap in execution on a processor:

$$\{proc(Bk_i) = proc(Bk_j)\} \wedge \{[st(Bk_i), ft(Bk_i)] \cap [st(Bk_j), ft(Bk_j)] \neq \phi\}$$
$$\Rightarrow proc(Pr_i) \neq proc(Pr_j). \tag{4.1}$$

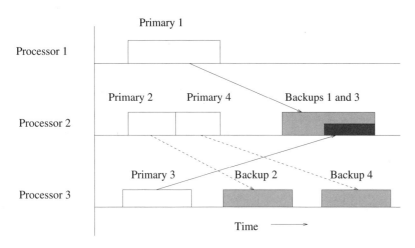

Figure 4.2
Backup overloading

Figure 4.2 depicts backup overloading. In this figure, Bk_1 and Bk_3, which are scheduled on processor P_2, overlap in execution, and their primaries Pr_1 and Pr_3 are scheduled on different processors P_1 and P_3, respectively. This backup overloading is valid under the assumption that there is at most one failure in the system (at any instant of time). However, this assumption is more optimistic than necessary, especially when the number of processors in the system is large.

In the GMM algorithm, the backup copy of a task is considered for scheduling immediately after its corresponding primary has been scheduled. The algorithm is informally stated in figure 4.3.

In each of steps (ii)–(iv), the search for fitting, adjusting, and overlapping begins at the end of the schedule and proceeds toward the start of the schedule of every processor. The depth of the search is limited to an input parameter $\overline{K}$. Since each of steps (ii)–(iv) takes $\overline{K}m$ time (where m is the number of processors), the worst-case time taken to schedule a primary copy is $2\overline{K}m$, whereas it is $3\overline{K}m$ for a backup copy.

This algorithm has the following limitations:

1. It does not support resource constraints among tasks, which is a practical requirement in most of the complex real-time systems.

2. It permits no more than one fault in the system.

3. It reclaims processor time only in cases of backup deallocation, but not when tasks complete early.

GMM Algorithm()
begin
    1. Order the tasks in nondecreasing order of deadline in the task queue.
    2. Choose the first (primary) and second (backup) tasks for scheduling:
        (a) Schedule the primary copy as early as possible by End Fitting() or
            Middle Fitting() or Middle Adjusting().
        (b) Schedule the backup copy as late as possible by Backup Overloading()
            or End Fitting() or Middle Fitting() or Middle Adjusting().
    3. **If** both primary and backup copies meet their deadline, accept them in the schedule.
    4. **else** reject them.
end.

(i) End Fitting(): Schedule the current task as the last task in the schedule of a processor.
(ii) Middle Fitting(): Schedule the current task somewhere in the middle of the schedule of a processor.
(iii) Middle Adjusting(): Schedule the current task somewhere in the middle of the schedule of a processor by changing the start and finish times of other tasks.
(iv) Backup Overloading(): Schedule the current task on a backup time interval if the primary copies corresponding to these backup copies are scheduled on two different processors.

Figure 4.3
GMM algorithm

4.5.3   The Distance Myopic Algorithm

Recently, a notion called *distance* has been introduced and its importance studied with a fault-tolerant extension to the myopic algorithm discussed in chapter 2. The myopic concept with distance *(distance myopic)* allows tasks to have resource constraints, permits more than one fault in the system, and can be integrated with reclaiming algorithms like the RV algorithm, discussed in chapter 3. The key features of the distance myopic algorithm are as follows:

• It uses a notion of *distance,* which decides the relative difference in position between the primary and backup copies of a task in the task queue.

• It allows a flexible level of backup overloading; this introduces a trade-off between number of faults and performance.

• It uses an RV-based algorithm to reclaim resources from both deallocated backups and tasks completing early.

    The following definitions are necessary to explain the distance myopic algorithm.

Definition 7: The scheduler fixes a *feasible schedule S*, which uses the worst-case computation time of a task for scheduling it and ensures that the timing, resource, and fault-tolerant constraints of all the tasks in S are met. A *partial schedule* is one that does not contain all the tasks in S.

Definition 8: EAT_k^s (EAT_k^e) is the earliest time at which resource R_k becomes available for shared (or exclusive) usage [17].

Definition 9: Let P be the set of processors and R_i be the set of resources requested by task T_i. The *earliest start time* of a task T_i, denoted as $EST(T_i)$, is the earliest time when its execution can be started, defined as

$$EST(T_i) = \max(r_i, \min_{j \in P}(avail\ time(j)), \max_{k \in R_i}(EAT_k^u)),$$

where *avail time(j)* denotes the time at which the processor P_j is available for executing a task, and the third term denotes the maximum among the available time of the resources requested by task T_i, in which $u = s$ for shared mode and $u = e$ for exclusive mode.

4.5.3.1 The Notion of Distance In a PB task model, every task T_i has two copies. In the distance myopic, both copies of a task T_i are placed in the task queue with a relative difference of $distance(Pr_i, Bk_i)$ in their positions. The primary copy of any task always precedes its backup copy in the task queue. Let n be the number of the currently active tasks, whose characteristics are known. (The algorithm does not know the characteristics of any new tasks that may arrive while scheduling the currently active tasks.) *distance* is an input parameter to the scheduling algorithm that determines the relative positions of the copies of a task in the task queue in the following way:

$$\forall T_i, distance(Pr_i, Bk_i) = \begin{cases} distance & \text{for the first } (n - (n \bmod distance)) \text{ tasks} \\ n \bmod distance & \text{for the last } (n \bmod distance) \text{ tasks.} \end{cases}$$

The following is an example task queue with $n = 4$ and $distance = 3$, assuming that the deadlines of tasks T_1, T_2, T_3, and T_4 are in nondecreasing order.

Pr_1	Pr_2	Pr_3	Bk_1	Bk_2	Bk_3	Pr_4	Bk_4

The positioning of backup copies in the task queue relative to their primaries can easily be achieved with minimal cost (1) by having two queues, one for primary copies (n entries) and the other for backup copies (n entries), and (2) merging these queues, before invoking the scheduler, based on the *distance* value, to get a task queue of $2n$ entries. The time taken for this merging is $2n$.

Distance Myopic()
begin
　　1. Order the tasks (primary copies) in nondecreasing order of deadlines in the task queue
　　　　and insert the backup copies at the appropriate *distance* from their primary copies.
　　2. Compute earliest start time $EST(T_i)$ for the first K tasks in the task queue, where K is the
　　　　size of the feasibility check window.
　　3. Check for strong feasibility: check whether $EST(T_i) + c_i \le d_i$ is true for all the K tasks.
　　4. **If** strongly feasible or no more backtracks are possible
　　　　(a) Compute the heuristic function $(H = d_i + W * EST(T_i))$ for the first K tasks, where W
　　　　　　is an input parameter.
　　　　　　　• When Bk_i of task T_i is considered for H function evaluation and Pr_i has not been
　　　　　　　　scheduled, set $EST(Bk_i) = \infty$.
　　　　(b) Choose the task with the *best* (smallest) H value to extend the schedule.
　　　　(c) **If** the best task meets its deadline, extend the schedule by the best task (best task is
　　　　　　accepted in the schedule).
　　　　　　　• **If** the best task is primary copy (Pr_i) of task T_i
　　　　　　　　　• Set $readytime(Bk_i) = ft(Pr_i)$. This is to achieve time exclusion for task T_i.
　　　　　　　　　• Set $exclude\ proc(Bk_i) = proc(Pr_i)$. This is to achieve space exclusion for
　　　　　　　　　　task T_i.
　　　　(d) **else** reject the best task and move the feasibility check window to the right by
　　　　　　one task.
　　　　(e) **If** the rejected task is a backup copy, delete its primary copy from the schedule.
　　5. **else** Backtrack to the previous search level and try extending the schedule with a task
　　　　having the next best H value.
　　6. **Repeat** steps (2–5) **until** termination condition is met.
end.

Figure 4.4
Distance-based myopic algorithm

4.5.3.2 The Distance-Based Fault Tolerant Myopic Algorithm   The myopic scheduling algorithm [17], discussed in chapter 2, is a heuristic search algorithm for scheduling real-time tasks with resource constraints. Each vertex in the search tree represents a partial schedule. A vertex is said to be *strongly feasible* if a feasible schedule can be generated by extending the partial schedule represented by that vertex with all unscheduled tasks within the *feasibility check window* (of size K) by considering them independently. The larger the size of the feasibility check window, the higher the scheduling cost and the more the look-ahead nature. The schedule from any particular vertex is extended only if the vertex is strongly feasible.

　　The fault-tolerant extensions to the original myopic algorithm using the distance concept are given in figure 4.4. Here, each task corresponds to a plan. The distance notion can be applied to any dynamic scheduling algorithm.

The termination condition for the algorithm is that either (1) all the tasks are scheduled or (2) all the tasks are considered for scheduling and no more backtracking is possible. The algorithm has the same complexity as the original myopic algorithm, which is $O(Kn)$. Note that the distance myopic algorithm can tolerate more than one fault at any point in time and that the number of faults is limited by the assumption that at most one of the copies of a task can fail. When a permanent processor failure is detected, the faulty processor is isolated from further scheduling until it gets repaired. In case of a transient fault, the processor on which the fault has occurred will still be considered for further scheduling.

Figure 4.5 is an example that shows the importance of the *distance* parameter for a set of independent tasks. The schedules in figure 4.5 are obtained using a fault-tolerant version of the myopic algorithm for *distance* $= 1$ to 5. Tasks i and ia denote the primary and backup copies of task T_i, respectively, which have the same worst-case computation time (c_i) and deadline (d_i). The values of K and W and the number of backtracks are taken to be 2, 1, and 0, respectively. When *distance* equals 1, 2, 3, or 5, the task set is not feasible because the backup version of task T_5 ($5a$) cannot be scheduled before its deadline 65, whereas the schedule obtained with *distance* set to 4 is feasible, as both copies of all 5 tasks meet their deadlines. Note that *distance* should be neither too low nor too high.

4.5.3.3 Implications of Distance

The interplay between *distance* and the size of the feasibility check window is an interesting result:

1. When *distance* is small, backup versions are positioned close to their respective primary versions in the task queue, and hence scheduling these backup versions may be postponed (termed as *backup postponement*) because of time and space exclusions. This causes an accumulation of more and more unscheduled backup versions of tasks. When this number exceeds K, the scheduler is forced to choose the best task (say T_b) from among these backup versions, which creates a hole in the schedule, since $EST(T_b)$ is greater than the *available time* of idle processors. This hole creation could be avoided by moving the feasibility check window until a primary task fell into it, but this approach is not considered since it increases the scheduling cost.

2. When *distance* is large, backup versions are positioned far apart from their respective primary versions in the task queue; that is, tasks (backup versions) having lower deadlines may be placed after some tasks (primary versions) having higher deadlines. This may lead to backtracking when the feasibility check window reaches these backup versions (termed as *forced backtrack*).

4.5.3.4 Flexible Backup Overloading in the Distance Myopic Algorithm

Here, we discuss how the distance myopic algorithm can employ a flexible level of backup overloading [3] to achieve a trade-off between faults and performance. In flexible overloading,

task (T_i)	r_i	c_i	d_i
T_1	0	10	35
T_2	0	15	40
T_3	0	15	55
T_4	0	10	60
T_5	0	10	65

| 1 | | 2a | 4 | 3a | 5a misses its deadline |

| 2 | 1a | 3 | 4a | 5 |

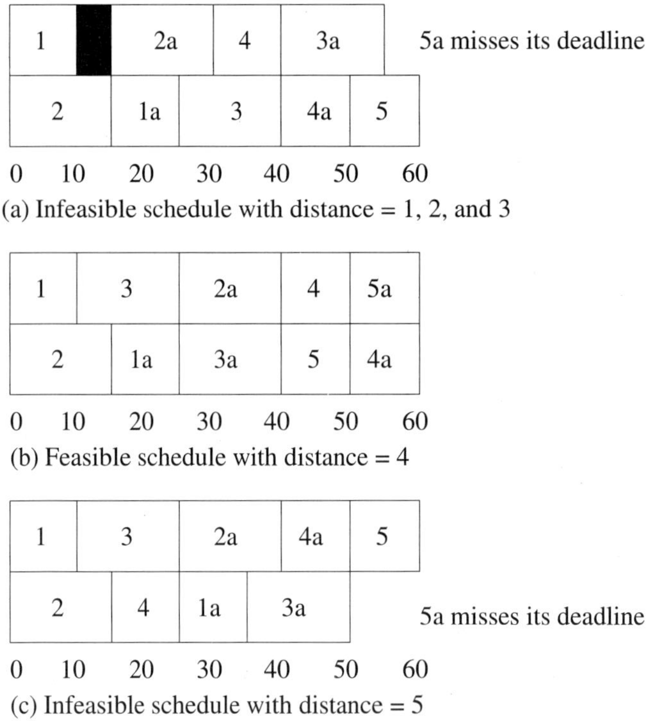

```
0    10    20    30    40    50    60
```
(a) Infeasible schedule with distance = 1, 2, and 3

| 1 | 3 | 2a | 4 | 5a |

| 2 | 1a | 3a | 5 | 4a |

```
0    10    20    30    40    50    60
```
(b) Feasible schedule with distance = 4

| 1 | 3 | 2a | 4a | 5 |

| 2 | 4 | 1a | 3a | 5a misses its deadline |

```
0    10    20    30    40    50    60
```
(c) Infeasible schedule with distance = 5

Figure 4.5
Task set and schedules for myopic algorithm with distance

processors are partitioned into different groups. Let $group(P_i)$ denote the group of which processor P_i is a member and m be the number of processors in the system. The rules for flexible backup overloading are as follows:

- Every processor is a member of exactly one group.
- For backup overloading to take place in a group, it must have at least three processors.
- The size of each group (*gsize*) is the same (except for one group, when $(m/gsize)$ is not an integer).
- Backup overloading can take place only among the processors within a group, according to the following:

$$Equation(4.1) \Rightarrow \{group(Proc(Bk_i)) = group(Proc(Pr_i)) = group(Proc(Pr_j))\}. \qquad (4.2)$$

Thus, the flexible overloading scheme permits up to $\lceil (m/gsize) \rceil$ number of faults at any instant of time, with the restriction of at most one fault in each group. In this scheme, as the number of faults permitted is increased, the flexibility in backup overloading is limited, and hence the guarantee ratio may drop [14]. This mechanism thus gives the system designer flexibility in choosing the desired degree of fault tolerance.

4.6   Scheduling of Real-Time Imprecise Computations

In this section, we discuss some of the algorithms proposed for scheduling imprecise computations of monotone and 0/1 constraint type. The algorithms to be discussed are for uniprocessor systems. To extend these algorithms to a multiprocessor system with m processors, the task set has to be first partitioned into m subsets, one subset assigned to each processor, and the uniprocessor algorithm applied on each subset.

4.6.1   Scheduling of Monotone Imprecise Computations

Before discussing the various algorithms that schedule imprecise computations (tasks), it is important to understand the types of error functions involved. For a monotone IC task T_i, the error ϵ_i is a function of the difference between the computation time o_i of its optional part O_i to the processor time σ_i alloted to the optional part; that is, $\epsilon_i = E_i(o_i - \sigma_i)$, where E_i is the error function. The error function $E_i(\sigma_i)$ is usually a monotonically nonincreasing function of σ_i.

In this context, an algorithm is optimal if, whenever feasible schedules that meet the ready time and deadline constraints of all tasks exist, it finds one that has minimum total error of all tasks. In [20], two preemptive scheduling algorithms have been proposed to schedule n imprecise computational tasks of monotone type onto a uniprocessor system. Each task is characterized by its ready time, computation time, and deadline. One of the

Algorithm F(T,M,O)

begin

1. Treat all mandatory tasks in M as optional tasks. Use the ED Algorithm to find a schedule S_t of the set T. **If** S_t is a precise schedule, stop. The resultant schedule has zero error and is optimal.

2. **else** use the ED Algorithm to find a schedule S_m of the set M. If S_m is not a feasible schedule, T cannot be feasibly scheduled. **Stop.**

3. **else** transform S_t into an optimal schedule S_o that is feasible and minimizes the total error using S_m as a template.

    Processor time adjustment process:

    $L_m(j)$ and initial values of $L_t(j)$ for $j = 1, 2, \ldots, k$ are given by S_m and S_t, respectively.

      (a) **For** $(j = k$ to 1 in steps of $-1)$

         i. **If** $(L_m(j) > L_t(j))$

            $\Delta = L_m(j) - L_t(j)$.

            Assign Δ units of processor time in $[a_j, a_{j+1}]$ to T(j).

            Reduce the amounts of processor time assigned to other tasks in X_j

               in $[a_j, a_{j+1}]$ by Δ units to accomplish this reassignment.

            Update the values of $L_t(1), L_t(2), \ldots, L_t(j)$ and modify S_t.

      (b) $S_o = S_t$

end.

Figure 4.6
Algorithm F

algorithms is optimal when the tasks have identical weights (i.e., E_i for every task T_i is the same), and its complexity is $O(n \log n)$. The other algorithm is optimal when the tasks have different weights, but its complexity is $O(n^2)$. In the rest of the section, we discuss the first algorithm in detail.

4.6.1.1 Scheduling Tasks with Identical Weights to Minimize the Total Error   The $O(n \log n)$ algorithm, called *Algorithm F,* used for optimally scheduling a set of n tasks having identical weights on a uniprocessor system, works as follows. The input task set $T = \{T_1, T_2, \ldots, T_n\}$ is decomposed into two sets: (1) the set of mandatory tasks (portions) $M = \{M_1, M_2, \ldots, M_n\}$ and (2) the set of optional tasks (portions) $O = \{O_1, O_2, \ldots, O_n\}$. The algorithm's output is an optimal schedule S_o that contains both precise and imprecise tasks. The attributes of a task T_i are r_i (ready time), c_i (worst-case computation time of the precise task), m_i (worst-case computation time of the mandatory part), o_i (worst-case computation time of optional part), and d_i (deadline).

The Algorithm F given in figure 4.6 uses the ED algorithm [20], whose complexity is $O(n \log n)$, as a subroutine. The ED algorithm is a variant of the classical EDF algorithm:

1. It is preemptive and priority-driven.

2. Priorities of tasks are assigned according to their deadlines.

3. Tasks with earlier deadlines have higher priorities.

4. At every instant, the processor is assigned to the task with the highest priority among the tasks that are ready to be executed, preempting any task with a lower priority if necessary.

In the ED algorithm, every task is terminated at its deadline even if it is not completed by that time, and no processor time is assigned to any task in the time interval after its deadline.

Note that the schedule S_t produced by step 1 in the algorithm need not be feasible; that is, some of the tasks may not complete even their mandatory parts before their deadlines. The idea behind step 3 is to make S_t feasible by taking away some processor time from tasks that have been allocated more than their mandatory requirement and allocating that time to tasks whose mandatory parts missed their deadline in S_t. The following definitions are needed to understand the step 3 of Algorithm F.

1. Time intervals $[a_j, a_{j+1}]$ for $j = 1, 2, \ldots, k$. Let a_1 be the earliest starting time and a_{k+1} be the latest finishing time of all tasks in schedule S_m. The time interval $[a_1, a_{k+1}]$ is partitioned according to S_m into disjoint intervals such that in S_m each processor is assigned to only one task in one interval and is assigned to different tasks in adjacent intervals. The quantity k denotes the number of such intervals.

2. The interval $[a_{k+1}, a_{k+2}]$. Let a_{k+2} be the latest finishing time of all tasks in schedule S_t. Clearly, $a_{k+2} \geq a_{k+1}$.

3. $M(j)$, for $j = 1, 2, \ldots, k$. $M(j)$ is the mandatory task portion that is scheduled in interval $[a_j, a_{j+1}]$ in S_m. Let $T(j)$ be the corresponding task.

4. X_j, for $j = 1, 2, \ldots, k + 1$. X_j is the set of tasks scheduled in interval $[a_j, a_{j+1}]$ according to schedule S_t.

5. $L_m(j)$, for $j = 1, 2, \ldots, k$. $L_m(j)$ is the total amount of processor time assigned to task $M(j)$ in interval $[a_j, a_{j+1}]$ and all later intervals according to schedule S_m. $L_m(j)$ is computed from S_m.

6. $L_t(j)$, for $j = 1, 2, \ldots, k$. $L_t(j)$ is the total amount of processor time assigned to task $T(j)$ in interval $[a_j, a_{j+1}]$ and all later intervals according to schedule S_t. $L_t(j)$ is initially given by S_t and is later modified during the adjustment process.

Consider the example task set (with $o_i = 2, \forall T_i, 1 \leq i \leq 5$) and its corresponding schedules given in figure 4.7. Step 1 of the algorithm produces schedule S_t and step 2 produces schedule S_m. Clearly, S_t is not a precise schedule (i.e., every task in it is not precise),

task (T_i)	r_i	d_i	c_i	m_i	o_i
T_1	0	12	7	4	3
T_2	2	14	6	2	4
T_3	5	16	6	4	2
T_4	5	18	3	2	1
T_5	10	19	4	1	3

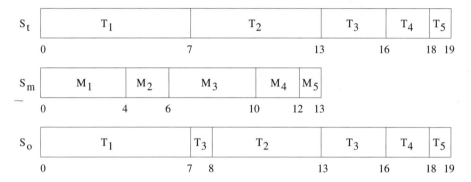

Figure 4.7
Task set and schedules for Algorithm F

and moreover it is not a feasible schedule because T_3 cannot complete even its mandatory portion before its deadline. But S_m is feasible, because every mandatory task finishes before its deadline in S_m. Step 3 of the algorithm starts from the right end of schedules S_m and S_t and proceeds as follows:

• The values of $L_m(j)$ are 4, 2, 4, 2, and 1 for $j = 1$ to 5, respectively. These values are fixed and obtained as per S_m. Initially, the values of $L_t(j)$ are 7, 6, 3, 2, and 1 for $j = 1$ to 5, respectively. These values are obtained as per S_t and correspond to the intervals in S_m. $S_t(j)$ may get modified as S_t changes.

• $L_t(5)$ and $L_t(4)$ are left unchanged because they are equal to $L_m(5)$ and $L_m(4)$, respectively.

• $L_t(3)$ is 3 and $L_m(3)$ is 4; therefore, one additional unit of processor time is assigned to $T(j)$, that is, the task corresponding to $L_m(3)$, which is T_3. This one unit is taken from a task in X_3 scheduled in the interval [6,10] of S_t. These tasks are T_1 (one time unit) and T_2 (three time units). Suppose we take one unit for T_3 from T_2, since T_2 has one unit in excess of its mandatory requirement. Therefore, S_t is modified by allocating the time interval [7,8] to T_3. The new values of $L_t(j)$ are 7, 5, 4, 2, and 1 for $j = 1$ to 5, respectively.

LDF Algorithm(T,M,O)
begin
    1. Use the ED Algorithm to find a schedule S_m of the mandatory set M.
    If S_m is not feasible, the task set T cannot be feasibly scheduled, stop.
    2. **else** do the following.
    Let $t_1, t_2, \ldots, t_n$ be the finish times, which are in non-increasing order, corresponding to
    $M_1, M_2, \ldots, M_n$, respectively.
    Let δ be the computation time of optional parts of all the tasks.
        (a) d_{n+1} = ready time of all tasks;   *real_deadline* = d_1
        (b) **For** ($j = 1$ to n in steps of 1)
            i. **If** (*real_deadline* $- t_j) \geq \delta$
                Schedule O_j; assign [*real_deadline* $- m_j - \delta$, *real_deadline*] to T_j
                real_deadline = min(*real_deadline* $- m_j - \delta, d_{j+1}$)
            ii. **else**
                Discard O_j; assign [*real_deadline* $- m_j$, *real_deadline*] to T_j
                real_deadline = min(*real_deadline* $- m_j, d_{j+1}$)
end.

Figure 4.8
LDF algorithm

• $L_t(2)$ and $L_t(1)$ are left unchanged becuase they are greater than $L_m(2)$ and $L_m(1)$, respectively. The original schedule S_t is transformed by allocating one unit of processor time to T_3 to make the schedule feasible. The optimal schedule S_o is given in figure 4.7.

4.6.2   Scheduling of Imprecise Computations with 0/1 Constraints

A schedule is said to satisfy the 0/1 constraint if every optional task in the schedule is either completed fully or discarded entirely. The problem of scheduling real-time tasks with 0/1 constraints to minimize the total error is NP-complete when the optional tasks have arbitrary computation times. An optimal schedule in this context is a feasible schedule in which the number of discarded optional tasks is minimum. Two optimal algorithms have been proposed in [20] for a special case in which all the optional tasks have equal computation times. The first algorithm is latest-deadline-first (LDF) algorithm, whose time complexity is $O(n \log n)$, for tasks having the same ready time. The second algorithm is depth-first-search (DFS) algorithm, whose time complexity is $O(n^2)$, for tasks having arbitrary ready times. Here, we discuss only the first algorithm in detail (figure 4.8). Step 1 of the algorithm checks whether the mandatory set M is feasible and produces a feasible schedule S_m. If M is feasible, this step inserts optional tasks into the schedule S_m. The idea behind step 2 is to schedule the mandatory tasks in S_m as late as possible (i.e., toward their

task (T_i)	d_i	m_i
T_1	5	2
T_2	7	2
T_3	9	3
T_4	11	3
T_5	16	2

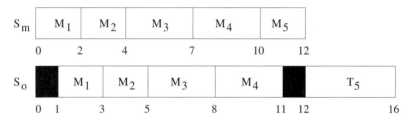

Figure 4.9
Task set and schedules for LDF algorithm

deadlines) starting from the *latest-deadline task* (i.e., the last task of S_m) and insert the optional tasks in the holes this adjustment creates.

Consider the example task set and its corresponding schedules given in figure 4.9. Step 1 of the algorithm produces schedule S_m, and S_o is the optimal schedule obtained by inserting optional tasks in schedule S_m. Note that in schedule S_o, task T_5 is precise. Also note that a hole is created between time units 11 and 12 because task T_4 cannot finish later than 11, which is its deadline.

4.6.3   Imprecise Scheduling of Periodic Tasks

Different performance metrics are used for different applications. Applications are classified as either error-noncumulative or error-cumulative. In an *error-noncumulative* application, instances of a periodic task are independent, and their inputs are precise. In such applications, only the average effect of errors in different periods are observable and relevant. Image and video transmission is an example of this type. In contrast, in *error-cumulative* applications, instances of a periodic task are dependent. In such cases, the imprecise output of an instance feeds imprecise input to its successor instances, which, to produce a precise output, therefore need to execute for a longer time than what is required when precise inputs are given. If this continues, at some point, the task will never produce a precise output no matter how long it executes. To avoid this effect, it is necessary to nullify the error that has accumulated over past periods by making instances at regular intervals produce a precise result. The simplification assumption is that the error accumulated over several consecutive periods is reset to zero when the optional task in the subsequent period completes and produces a precise result. An example of this type of application is tracking and control.

4.7   Other Work on Fault-Tolerant Scheduling of Real-Time Tasks

In this section, we briefly discuss some other results in fault-tolerant scheduling of real-time tasks that do not fit exactly into any of the above fault-tolerant approaches.

4.7.1 (m, k)-Firm Deadline Task Model

A periodic task is said to have an (m, k)-firm guarantee requirement if it is adequate to meet the deadlines of m out of any k consecutive instances of the task, where m and k are two positive integers with $m \leq k$ [18]. The main advantage of this guarantee model is that one can represent a wide range of tolerance to deadline misses by properly choosing the values of m and k. In particular, the traditional hard deadline requirement can be represented as a $(1, 1)$-firm guarantee requirement, and a soft deadline requirement of a bound on the fraction of deadline misses can be approximated by picking a large value for k and choosing m such that m/k equals the desired fraction. However, for most values of m and k, $m < k$, the (m, k)-firm guarantee requirement is less stringent than the hard deadline requirement but more stringent than the soft deadline requirement. Radar tracking and automobile control are some of the applications that use an (m, k)-firm guarantee model, wherein a few deadline misses of control law computation can be tolerated, especially if the deadline misses are adequately spaced.

Formally, each periodic task T_i is characterized by (c_i, p_i, m_i, k_i), where the parameters denote the computation time, period, m, and k values of the task, respectively. Strictly speaking, the (m, k)-firm guarantee model is not a fault-tolerant technique; rather, it provides scheduling flexibility, similar to the IC model, by trading off result quality to meet task deadlines. The difference between IC model and (m, k)-firm model is that in the former case each instance is divided into mandatory and optional parts, whereas in the latter case, each instance of a task T_i is classified as either mandatory or optional such that if the mandatory instances meet their respective deadlines then T_i's (m_i, k_i)-firm guarantee requirement is satisfied.

Recently, an algorithm was proposed in [18] for scheduling periodic tasks with (m, k)-firm guarantee requirements on a uniprocessor system. This algorithm aims at reducing the effective utilization of the system by selectively discarding task instances during overload. The algorithm is based on RMS scheduling policy (discussed in chapter 2). The crux of the algorithm involves (1) classifying the instances of a task as either mandatory or optional and (2) assigning a priority to each instance. The classification of instances of T_i as mandatory or optional is based on the values of m_i and k_i. More specifically, instances of T_i arrive at times ap_i, for $a = 0, 1, 2, \ldots$. An instance activated at time ap_i is classified as mandatory if $a = \lfloor \lceil \frac{am_i}{k_i} \rceil \cdot \frac{k_i}{m_i} \rfloor$ and as optional otherwise. The algorithm assigns a priority to mandatory instances of a task in such a way that their deadlines are guaranteed; it assigns the lowest priority to the optional instances, and they are not guaranteed to meet their respective deadlines. The mandatory instances of all the tasks are assigned priorities based on rate-monotonic policy; that is, the mandatory instances of T_i are assigned a higher priority than the mandatory instances of T_j if and only if $p_i < p_j$. The highest-priority instance among those awaiting execution is executed first. The currently executing instance is preempted if a new instance arrives and its priority is higher than that of the currently executing instance.

4.7.2 Determining Redundancy Levels

As discussed earlier, there are generally trade-offs between task performance and task reliability. Increasing the redundancy level for a task decreases the probability that the task will fail after being accepted, at the same time decreasing the schedulability of the system, that is, the number of tasks that get scheduled. This implies trade-offs involving the fault tolerance of the system, the rewards provided by guaranteed tasks that complete successfully, and the penalties due to tasks that fail after being guaranteed or that fail to be guaranteed. In this context, an approach is proposed in [25] to determine the degree of redundancy for a given set of tasks so as to maximize the total performance index, which is a performance-related reliability measure.

This approach is used in dynamic planning-based scheduling, in which decisions are made as tasks arrive. In a system using such scheduling with m processors, n tasks arrive at any particular point. The approach tries to find a redundancy level for the tasks such that the overall performance index is maximized by capturing both performance and reliability requirements. Once a task redundancy level is determined, a task is said to be guaranteed if that number of copies of the task are all scheduled to complete before the task's deadline. Suppose a task T_i provides a reward V_i if it completes successfully once it is guaranteed, a penalty P_i if it fails after being guaranteed, and penalty Q_i if it is not guaranteed. Let R_i be the reliability of a task and F_i be its failure probability, where $R_i = 1 - F_i$. The redundancy level of a task T_i and the failure model of the processors affect R_i. The performance index PI_i for task T_i is defined as

$$PI_i = \begin{cases} V_i R_i - P_i F_i, & \text{if } T_i \text{ is guaranteed.} \\ -Q_i, & \text{if } T_i \text{ is not guaranteed.} \end{cases}$$

task (T_i)	task attributes			penalty/reward		
	r_i	c_i	d_i	V_i	P_i	Q_i
T_1, T_2, T_3, T_4	0	10	10	10	100	1

u	$PI = \sum_{i=1}^{4} PI_i$
1	$4(10 * 0.9 - 100 * 0.1) = -4$
2	$2(10 * 0.99 - 100 * 0.01) - 2 \approx 16$
3	$1(10 * 0.999 - 100 * 0.001) - 3 \approx 7$
4	$1(10 * 0.9999 - 100 * 0.0001) - 3 \approx 7$

Figure 4.10
Task set and performance indices for redundancy level determination

Then the performance index for a task set containing n tasks is defined as

$$PI = \sum_{i=1}^{n} PI_i.$$

As an illustration, let us consider a set of four tasks whose characteristics are given in the first table of figure 4.10. Let the number of processors be four and each processor have a reliability of 0.9. Then the reliability of a task is 0.9 when its redundancy is 1, 0.99 when its redundancy is 2, and so on. The second table in figure 4.10 shows the performance index for different redundancy levels (u). The maximum performance index is reached when all scheduled tasks have their redundancy level at 2. From the values of PI, the redundancy level is not enough if $u < 2$ and too much if $u > 2$.

4.7.3 Scheduling with Fault Detection and Location

Several schemes for detecting and locating faulty processors through self-diagnosis (where the tasks to be scheduled themselves are used to perform health checking) in multiprocessor systems have recently been studied. These schemes attempt to start multiple copies (versions) of the tasks on available idle processors simultaneously and compare the results generated by the copies to detect or locate faulty processors.

Fault detection and location in non-real-time multiprocessor systems using self-diagnosis have been discussed in [2] and [24]. [2] describes a scheme in which a task is started (primary version) on any available idle processor. Other copies of the task (secondary versions) are started simultaneously on other idle processors, if there are any. The results generated are then compared to detect if any of the processors are defective. The performance metric used is

$$\Pi(n, \rho) = \frac{\text{number of secondary tasks completed}}{\text{number of primary tasks completed}} * 100,$$

where n is the number of processors and ρ is the average system load. It is worth noting that only the detection of a fault, not which of the processors is defective, is possible in this approach. [24] extends this by proposing three schemes in which the faulty processors themselves can be identified. The basic idea is to start more than one secondary version whenever possible. The performance metrics used are fault detection capability (FDC) and fault location capability (FLC). FDC gives the average amount of time for which a processor is checked by two or more processors, whereas FLC gives the average amount of time a processor is checked by three or more processors. They are defined as

$$FDC(n, \rho) = \left(\frac{1}{n}\right) \sum_{i=2}^{n} \frac{i * \gamma_i}{\mu_i} * 100;$$

$$FLC(n, \rho) = \left(\frac{1}{n}\right) \sum_{i=3}^{n} \frac{i * \gamma_i}{\mu_i} * 100;$$

where γ_i is the average number of tasks that complete with i versions and $1/\mu_i$ is the average service time (execution time) of the tasks that complete with i versions.

In real-time systems, in addition to the guarantee ratio, which is the primary performance metric, other metrics, namely, time spent on fault detection (TFD) and time spent on fault location (TFL) are also important when self-diagnosis is performed. Therefore, in these systems, any algorithm that attempts to perform self-diagnosis must tackle two problems: selecting the correct task to extend the schedule and scheduling the right number of versions (δ_i) of the selected task so that tasks' timing requirements are met.

In [11], an algorithm has been proposed to schedule real-time tasks with self-diagnosis capability. The algorithm is a variation of the myopic algorithm discussed in chapter 2. It solves the first problem by using the same heuristic function $h()$ as that of the myopic algorithm. To determine δ_i, it uses another heuristic function, $\mathcal{R}(T_i)$. Three different heuristics—the greedy heuristic, the look-ahead heuristic, and the spare-capacity heuristic—have been proposed for determining δ_i.

4.7.3.1 The Greedy Heuristic The greedy algorithm attempts to schedule as many versions as possible for a task. The heuristic function $\mathcal{R}(T_i)$ is defined as

$$\delta_i \leftarrow \max j \text{ such that } EST_{ij} + c_i \leq d_i (j = 1 \ldots p),$$

where c_i and d_i are the worst-case computation time and deadline of task T_i, respectively; p is the number of processors; and EST_{ij} is defined as the earliest time at which j versions of T_i can be started.

Thus the number of versions (j) scheduled is based on EST_{ij}, which is the maximum of (1) the ready time of T_i, (2) processor available time, and (3) resource available time of the resources requested by T_i. The basic problem with the greedy approach is that it does not consider the timing requirements of the unscheduled tasks. It blindly introduces secondary versions and corrects the error entirely with backtracks.

4.7.3.2 The Look-Ahead Heuristic The look-ahead algorithm attempts to overcome the problem associated with the greedy algorithm by examining the laxities of the tasks within the feasibility check window (used in the myopic algorithm) before deciding δ_i. The heuristic function $\mathcal{R}(T_i)$ first scans the feasibility check window and determines the number of tasks whose laxities (latest start times) are smaller than that of the scheduled finish time of T_i. Let t be the number of such tasks. Clearly these t tasks have to be scheduled before T_i finishes. Since these t tasks have to share the p processors,

$$\delta_i = \begin{cases} \lfloor p/t \rfloor & \text{if } p > t. \\ 1 & \text{otherwise.} \end{cases}$$

The look-ahead algorithm has its own problem, however: It blindly introduces a large number of secondary versions for the first few tasks, and hence is left with a large number of tasks to be scheduled in a short time span, thereby reducing schedulability.

4.7.3.3 The Spare-Capacity Heuristic The spare-capacity algorithm overcomes the problem associated with the look-ahead algorithm, basically by determining the spare capacity, in terms of processor and resources, at a given point of time. The heuristic function $\mathcal{R}(T_i)$ calculates the spare capacity and using this knowledge determines δ_i.

In summary, the greedy heuristic ignores the timing and resource requirements of unscheduled tasks, the look-ahead heuristic ignores the resource requirements of unscheduled tasks, and the spare-capacity heuristic takes into account both timing and resource requirements of unscheduled tasks while deciding the redundancy level of a task.

From simulation studies, it was concluded in [11] that the spare-capacity heuristic offers a better guarantee ratio (performance) than the other two heuristics and that its performance is very close to that of the myopic algorithm with the added value of achieving fault detection and location.

4.7.4 Integrated Fault-Tolerant Scheduling

The different techniques employed for fault detection in the three approaches (TMR, RB, IC) often make one approach preferable to the other in certain applications. Also, some applications can include tasks requiring more than one fault-tolerant approach [16]. Hence, it is necessary to have a single fault-tolerant scheduling algorithm that supports different approaches. One such algorithm is described below.

In [13], an integrated scheduling algorithm, a variant of myopic scheduling, has been proposed to schedule tasks having TMR, PB, and IC fault tolerance requirements. In this algorithm, for scheduling a task with a TMR fault tolerance requirement, three versions of a task are scheduled concurrently on three different processors (space exclusion only). Since all the versions of the task are assumed to have the same characteristics, it suffices to have only one task in the task queue at a time. When such a TMR task is considered for scheduling, the scheduler knows that three versions are to be scheduled. While computing $EST(T_i)$ of a TMR task T_i, the scheduler has to find the *earliest time* at which three processors (instead of one) and three copies of the resources required by T_i are available.

Scheduling of tasks having PB fault tolerance requirements is the same in this algorithm as in the distance myopic algorithm. For scheduling of tasks with IC fault tolerance requirements, the primary copy is treated as having both mandatory and optional parts, and the backup copy is treated as having the mandatory part alone. These two versions of the task are scheduled with time exclusion, but need not be with space exclusion; that is, the copies of a task could be scheduled on the same processor. The primary version of a task precedes its backup in time in the schedule. The task queue contains both the primary and backup copies of each task (the same as in the PB model). The $EST()$ calculation and other scheduling steps are the same as those for the PB model.

4.7.5   An Allocation Heuristic

The problem of allocating a set of periodic tasks, each of which, for fault tolerance purposes, has multiple versions, among the minimum number of processors such that the copies of a task are scheduled on different processors, is NP-complete. This motivates the need for heuristic algorithms to solve the problem in a reasonable amount of time. An allocation heuristic has been proposed in [15] that is proven to have a tight upper bound. The number of processors, N, required by the heuristic to feasibly schedule a set of tasks and the minimum number of processors, N_o, required to feasibly schedule the same set of tasks are related by $N \leq 2.33 N_o + k$, where k is the maximum degree of redundancy of a task. The allocation heuristic partitions the task set into N subsets, one per processor. On each individual processor, RMS guarantees that the tasks meet their deadlines. The resultant schedule obtained using this approach will be preemptive, since RMS is an optimal fixed-priority preemptive scheduling algorithm.

4.8   Summary

• Fault tolerance is informally defined as a system's ability to deliver the expected service even in the presence of faults. Based on the failure mode, hard real-time systems are often classified as fail-safe or fail-operational. In a fail-safe system, safe states can be identified that can be accessed in case of failure, whereas in a fail-operational system, such safe states cannot be identified; this means that the system must deliver a minimal level of service even in the case of failure.

• Fault tolerance can be expressed in terms of reliability and availability. Reliability is the probability of surviving over an interval of time. Availability is the probability of being operational at a given instant.

• Faults can be classified based on duration as permanent, intermittent, or transient; based on output behavior as malicious or nonmalicious; and based on correlation with other faults as correlated or independent.

• The basic principle of fault-tolerant design is redundancy. There are four basic approaches to achieve redundancy, namely, hardware redundancy, software redundancy, temporal redundancy, and information redundancy.

• The design methodology for fault-tolerant systems has often been characterized by the trade-off between time and space. In real-time systems, since timeliness is more crucial, the tendency is to trade space for time.

• Four techniques have evolved for fault-tolerant scheduling of real-time tasks, namely, N-modular redundancy, N-version programming, recovery blocks, and imprecise computations.

• There are three approaches for the fault-tolerant scheduling of dynamically arriving hard real-time tasks, depending on the nature of application: the dynamic planning-based approach, overallocation of resources statically, and fault tolerance based on resource availability.

• Two dynamic planning-based algorithms are discussed for recovery block based fault-tolerant scheduling, namely, the GMM algorithm and the fault-tolerant version of the myopic algorithm. The GMM algorithm uses strategies such as backup overloading and backup deallocation, whereas the fault-tolerant myopic algorithm uses a concept called distance, which determines the relative difference in position between different copies of a task in the task queue, in addition to these strategies. The GMM algorithm handles independent tasks and can tolerate at most one fault, whereas the fault-tolerant myopic algorithm handles resource constraints among tasks and can tolerate more than one fault.

• For scheduling IC tasks of monotone type with tasks having identical weights, an optimal algorithm to minimize the total error is discussed. The problem of optimal scheduling of IC tasks with 0/1 constraint, to minimize the total error, is NP-complete when the optional parts of tasks have arbitrary computation times. An optimal algorithm for a special case in which all the optional parts have equal computation times with the same ready times is discussed.

• In some applications, a periodic task can be characterized by an (m, k)-firm guarantee model, in which it is adequate to meet the deadlines of m out of any k consecutive instances of the task.

• In real-time systems, any algorithm that attempts to perform self-diagnosis must tackle two problems. The first is to select the correct task to extend the schedule, and the second is to schedule the right number of versions of the selected task so that tasks' timing requirements are met.

• An algorithm that uses a performance-related reliability measure to determine the degree of redundancy is discussed. Integrating different fault-tolerant approaches into a single scheduling algorithm is also discussed.

Exercises

1. What are the different causes of system failure? Discuss.

2. What are the methods of fault detection? Discuss.

3. Does a system with high reliability mean high availability or vice versa?

4. What features distinguish forward and backward recovery schemes? To which category does imprecise computation belong?

5. What needs to be done to apply the algorithms used for scheduling tasks with PB fault tolerance to imprecise tasks with 0/1 constraints?

6. In a multiprocessor system with m processors, under what condition(s) is backup overloading not possible?

7. For the task set shown in figure 4.5, find the values of K for which feasible schedules exist when *distance* is 4. Show the schedules. (Assume that the values of W and number of backtracks are 1 and 0, respectively.)

8. Construct schedules for the set of tasks in figure 4.11 using distance myopic algorithm with *distance* equal to 1 and 3. Are these schedules feasible? (Assume that the values of K, W, and number of backtracks are 2, 1, and 0, respectively.)

9. Construct schedules S_t, S_m, and S_o for the imprecise computational tasks of monotone type in figure 4.12. Calculate the total error assuming equal weight to each task. In the figure, r_i and d_i denote the ready time and deadline of T_i, and c_i, m_i, and o_i denote the computation time of entire task, mandatory part, and optional part, respectively.

10. Construct schedules S_m and S_o for the imprecise computational tasks with 0/1 constraints for the task set in the previous question, with the modification that the ready times (r_i) of the tasks are 0 and the computation times of the optional parts (o_i) of the tasks are 2.

task	c_i	d_i
T_1	28	110
T_2	14	113
T_3	41	118
T_4	25	134

Figure 4.11
Exercise 4.8 task set

task (T_i)	r_i	d_i	c_i	m_i	o_i
T_1	0	7	5	3	2
T_2	3	12	7	4	3
T_3	4	14	6	2	4
T_4	6	16	6	4	2
T_5	4	18	3	2	1
T_6	10	19	4	1	3

Figure 4.12
Exercises 4.9 and 4.10 task set (imprecise)

task	task attributes			penalty/reward		
	r_i	c_i	d_i	V_i	P_i	Q_i
$T_1, T_2, \ldots, T_{10}$	0	10	10	10	100	2

Figure 4.13
Exercise 4.11 task set (with penalty/reward attributes)

11. Calculate the redundancy level for the task set in figure 4.13 with a multiprocessor system having 10 processors. Determine the best redundancy level for each task that maximizes the PI of the system. Assume that each processor has a reliability of 0.9 and that all tasks have the same redundancy level. In the figure, r_i, c_i, and d_i denote the ready time, computation time, and deadline, respectively, of a task T_i, and V_i, P_i, and Q_i denote the reward for successful completion of a guaranteed task, the penalty for unsuccessful completion of a guaranteed task, and the penalty for not being able to guarantee a task, respectively.

12. In an adaptive fault-tolerant scheduling, there is a flexibility in choosing the fault-tolerant approach, if the task permits so. If TMR and PB are the choices, when should a designer choose TMR and when should he/she choose PB?

References

[1] L. Chen and A. Avizienis. "N-version programming: A fault-tolerance approach to reliability of software operation." In *Proc. IEEE Fault-Tolerant Computing Symp.,* pp. 15–22, 1988.

[2] A. Dahbhura, K. Sabnani, and W. Hery. "Spare capacity as a means of fault detection and diagnosis in multiprocessor systems." *IEEE Trans. Computers,* vol. 38, no. 6, pp. 881–891, June 1989.

[3] S. Ghosh, R. Melhem, and D. Mossé. "Fault-tolerance through scheduling of aperiodic tasks in hard real-time multiprocessor systems." *IEEE Trans. Parallel and Distributed Systems,* vol. 8, no. 3, pp. 272–284, Mar. 1997.

[4] O. González, H. Shrikumar, J. A. Stankovic, and K. Ramamritham. "Adaptive fault-tolerance and graceful degradation under dynamic hard real-time scheduling." In *Proc. IEEE Real-Time Systems Symp.,* 1997.

[5] K. Kim and J. Yoon. "Approaches to implementation of reparable distributed recovery block scheme." In *Proc. IEEE Fault-Tolerant Computing Symp.,* pp. 50–55, 1988.

[6] H. Kopetz and P. Veríssimo. "Real-time and dependability concepts." In *Distributed Systems* (Sape Mullender, ed.), pp. 411–446, Addison-Wesley, 1994.

[7] C. M. Krishna and K. G. Shin. *Real-Time Systems.* McGraw-Hill International, Singapore, 1997.

[8] J. H. Lala and R. E. Harper. "Architectural principles for safety-critical real-time applications." *Proc. IEEE,* vol. 82, no. 1, pp. 25–40, Jan. 1994.

[9] A. L. Liestman and R. H. Campbell. "A fault-tolerant scheduling problem." *IEEE Trans. Software Engg.,* vol. 12, no. 11, pp. 1089–1095, Nov. 1986.

[10] J. W. S. Liu, K. J. Lin, W. K. Shih, A. C. Yu, J. Y. Chung, and W. Zhao. "Algorithms for scheduling imprecise computations." *IEEE Computer,* vol. 24, no. 5, pp. 58–68, May 1991.

[11] K. Mahesh, G. Manimaran, C. Siva Ram Murthy, and A. K. Somani. "Scheduling algorithms with fault detection and location capabilities for real-time multiprocessor systems." *Journal of Parallel and Distributed Computing,* vol. 51, no. 2, pp. 136–150, June 1998.

[12] L. V. Mancini. "Modular redundancy in a message passing system." *IEEE Trans. Software Engg.,* vol. 12, no. 1, pp. 79–86, Jan. 1986.

[13] G. Manimaran and C. Siva Ram Murthy. "A new scheduling approach supporting different fault-tolerant techniques for real-time multiprocessor systems." *Journal of Microprocessors and Microsystems,* vol. 21, no. 3, pp. 163–173, Dec. 1997.

[14] G. Manimaran and C. Siva Ram Murthy. "A fault-tolerant dynamic scheduling algorithm for real-time multiprocessor systems and its analysis." *IEEE Trans. Parallel and Distributed Systems,* vol. 9, no. 11, pp. 1137–1152, Nov. 1998.

[15] Y. Oh and S. H. Son. "Enhancing fault-tolerance in rate-monotonic scheduling." *Real-Time Systems,* vol. 7, no. 3, pp. 315–329, May 1994.

[16] J. H. Purtilo and P. Jalote. "An environment for developing fault-tolerant software." *IEEE Trans. Software Engg.,* vol. 17, no. 2, pp. 153–159, Feb. 1991.

[17] K. Ramamritham, J. A. Stankovic, and P.-F. Shiah. "Efficient scheduling algorithms for real-time multiprocessor systems." *IEEE Trans. Parallel and Distributed Systems,* vol. 1, no. 2, pp. 184–194, Apr. 1990.

[18] P. Ramanathan. "Graceful degradation in real-time control applications using (m, k)-firm guarantee." In *Proc. IEEE Fault-Tolerant Computing Symp.,* pp. 132–141, 1997.

[19] B. Randell. "System structure for software fault-tolerance." *IEEE Trans. Software Engg.,* vol. 1, no. 2, pp. 220–232, June 1975.

[20] W. K. Shih, J. W. S. Liu, and J. Y. Chung. "Algorithms for scheduling imprecise computations with timing constraints." *SIAM J. Computing,* vol. 20, no. 3, pp. 537–552, June 1991.

[21] K. G. Shin and P. Ramanathan. "Real-time computing: A new discipline of computer science and engineering." *Proc. IEEE,* vol. 82, no. 1, pp. 6–24, Jan. 1994.

[22] A. K. Somani. "Sequential fault occurrence and reconfiguration in system level diagnosis." *IEEE Trans. Computers,* vol. 39, no. 12, pp. 1472–1475, Dec. 1990.

[23] A. K. Somani and N. H. Vaidya. "Understanding fault-tolerance and reliability." *IEEE Computer,* vol. 30, no. 4, pp. 45–50, Apr. 1997.

[24] S. Tridandapani, A. K. Somani, and U. R. Sandadi. "Low overhead multiprocessor allocation strategies exploiting system spare capacity for fault detection and location." *IEEE Trans. Computers,* vol. 44, no. 7, pp. 865–877, July 1995.

[25] F. Wang, K. Ramamritham, and J. A. Stankovic. "Determining redundancy levels for fault-tolerant real-time systems." *IEEE Trans. Computers,* vol. 44, no. 2, pp. 292–301, Feb. 1995.

5 Resource Management in Distributed Real-Time Systems

Overview

In the previous chapters, we discussed the problem of resource management in multi-processor real-time systems. In this chapter, we consider the resource management problem in distributed real-time systems. We first introduce a generic layered architecture for resource management in distributed real-time systems and then discuss each layer of this architecture in detail. Then, we present some well-known scheduling algorithms for distributed real-time systems. Finally, we present a comparative study of these algorithms.

5.1 Introduction

The scheduling of tasks in distributed real-time systems has recently attracted many researchers. The demand for more and more complex real-time applications, which have high computational needs with timing constraints and fault tolerance requirements, have led to the choice of distributed systems as a natural candidate for supporting such real-time applications, because of their potential for high performance and reliability. The nodes in a distributed real-time system are connected through a point-to-point or multiple access network, and each node has at least one processor. The presence of multiple nodes enables the system to improve its performance by migrating tasks from heavily loaded nodes to lightly loaded nodes to meet the tasks' deadlines. The presence of multiple disjoint paths between nodes in such networks makes them robust to link and node failures. Also, because it is possible to support simultaneous transmission on different links, these networks provide a higher total throughput [5]. In multiple access networks, all the nodes share a single medium (link) for communication. These networks can tolerate node failures but may not tolerate link failures.

As noted several times previously, the problem of meeting task deadlines is of great importance in real-time systems, because failure to meet task deadlines may result in severe consequences, possibly loss of human life. Similarly, the problem of providing predictable intertask communication is of great significance in real-time systems, because unpredictable delays in the delivery of messages can affect the completion time of tasks participating in the message communication.

5.1.1 Tasks, Messages, and System Models

In this section, we first describe task and message models, and then make some assumptions about the distributed system.

Real-time tasks can be classified into two categories: periodic tasks, which are time-driven, and aperiodic tasks, which are event-driven. Similarly, real-time messages can be classified into two categories: periodic messages (also known as synchronous messages) and aperiodic messages (also known as asynchronous messages).

Periodic Messages: Periodic tasks generate periodic messages. The periodicity of the message stream spaces the arrival times of periodic messages. If the delays encountered in sending a periodic message exceed its period, it is considered to be lost. Periodic messages are often used for sending sensory data and intertask communication between periodic tasks.

Aperiodic Messages: The arrival pattern of aperiodic messages is stochastic in nature, as opposed to the deterministic nature of periodic messages. Like those of aperiodic tasks, the characteristics of aperiodic messages are known only on their arrival. Each aperiodic message has an end-to-end deadline, and it must reach its intended destination before the deadline. Otherwise, it is considered to be lost. Aperiodic tasks are often used to carry alert messages or for communication between aperiodic tasks.

5.1.2   Distributed System

A distributed system consists of uniprocessor or multiprocessor nodes connected through a multihop or multiple access network. The processors in each node of the system are identical, but the number of processors may vary from node to node. In multihop networks, no assumption is made about the nodes' interconnection. Activities at a node such as local scheduling, global scheduling, and message scheduling are assumed to be periodic tasks, and they may run on a dedicated processor.

Periodic tasks are scheduled a priori onto a set of processors in each node of the distributed system. Message exchanges among periodic tasks are assumed to flow through the a priori established periodic real-time channels [2].[1] Aperiodic tasks arrive at each node independent of the task arrivals at other nodes of the distributed system.

5.2   Scheduling in Distributed Real-Time Systems

In this section, we first define the scheduling problem and then present a generic framework for scheduling of tasks in distributed real-time systems.

5.2.1   The Scheduling Problem and Metrics

The scheduling problem in distributed real-time systems involves how to schedule aperiodic tasks that arrive dynamically at each node onto the processors of the distributed system before their deadlines, and simultaneously schedule the messages that are exchanged among communicating tasks before their deadlines.

---

1. A channel with a guaranteed quality of service.

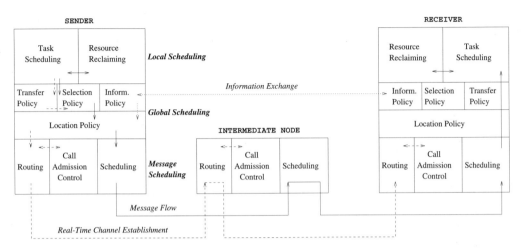

Figure 5.1
Layered architecture of a node in a distributed real-time system

Classical task-scheduling theory in a multiprocessor system typically uses metrics such as minimizing schedule length and the sum of completion times. The traditional load-balancing algorithms in a distributed system attempt to maximize throughput and fairness and minimize response time. In real-time systems, these metrics have secondary importance since they do not directly address the fact that individual tasks have deadlines. The metric used in a dynamic real-time system is, instead, the guarantee ratio. The objective of any dynamic real-time scheduling algorithm is to improve the guarantee ratio.

5.2.2   An Architecture for Distributed Real-Time Scheduling

Figure 5.1 depicts a three-layered architecture of a node in a distributed real-time system. The top layer (layer 3) is used for local scheduling, the middle layer (layer 2) handles global scheduling, and the bottom layer (layer 1) takes care of message scheduling. Layer 3 interacts with layer 2, and layer 2 interacts with layer 1. The local scheduling does not depend on whether the network is multihop or multiple access, but the global scheduling does. Each of these layers is briefly described below:

1. *Local scheduling.* Local scheduling deals with the scheduling of dynamically arriving real-time tasks onto the processor(s) and resource(s) of a uniprocessor or multiprocessor system satisfying the timing constraints and resource and fault tolerance requirements of the tasks and running a resource reclaiming algorithm in an attempt, by exploiting the run-time execution of tasks, to reclaim part of the resources assigned originally based on worst-case estimates. Dynamic scheduling for multiprocessor systems is discussed in

chapter 2, resource reclaiming is discussed in chapter 3, and fault-tolerant scheduling is discussed in chapter 4. Algorithms for scheduling tasks in a uniprocessor system can be found in chapter 2 and in [3, 6].

2. *Global scheduling.* The aim of global scheduling is to migrate tasks from a heavily loaded node (sender) to a lightly loaded node (receiver) if it is not possible to schedule them locally. This is achieved through the following four interrelated modules (also known as policies):

• *Information policy.* This dictates how information should be exchanged among different nodes, that is, what information is to be collected and when it is to be collected.

• *Transfer policy.* This decides when tasks are to be migrated from the current node, which is heavily loaded.

• *Selection policy.* This decides which tasks are to be transferred from the current node, which is heavily loaded.

• *Location policy.* This governs the choice of a suitable node (receiver), which is lightly loaded, for a task transfer.

3. *Message scheduling.* The message scheduler at a node is responsible for scheduling:

• Statically guaranteed periodic messages. These are the messages generated by periodic tasks.

• Dynamically arriving aperiodic messages. These are the messages generated by aperiodic tasks.

• Messages that constitute a task during task transfer from a heavily loaded node to a lightly loaded node. The messages constituting a task are periodic, but task transfer is aperiodic. Therefore, a real-time channel has to be established for a transfer and torn down after the task transfer.

All these types of messages require a bound on delay. As mentioned earlier, the nodes of the distributed system can be connected through either a multihop or a multiple access network. The fundamental difference between these two is that a node in the former has a choice to route (schedule) messages on different links, whereas in the latter all nodes contend for a single link. In a distributed real-time system, periodic message communication is constant-bit-rate (CBR) traffic and requires deterministic guarantees. CBR traffic is characterized by a peak-rate model. In a peak-rate model, the parameters are (1) minimum interarrival time, (2) maximum packet length, and (3) end-to-end deadline. On the other hand, aperiodic message communication is variable-bit-rate (VBR) traffic. Peak-rate models overstate the bandwidth needs for all VBR traffic. Therefore, statistical guarantees are more suitable for aperiodic message communications. Message scheduling in multihop networks and multiple access networks is discussed in chapters 7 and 10, respectively.

5.2.3 Information Flow in the Architecture

In figure 5.1, the arrows show the paths of interaction between different modules within or across layers. These interactions are described below:

Local Scheduling

1. The task-scheduling module schedules tasks onto processors, the processors execute the tasks, run the resource reclaiming algorithm, and inform the task scheduler of the amount of time reclaimed so that this time can be incorporated in scheduling subsequent tasks.

Global Scheduling

2. The transfer policy decides whether tasks are to be migrated, and the selection policy selects the tasks to be transferred and then passes the tasks to the location policy for migration.

3. The information policy exchanges state information with the information policy of other nodes.

4. The location policy receives state information from the information policy and decides the best receiver node for the task migration.

5. The location policy then contacts the routing component of the message scheduling to establish a real-time channel for migrating the task.

Message Scheduling

6. The routing component selects the best link for migrating the task (neighboring node), based on the routing algorithm used, then consults the call admission control module to determine whether the channel request can be admitted on the selected link.

7. If the call admission is not successful, the routing algorithm may select the next-best link or reject the call.

8. If the call admission is successful, the resources requested by the call, such as bandwidth and buffers, are reserved, and the call request is passed on to the neighboring node.

9. The routing components of the intermediate nodes[2] perform the same function until the receiver node is reached.

10. Once a channel is established, the scheduling component of the message scheduling module takes the task from the location policy and migrates it through the established channel.

---

2. In a multiple access network, there is no intermediate node.

11. At the receiver node, the scheduling component of the message scheduling module receives the task and gives it to the task scheduler of the node for scheduling.

12. The channel is torn down after the task migration is over.

5.3   Global Scheduling

5.3.1   Load Index

The key issue in global scheduling is identifying a suitable load index. A *load index* is a quantitative measure of a node's load. The load indices proposed for load balancing in non-real-time systems, such as task queue length and processor utilization over a period of time, are inadequate for real-time systems since they fail to take into account the deadlines of individual tasks. In a real-time system, a good load index must take into account the deadlines/laxity of tasks together with the other parameters such as length of the task queue and processor utilization.

5.3.2   Transfer Policy

The transfer policy at a node determines whether the node is in a suitable state to participate in a task transfer either as a sender or as a receiver. The transfer policy is composed, broadly speaking, of two categories of policies: (1) threshold-based policies and (2) relative-load policies.

5.3.2.1   Threshold-Based Policies   Thresholds are parameters in terms of which a node's current load can be expressed in three different states, namely, light, medium, and heavy. If the node's load is (1) above the upper threshold, it is said to be in heavy state, (2) below the lower threshold, it is in light state, and (3) between the two thresholds, it is in medium state. In threshold-based transfer policies, the load state of nodes determines their role in task transfer. When a task arrives at a node and the node is in heavy state, it becomes a *sender,* and passes the task off to a less congested node, if it can find one. When it is in light state, the node is a potential *receiver* and can accept tasks from other nodes. When the node is in medium state, it is neither a sender nor a receiver of tasks. Depending on the algorithm under which a particular system operates, the upper and lower thresholds may or may not have the same value. The simplest threshold-based policy is the *random-threshold algorithm,* in which a node that finds its load exceeding the threshold simply sends excess tasks to another node selected at random.

5.3.2.2   Relative-Load Policies   Relative-load policies consider the load of a node in relation to loads at other nodes in the system in making transfer decisions. For example, a relative policy might consider a node to be a suitable receiver for a task if its load is less by some fixed value δ than the average system load. Alternatively, if the load at the node is more than the average system load by δ, then it may be a sender.

5.3.3 Selection Policy

Once a transfer policy decides that a particular node is a sender, a selection policy selects a task or a set of tasks for task transfer, choosing to send either (1) the task that has the least laxity or (2) the task that has the most laxity. The rationale behind the least-laxity approach is to make the sender node light (in terms of laxity) as early as possible, whereas the most-laxity approach aims at making the node light in the long term. The selection policy must consider several factors in selecting a task for transfer:

• The *end-to-end delay* incurred in transferring a task from a sender to a receiver. This is very crucial, because a real-time task has deadline associated with it. In other words, a task transfer is useful only if the task reaches its destination before its deadline.

• Task *affinity* to nodes. Some tasks may have *affinity* to some nodes because only those nodes have the resources required by these tasks.

• The *value* of the task. In real-time systems, tasks may have value (which defines the utility) associated with them. Meeting the deadline of a task with a higher value increases overall system value more than meeting the deadline of a task with a lower value.

5.3.4 Location Policy

The location policy at a node determines the receiver node to which a task should be transferred. Most existing location policies find a suitable receiver node through *polling:* A node polls another node to find out whether it is willing to accept a new task, according to the transfer policy of the potential recipient node, as discussed in section 5.3.2. Nodes can be polled either serially or in parallel and can be selected for polling in a number of ways: random choice, using knowledge acquired during earlier polls, based on neighborhoodness of the potential recipients, or in broadcast mode. The broadcast is the extreme case, in which the polling message is sent to every other node in the system.

The major drawbacks of the polling approach are (1) the delay involved in probing the nodes and (2) the fact that a suitable receiver may not be identified within the polling limit if the system has only a few lightly loaded nodes, causing tasks to miss their deadlines. Location policies are broadly classified as *sender-initiated* (in which potential senders search for suitable receivers), *receiver-initiated* (in which potential receivers search for suitable senders), and *symmetrically initiated* (in which both senders and receivers search for complementary nodes).

5.3.5   Information Policy

The information policy of a node decides when that node collects information about the states of other nodes in the system, what information is collected, and where it is collected from. There are three types of information policies: (1) demand-driven, (2) periodic, and (3) state-change-driven.

5.3.5.1   Demand-Driven Policies   A demand-driven policy is a decentralized policy in which a node collects the state information of other nodes only when it becomes either light (receiver) or heavy (sender), making it a potential participant in task transfer. A demand-driven policy is inherently dynamic, as its action depends on the change of the node's state. Such a policy may be sender-initiated, receiver-initiated, or symmetrically initiated.

5.3.5.2   Periodic Policies   Periodic policies may be either centralized or decentralized, but in either case they simply collect information about the state of other nodes periodically (i.e., at fixed time intervals). Periodic information policies do not adapt their activity to the system state very well. The choice of the period is crucial in determining the system performance. A shorter period (meaning higher frequency of information collection) results in more recent state information but higher overhead, whereas higher period (lower frequency of information collection) results in potentially obsolete information but lower overhead. It is crucial to ensure that the overhead incurred in exchanging periodic information does not offset the gain obtained by using the periodic policies. Since they make state information available in a timely and predictable manner, periodic policies are more suitable for real-time systems than the other two approaches.

5.3.5.3   State-Driven Policies   In state-driven policies, which may be either centralized or decentralized, nodes disseminate information about their states to the other nodes in the system whenever their states change. This policy differs from the demand-driven policy in that it involves a node's disseminating information about its state to other nodes, rather than collecting information about other nodes from them.

5.4   Work on Global Scheduling

Many algorithms have been proposed for load balancing in distributed non-real-time systems and global scheduling in distributed real-time systems. Most of these algorithms incorporate the functionalities of more than one of the policies discussed above. In this section, we discuss three different algorithms, namely, focused addressing with bidding (FAB) [16], the buddy set–based algorithm [13], and integrated scheduling of tasks and messages [10], that have been proposed for global scheduling.

5.4.1 Focused Addressing with Bidding

5.4.1.1 Information Policy In the FAB algorithm [16], each node maintains a status table that indicates which tasks it has already committed to run. These include the set of periodic tasks (which are preassigned statically) and any additional aperiodic tasks that it may have accepted. In addition, it maintains a table of the surplus computational capacity at every node in the system. The time axis is divided into fixed-size intervals (called *windows*), and each node periodically sends to its colleagues a message telling the fraction of the next window that is free (i.e., not already allotted to any task). Since the state exchange is not instantaneous, because of the delay involved in sending the message, this information may never be completely up to date.

5.4.1.2 Transfer and Selection Policies When an aperiodic task arrives at a node, the task scheduler of that node checks whether the newly arrived task can be guaranteed without violating the guarantees that have already been given. If the task is not schedulable at the local node, then it is eligible to be transferred to another (light) node, provided the task has enough laxity to permit this. That is, the schedulability check performs the function of transfer policy, and the selection policy is implicit, since every task that fails the schedulability check is considered for migration.

5.4.1.3 Location Policy If the transfer policy of a node decides to transfer a task and the task to be transferred is also selected, then the next step is the identification of a suitable receiver, which occurs as follows:

• The overloaded node checks its surplus information and selects the node (called the *focused node*) n_s that it believes to be the most likely to be able to execute that task successfully by its deadline.

• The node then transfers the task to the identified receiver.

• Since the information it has transmitted about its surplus capacity may not be up to date, the receiver node to whom the task is transferred may not have enough computational capacity to execute the migrated task. To overcome this problem, in parallel with the task transfer, the sender also sends a request for bid (RFB) message to other lightly loaded nodes. The RFB contains the characteristics of the task (T_i), such as its computation time (c_i), deadline (d_i), and resource requirements, and asks any node that can meet the requirements of the task to send a bid to the focused node n_s stating how quickly it can process the task.

The node that is sending the RFBs (that is, the originating node) computes the sum (t_{bid}) of (1) the estimated time it will take the RFB to reach its destination, (2) the estimated time it will take each of the intended destination nodes to respond with a bid, and

(3) the estimated time it will take to transmit the bid to the focused node. It also computes the latest time ($t_{transfer}$) at which the focused node can transfer the task to a bidder without the task missing its deadline, which is given by

$$t_{transfer} = d_i - (\text{current time} + \text{time to migrate the task} + c_i).$$

• If $t_{bid} \leq t_{transfer}$ for a particular destination node, then an RFB is sent to that node.

• When a node n_t receives an RFB, it performs a schedulability check to see whether it can guarantee the new (transferred) task without jeopardizing the guarantees that have been provided for the previously scheduled tasks. It accomplishes this as follows:

(a) It estimates the arrival time ($t_{arrival}$) of the transferred task and how long it will take to be either guaranteed or rejected:

$$t_{arrival} = \text{current time} + \text{time for bid to be received by } n_s$$
$$+ \text{time taken by } n_s \text{ to make decision}$$
$$+ \text{time taken to transfer the task}$$
$$+ \text{time taken by } n_t \text{ to either guarantee or reject the task.}$$

(b) It calculates the surplus computation time ($t_{surplus}$) that it currently has between $t_{arrival}$ and the deadline of the task d_i by estimating the computational time already committed in the interval $[t_{arrival}, d_i]$:

$$t_{comp} = \text{time allotted to periodic tasks in } [t_{arrival}, d_i]$$
$$+ \text{time needed in } [t_{arrival}, d_i] \text{ to execute already accepted aperiodic tasks}$$
$$+ \text{fraction of recently accepted bids}$$
$$* \text{time needed in } [t_{arrival}, d_i] \text{ to honor pending bids.}$$
$$t_{surplus} = d_i - \text{current time} - t_{comp}.$$

• If $t_{surplus} < c_i$, then no bid is sent out; otherwise n_t sends out a bid to n_s. The bid contains $t_{arrival}$, $t_{surplus}$, and an estimate of how long a task transferred to n_t will have to wait before it is either guaranteed or rejected.

• If n_s is unable to guarantee the transferred task locally, it can review the bids it gets to see which other node is most likely to be able to do so, and transfer the task to that node. It evaluates the bids as follows:

(a) For each bidding node n_k, n_s computes the estimated arrival time $\eta(k)$ of the task at that node. Let $t_{surplus}(k)$ and $t_{arrival}(k)$ be the values of $t_{surplus}$ and $t_{arrival}$ contained in the bid received from node n_k.

(b) Then, n_s computes the following quantity for each bid:

$$t_{est}(k) = t_{surplus}(k) \frac{d_i - \eta(k)}{d_i - t_{arrival}(k)}.$$

(c) Let $t_{est}(j)$ be the maximum such value. If n_s cannot itself guarantee the task, it transfers the task to node n_j.

An important point to be noted is that the kind of time estimates used for bid calculation, average computation time or worst-case computation time, affects whether the resulting bids are aggressive or conservative. If the worst-case computation times are used, the bids will be very conservative, whereas they will be less conservative if average computation times are used.

5.4.2 Buddy Strategy

Another interesting algorithm for global scheduling is based on buddy sets. This algorithm differs from the FAB algorithm in the manner in which the receiver nodes are determined.

5.4.2.1 Transfer Policy In the buddy set–based algorithm, each node has three states of loading: under, full, and over, governed by threshold parameters T_U, T_F, and T_V, respectively. The node's load at any given time is determined by the number of tasks awaiting service in its task queue. If the queue length is Q, the node is said to be in

state U (underloaded), if $Q \le T_U$.
state F (fully loaded), if $T_F < Q \le T_V$.
state V (overloaded), if $Q > T_V$.

States U, F, and V correspond to the states light, medium, and heavy, respectively.

5.4.2.2 Information, Selection, and Location Policies The information policy in the buddy set–based algorithm is state-driven. When a node makes a transition out of or into state U, it announces its state to a subset of nodes that is called its *buddy set*. (How the membership of the buddy set is determined is addressed below.) The selection policy is implicit, as each newly arriving task is considered for migration if it cannot be guaranteed locally. The location policy of each node is always aware, because of the way the information policy works, of whether any member of its buddy set is in state U. If the node is overloaded, it finds an underloaded member, if any, exists in its buddy set to which to transfer the task.

5.4.2.3 Important Issues There are three important issues to be addressed in the buddy strategy: (1) how the buddy set is chosen, (2) the choice of threshold parameters, and

(3) preventing too many task transfers to the same destination due to the nature of the buddy set. Each of these issues is discussed here in turn.

- *Choosing a buddy set.* In a multihop network, the cardinality of the buddy set is very crucial. If the buddy set is too large, the state exchange messages will heavily load the network. If the set is too small, the communication cost will be low, but the over-loaded nodes will have a smaller chance of success in finding an underloaded node in their buddy sets. One way to reduce the communication cost is to make the neighbors (in terms of hops) of any node the members of its buddy set. In that case, the size of the buddy set will depend on the network topology. On the other hand, in a multiple access network, the buddy set comprises all other nodes, and thus its size has no im-pact on system performance, since the nodes are connected through a bus that is the broadcast medium, and hence every node receives state exchange information in a sin-gle hop.

- *Choice of threshold parameters.* The proper values for the threshold parameters T_U, T_F, and T_V are crucial in determining system performance. In general, the greater the value of T_V, the lower the rate at which tasks are transferred from one node to another. The choice of values for the threshold parameters depends on the size of the buddy set, current load, topology of the network, and bandwidth of the network.

- *Excessive task transfers to a node.* Suppose a node is in the buddy set of many over-loaded nodes and sends state change information to each of its buddy nodes saying it is now underloaded. This can result in each of the overloaded nodes transferring tasks simul-taneously to that node, making it heavy. This can eventually result in *thrashing,* that is, a situation in which a task undergoes too many transfers. To reduce the probability of this happening, an ordered list of preferred nodes is created at each node, with closer nodes given higher preference than those more distant. An overloaded node uses this list to look for underloaded nodes and transfers the task(s) to the first underloaded node in the list. If the lists of different nodes are ordered differently (as they should be, given the different relative proximities of each node to other nodes), the probability of a node's being simul-taneously dumped with tasks from a number of other nodes, resulting in a heavy load, is reduced.

5.5   An Integrated Approach to Distributed Real-Time Scheduling

In this section, we discuss a scheme [10] (we call it an *integrated scheme*) that inte-grates all three scheduling components (local, global, and message) in an attempt to provide a complete solution to distributed real-time scheduling. Earlier solutions for the problem considered one component at a time, ignoring the demands of the other two components. The integrated scheme has all the three components and also takes into account the *interactions* among them, which are shown to be very important in improving the guarantee ratio. The integrated scheme has the following components and interactions.

1. *Local scheduling.* The Spring (myopic) scheduling algorithm (discussed in chapter 2) with RV-based reclaiming algorithms (discussed in chapter 3) is used for local scheduling.

2. *Global scheduling*

• *Information policy.* A Maekawa set [9]–based state exchange protocol is used, which exchanges both processor and link load information. The information policy is periodic.

• *Transfer policy.* An adaptive load determination algorithm is used. The transfer policy is relative.

• *Location policy.* A new heuristic algorithm is used that takes into account the states of both *nodes* and *links* of the network and the existing connection status from (or through) the current node. The location policy is sender-initiated (knowledge-based).

3. *Message scheduling.* When the nodes of the distributed system are connected by a multihop network, hierarchical round robin (HRR) (discussed in chapter 7) is used for message scheduling. When a multiple access network is employed, the preorder deterministic collision resolution protocol (discussed in chapter 10) is used.

4. *Interactions.* The set of interactions between the message scheduler and transfer policy, and between the message scheduler and location policy, is considered to improve the schedulability of the system.

   The schematic of a node (consisting of various modules) in a distributed real-time system with integrated scheduling is shown in figure 5.2. In the rest of the section, we discuss the functionality of each of these modules and their interactions. (Note that in a multiple access network, link state information is of no utility.)

5.5.1   Global Scheduling

In this section, we first define the state of a node and then describe information, transfer, and location policies used in the integrated scheme.

5.5.1.1   State of a Node   Most of the existing works consider the state of a node only in terms of the load on the processors for task transfer. When a node is heavily loaded, it finds a suitable receiver based on its location policy and then transfers a task to it. The choice of receiver node is made without considering the state of the links between the two

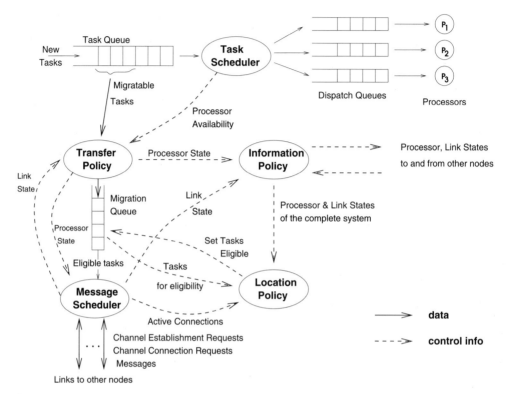

Figure 5.2
Schematic of a node in the distributed real-time system

nodes. If none of the routes to the receiver node is able to provide the required real-time channel for the task migration, however, then the identified receiver node may not be the best choice or even a plausible choice at all; that is, there is no guarantee that the task will be migrated to the receiver in time to execute before its deadline. Also, even if there is a routing path that will enable the task to migrate between the two nodes, it might be costlier than the routing path to another possible receiver that has not been considered (or was considered and rejected in favor of the node chosen). This may result in poor performance.

The above problem motivates us to define the state of a node as a combination of the load on its processors as well as that on its links. The processors of a node, based on their load, denoted as *NodePLoad*, (*processor state*), can be in light state, medium state, or heavy state. The processor state of a node is determined based on the average processor load of the system (*SysPLoad*) and a parameter called *processor load offset* (*Poffset*). The processor load of a node is in

light state,   if $(SysPLoad - NodePLoad) > Poffset$.

heavy state,   if $(NodePLoad - SysPLoad) > Poffset$.

medium state,   otherwise.

Similarly, the link state of a node is determined based on the average link state of the system (*SysLLoad*) and a *link load offset* (*Loffset*) parameter. The load offset parameters (*Poffset*, *Loffset*) are input parameters and depend on the load fluctuation in the system. When the fluctuation is great, the values of these parameters have to be large compared to their values when the fluctuation is less. A node is *qualified* to be a receiver for task transfer from a sender only when its processor state is light and the link states along the route (including its own link state) from the sender node to the receiver node are in either light or medium state. A node is defined as being in heavy state if its processor state is heavy, irrespective of its link state.

5.5.1.2 Information Policy   Here, we present an algorithm for information policy in a distributed real-time system with integrated task scheduling based on the Maekawa set used in the distributed mutual exclusion algorithm [9]. In this algorithm, the sender does not probe nodes for their readiness to receive a task at the time it has a task it needs to transfer. Instead, it collects information about potential receivers in advance. This is essential in real-time systems, since probing nodes is a time-consuming process, and hence a task has a high chance of missing its deadline because of the time required for probing. Maekawa sets are chosen in such a way as to give equal responsibility to every node in state information exchange, using a minimal number of messages, with decentralized control.

Data Structures: Each node maintains the following three sets to ensure an efficient information policy:

- Request set. Set of nodes to which it sends requests for state information.
- Inform set. Set of nodes to which it sends information about its state.
- Status set. Set of nodes whose state information it maintains.

The following is an example of Maekawa sets for a distributed system with seven nodes. R_i, I_i, and S_i denote the request set, inform set, and status set of node i, respectively. As figure 5.3 shows, each node maintains information on the status of only three nodes, and each node's status information is maintained by exactly three nodes.

$R_1 = I_1 = \{1, 2, 4\}$	$S_1 = \{1, 5, 7\}$
$R_2 = I_2 = \{2, 3, 5\}$	$S_2 = \{1, 2, 6\}$
$R_3 = I_3 = \{3, 4, 6\}$	$S_3 = \{2, 3, 7\}$
$R_4 = I_4 = \{4, 5, 7\}$	$S_4 = \{1, 3, 4\}$
$R_5 = I_5 = \{5, 6, 1\}$	$S_5 = \{2, 4, 5\}$
$R_6 = I_6 = \{6, 7, 2\}$	$S_6 = \{3, 5, 6\}$
$R_7 = I_7 = \{7, 1, 3\}$	$S_7 = \{4, 6, 7\}$

Figure 5.3
Maekawa sets for seven nodes

The request set is constructed using the finite projective plane method, and its size is $O(\sqrt{N})$ [9], where N is the number of nodes. The inform set is identical to the request set. The status set of a node is the set of all nodes whose request contains that node. In Maekawa sets, for any two nodes i and j, one of the following holds:

1. The inform sets of the two nodes overlap: The request set of one of the nodes overlaps with the inform set of the other node, and hence mutual state information exchange occurs in at most two steps.

2. Each node's request set contains the other node: Hence, mutual state information exchange occurs in one step.

Thus, the information policy algorithm for integrated scheduling aims to capture the complete state of the system for determining the best receiver for a task to be transferred from a heavily loaded node (i.e., the sender) in a very short duration of time (at most two steps) and simultaneously to keep the number of state exchange messages small. Thus, a node can collect system load information by requesting information from only $O(\sqrt{N})$ nodes, each of which sends information about $O(\sqrt{N})$ nodes.

In the integrated scheduling scheme under discussion here, nodes exchange state messages containing the state of both their processors and their links. This aids in identifying the actual best receiver node, overcoming the problems identified in section 5.5.1.1. If state information is to be exchanged periodically among nodes as dictated by the Maekawa set, then permanent real-time channels are needed.

5.5.1.3 Transfer Policy   To decide which tasks are to be migrated from a node and when they are to be migrated, the node's transfer policy needs to determine the state of the processors of potential recipients, which depends on (1) the current load on the processors, (2) the past load within some specified time interval, and (3) an estimate of the future load. Having ascertained the state of the intended recipient, the transfer policy can then use the

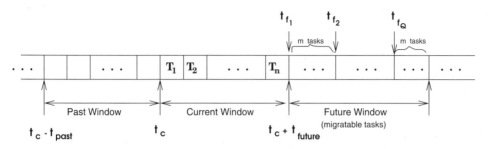

Figure 5.4
Task queue as viewed by the transfer policy in the integrated scheme

link state of the recipient node to move the tasks from the task queue to the migration queue (figure 5.2). In the *integrated scheme,* the processor state is computed using the heuristic described below.

The task queue is divided into three regions, namely, the past window, the current window, and the future window, as in figure 5.4. Let t_c be the time at which the current window begins, that is, the present time. T_p is the set of tasks in the past window that the scheduler has feasibly scheduled between times $(t_c - t_{past})$ and t_c. T_c is the set of tasks whose deadline is between t_c and $(t_c + t_{future})$. T_f is the set of *FUT_WIN_SIZ* tasks with deadline greater than $(t_c + t_{future})$. t_{past}, t_{future}, and *FUT_WIN_SIZ* are input parameters. Let $T_{f1}, T_{f2}, \ldots, T_{fQ}$ be equal partitions of the set T_f whose cardinalities (denoted as $|T_f|$) are m, where m is the number of processors in the current node, except possibly that of T_{fQ}, whose cardinality may be less than m and $Q = \lceil |T_f|/m \rceil$. t_{f1} is the estimated start time of the tasks in the first partition T_{f1} and is computed as

$$t_{f1} = t_c + \frac{C_{av} * |T_c|}{m}, \tag{5.1}$$

where C_{av} is the average worst-case computation time of the tasks in T_{f1}. Then the estimated start time of the tasks in the kth partition is computed as

$$t_{fk} = t_{f(k-1)} + C_{av}, \quad 2 \le k \le Q. \tag{5.2}$$

The overall laxity of tasks in a node depends on the laxity of tasks in the past and future windows, and this quantity is the processor load index, denoted as *NodePLoad*, of the node:

$$NodePLoad = \frac{\sum_{\tau_i \in T_p}(d_i - f_i)}{|T_p|} + W\_LDF * \left(\sum_{k=1}^{Q} \frac{\sum_{\tau_i \in T_{fk}}(d_i - t_{fk} - c_i)}{|T_{fk}|} \right) /Q, \tag{5.3}$$

where d_i, f_i, and c_i are the deadline, finish time, and worst-case computation time of task τ_i, respectively, and W_LDF is an input parameter that represents the weight associated with the future load estimation.

Based on information about the processor state and the link state of the intended recipient, the transfer policy decides to move tasks from the task queue to the migration queue. It calculates the number, M, of tasks to be moved as follows and selects the tasks of least laxity first.

$$M = \min \left\{ \frac{FUT\_WIN\_SIZ * (NodePLoad - SysPLoad)}{NodePLoad}, FUT\_WIN\_SIZ \right\}. \qquad (5.4)$$

5.5.1.4 Location Policy The function of a node's location policy is to identify suitable receivers for the tasks in the node's migration queue. In the integrated scheme, it does this based on (1) the node and link states of the entire distributed system (obtained from the information policy) and (2) the availability of currently active real-time channels for task migration from the current node (obtained from the message scheduler) to other nodes. The location policy does the following:

1. It picks up one or more tasks from the migration queue and identifies light receivers for them, with an associated routing path. During this process it might decide to send a group of tasks to the same destination, if the state of the receiver permits it. Sending a group of tasks to the same destination eliminates the channel establishment overhead for subsequent tasks by using the same channel.

2. It places tasks into the migration queue after filling information related to task transfer, such as destination node, routing path to the destination node, and task grouping identification, in the data structures associated with task migration. Tasks with all this information filled in are said to be *eligible tasks* for migration.

5.5.2 Message Scheduling

The tasks in the migration queue that have been marked eligible by the location policy are considered for transfer by the message scheduler. The HRR scheduling algorithm [4] is used for message scheduling in the integrated scheme presented here. Before it can be used to transfer a task from a sender to a receiver, a real-time channel has to be established that meets the specifications of a required quality of service (QoS) requested by the source node in terms of delay bound. The message traffic is characterized as periodic, with a rate determined by the laxity of the task to be transferred: lower task laxity requires a higher rate. Before a task can start migrating, a real-time channel for the transfer must be established so that the resources required for the transfer are reserved along the channel throughout the call duration (i.e., task migration). Otherwise, another node that has also sensed the same link as light might try to migrate a task over that link, which will make either or both the migrations miss their deadline for reaching their respective destinations. Source routing (which is computed by the location policy) is used during channel establishment, when the call admission test has to be carried out. Once the channel has been established, data transfer (task migration) begins, at the rate specified at the time of channel establishment. After the task is migrated, the channel is torn down.

5.5.2.1   Real-Time Channel Requirements   The integrated scheme presented here requires the following real-time channels for sending application data and signaling information:

• Permanent real-time channels for state exchange messages, which are used as part of the information policy. These are multicast channels (chapter 9) among the nodes, as determined by the Maekawa set.

• Permanent real-time channels for sending requests for channel establishment.

• Permanent real-time channels with variable bandwidth (over time) for exchanging aperiodic messages generated on completion of aperiodic tasks. These channels must exist among all pairs of nodes and meet some approximate performance requirements.

• Nonpermanent channels for migrating tasks from a heavily loaded node to a lightly loaded node. Each of these channels is torn down after the task for which it is created is migrated.

5.5.3   Interactions among Modules of a Node

In this section, we establish the motivation for establishing interaction among various modules of a node and discuss the kinds of interactions that will improve the system's guarantee ratio. The interactions considered here arise as a result of the message scheduling that controls link resources.

5.5.3.1   Interaction between the Message Scheduler and Transfer Policy   The motivation for interaction between the message scheduler and transfer policy is given below, and figure 5.5 shows its effect.

1. If the message scheduler and transfer policy do not interact, the transfer policy might move unadmitted tasks from the task queue (TQ) to the migration queue (MQ) without knowing the state of the link between the sender and recipient nodes. If the links between the nodes happen to be heavily loaded, the message scheduler may not be able to transfer the tasks or may not be able to do so in time for them to meet their deadlines. Had they

action by	processor state	link state	action taken
	heavy	light	move tasks from TQ to MQ
Transfer	heavy	heavy	don't move tasks
Policy	light	–	don't move tasks
	medium	–	don't move tasks
	heavy	–	reject incoming channel requests
	medium	light	accept/reject is decided by CAC
Message	medium	medium	reject incoming channel requests
Scheduler	medium	heavy	reject incoming channel requests
	light	–	accept/reject is decided by CAC

Figure 5.5
Effect of interaction between message scheduler and transfer policy

instead remained in the sender node's task queue, they might have been scheduled successfully in the original node using the resources (processor and resource times) reclaimed by
the resource reclaiming algorithm.

2. Similarly, due to the same lack of interaction, the call admission control (CAC) of a
node's message scheduler might accept incoming channel requests even if the processor of
the node to which it belongs is in heavy state. This would saturate the link with a level of
usage such that task migration from the node is not possible, which will also result in the
missing of task deadlines.

5.5.3.2 Interaction between the Message Scheduler and Location Policy The location policy uses information obtained from the message scheduler about the active connections from the current node to decide whether some of the tasks in the migration queue can
be transferred using already established migration channels. This reduces channel establishment time, which is crucial in the context of real-time systems. The message scheduler
then establishes channels to the appointed destinations for any remaining eligible tasks in
the migration queue—those that cannot be migrated on existing channels—using the routing path specified by the location policy.

The chances of more than one heavily loaded node transferring tasks to the same lightly
loaded node, even if there are many lightly loaded nodes in the system, are very small
because the sender node establishes the channel to a receiver node before transferring a
task to it. If the receiver node has changed state since it last sent out status information
because a sender node has successfully established a channel with it, it can always reject the
channel requests from other senders. The rejected senders then try their next-best receivers

for their task transfer, and so on, provided the tasks meet their deadline by transferring to other nodes.

5.5.4 Simulation Studies

Manimaran et al. [10] have conducted simulation studies that compare the integrated scheme with focused addressing and the random scheme. The studies also quantify the benefits obtained by making use of link state information and interactions among components. The simulations have been carried out for a distributed system of nine nodes connected as a 3×3 mesh topology. Each node comprises eight processors used for executing tasks. The tasks for the simulations have been generated in the following way:

• It is important to generate a proper load at each node to study the effect of task migration in distributed real-time task scheduling. If all the nodes have the same task load, there will be no migration, since global scheduling migrates tasks based on the node's load relative to others. Therefore, it is important to use a proper load distribution function to achieve different loads at different nodes. In our studies, the interarrival time of the tasks is based on a distribution whose mean is obtained by the formula $A * b^i$ for the ith node, where $A > 0, b > 1, i = 0, 1, 2, 3, \ldots$, as given in [11]. In the formula, the lower the value of b or A, the smaller the interarrival time of tasks and hence the higher the task load in the system.

• The worst-case computation time (WCC) of a task is uniformly chosen in the interval [40, 60].

• The deadline of a task is uniformly distributed in the interval $[WCC, (1 + \alpha) * WCC]$, where $\alpha > 0$ is an input parameter, denoted as the laxity parameter.

The values of A, b, the feasibility check window size (used in the Spring scheduling), and α have been taken as 3, 1.3, 18, and 4, respectively (if not specified otherwise). The average single hop time has been taken as 15 time units, and each link was assumed to have a total bandwidth of 30 units. The minimum and maximum bandwidth (rate) required per connection is 6 and 10 units, respectively. The information exchange period of the information policy is taken as 100. The load estimation and transfer policy are the same for all algorithms studied here, as described in section 5.5.1.3. The curves in figures 5.7–5.13 depict results for the following global scheduling schemes:

1. *No migration.* Each node schedules its tasks locally and there is no migration at all.

2. *Random.* The receiver (location policy) for migration of a task is randomly selected. Here, no information policy exists.

3. *Random + Interxn*. The receiver is selected as in the random policy, but with inter-actions between the message scheduler and the global scheduling policies.

4. *Focused*. The location policy considers only the state of the processor(s) of the nodes in selecting a potential receiver for migration of tasks [16]. Each node knows the status of the entire system (information policy) obtained through the periodic state exchange policy based on Maekawa sets or some other means.

5. *Focused + Interxn*. The receiver is selected as in (4), but with interactions between the message scheduler and the global scheduling policies.

6. *Integrated*. In this full-fledged scheme, a Maekawa set–based information policy, interactions between the message scheduler and global scheduling policies, and informa-tion about both processor and link states are all used to identify the receiver.

For all the above algorithms, before migrating a task, we establish a real-time channel, as discussed in section 5.5.2. When evaluating the effectiveness of different algorithms in a real-time system, it is necessary to equate the scheduling costs of the algorithms. In the experiments, we accomplished this by adding the worst-case computation time of the algorithm under evaluation to the worst-case computation time of every task. This means that *WCC* for a given task is higher for complex algorithms than for simple algorithms.

Local scheduling has the same cost for all the algorithms studied here, hence its cost is taken as zero, whereas the costs of information policy, location policy, and message scheduling are different for different algorithms. For example, the information policy incurs no cost in random policy, since no information is exchanged. The algorithms that include interactions have higher costs than their no-interaction counterparts (since transfer and location policies and message scheduling all have higher costs). The costs of the different algorithms are computed based on their worst-case execution times. The cost of no migration is taken as 0. The cost of location policy for a random policy, focused addressing, and the integrated scheme are taken as 4, 4, and 5, respectively. Additional costs of 4 units are added for schemes that consider interactions. Note that the integrated scheme $(5 + 4 = 9)$ costs more than other algorithms because it uses link state information and has interactions also. Figure 5.6 specifies the different parameters considered in the simulation.

5.5.4.1 Effect of Task Load Figure 5.7 studies the effect of varying the task load on each of the algorithms, which we accomplish here by varying the parameter b. A lower value of b means a lower interarrival time and a higher task load. As the figure shows, initially, at higher loads, a decrease in load increases the guarantee ratio for all the algorithms. After a point $(b = 1.25)$, depending on the algorithm, the guarantee ratio

parameter	explanation
TaskLaxity	laxity parameter which decides the deadline of tasks
TaskLoad	amount of system wide computation demand per processor per unit time
Proc.perNode	number of processors per node
Bandwidth	bandwidth of each of the links
TaskSize	average size of the task (15 units)
Topology	variation in topology

Figure 5.6
Simulation parameters

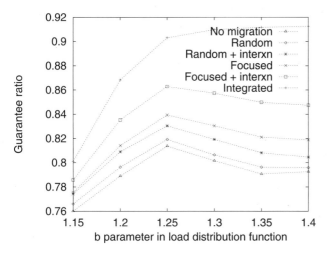

Figure 5.7
Effect of task load on guarantee ratio

either saturates or starts decreasing, because the load is well balanced among nodes; that is, all the nodes are equally light, and hence the nodes have no need to migrate tasks most of the time. If the load imbalance among nodes can be increased by employing a different load distribution function, other than Ab^i, one would expect that decrease in load continues to increase the guarantee ratio.

5.5.4.2   Effect of Task Laxity   As expected, the guarantee ratio of a system increases with increases in the laxities of tasks, as shown in figure 5.8. Algorithms that consider

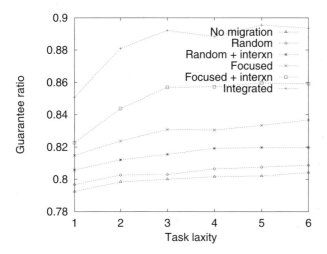

Figure 5.8
Effect of task laxity on guarantee ratio

interactions are able to show considerable improvement in guarantee ratio over their no-interaction counterparts. The use of link state information further improves the guarantee ratio.

5.5.4.3   Effect of Number of Processors   Examining the effect of the number of processors enables us to study the scalability of each framework. The guarantee ratio of the system increases with the increase in the number of processors available to execute the tasks at each node, as figure 5.9 shows. When the task load at each node is held constant, an increase in the number of processors makes the node lighter and hence increases the guarantee ratio. For very low and very high numbers of processors, different algorithms offer less difference in the guarantee ratio, since the system is heavy in the former case and light in the latter. Therefore, the guarantee ratio is poor for all the algorithms for a small number of processors and is better for all the algorithms for a large number (for 12 processors, for example, every algorithm guarantees about 95% of the tasks). Only for intermediate values of processors (6, 8, and 10) is the difference in guarantee ratio among algorithms noticeable.

5.5.4.4   Effect of Link Bandwidth   In figure 5.10, the effect of varying the link bandwidth is studied. As link bandwidth increases, the guarantee ratio also increases for all the algorithms, except for that with no migration, because increasing bandwidth increases the chances of establishing real-time channels for migrating tasks. (The guarantee ratio

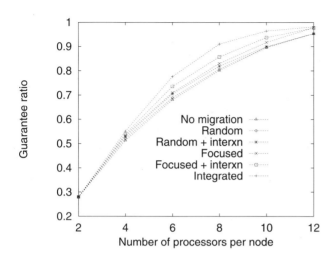

Figure 5.9
Effect of number of processors on guarantee ratio

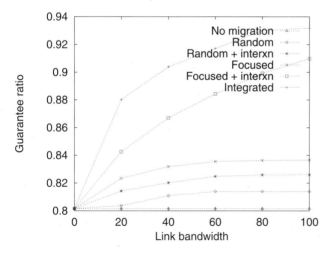

Figure 5.10
Effect of link bandwidth on guarantee ratio

of the algorithm with no migration is constant for all values of link bandwidth, since the algorithm does not use links, as there is no migration.) It can be seen from figure 5.10 that when link bandwidth is 0, every algorithm behaves like the no-migration algorithm. It is also apparent that an increase in link bandwidth increases the guarantee ratio significantly more in the integrated scheme than in the other algorithms. This is because the integrated scheme makes use of link state information effectively in deciding on the receiver. At a sufficiently high link bandwidth, bandwidth is no longer a potential bottleneck for task migration, and since we use the same load estimation and transfer policy for all the migrating algorithms, we can expect the same value of guarantee ratio (this behavior is not shown in figure 5.10). In fact, if bandwidth is increased beyond a point (much beyond 100), the guarantee ratio becomes the same for every migrating algorithm.

5.5.4.5   Effect of Network Topology   The effect of network topology on the guarantee ratio is studied to enable us to evaluate the performance of focused addressing and integrated scheme under widely varying network topologies. The topologies considered are 3×3 mesh (an example of dense topology) and 9-node ring (an example of sparse topology), and the link bandwidth and task load are varied. From figure 5.11, it can be seen that these algorithms offer a better guarantee ratio on mesh than on ring. This is because of rich connectivity in the mesh, which leads to the existence of many paths between any pair of nodes and hence greater flexibility when establishing real-time channels for task migration; that is, if there is not enough bandwidth on a particular path for a real-time channel, a large number of alternate paths can be tried.

5.5.4.6   Effect of Scheduling Costs   The scheduling cost of the various algorithms has been varied here over a range of values (k) since the costs of the algorithms are implementation dependent. This experiment enables us to study the trade-off between the scheduling cost of an algorithm and the gain (in terms of guarantee ratio) that it offers. For example, when the scheduling cost of an algorithm is very high, the gain it offers may be nullified by its cost. For this experiment, the cost of algorithms with interactions is taken as $2(k + 1)$, and algorithms without interactions take a cost of k. The cost of no migration is 0. From figure 5.12, it can be seen that the integrated scheme performs better than the other algorithms over a wide range of values of algorithm costs.

5.5.4.7   Effect of Information Exchange Period   In this experiment, the period of information exchange in the Maekawa set–based information policy has been varied. For this experiment, the link bandwidth and b (load parameter) are taken as 60 and 1.15, respectively. It can be noted from figure 5.13 that the performance of the no-migration and random policies is flat for all values of exchange period, since no information is exchanged

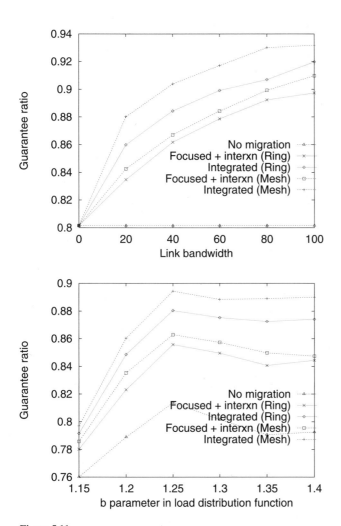

Figure 5.11
Effect of network topology on guarantee ratio

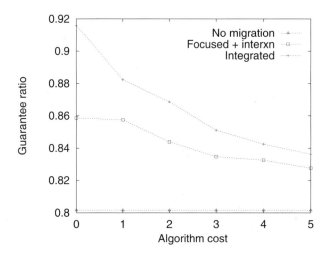

Figure 5.12
Effect of scheduling cost on guarantee ratio

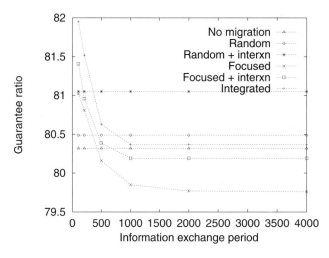

Figure 5.13
Effect of information exchange period on guarantee ratio

in either policy. It can also be seen that as the exchange period increases, the system's performance decreases because the system (load) information available becomes more and more obsolete, and hence the potential receivers identified might actually be in heavy state by the time a task transfer can be set up. This trend is applicable for all the algorithms that use an information policy. When the exchange period is too large, some algorithms that use an information policy perform even worse than the no-migration algorithm. For example, when the period is 1,000 and above, the focused addressing algorithms perform worse than random policies and no migration.

5.5.4.8   Summary and Conclusions of the Simulation Studies   From the graphs plotted in figures 5.7–5.13, we conclude that the system's guarantee ratio can be improved to a large extent by considering link state information and the interaction between the various modules of the node. In all the graphs, the performance improvements obtained can be interpreted as follows:

• The difference in the guarantee ratio due to interactions can clearly be seen by comparing the graph of each algorithm that considers interactions with that for its corresponding no-interaction algorithm.

• The difference in the guarantee ratio between focused addressing and a random policy is the result of performance improvement due to the Maekawa set–based information policy in focused addressing.

• The difference in the guarantee ratio between the integrated scheme and focused addressing with interaction is due to the use of link state information in the integrated scheme in determining the receiver nodes for tasks.

The plots in figures 5.7–5.13 show that algorithms that migrate tasks always give better guarantee ratios than schemes with no migration. Among the different migrating algorithms, the integrated scheme offers a better guarantee ratio than focused addressing and a random policy (with and without interactions). Also, it can be seen that an algorithm with interactions performs better than its noninteraction counterpart. Moreover, focused addressing performs better than a random policy because of the former's information policy.

The results of the simulation studies lead us to a number of conclusions that can be summarized as follows:

• The capacity for task migration always improves a system's guarantee ratio. This means that global scheduling is important in scheduling of tasks in distributed real-time systems.

• The use of link information in deciding on a receiver for task migration also always improves a system's guarantee ratio.

• Interactions between the message scheduler and global scheduling policies always improve the guarantee ratio as well. This was shown to be true for all the algorithms studied.

• The integrated scheme combines all the above performance enhancement features and offers a better guarantee ratio than the focused addressing and random algorithms for all the simulated conditions.

5.6 Summary

• Scheduling in distributed real-time systems involves scheduling of tasks within a node *(local scheduling)*, migration of tasks to other nodes *(global scheduling)* if it is not possible to schedule them locally, and scheduling of messages on communication links *(message scheduling)* to support intertask communication.

• Local scheduling involves scheduling and resource reclaiming. Global scheduling is governed by information, transfer, selection, and location policies. Message scheduling involves channel establishment and run time message scheduling on the established channel.

• One of the key issues in global scheduling is identifying a suitable load index, which should take into account parameters such as task laxities, processor utilization, and task queue length.

• Load information is exchanged among nodes through the information policy, which can be demand-driven, periodic, or state-driven. The transfer policy decides when to transfer tasks, and can be threshold-based or relative-load-based.

• The selection policy decides which tasks are to be migrated. This selection depends on each task's laxity, value, and affinity, if any. The location policy determines a suitable receiver node for each task selected for transfer. This can be accomplished by polling, through a random choice, or based on knowledge about the system. The policy can be sender-initiated, receiver-initiated, or symmetrically initiated.

• The focused addressing scheme with bidding is demand-driven (information policy), threshold-based (transfer policy), and sender-initiated-polling-based (location policy).

• The buddy set algorithm is state-change-driven (information policy), threshold-based (transfer policy), and sender-initiated knowledge-based (location policy).

• The integrated scheme is periodic (information policy) using Maekawa set, relative-load-based (transfer policy), and sender-initiated knowledge-based (location policy).

• Use of information about link state together with information about processor state when deciding on the receiver nodes for tasks improves the performance of distributed real-time systems. Allowing interactions among local, global, and message schedulers also improves performance.

Exercises

1. What is the difference between load balancing and load sharing?

2. Compare preemptive and non-preemptive migration strategies.

3. Compare periodic and demand-driven information policies.

4. What is the difference between demand-driven and state-change-driven information policies?

5. Compare sender-initiated and receiver-initiated algorithms.

6. Which are more stable: sender-initiated or receiver-initiated algorithms? Explain.

7. Under what conditions may task migration not be effective?

8. Compare Maekawa sets and buddy sets.

9. When is interaction between message scheduler and transfer policy less effective than it generally is?

10. Give an algorithm for constructing a Maekawa set. Using your algorithm, construct a set with ($N =$) 14 nodes. (*Hint:* The cardinality of the set can be $2\sqrt{N} - 1$.)

References

[1] T. Casavant. "A taxonomy of scheduling in general-purpose distributed computing systems." *IEEE Trans. Software Engg.,* vol. 14, no. 2, pp. 141–153, Feb. 1988.

[2] D. Ferrari and D. C. Verma. "A scheme for real-time channel establishment in wide-area networks." *IEEE JSAC,* vol. 8, no. 3, pp. 368–379, Apr. 1990.

[3] M. Joseph (ed.). *Real-Time Systems Specification, Verification and Analysis.* Prentice Hall (International Series in Computer Science), London, 1996.

[4] R. Kalmanek, H. Kanakia, and S. Keshav. "Rate controlled servers for very high-speed networks." In *Proc. IEEE GLOBECOM,* pp. 12–20, Dec. 1990.

[5] D. D. Kandlur, K. G. Shin, and D. Ferrari. "Real-time communication in multihop networks." *IEEE Trans. Parallel and Distributed Systems,* vol. 5, no. 10, pp. 1044–1056, Oct. 1994.

[6] C. M. Krishna and K. G. Shin. *Real-Time Systems.* McGraw-Hill International, Singapore, 1997.

[7] P. Krueger and N. G. Shivaratri. "Adaptive location policies for global scheduling." *IEEE Trans. Software Engg.,* vol. 20, no. 6, pp. 432–444, June 1994.

[8] V. O. K. Li and W. Liao. "Distributed multimedia systems." *Proc. IEEE,* vol. 85, no. 7, pp. 1063–1108, July 1997.

[9] M. Maekawa. "A $\sqrt{N}$ algorithm for mutual exclusion in decentralized systems." *ACM Trans. Computer Systems,* vol. 2, no. 2, pp. 145–158, May 1985.

[10] G. Manimaran, M. Shashidhar, A. Manikutty, and C. Siva Ram Murthy. "Integrated scheduling of tasks and messages in distributed real-time systems." *Journal of Parallel and Distributed Computing Practices,* vol. 1, no. 2, pp. 75–84, June 1998.

[11] K. Ramamritham, J. A. Stankovic, and W. Zhao. "Distributed scheduling of tasks with deadlines and resource requirements." *IEEE Trans. Computers,* vol. 38, no. 8, pp. 1110–1123, Aug. 1989.

[12] H. G. Rotithor. "Taxonomy of dynamic task scheduling schemes in distributed computing systems." *IEE Proc. Computers and Digital Techniques,* vol. 141, no. 1, pp. 1–10, Jan. 1994.

[13] K. G. Shin and Y. G. Chang. "Load sharing in distributed real-time systems with state-change broadcasts." *IEEE Trans. Computers,* vol. 38, no. 8, pp. 1124–1142, Aug. 1989.

[14] N. G. Shivaratri, P. Krueger, and M. Singhal. "Load distributing for locally distributed systems." *IEEE Computer,* vol. 25, no. 12, pp. 33–44, Dec. 1992.

[15] J. A. Stankovic. "Stability and distributed scheduling algorithms." *IEEE Trans. Software Engg.,* vol. 11, no. 10, pp. 1141–1152, Oct. 1985.

[16] J. A. Stankovic, K. Ramamritham, and S. Cheng. "Evaluation of a flexible task scheduling algorithm for distributed hard real-time systems." *IEEE Trans. Computers,* vol. 34, no. 12, pp. 1130–1143, Dec. 1985.

[17] P. Veríssimo and H. Kopetz. "Design of distributed real-time systems." In *Distributed Systems* (Sape Mullender, ed.), pp. 511–530, Addison-Wesley, 1994.

6 Scheduling of Object-Based Tasks in Distributed Real-Time Systems

Overview

In this chapter, we focus on a newly emerging software design methodology, the object-based technique. We first review the utility of this technique in real-time systems, then discuss programming, scheduling, and concurrency models of object-based tasks. Next we present an algorithm for the scheduling of object-based tasks in distributed real-time systems and illustrate this algorithm with an example. Finally, we introduce a higher-level abstraction, called the dynamic path paradigm, based on the object-based task abstraction.

6.1 Introduction

Evaluation of the software development process reveals evidence that there is a software crisis, in that the rate at which new software is developed and maintained does not keep pace with the growth in software needs. The main reasons for this crisis are

- the complexities of the problem domain,
- the difficulties of managing the developmental process,
- the flexibility possible through software,
- the problem of characterizing discrete system behavior, and
- humans' inherent limitations in dealing with complexity.

Two prominent methodologies have evolved to deal with this crisis [10]: (1) algorithmic decomposition and (2) object-based decomposition.

6.1.1 Algorithmic Decomposition

Algorithmic decomposition decomposes a system into a set of modules, each of which represents a major step in the system's functionality. However, the algorithmic decomposition approach has the following disadvantages [1]:

1. inability to adequately address data abstraction and information hiding,
2. inability to utilize the natural concurrency of problem domains, and
3. lack of responsiveness to changes in the problem space.

6.1.2 Object-Based Decomposition

Object-based decomposition decomposes a system according to key abstractions in the problem domain and identifies objects derived directly from the problem domain. The solution to a particular problem is viewed as a set of autonomous agents that collaborate to perform some high-level behavior.

Object-based design and methodology has the advantage of striving to mitigate the three major disadvantages of the algorithmic approach [12]. Further, it also offers a mechanism for software reuse. A reusable software component

1. makes it possible to formally express data structures and algorithms,

2. supports software engineering principles such as abstraction, encapsulation, and modularity, and

3. offers a mechanism for software reuse.

The software reusability and the close-to-real-world abstraction the object-based decomposition technique provides makes it a good solution to tackle the software crisis. As a result, the software community has come to prefer object-based decomposition over algorithmic decomposition as the ideal methodology for quality software development.

6.1.3   Significance of Object-Based Techniques in Real-Time Systems

The most important characteristic of real-time software is that it must be *dependable.* This dependability is ensured only if the software is *correct, reliable,* and *safe.* These factors, in addition to the complexity of software, make real-time software development a tedious process. Object-based techniques (reusable software components) provide various advantages over algorithmic approaches that can help conquer the difficulties in ensuring the above software characteristics.

The term *object-oriented* means object-based with the inclusion of such issues as inheritance and polymorphism. However, inheritance causes unpredictable system behavior because of its property of dynamic binding. The object-oriented technique as such is thus not suited to real-time systems, for which predictability is a very important requirement.

6.2   Programming Model

6.2.1   Abstract Data Types and Abstract Data Objects

Abstract data types (ADTs) and abstract data objects (ADOs) are basic units in object-based design [10]. Each ADT/ADO (also generally called *software components*) contains a set of data values and a set of methods. A typical ADT defines and exports [17] a type to be used for declaring variables and operations (or methods) to manipulate variables of the provided type.

The creation of data values (or objects) from ADTs is a two-step process. First, the ADT is instantiated to create a *facility* that contains the defined type and a set of methods used to manipulate the variables declared to be of the type. Second, the type exported by the ADT is used to declare variables, that is, to create objects. Multiple variables may be managed by a single set of methods, creating a contention in accessing ADTs that must be taken into account in the real-time scheduling context. ADTs are supported by languages such as Ada, C++, Clu, and Modula-2.

ADO is a restricted form of ADT in the sense that it does not export a type like the ADT. It does, however, encapsulate state (data) as in an ADT. Creating data values (objects) from ADOs is a single-step process in which the instantiation of the ADO yields an object containing data values and a set of methods for manipulating the data values. Thus two objects created from the same ADO each have their own copy of the methods set.

The differences between ADTs and ADOs are illustrated through the design of an automated medical treatment system, described in [14]. Computers are used in such systems because they can manage patient care through periodic monitoring of patients' vital signs and adjusting the treatment doses in response to observed values. We consider here a typical scenario in which an automatic medical treatment system is monitoring three postsurgery cardiac patients. It is assumed that all three patients are admitted to a single ward. The patients are critically ill, so the system checks their health conditions every minute, and they receive nourishment intravenously, breathe with the assistance of a respirator, and receive medication to control blood pressure. The system must

• calculate the calorific needs of the patients (a function of the level of glucose in the blood),

• calculate the rate at which oxygen is to be given through the respirator (determined by examining the level of oxygen in patient's blood), and

• calculate the rate at which the blood pressure medication is to be given (calculated by considering the patient's heart rate).

Figures 6.1 and 6.2 show the implementation of the above system using ADTs and ADOs, respectively. The implementation in figure 6.1 has six ADTs: *ward_ADT, patient_ADT, feeder_ADT, respirator_ADT, blood_pressure_medicator_ADT,* and *record3_ADT.* (To simplify the diagram, the implementation of ADTs other than *ward_ADT* and *patient_ADT* is omitted here.) The ADTs *feeder_ADT, respirator_ADT,* and *blood_pressure_medicator_ADT* correspond to the different types of treatment. A patient is represented by *patient_ADT,* and *ward_ADT* represents a ward. The ADT *patient_ADT* exports a

S1 :   MODULE ward_ADT

S2 :   LOCAL DECLARATIONS

S3 :   FACILITY p IS patient_ADT

S4 :   FACILITY rec3 IS record3_ADT(p.patient,
                        p.patient,p.patient)

S5 :   EXPORTS

S6 :   TYPE ward IS REPRESENTED AS rec3.record3

S7 :   OPERATION check_treatment(IN OUT w: ward)

S8 :   VARIABLE p1,p2,p3: p.patient

S9 :   rec3.access_field1(w,p1)

S10:   rec3.access_field2(w,p2)

S11:   rec3.access_field3(w,p3)

S12:   p.monitor_and_adjust(p1)

S13:   p.monitor_and_adjust(p2)

S14:   p.monitor_and_adjust(p3)

S15:   rec3.access_field1(w,p1)

S16:   rec3.access_field2(w,p2)

S17:   rec3.access_field3(w,p3)

S18:   END check_treatment

S19:   END ward_ADT

S20 : MODULE patient_ADT

S21 : LOCAL DECLARATIONS

S22 :   FACILITY f IS feeder_ADT

S23 :   FACILITY r IS respirator_ADT

S24 :   FACILITY b IS blood_pressure_medicator_ADT

S25 :   FACILITY r3 IS record3_ADT(f.feeder,
                        r.respirator, b.blood_pressure_medicator)

S26 : EXPORTS

S27 :   TYPE patient IS REPRESENTED AS r3.record3

S28 :   OPERATION monitor_and_adjust(IN OUT p: patient)

S29 :   VARIABLE fd: f.feeder, rsp: r.respirator

S30 :   VARIABLE bpm: b.blood_pressure_medicator

S31 :   r3.access_field1(p,fd)

S32 :   f.monitor(fd)

S33 :   r3.access_field2(p,rsp)

S34 :   r.monitor(rsp)

S35 :   r3.access_field3(p,bpm)

S36 :   b.monitor(bpm)

S37 :   f.adjust(fd)

S38 :   r.adjust(rsp)

S39 :   b.adjust(bpm)

S40 :   r3.access_field1(p,fd)

S41 :   r3.access_field2(p,rsp)

S42 :   r3.access_field3(p,bpm)

S43 :   END monitor_and_adjust

S44 : END patient_ADT

S45 : TASK ward_monitor

S46 : LOCAL DECLARATIONS

S47 :   FACILITY wd IS ward_ADT

S48 :   VARIABLE w1,w2: wd.ward

S49 :   OPERATION monitor

S50 :   wd.check_treatment(w1)

S51 :   wd.check_treatment(w2)

S52 :   nextstart = nextstart + PERIOD

S53 :   END monitor

S54 : END ward_monitor

Figure 6.1
ADT implementation of automated patient monitoring system

type *patient* and an operation *monitor_and_adjust* to monitor a patient, whereas *ward_ ADT* exports a type *ward* and an operation *check_treatment* to monitor the patients in a ward. The type *patient,* exported by *patient_ADT,* is created in *ward_ADT* by instantiating *patient_ADT* (*S3*). *ward_ADT* declares variables of the type *patient* (*S8*). The method *check_treatment* in *ward_ADT,* which monitors the patients in the ward, accesses the variables of type *patient* by calling *monitor_adjust.* Implementation of *ward_ADT* contains one more module, namely, *record3_ADT,* which is an example of a generic ADT. It is parameterized in *ward_ADT* by three types that correspond to the three patients in the ward (*S4*). *patient_ADT* also uses *record3_ADT,* but for different types, namely, the feeder, respirator, and blood pressure medicator.

The *check_treatment* operation in *ward_ADT* receives a parameter of type *ward,* which monitors the vital signs and adjusts the treatment of each patient in the ward. This is accomplished by (1) swapping each field out of the ward record (calls operation *access_ field1, access_field2,* and *access_field3* of *record3_ADT*) [2], (2) monitoring each patient by calling *monitor_and_adjust,* and (3) swapping each field back into the ward record. The operation *monitor_and_adjust* in *patient_ADT* also functions in a similar way. It receives a parameter of type *patient_ADT* and gets the fields corresponding to the three treatments for the patient record, monitors each of the vital signals (*f.Monitor, r.Monitor,* and *b.Monitor*), and adjusts treatments accordingly.

It should be noted that *record3_ADT* is used both in *ward_ADT* and *patient_ADT.* The local declarations in *ward_ADT* and *patient_ADT* create two different *facilities,* however, one for keeping track of the patients and the other for monitoring the different types of treatments.

Since each patient must be monitored every minute, monitoring is implemented as a periodic task with period 60 seconds. Thus, the periodic task *ward_monitor* will be executing periodically, which involves a call to the operation *check_treatment* of *ward_ADT.*

Figure 6.2 shows the implementation of the same system using ADOs. It can be seen that no *facility* is created in figure 6.2, unlike in figure 6.1. Further, ADOs do not export any type or any operation. The way in which methods are called is different in figures 6.1 and 6.2. In figure 6.1, methods are called with the syntax *facility.operation(object, otherparameters),* where *object* is created from an ADT, by declaring variables of the type exported by the ADT. But in the ADO implementation, methods are called with the syntax *object.operation(otherparameters),* where *object* is created by instantiating the ADO. Thus, in an ADT different objects share methods, whereas each object created from an ADO has its own set of methods. For example, the objects created corresponding to the three patients in this example share the operation *monitor_and_adjust* in figure 6.1, whereas in figure 6.2, each of the objects, corresponding to each patient, has its own copy of *monitor_and_adjust.*

```
S1  :  MODULE ward_ADO
S2  :  LOCAL DECLARATIONS
S3  :     FACILITY rec3 IS record3_ADT(patient_ADO,
                      patient_ADO,patient_ADO)
S4  :     OPERATION check_treatment()
S5  :         VARIABLE p1,p2,p3: patient_ADO
S6  :         rec3.access_field1(w,p1)
S7  :         rec3.access_field2(w,p2)
S8  :         rec3.access_field3(w,p3)
S9  :         p1.monitor_and_adjust()
S10:          p2.monitor_and_adjust()
S11:          p3.monitor_and_adjust()
S12:          rec3.access_field1(w,p1)
S13:          rec3.access_field2(w,p2)
S14:          rec3.access_field3(w,p3)
S15:      END check_treatment
S16:   END ward_ADO
```

```
S17 : MODULE patient_ADO
S18 : LOCAL DECLARATIONS
S19 :     FACILITY r3 IS record3_ADT(feeder_ADO,
                      respirator_ADO, blood_pressure_medicator_ADO)
S20 :     OPERATION monitor_and_adjust()
S21 :         VARIABLE f1: feeder_ADO, r1: respirator_ADO
S22 :         VARIABLE b1: blood_pressure_medicator_ADO
S23 :         r3.access_field1(p,f1)
S24 :         f1.monitor()
S25 :         r3.access_field2(p,r1)
S26 :         r1.monitor()
S27 :         r3.access_field3(p,b1)
S28 :         b1.monitor()
S29 :         f1.adjust()
S30 :         r1.adjust()
S31 :         b1.adjust()
S32 :         r3.access_field1(p,f1)
S33 :         r3.access_field2(p,r1)
S34 :         r3.access_field3(p,b1)
S35 :     END monitor_and_adjust
S36 : END patient_ADO
```

```
S37 : TASK ward_monitor
S38 : LOCAL DECLARATIONS
S39 :     VARIABLE w1,w2: ward_ADO
S40 :     OPERATION monitor
S41 :         w1.check_treatment()
S42 :         w2.check_treatment()
S43 :         nextstart = nextstart + PERIOD
S44 :     END monitor
S45 : END ward_monitor
```

Figure 6.2
ADO implementation of automated patient monitoring system

6.2.2   Stateful and Stateless Objects

Software components in object-based design can be either *stateful* or *stateless*. Stateful objects have a state associated with them. Stateless objects, on the other hand, have no state variables associated with them. Usually, all methods belonging to a stateful object are executed on one processor only, and that processor contains the data store of that stateful object. Executing methods of a stateful object on different processors may increase overhead, as the consistency of the object data store has to be maintained. No such overhead is involved in the case of stateless objects.

6.2.3   Environment-Dependent Objects

Some software components that represent resources in an object-based system are called *environment-dependent software components,* and the objects created at run time are called *environment-dependent objects.* If different methods of an environment-dependent object are executed on different processors, this would imply considerable overhead to main the synchronization of the resource utilization.

6.3   Scheduling Model

6.3.1   Semi-Preemption Model

The points at which the methods of a software component make external procedure (method) calls are known as *preemption points.* [10] describes a semi-preemption model, in which methods may be preempted only at predefined preemption points, such as external procedure calls and blocking device accesses. The approach is a compromise between full preemption, in which methods may be preempted at any point, and no preemption, in which methods may not be preempted at all. In the semi-preemption model, preemption is allowed, but the context-switching overhead encountered in full preemption is reduced. Two consecutive preemption points constitute a non-preemptable entity called a *bead.* Beads can be of two types, computation beads and communication beads. A *computation bead* is the execution of sequential code. The communication between two methods constitutes a *communication bead.* Thus every method is some combination of one or more computation beads.

6.3.2   Object-Based Real-Time Task Model

An object-based real-time application can be designed as described below. This design procedure is summarized in figure 6.3.

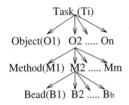

Figure 6.3
Object-based task model

• The application is designed in such a way that there are a number of tasks $T = \{T_1, T_2, \ldots, T_t\}$.

• Each task contains a set of objects that are the instances of software components spread over a set of programs. Each object can be

• an ADT or an ADO,

• stateful or stateless, and

• environment-dependent or not.

• Each object contains a set of methods.

• Each method is split into beads according to the semi-preemption model.

Resource requirements of tasks are represented at method level. If a task needs to access a particular resource, a method of the environment-dependent software component must be called. If two different tasks try to call a method of an environment-dependent software component at the same time, one of them has to wait. Thus resource constraints are modeled in the same way as contention for access to a shared software component.

Thus the execution of an *object-based task* spans a set of programs, starting from one program and switching to other programs through method calls.

6.4 Concurrency Model

Even though the reusable software components in the object-based implementation of an application have advantages such as abstraction and encapsulation, execution efficiency may have to be sacrificed due to [18]

1. contention for access to shared software components.

2. large number of procedure calls.

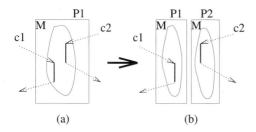

Figure 6.4
(a) Contention to access a method (b) Cloning to resolve contention

Techniques that use the parallelism inherent among the objects can help overcome these disadvantages. Two such techniques are (1) cloning and (2) asynchronous remote procedure calls.

6.4.1 Cloning

Contention among ADTs will occur to access the multiple data items they manage. One way to resolve such contention is to *clone* (or replicate) the software component on another processor so that more than one data item can be processed at a time. Figure 6.4(a) shows an example of the contention created by two methods $c1$ and $c2$ calling the same method M. The two calls have to be serialized and cannot be executed concurrently. However, when method M is cloned across two processors (figure 6.4(b)), the two calls to it have no interrelation and can thus be executed in parallel, if required. The fact that stateful software components have a state associated with them makes cloning of such components a costly operation. It is therefore assumed that only stateless software components can be cloned. Thus environment-dependent software components are nonclonable. As the number of stateful software components and environment-dependent software components in a system increases, the chances of cloning decrease, and hence schedulability also decreases.

6.4.2 Synchronous and Asynchronous Remote Procedure Calls

Each software component or object in an object-based system has a set of methods operating on the data encapsulated in the object. At run time, these objects communicate with each other through method calls. If the caller and callee are assigned to the same processor (or site), then the method call can be implemented through a local procedure call (LPC). When the caller and callee are on different sites, however, the method call is implemented by a remote procedure call (RPC). Figure 6.5 illustrates the distinction between an LPC and an RPC across two methods $M1$ and $M2$. An RPC can be either a synchronous RPC

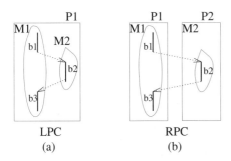

Figure 6.5
(a) LPC (b) RPC

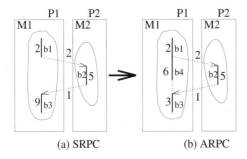

Figure 6.6
(a) SRPC (b) ARPC

(SRPC) or an asynchronous RPC (ARPC). In SRPCs, the caller gets blocked after the call until the callee returns. In ARPCs, the caller can continue its execution in parallel with the callee until the caller needs the results from the callee. In Figure 6.6(a), where the method call from $M1$ to $M2$ is implemented as an SRPC, b_3, which has nine units of computation time, has to wait for b_2 to finish execution. However, if b_3 does not need the result of b_2 to start execution, then b_3 can be executed in parallel with b_2, as an ARPC, shown in figure 6.6(b). Here the original bead b_3 is split into two beads b_3 and b_4, of which b_4 can be executed in parallel with b_2.

6.4.3   Identifying Cloning and ARPCs in an Object-Based Real-Time Application

To identify the cloning and ARPC potentialities in an object-based real-time application, static analysis of the application code must be conducted. This involves identifying certain relationships in the code on the statement, method, and instance levels [17].

A parallel virtual machine model for executing programs that use ADTs employing ARPCs has been designed in [14]. This constructs certain dependency, precedence, and call graphs to model the above relationships and then identify the ARPCs and cloning requirements in the application.

6.5   Example Application: Mine Pump

An object-based design of a mine pump and control system [3] is chosen to illustrate the object-based real-time task model. For simplicity, we consider only a part of the system, which has two tasks, *MethaneMonitor* and *AirflowMonitor*, which monitor the level of methane and airflow in the mine. Sensors are present in the mine to detect methane level and airflow level. If the methane level exceeds a certain threshold, then the pump that pumps out the water percolating into the mine is switched off to avoid explosion. If the methane level exceeds the threshold or airflow level decreases to below a certain threshold, an alarm is sent to inform the mine's operator. *AirFlowMonitor* makes an additional check on the ratio of the methane level stored in *Status* to the airflow level sensed, to ensure safety. The software component *Status* tracks the methane level and airflow level in the mine. Readings from all sensors, and a record of the operation of the pump, are logged in *Status* for later analysis.

The pseudocode of these two tasks is shown in figure 6.7. The execution time needed for code segments is shown in the comments. The 2-tuples shown in the comments for each method invocation denote the amount of data communicated from caller to callee and vice versa. Figure 6.8 shows the comprehensive entity invocation graph (CEIG) of the application. Software components (or objects) are denoted by circles or ovals, and the methods in the software components are shown as a sequence of solid straight lines. Method calls are denoted by dotted lines. The weights associated with the solid and dotted lines indicate the computation and communication times required, respectively. The CEIG is obtained from the application code by performing a static analysis.

In figure 6.8, the software component *OperatorAlarm* has a method *Alarm* shared by *MethaneMonitor.Monitor* and *AirflowMonitor.Monitor*. The calls to *OperatorAlarm.Alarm* from both are ARPCs in which five units of *MethaneMonitor.Monitor* and four units of *AirflowMonitor.Monitor* can go in parallel with *OperatorAlarm.Alarm*. The call to *Status.Read* from *AirflowMonitor.Monitor* is an SRPC. *Status.Write* takes four and five time units to execute calls from *MethaneMonitor.Monitor* and *AirflowMonitor.Monitor*, respectively. Status is a stateful software component, since it keeps track of the methane and airflow levels in the mine. *OperatorAlarm* and *Logger* are stateless software components.

task MethaneMonitor
data SensorReading,MethaneThreshold,Period
procedure Monitor
begin
.... read hardware register into SensorReading. /* 1 Time Unit (TU) */
if (*SensorReading* > *MethaneThreshold*) /* 1 TU */
Controller.Stop; /* (2,0)*/
.... /* 2 TU */
OperatorAlarm.Alarm(Methane); /* (2,0)*/
.... in parallel with OperatorAlarm /* 5 TU */
endif
.... /* 3 TU */
Status.Write(SensorReading,Methane); /* (2,1)*/
.... in parallel with Status /* 8 TU */
.... /* 1 TU */
Logger.MLog() /* MethaneLog; */ /* (1,0)*/
NextStart = NextStart + Period; /* 1 TU */
delay until NextStart;
end MethaneMonitor

task AirflowMonitor
data SensorReading,Reading,Ratio,AirflowThreshold,Period
procedure Monitor
begin
.... read hardware register into SensorReading /* 1 TU */
Status.Read(Reading,Methane); /* (1,2)*/
Ratio = SensorReading/Reading; /* 1 TU */
if ((*Ratio* < *MinRatio*)**or**(*SensorReading* <= *Airflow*)) /* 1 TU */
OperatorAlarm.Alarm(Airflow); /* (3,0)*/
.... in parallel with OperatorAlarm /* 4 TU */

Figure 6.7
Pseudocode of mine pump and control system

endif
.... /* 2 TU */
Status.Write(SensorReading,Airflow); /* (2,1)*/
.... in parallel with Status /* 4 TU */
.... /* 1 TU */
Logger.ALog(); /* (1,0)*/
.... in parallel with Logger /* 4 TU */
NextStart = NextStart + Period; /* 1 TU */
delay until NextStart;
end AirflowMonitor

software component Controller
data PumpStatus,SafetyStatus;
procedure Stop; /* 3 TU */
procedure Start; /*This method is not considered in this example*/
end Controller

software component Status
data MethaneValue,AirflowValue;
procedure Read(Reading,Type); /* 3 TU */
procedure Write(Reading,Type); /* 4,5 TU */
end Status

software component OperatorAlarm
procedure Alarm(AlarmSource); /* 4 TU */
end OperatorAlarm

software component Logger
procedure MLog(MethaneLevel); /* 4 TU */
procedure ALog(AirflowLevel); /* 3 TU */
end Logger

Figure 6.7 *(continued)*

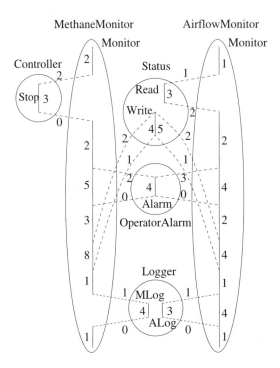

Figure 6.8
Mine pump and control system

6.6 A Scheduling Algorithm for Object-Based Periodic Tasks in Distributed Real-Time Systems

6.6.1 Problem Statement

The application depicted in this section is designed in such a way that there are t periodic tasks $T = \{T_1, T_2, \ldots, T_t\}$, where the structure of a task is as shown in figure 6.3 and as described in section 6.3.2. Each task T_i is assumed to be periodic with period P_i (and the computation time of the task is defined at the bead level).

The problem is to statically (i.e., pre–run time) schedule these t periodic tasks on a distributed system that is a collection of processors (or sites) connected by a multiple access network employing time division multiple access (TDMA) protocol. The least common multiple (LCM) of all the task periods is taken, and this period is referred to as the *planning cycle*. LCM/P_i instances of each task T_i are scheduled within the planning cycle, the ith instance being scheduled to start not earlier than $(LCM/P_i) * (i - 1)$ and scheduled to finish not later than $(LCM/P_i) * i$. The schedule has to take care of all precedence and resource constraints among tasks generated by software component contention, resource requirements, bead order in a method, and so forth.

6.6.2 Notation

For each computation (communication) bead B, $E(B)$ denotes the computation (communication) time of the bead. Since a method is composed of one or more beads, $E(M_{ij})$ stands for the sum of the computation times of all the beads of the method M_{ij}. $NM(M_{ij})$ denotes the total number of calls made to M_{ij} by all tasks for all periods up to the LCM of the task periods. The execution time of a task, denoted by $E(T_i)$, is the sum of the execution times of all the methods present in the implementation of the task.

6.6.3 Work on Object-Based Real-Time Task Scheduling

Pre–run time scheduling algorithms in which contention for access to both physical shared resources (processors, devices, and communication channels) and logical shared resources (software components) is avoided by preallocating those resources are suitable choices for object-based systems. As mentioned in chapter 2, pre–run time scheduling algorithms are classified into static table-driven and static priority-driven algorithms [5].

Many static table-driven heuristic scheduling algorithms [4, 6, 16] have been proposed for non-object-based real-time systems. The approach taken here differs from those algorithms in the following ways:

1. They consider a module and submodule to be a task and a subtask, respectively. Since the task model here consists of finer-grained entities like reusable software components, schedulability and resource utilization are enhanced.

2. In their models intertask/intratask communication is possible only at the end of execution of a subtask (or task). But the model of this section allows the methods to communicate during their execution.

3. The way the parallelism within tasks is exploited is different in the model of this section than in those algorithms. Even though [6] exploits parallelism within a task by distributing the subtasks on different sites, it differs from parallelism exploitation techniques such as cloning and introduction of ARPCs.

Most of the existing literature in object-based scheduling tries to find ways to overcome the difficulties involved in using reusable software components, such as execution overhead due to a large number of procedure calls and contention for shared software components [9, 10, 13, 17, 18]. One exception is [11], in which software components are assigned and scheduled on processors based on interprocess parallelism and processor utilization computed using probabilistic techniques. An algorithm to assign reusable software components that exploits intermodular parallelism with a minimum number of processors through the introduction of ARPCs is described in [13]. A model for pre–run time scheduling of object-based distributed real-time systems composed of ADTs and ADOs is proposed in [9, 10]. In addition, [9] and [10] present an incremental scheduling approach that constructs an initial schedule and modifies it by enhancing concurrency through the introduction of ARPC and cloning, until a feasible schedule is obtained. The study in [18] presents compiler techniques for identifying concurrency among software components via ARPCs and cloning in the context of an incremental scheduling algorithm. The work presented in this section (also in [8]) differs from the work in [18] in that the model here considers periodic tasks having precedence constraints among them compared to the multiple independent tasks considered in [18].

6.6.4   The Scheduling Algorithm

The scheduling approach proposed in [8] has two main parts: *allocation* and *scheduling*. The algorithm allocates software components/methods to processors (or sites) and schedules the beads of the methods of software component instances (objects) on the corresponding processors. The following issues have to be dealt with in making allocation and scheduling decisions:

1. whether two software components whose objects are communicating should be placed on the same site

2. to which site a software component should be allocated

3. at what time the beads and hence the methods should start execution

4. whether a method is to be cloned

5. if a method is to be cloned, then to which site it should be cloned

6. whether the schedule constructed is load balanced.

Since the potential search space in which to find a feasible schedule is very large, heuristics are used to reduce the size of the search space to manageable levels. We first give an overview of the scheduling approach and the details follow that.

1. *Constructing comprehensive entity invocation graph.* A CEIG that contains all the instances of periodic tasks up to the LCM is constructed.

2. *Clustering step.* The clustering heuristic takes into account *communication, parallelism,* and factors that contribute to *load balance* among *entities* such as software components and methods of software components. The aim of the clustering step is to minimize the communication volume among entities by exploiting maximum parallelism among

them by considering load balance, such that task deadlines can be met. Depending on a tunable parameter called the parallelism and communication factor (*PCF*), some communicating entities are clustered together, whereas others are declustered.

3. *Constructing modified comprehensive entity invocation graph.* After the clusters have been created in the previous step, the CEIG is modified to get the modified comprehensive entity invocation graph (MCEIG) by setting communication among the communicating entities to zero. Then the latest start time (LST) of each bead is calculated by traversing the MCEIG from bottom to top.

4. *Allocation and scheduling step.* Allocation and scheduling in this model involves a heuristic search technique in which the software components/methods are allocated onto different processors and the beads of the methods are then scheduled on the processors. This step consists of (1) generation of mappings of ready beads from a ready queue onto the processors available at any time, (2) checking the validity of a mapping, (3) checking each search point for feasibility, and (4) cloning to increase schedulability.

If it is not possible to find a feasible schedule using this method, the value of *PCF* can be changed to make a new clustering and steps 2–4 are then repeated. In the rest of this section, we describe each of the algorithmic steps in detail.

6.6.5   Construction of the CEIG

The algorithm presented in this section attempts to construct a feasible schedule for all task instances for a duration equal to the planning period. The first instance of each periodic task is assumed to start at 0. The ith periodic task with period P_i will have $\frac{LCM}{P_i}$ instances present in the CEIG. The jth instance of the ith periodic task, for $j = 1, 2, \ldots, \frac{LCM}{P_i}$, with period P_i, must finish its execution in the interval $(P_i * (j - 1), P_i * j)$. The first bead of the first method of the jth instance of the ith periodic task should not start before $(j - 1) * P_i$. Similarly the last bead of the last method of the jth instance of the ith task should finish before $j * P_i$.

6.6.6   Clustering/Declustering Step

Clustering/declustering can be applied at the software component level or the method level. It captures the parallelism and communication among the software components/methods and the factors that contribute to load balance. The clustering heuristic applied to software components is presented first, and the method-level clustering heuristic follows in section 6.7.1.

   If by assigning two communicating software components to different sites, it is possible to shorten their completion time, the situation is referred to as *gain;* otherwise it is called *loss. Communicating* software components are those whose objects, instantiated from them at run time, are communicating with each other. By *shortening* the completion time of a software component, we mean reducing the execution time of its methods. Gain can occur only for ARPCs. Loss occurs for all SRPCs and those ARPCs where communication dominates the parallelism. The total gain/loss is the sum of the gain/loss of all the method calls among the communicating software components. The clustering heuristic captures the gain or loss involved among the software components.

Different clustering heuristics are applied to the gain and loss cases, since the purpose is to maximize gain and minimize loss. The gain/loss among two communicating software components is calculated by aggregating the gain/loss for each communicating method pair among the software components. Before explaining the clustering heuristic, some notations are introduced that are common to both gain and loss cases.

Let M_{ij} and M_{pq} be two communicating methods and let M_{ij} call M_{pq}, $NMC(M_{ij}, M_{pq})$ times. The net advantage (*NADV*) in assigning them to two different sites is

$$NADV_{ijpq} = \sum_{k=1}^{NMC(M_{ij}, M_{pq})} ([pt_k + E(M_{pq})] - \max(pt_k, cs_k + cr_k + E(M_{pq}))),$$

where $pt_k = \sum B_{ijl}$ is the sum of the execution times of the beads of M_{ij} that can execute in parallel with the kth call to M_{pq}, and cs_k and cr_k denote the amount of data communicated from M_{ij} to k^{th} call of M_{pq} and vice versa. The first term in *NADV* denotes the time needed to execute M_{ij} and $M_{p_k q_k}$ if they are assigned to the same site. The second term denotes the time they take if executed on different sites. Together these two terms denote the gain/loss for one method call. Similarly for two communicating software components C_i and C_p, the net gain/loss among them, that is, the net advantage among software components (*CNADV*), is defined as $CNADV_{ip} = \sum NADV_{ijpn} * NM(M_{ij}) + \sum NADV_{pnij} * NM(M_{pn})$, for all method calls M_{ij} to M_{pn} from C_i to C_p and all method calls M_{pn} to M_{ij} from C_p to C_i.

6.6.6.1 Clustering Heuristic for Gain Cases

For gain cases, if the communicating software components are assigned to different sites, then it is possible to exploit parallelism by introducing some communication into the channel. $CNADV_{ip}$ can be calculated for all communicating software components C_i and C_p, and a threshold value can be chosen for *PCF* so that all those software component pairs with $CNADV_{ip} \leq PCF$ are clustered and others are declustered. Here the aim is to exploit the ARPC calls having maximum parallelism. It is not desirable to consider only $CNADV_{ip}$ since it is calculated by adding *NADV* values which account for only those beads that be executed in parallel.

Consider a situation in which a method M_{pq} is called by two different methods M_{ij} and M_{kl}. Assume $E(M_{ij}) > E(M_{kl})$ and $NADV_{ijpq} < NADV_{klpq}$. By considering *NADV* values,

M_{ij} and M_{pq} will be clustered together, since the amount of parallelism between M_{ij} and M_{pq} is less than that between M_{kl} and M_{pq}. A schedule constructed in such a way will have a much greater load imbalance compared to a clustering in which M_{pq} and M_{kl} are put together. Since $(E(M_{ij}) + E(M_{pq})) > (E(M_{pq}) + E(M_{kl}))$, a reduction in $(E(M_{pq}) + E(M_{kl}))$ will be less significant (exploiting parallelism among M_{pq} and M_{kl}) for the overall schedule compared to the reduction in $(E(M_{ij}) + E(M_{pq}))$ (exploiting parallelism among M_{ij} and M_{pq}), because beads that do not take part in the computation of *NADV* still have a role in deciding on a good schedule. Therefore, exploiting the ARPC parallelism in the method pair that has the largest gain need not generate a load-balanced schedule. So the clustering heuristic takes the load balance factor into account. Thus if the time two methods take to finish execution when they are clustered is very large, then it is better to exploit the parallelism among them so that load will be balanced.

The algorithm applies the following gain heuristic (*GH*) function to all communicating software components C_i and C_p:

$$GH_{ip} = \frac{CNADV_{ip}}{G_{\max}} + \frac{E(C_i) + E(C_p)}{EP_{\max}},$$

for all $CNADV_{ip} > 0$. $G_{\max} = \max[\max(CNADV_{ip})]$, for all communicating software components C_i and C_p, is the maximum of the gains among all communicating software component pairs. Similarly $EP_{\max} = \max[\max(E(C_i) + E(C_p))]$ is the maximum among all the software component pairs, where $E(C_x) = \sum E(M_{xj}) * NM(M_{xj})$ is the sum of the execution time of beads of all the methods of the software component C_x for all tasks for all periods up to the LCM. The first fraction in the equation for GH_{ip} is normalized with respect to maximum gain, and the second fraction is normalized with respect to maximum software component pair execution time. Both range from 0 to 1; thus the value of GH_{ip} ranges from 0 to 2. The higher the value of GH_{ip}, the better it is for the two components to be assigned to different sites, since it indicates either high gain when they are on different sites or high load when they are on the same site.

6.6.6.2 Clustering Heuristic for Loss Cases

For gain cases, the clustering heuristic tries to exploit the parallelism among the software components by checking for load imbalance, if those components are assigned to the same site. Our aim in those cases is to decluster the components onto different sites. But software component pairs that result in loss when they are assigned to different sites are treated in the opposite way.

Clearly, allocating two software components to different sites with loss as a result will increase overall completion time of the task and inject unnecessary communication into the channel. So loss among the software components is to be minimized. But just as for the gain cases, concentrating only on the loss cases may generate highly imbalanced schedules.

The load balancing factor considered by the clustering heuristic takes into account the load when software components are assigned to different sites, including the communication among the objects created from those components. The higher the load resulting from assignment of those components to different sites, the better to put them on the same site. Let $LTEMP$ be defined as follows for all communication software components C_i and C_p:

$$LTEMP_{ip} = \frac{CNADV_{ip}}{L_{min}} + \frac{E(C_i) + E(C_p) + COMM_{ip} + COMM_{pi}}{EPC_{max}},$$

for all $CNADV_{ip} \leq 0$. $L_{min} = \min[\min(CNADV_{ip})]$, for all C_i and C_p, is the maximum of the losses among all software component pairs. Similarly, $EPC_{max} = \max[\max(E(C_i) + E(C_p) + COMM_{ip} + COMM_{pi})]$ is the maximum among all software component pairs, where $COMM_{ip}$ denotes the communication from C_i to C_p, which is the sum of communications among all method pairs of C_i and C_p for all tasks and for all periods up to LCM. The higher the value of $LTEMP_{ip}$, the better it is that the two components in question are assigned to the same site, since it indicates either high loss or high load when they are on different sites. Uniformity in the heuristic is lost, since a high value for GH_{ip} indicates declustering but a high value for $LTEMP_{ip}$ indicates clustering. So to make the heuristic uniform for both gain and loss cases, it is modified to $LH_{ip} = 2 - LTEMP_{ip}$. Thus a lower value means clustering and a higher value means declustering for both GH_{ip} and LH_{ip}.

Heuristic values are calculated for all software component pairs. For each pair, depending on the value of $CNADV$, GH (gain) or LH (loss) is applied. GH and LH values are then combined and arranged in ascending order. The tunable parameter PCF is set to the maximum value among GH and LH. This parameter will cluster all the software components. If the schedule constructed does not meet the deadline, the value of PCF is decremented so that some software components will go to different sites, and the parallelism among them is exploited. If clusters of unlimited size are allowed, many values of PCF may generate clusters that have high load imbalances. So it is necessary to limit the number of software components in any given cluster. Therefore, software components can be added to a cluster only until the sum of their execution times in the cluster does not exceed a limit whose value is equal to

$$ClusterRatio * \frac{\sum E(C_i)}{Number\_of\_processors},$$

for all i and for all tasks up to the LCM. By varying $ClusterRatio$, the number of software components added to a cluster can be controlled, since $ClusterRatio$ determines the maximum load that a cluster can sustain.

6.6.7 Constructing the MCEIG

After clustering decisions are made, the CEIG is modified to the MCEIG by setting the communication between the methods of clustered software components to 0. The LST of the beads in the MCEIG is then computed. Let B be a bead belonging to a method that is present in task T_i. The LST of B is $D - LP$, where LP is the longest path from B up to and including the computation time of beads in the path and the communication between the beads in the path and D denotes the deadline of the task to which B belongs. If the bead starts later than LST, then the task to which it belongs will definitely miss the deadline.

6.6.8 Allocation and Scheduling

Once a software component is allocated to a particular site, all the objects instantiated from it, and hence all the methods of the objects, and hence all the beads of the methods, are executed on the same site. A software component is allocated to a site when it is accessed for the first time, by calling any method of it. When the first bead of that method is to be scheduled, the software component is allocated to a site. If the software component has the flexibility to be allocated to more than one site, it is allocated to the site having the least load at the moment it needs to be allocated. A site may execute more than one method at a time by interleaving their beads. A site's load at a particular moment is the remaining execution time of the currently executing methods, which is equal to the sum of the execution time of beads of those methods that have yet to be executed.

Since both communication and computation beads are assumed to be non-preemptable, when a bead becomes ready for execution, if the site or communication channel on which it is to be scheduled is busy, it will wait till that site or that communication channel becomes free. Thus at any point in the search for a schedule, the beads are mapped to the resources idle at that time. Other than processors and communication channels, all other resources are accessed through method calls of the software component representing the resource. If the resource a particular task needs is not available, this means that some other task has called some method of the software component representing the resource. So the former task has to wait until the latter task finishes execution.

In the allocation and scheduling step, a ready queue (RQ) is maintained that contains the beads that are ready to execute. A bead becomes ready when all its predecessors have completed execution and when its start time constraint is met. The RQ is ordered according to increasing LST of the beads it contains. When two beads have the same LST, the bead with the greater number of successors is placed first. The following subsections discuss the substeps of the allocation and scheduling step.

6.6.8.1   Systematic Generation of Mappings   The mapping of the beads in the RQ defines their assignment to the available processors and communication channel at the time the mapping is made. Mappings are generated using a lexicographic mapping generator [6]. The use of such a scheme reduces the amount of information that has to be maintained during the schedule search where only the most recently used mapping at any point in the search needs to be kept as part of the search structure.

6.6.8.2   Testing the Validity of a Mapping   A mapping should satisfy the following conditions:

1. Communication beads must be allocated to a communication channel.

2. If a site has already been allocated to a method, then the beads of that method should not be allocated to other sites.

6.6.8.3   Testing for Feasibility   Whenever either of the following conditions are satisfied, the current search point will not lead to a feasible schedule:

1. The time at the current search point is greater than the LST of any single bead in the ready list.

2. For any bead B, (current time + computation time of predecessors of B) is greater than the LST of B.

6.6.8.4   Cloning to Increase Schedulability   Allocation at the software component level lacks flexibility, since when allocation is conducted at that level, all the methods of the software component must be executed on the same site. That is, a software component C_i's invocation of a method M_{ij} may have to wait, since the execution of M_{ij} may be in progress for a previous invocation of M_{ij}. Such a conflict can be detected by (a) checking for the execution of a bead B_{ijk} of method M_{ij} on the site allocated to C_i, or (b) checking for the presence of a bead B_{ijk} of method M_{ij} in RQ. Let *DELAY* be the amount of time the second invocation of M_{ij} has to wait to start its execution, and let the LST of the first bead of M_{ij} (second invocation) be L. *DELAY* is the sum of (1) the time required to finish the execution of all the remaining beads of the first invocation of M_{ij}, (2) the time required to finish the execution of all the remaining methods called by the first invocation of M_{ij}, and (3) the time required to finish the execution of beads present in the RQ whose LST is less than L. If *CurrentTime* + *DELAY* > L, this means that, if the second invocation of M_{ij} waits to execute on the site allocated to C_i, the time at which M_{ij} can start execution will exceed its LST, and hence it will miss the deadline. To overcome this difficulty, the methods of the software component will be cloned on another processor, so that more than one method of the software component can be executed in parallel. The second invocation of M_{ij} will thus be executed on a different site than the first.

6.7 Scheduling the Mine Pump Application

The mine pump example discussed earlier in the chapter is now used to show the working of the scheduling algorithm presented above. Both *MethaneMonitor* and *Airflow-Monitor* are assumed to have period 35, and thus their LCM is 35. The total number of times *OperatorAlarm.Alarm* is called by other methods is $NM(OperatorAlarm.Alarm) = 2$. Similarly, $E(MethaneMonitor.Monitor) = 2 + 2 + 5 + 3 + 8 + 1 + 1 = 22$, and $NMC(MethaneMonitor.Monitor, OperatorAlarm.Alarm) = 1$.

Figure 6.9 shows the calculation of gain and loss. Assigning 2, 1.63, and 1.51 to *PCF* will not generate a feasible schedule, since it will cluster all software components. But when $PCF = 1.04$, the clusters made are (*MethaneMonitor, Controller,* and *Logger*) and (*AirflowMonitor, Status, OperatorAlarm*). This exploits the parallelism that is present among (*MethaneMonitor, OperatorAlarm*) and (*MethaneMonitor, Status*). Since the two tasks have high computational requirements, it is not possible to generate a feasible schedule with one or two processors. But if there is a third processor, the parallelism among both the above pairs can be extracted, and the tasks will meet their deadlines. The schedule generated by the algorithm is shown in figure 6.10, in which three processors are denoted as P1, P2, and P3, and the communication channel is denoted as C. Each of the beads in the schedule is marked with an abbreviation of the name of the method to which it belongs: MM (*MethaneMonitor.Monitor*), AM (*AirflowMonitor.Monitor*), SR (*Status.Read*), SW (*Status.Write*), OA (*OperatorAlarm.Alarm*), LM (*Logger.MLog*), LA (*Logger.ALog*), and CS (*Controller.Stop*). OA(AM) means OA is called from AM. Similarly, communication beads MM(OA) means MM calls method OA and parameters are passing from MM to OA.

6.7.1 Method-Level Clustering/Declustering

In the example application, if the last bead of the method *MethaneMonitor.Monitor* has computation time equal to 2 units compared to the 1 unit shown in figure 6.8, its completion time will become 36, and it will not meet its deadline. The drawback of software component level clustering is that it is applied to software components that are coarse-grained in comparison to their methods, and hence this type of clustering lacks flexibility. Applying the clustering heuristic to the methods of the software components, rather than the components themselves, makes it possible to exploit the parallelism at a finer granularity that favors schedulability. Also, at the method level, clustering heuristics are applied to the gain and loss cases.

6.7.1.1 Method-Level Clustering Heuristic for Gain Cases As defined in section 6.6.6, $NADV_{ijpq}$ denotes the net advantage in assigning two communicating methods

caller software component (E(softwarecomponent))	callee software component (E(softwarecomponent))	comm. times	CNADV gain/loss	EP/ EPC	norm. gain/loss	norm. EP/EPC	GH/ LH
MethaneMonitor(22)	Status(12)	(2,1)	4	34	$\frac{4}{4}$	$\frac{34}{34}$	2
MethaneMonitor(22)	OperatorAlarm(8)	(2,0)	3	30	$\frac{3}{4}$	$\frac{30}{34}$	1.63
AirflowMonitor(19)	Logger(7)	(1,0)	3	26	$\frac{3}{4}$	$\frac{26}{34}$	1.51
AirflowMonitor(19)	OperatorAlarm(8)	(3,0)	1	27	$\frac{1}{4}$	$\frac{27}{34}$	1.04
MethaneMonitor(22)	Logger(7)	(1,0)	−1	30	$\frac{-1}{2}$	$\frac{30}{37}$	0.69
MethaneMonitor(22)	Controller(3)	(2,0)	−2	27	$\frac{-2}{2}$	$\frac{27}{37}$	0.27
AirflowMonitor(19)	Status(12)	(3,3)	−2	37	$\frac{-2}{2}$	$\frac{37}{37}$	0

Figure 6.9
Software component level clustering heuristic value calculation

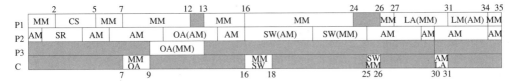

Figure 6.10
Schedule constructed by the algorithm (software component level clustering)

M_{ij} and M_{pq} to different sites. Our aim here is to exploit the ARPC calls, ensuring maximum parallelism by considering load balance. Thus the method-level clustering heuristic for gain cases is

$$GH_{ijpq} = \frac{NM(M_{ij}) * NADV_{ijpq}}{G_{max}} + \frac{NM(M_{ij}) * (E(M_{ij}) + CE(M_{pq}))}{EP_{max}},$$

for all $NADV_{ijpq} > 0$. $G_{max} = \max[\max(NM(M_{ij}) * NADV_{ijpq})]$, for all communicating methods M_{ij} and M_{pq}, is the maximum of all the gains among all communicating methods. $CE(M_{pq})$ denotes $\sum_{1}^{NMC(M_{ij},M_{pq})} E(M_{pq})$. $EP_{max} = \max[\max(E(M_{ij}) + CE(M_{pq}))]$ is the maximum among all the method pairs. As with the software component level clustering, the values of GH_{ijpq} range from 0 to 2. The higher is the value of GH_{ijpq}, the better it is for the two methods to be assigned to different sites, and the lower that value, the better for the two methods to be assigned to the same site.

6.7.1.2   Method-Level Clustering Heuristic for Loss Cases   The method-level clustering heuristic for loss cases is similar to the software component level clustering heuristic discussed in section 6.6.6.2. Let $LTEMP_{ijpq}$ be defined as follows:

$$LTEMP_{ijpq} = \frac{NM(M_{ij}) * NADV_{ijpq}}{L_{min}} + \frac{NM(M_{ij}) * (E(M_{ij}) + LCE(M_{pq}))}{EPC_{max}}$$

for all $NADV_{ijpq} \leq 0$. $L_{min} = \min[\min(NADV_{ijpq})]$, for all M_{ij} and M_{pq}, is the maximum of the losses for all method pairs. $LCE(M_{pq})$ denotes $\sum_{1}^{NMC(M_{ij},M_{pq})} (E(M_{pq}) + COMM_{ijpq})$, where $COMM_{ijpq}$ denotes the communication from M_{ij} to M_{pq} for all invocations of every task for each period up to LCM. $EPC_{max} = \max[\max(E(M_{ij}) + LCE(M_{pq}))]$ is the maximum among all method pairs. The higher the value of $LTEMP_{ijpq}$, the better it is for the two methods to be assigned to the same site, since it indicates either high loss or high load when they are on different sites. Uniformity in the heuristic is again lost, since a high value for GH_{ijpq} indicates declustering but a high value for $LTEMP_{ijpq}$ indicates clustering. To make the heuristic uniform for both gain and loss cases, the heuristic is modified to $LH_{ijpq} = 2 - LTEMP_{ijpq}$. Thus a lower value indicates clustering is advantageous and a higher value means declustering is advantageous for both GH_{ijpq} and LH_{ijpq}.

The heuristic values are calculated for all method pairs. As in software component level clustering, for each method pair, depending on the value of *NADV*, *GH* (gain) or *LH* (loss) is applied. Setting to the maximum value among *GH* and *LH* clusters all the methods. If this does not generate a feasible schedule, the value of *PCF* is decremented to exploit the parallelism among the methods by forcing them to go to different sites. Methods can be added to a cluster until the sum of their execution times in the cluster does not exceed a limit equal to

$$ClusterRatio * \frac{\sum E(C_i)}{Number\_of\_processors},$$

for all *i* and for all tasks up to the LCM.

Once a method is allocated to a particular site, all the calls made to it, and hence all the beads of the method, are executed on the same site. A method is allocated to a site when it is accessed for the first time, by calling it. When the first bead of that method is to be scheduled, the method is allocated to a site. All the methods of environment-dependent and stateful software components must be executed on the same site. All the methods of an environment-dependent (or stateful) software component are assigned to the cluster to which the first method of the environment-dependent (or stateful) software component that encounters the clustering decision is assigned. If the method (or environment-dependent or stateful software component) has the flexibility to be allocated to more than one site, it is allocated to the site having the least load at the moment it needs to be allocated. All the other substeps of allocation and scheduling are same as in section 6.6.8.

If the execution time of the last bead of *MethaneMonitor.Monitor* in figure 6.8 is increased from 1 to 2, the schedule constructed by the software component level clustering algorithm shown in figure 6.10 will not meet its deadline. A feasible schedule can be constructed by applying the clustering heuristic at the method level. The application of the method-level clustering heuristic to the example produces the heuristic function values shown in figure 6.11. Assigning 2, 1.72, and 1.44 to *PCF* does not generate a feasible schedule. When *PCF* = 1.13, the clusters generated are (*AirflowMonitor.Monitor, Status.Read, Status.Write, OperatorAlarm.Alarm*) and (*MethaneMonitor.Monitor, Controller.Stop, Logger.MLog*). This exploits the parallelism that is present among *AirflowMonitor.Monitor* and *Logger.ALog* and helps the example application to meet its deadline. Figure 6.12 shows the feasible schedule generated by the method-level clustering algorithm.

caller method (M) $(E(M) * NM(M))$	callee method (M) $(E(M) * NM(M))$	comm. times	NADV gain/loss	EP/ EPC	norm. gain/loss	norm. EP/EPC	GH/ LH
MethaneMonitor.Monitor(23)	Status.Write(9)	(2,1)	4	32	$\frac{4}{4}$	$\frac{32}{32}$	2
MethaneMonitor.Monitor(23)	OperatorAlarm.Alarm(8)	(2,0)	3	31	$\frac{3}{4}$	$\frac{31}{32}$	1.72
AirflowMonitor.Monitor(19)	Logger.ALog(3)	(1,0)	3	22	$\frac{3}{4}$	$\frac{22}{32}$	1.44
AirflowMonitor.Monitor(19)	Status.Write(9)	(2,1)	1	28	$\frac{1}{4}$	$\frac{28}{32}$	1.13
AirflowMonitor.Monitor(19)	OperatorAlarm.Alarm(8)	(3,0)	1	27	$\frac{1}{4}$	$\frac{27}{32}$	1.09
MethaneMonitor.Monitor(23)	Logger.MLog(4)	(1,0)	−1	28	$\frac{-1}{3}$	$\frac{28}{28}$	0.67
MethaneMonitor.Monitor(23)	Controller.Start(3)	(2,0)	−2	28	$\frac{-2}{3}$	$\frac{28}{28}$	0.33
AirflowMonitor.Monitor(19)	Status.Read(3)	(1,2)	−3	25	$\frac{-3}{3}$	$\frac{25}{28}$	0.11

Figure 6.11
Method-level clustering heuristic value calculation

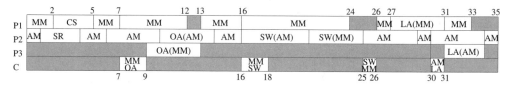

Figure 6.12
Schedule constructed by the algorithm (method level clustering)

6.8   The Dynamic Path-Based Paradigm

In this section, we discuss the *dynamic path-based paradigm* [15], which, as its name indicates, is based on *dynamic paths*. The notion of a dynamic path is useful for describing systems with dynamic variability, wherein the behavioral characteristics of the various tasks cannot be determined statically. The dynamic path-based paradigm is convenient for specifying end-to-end system objectives and for analyzing the timeliness, dependability, and scalability of distributed real-time systems. It is being considered an important paradigm for building real-time systems for the following reasons:

• When the real-time system is highly dynamic, its loading can vary significantly over time with no upper bound. Therefore a system description that can accommodate this dynamic variability is required, and any static resource allocation scheme (based on an artificially imposed upper bound) will lead to poor resource utilization.

• Most of the system specifications directly translate into timeliness constraints (deadlines) only for higher-level execution paths. Therefore a task-based description of the system will require imposing artificial deadlines on individual tasks, whereas the problem specification imposes a timeliness constraint only on the execution of a sequence of tasks.

• Scheduling paths as a whole rather than individual tasks (that constitute these paths) makes more sense, especially in the context of failures. For example, consider a path consisting of a sequence of four tasks. Suppose the first two tasks execute successfully but the third task is not schedulable. In this case, the execution of tasks 1 and 2 results in a wastage of resources. A much better strategy would have been to initiate executions of tasks 1 and 2 only if the entire path is schedulable.

• Paths being an abstraction of larger granularity than tasks, the scheduling algorithm has a smaller number of scheduling entities to be handled in the case of a dynamic path-based scheduler. This lowers the scheduling cost.

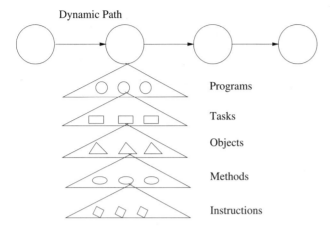

Figure 6.13
Software architecture of dynamic paths

6.8.1   Dynamic Paths

A dynamic path is an abstraction of larger granularity than the traditional task abstraction. Figure 6.13 illustrates the layers of software that make up any stage in a dynamic path. A particular software component in a dynamic path is usually composed of a collection of executable programs. These programs are composed of concurrent threads of control (tasks), which are in turn implemented in terms of objects/packages. The objects encapsulate a set of methods (procedures) composed of program instructions. As defined in [15], a dynamic path consists of a data/event source, a data/event stream, and a data/event consumer. The data/event source produces data/events, which cause the data/event consumer to perform processing. Based on the nature of the source and consumer, dynamic paths can be classified into the following categories:

• *Transient path.* A transient path (TP) consists of an event source, an event stream, and an event consumer. A TP is activated by an event, which causes the consumer to initiate an action. The response to the event must occur within a specified amount of time, which is the *required latency* or *activation deadline* of the path. Usually, timeliness is very critical for TPs, and this activation deadline is hard.

• *Continuous path.* A continuous path (CP) consists of a data source, a data stream, and a data consumer. The data stream is a set of data elements with attributes. The data source cyclically produces updates about the attributes of the elements in the data stream, which are processed by the data consumer. The set of elements in the data stream can change with time. CPs can be characterized by their *cycle deadline,* which is the time by which all the elements in the data stream must have been processed once. *Tactical throughput* (the number of elements processed per unit time) and *data interprocessing time* (the time interval between successive updates to a data element) are measures that characterize the timeliness of a CP.

• *Quasi-continuous path.* A quasi-continuous path (QCP) is activated and deactivated by events. However, between the activation and deactivation events, a QCP behaves like a CP, cyclically processing the items in a data stream. Each QCP has a *deactivation deadline,* which is the time by which it must be deactivated. This deadline is usually determined upon activation.

6.8.2   Scheduling at the Path Level

In a traditional task-level description of a distributed real-time system, the entities that are used for scheduling purposes are *tasks.* However, when the system is described in terms of the dynamic path-based paradigm, a scheduling strategy based on *paths* is more appropriate, as discussed above.

6.8.2.1   Static Scheduling   In the dynamic path-based paradigm, the continuous paths generated by assuming a load equal to the system's minimum load are scheduled by means of an off-line scheduler using an algorithm similar to the one discussed in [17]. The algorithm works as follows (refer to figure 6.14):

• An initial schedule is constructed based on sequential execution.

• The initial schedule is evaluated to see if all timing constraints are satisfied and if the schedule can be improved.

• If improvement is required, then a set of *critical paths* is identified (which are the bottlenecks in a feasible schedule because of their completion times). The candidates for these critical paths are evaluated based on their effect on the entire schedule, the utilization and availability of resources, and the amount of concurrency that can be produced if they are parallelized.

• The execution times of the selected critical paths are then reduced through concurrency exploiting techniques such as ARPCs and cloning, and a new schedule is once again constructed and tested for feasibility.

• These last two steps are repeated until either a feasible schedule is constructed or there is no further chance of exploiting concurrency.

The concurrency analysis of these paths, along with the computation of their schedule, can be conducted completely off-line and stored as a table for use during dispatch.

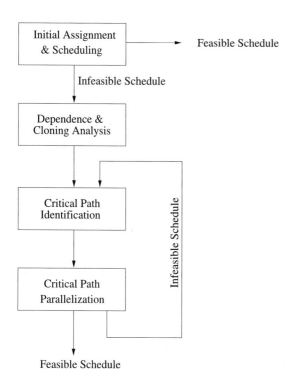

Figure 6.14
Structure of off-line scheduler

6.8.2.2 Dynamic Scheduling For dynamically arriving transient paths and for continuous paths generated by loads exceeding the minimum load, the scheduling strategy presented in [7] can be used. Figure 6.15 illustrates the major steps in the algorithm:

- Upon arrival, a path P_i is first subjected to a feasibility test (path admission test) that involves computing the laxity $L_i = D_i - (AT_i + C_i)$, where D_i, AT_i, and C_i are deadline, arrival time, and computation time of P_i, respectively, and checking whether the path has sufficient laxity to allow for running of the scheduler itself. If the path has enough slack time L_i such that

$$L_i > WCET_{guarantee} + WCET_{parallelize} + K_{cs} + P_{scheduler} + K_d,$$

where $WCET_{guarantee}$ is the worst-case execution time of the guarantee routines, $WCET_{parallelize}$ is the worst-case execution time of the parallelizing routines, K_{cs} is the overhead for the context switch between scheduler and parallelizing routine, $P_{scheduler}$ is

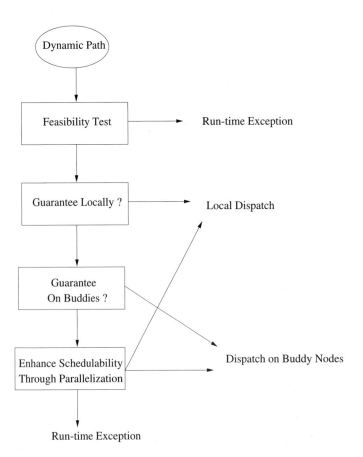

Figure 6.15
Structure of on-line scheduler

the period of the scheduler, and K_d is the dispatching overhead, then the path is scheduled either locally or on a set of processing nodes (PNs). If the path fails the admission test, a run time exception is raised.

- The guarantee routine computes the latest start time, $LST_i = D_i - C_i$, of the path and checks whether there exists a time interval (t_p, t_q) at the local PN such that $t_p \leq LST_i, D_i \leq t_q$, and there is a free time slot $FTS \in (t_p, t_q)$ such that the length of FTS is greater than $C_i + K_{cs}$. If this is satisfied, then the path can be scheduled on the local PN with a start time equal to the start time of FTS.

- If the path cannot be scheduled on the local PN, then information from a set of *buddy nodes* (in physical proximity to this local node) is checked to see if the path can be guaranteed on one of them. Here, a possible free time slot on a buddy node must accommodate for the time to load and context switch that path on the transferred node.

• If none of the buddies can guarantee the dynamic path because their surplus time is insufficient to do so, then the path is parallelized to reduce its completion time and allow it to run on a set of buddy nodes that has an amount of surplus time less than the path's execution time. Those nodes that have some surplus time during the interval (t_p, t_q) but not enough to run the unparallelized path may now be able to be used (to run the parallelized path).

• If the path cannot be scheduled even after parallelizing in the previous step, a run time exception is once again raised.

For the parallelization of the paths in the last step, techniques similar to the ones in the off-line scheduling algorithm, such as cloning and ARPCs, are employed. Also, the parallelized schedule, along with the reduced completion time for every dynamic path that could be created in the system, is maintained in a table. Thus during run time, when a guarantee routine fails, the parallelizing routine needs only to consult this table in conjunction with the surplus time information from the buddy nodes.

6.9 Summary

• A software crisis is a phenomenon in which the rate at which software is developed and maintained does not keep pace with its demand.

• Algorithmic decomposition and object-based decomposition are (currently) the two main solutions to the software crisis.

• The object-based technique has the advantages of abstraction, encapsulation, modularity, and reusability. These have made the object-based technique a preferable solution to the algorithmic approach for software development. The object-based technique has also emerged as a good tool for tackling the software crisis.

• Real-time systems need to be dependable. Thus, software for such systems has to be correct, reliable, and safe. The properties of object-based techniques make them well-suited to develop dependable real-time software and also to tackle the complex nature of such software.

• The object-based technique does have some disadvantages: a large number of procedure calls and the contention among methods to access objects.

• In an attempt to solve these two problems, the chapter presented a pre–run time scheduling algorithm for object-based tasks on distributed systems. This algorithm uses ARPCs and cloning to achieve parallelism.

• The dynamic path is a higher-level abstraction than the conventional task abstraction and is useful for describing systems with dynamic variability.

• The dynamic path-based paradigm, which is based on dynamic paths, is convenient for specifying end-to-end system objectives and for analyzing the timeliness, dependability, and scalability of distributed real-time systems.

Exercises

1. What is the software crisis? Do you think it really exists? If it does, do you think it should be called a *crisis*? If it does not, why not?

2. What are the advantages of object-based techniques? Why are object-based techniques, but not object-oriented techniques, used in real-time systems software?

3. What is the difference between

(a) LPC and RPC?

(b) SRPC and ARPC?

4. What types of objects are difficult to clone? Why?

5. Outline the main steps of the algorithm presented in the chapter for scheduling object-based real-time tasks on distributed systems.

6. Two methods, M_{11} and M_{21}, belonging to different objects O_1 and O_2 respectively, communicate as shown in figure 6.16.

(a) Calculate the value of $NADV_{11,21}$.

(b) Calculate the value of $CNADV_{1,2}$, given that M_{11} is called three times up to the planning cycle.

(c) Calculate the value of $CNADV_{2,1}$.

(d) Calculate the value of the gain/loss heuristic, given that M_{11} and M_{21} are the only methods in their respective objects—O_1 and O_2—and that M_{21} is not called by any other method in the planning cycle. $G_{max} = 30$; $L_{min} = -30$; $EPC_{max} = 75$; $EP_{min} = 50$.

7. An object-based real-time application for a mine pump and control system is given in figure 6.17. Both tasks *SafetyChecker.Check* and *MethaneMonitor.Monitor* have a deadline of 22 time units. Status is a stateful object. All other objects are stateless and non-environment-dependent.

(a) Identify the SRPCs and the ARPCs.

(b) Construct the schedule for this task graph using the algorithm presented in this chapter. Use method-level clustering.

(c) Does the algorithm produce a feasible schedule?

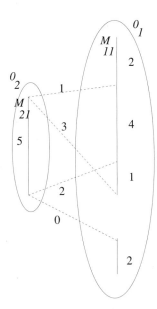

Figure 6.16
Exercise 6.6: Communication between methods M_{11} and M_{21}

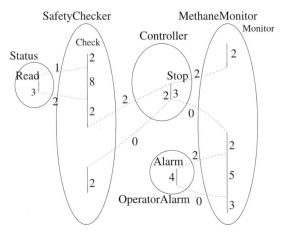

Figure 6.17
Exercise 6.7: Mine pump and control system

References

[1] G. Booch. *Software Components with ADA*. Benjamin/Cummings, California, 1987.

[2] D. E. Harms and B. W. Weide. "Copying and swapping: Influences on the design of reusable software components." *IEEE Trans. Software Engg.*, vol. 17, no. 5, pp. 424–435, May 1991.

[3] M. Joseph (ed.). *Real-Time Systems Specification, Verification, and Analysis*. International Series in Computer Science, Prentice Hall, London, 1996.

[4] D. T. Peng and K. G. Shin. "Static allocation of periodic tasks with precedence constraints in distributed real-time systems." In *Proc. Intl. Conf. on Distributed Computing Systems,* June 1989.

[5] K. Ramamritham and J. A. Stankovic. "Scheduling algorithms and operating systems for real-time systems." *Proc. IEEE,* vol. 82, no. 1, pp. 55–67, Jan. 1994.

[6] K. Ramamritham. "Allocation and scheduling of precedence-related periodic tasks." *IEEE Trans. Parallel and Distributed Systems,* vol. 6, no. 4, pp. 412–420, Apr. 1995.

[7] B. Ravindran and L. R. Welch. "Exploiting parallelism in high performance embedded system scheduling." In *Proc. IEEE Intl. Conf. on High Performance Computing,* Trivandrum, India, 1996.

[8] I. Santhoshkumar, G. Manimaran, and C. Siva Ram Murthy. "A pre-run-time scheduling algorithm for object-based distributed real-time systems." *Journal of Systems Architecture,* vol. 45, no. 14, pp. 1169–1188, July 1999.

[9] J. P. C. Verhoosel, D. K. Hammer, G. Yu, and L. R. Welch. "Pre-run-time scheduling for object-based, concurrent, real-time applications." In *Proc. Workshop on Real-Time Applications,* July 1994.

[10] J. P. C. Verhoosel, D. K. Hammer, E. Y. Luit, L. R. Welch, and A. D. Stoyenko. "A model for scheduling of object-based distributed real-time systems." *Real-Time Systems,* vol. 8, no. 1, pp. 5–34, Jan. 1995.

[11] J. P. C. Verhoosel, L. R. Welch, D. K. Hammer, and E. J. Luit. "Incorporating temporal considerations during assignment and pre-run-time scheduling of objects and processes." *Journal of Parallel and Distributed Computing,* vol. 36, no. 1, pp. 13–31, July 1996.

[12] B. W. Weide, W. F. Ogden, and S. H. Zweben. "Reusable software components." In *Advances in Computers* (M.C. Yovits, ed.), vol. 33, pp. 1–65, Academic Press, 1991.

[13] L. R. Welch. "Assignment of ADT modules to processors." In *Proc. Intl. Parallel Processing Symp.,* Mar. 1992.

[14] L. R. Welch. "A parallel virtual machine for programs composed of abstract data types." *IEEE Trans. Computers,* vol. 43, no. 11, pp. 1249–1261, Nov. 1994.

[15] L. R. Welch. "Large-grain, dynamic control system architectures." In *Proc. Workshop on Parallel and Distributed Real-Time Systems,* IEEE, Geneva, 1997.

[16] J. Xu and D. L. Parnas. "Scheduling processes with release times, deadlines, precedence, and exclusion relations." *IEEE Trans. Software Engg.,* vol. 16, no. 3, pp. 360–369, Mar. 1990.

[17] G. Yu and L. R. Welch. "A novel approach to off-line scheduling in real-time systems." *Informatica,* vol. 19, no. 1, pp. 71–83, Feb. 1995.

[18] G. Yu. "Identifying and exploiting concurrency in object-based real-time systems." Ph.D. diss., New Jersey Institute of Technology, Jan. 1996.

7 Real-Time Communication in Wide Area Networks

Overview

In this chapter, we first discuss the need for real-time communication in wide area networks. Then we describe the traffic models and performance requirements of real-time applications. We next present an architecture for resource management in real-time networks and discuss each of its components in detail. Then we discuss switching architecture. Finally, we present a classification of message scheduling disciplines and describe several well-known scheduling algorithms under each of these classes.

7.1 Introduction

The technological advances in the last decade have revolutionized communication systems. The speed and capacity of various components in a communication system, such as transmission media, switches, processors, and memory, have grown either linearly or in many cases exponentially in the past decade. The advent of high-speed networking has introduced opportunities for new applications, such as real-time distributed computation, remote control systems, video conferencing, medical imaging, and scientific visualization.

The characteristics of real-time applications differ significantly from those of corresponding non-real-time systems. Real-time communication is distinguished by the fact that the value of the communication depends on the times at which the messages are delivered to the recipient. Typically, the desired delivery time for each message across the network is bounded by a specific maximum delay or latency, resulting in a deadline being associated with each message. If a message arrives at the destination after its deadline has expired, its value to the application may be greatly reduced.

Similar to real-time computing applications, real-time communication applications are commonly classified as either *soft* or *hard*. They differ in the following way:

- Soft real-time applications can tolerate some amount of lost messages, whereas hard real-time applications have zero loss tolerance.

- In general, soft real-time applications have less stringent service requirements and thus allow the network that runs them to maximize its utilization, whereas hard real-time applications require deterministic predictability on network delays, and hence maximizing the network utilization is of secondary importance.

Most real-time applications have stringent performance requirements in terms of throughput, delay, delay jitter, and loss rate. The *delay jitter* of a real-time connection is the maximum variation in delay experienced by messages that travel across the connection. For example, if the minimum delay seen by a message on a particular connection is 1 msec and the maximum delay is 5 msec, then the delay jitter of that connection is 4 msec. Many real-time applications, particularly those that are interactive, require a bound on jitter, in addition to a bound on delay. For example, continuous media traffic (e.g., video and audio playback) is sensitive to both delay and delay jitter but can tolerate occasional message loss. Discrete media traffic (e.g., file transfer and image retrieval) requires error-free service but is tolerant of both delay and delay jitter. Some applications have specific requirements that the network that runs them must also support. For example, video conferencing requires multicast service for group distribution, and interactive television requires switched point-to-point services and asymmetric bandwidth between the upstream (user to the video server) and the downstream (video server to user) directions. There is an ever-increasing demand for network services that support these applications.

One of the most important issues in providing performance guarantees is the choice of the message service discipline (message scheduling) at the intermediate node (switch). In a packet switching network, messages from different connections interact with each other at each switch. The message scheduling algorithms at the switches determine the order in which the packets from different connections are serviced. Recently, a number of message scheduling algorithms have been proposed that aim at providing per-connection performance guarantees in the context of high-speed packet switching networks. Some of these algorithms provide deterministic guarantees, some provide statistical guarantees, and some provide both. Hard real-time communication requires deterministic guarantees, whereas for soft real-time communication, such as multimedia, statistical guarantees suffice.

7.2 Service and Traffic Models and Performance Requirements

In this section, we discuss service models, traffic characterization, and performance requirements of real-time applications, as well as some related issues.

7.2.1 Approaches to Real-Time Communication

There are several mechanisms for supporting real-time communication in wide area networks.

1. *Pure circuit switching* can easily provide real-time guarantees on message delivery. However, it sets aside a fixed portion of network bandwidth according to the peak band-

width requirement of each connection. Since most real-time traffic is bursty in nature, this leads to low effective bandwidth utilization.

2. *Pure packet switching* can efficiently utilize network bandwidth but cannot provide real-time guarantees.

3. *Packet-oriented switching,* in which a virtual channel is established before transmission begins, employs statistical multiplexing to utilize bandwidth efficiently. Asynchronous transfer mode (ATM) technology is an example of this technique. ATM networks combine the high speeds of optical fibers, fast switching (with their simple protocol), service independence (by sending all traffic in short fixed-length packets called *cells*), and bandwidth on demand (with their dynamic allocation of bandwidth using statistical multiplexing).

7.2.2 Types of Service

A network can provide three levels of service to the applications it runs. The first two are guaranteed services, whereas the third is nonguaranteed.

1. *Guaranteed service.* Also termed *deterministic* or *hard guaranteed service,* this approach is conservative in resource reservation and is the simplest method for real-time services.

2. *Predictive service.* This service is meant for adaptive applications that can tolerate occasional violation of the delay bound. It provides a sufficiently reliable (but not absolute) delay bound, depending on the actual load on the network at any given time. Multimedia playback applications function well with this category of service.

3. *As-soon-as-possible service.* This is best-effort service with priorities, the highest to be given to interactive burst traffic and the lowest to asynchronous bulk transfer. This category of service provides no guarantees, and no resources are reserved for it, but it uses the resources alloted to the first two categories when they are idle.

The channels corresponding to these services have two phases, namely, the *channel establishment phase* and the *run time scheduling phase.* During the channel establishment phase, call admission control is performed at each node along the routing path of the call to decide whether enough resources are available to support the connection. To make this decision, the network load must be known. For guaranteed service, the network load is based on the prespecified characterization of existing connections. In the case of predictive service, it is based on the current measured traffic. Since the measured network load may vary, predictive service provides a less reliable service commitment than guaranteed service, but its utilization of network resources is superior.

7.2.3   Characterization of Real-Time Traffic

Most real-time sources generate traffic that falls into one of the following two categories:

• *Constant bit rate.* In constant bit rate (CBR) traffic, fixed-size packets are generated at regular intervals. The data generated by sensors often falls into this category. Certain real-time applications, such as air-traffic control, generate data that have less redundancy and that are too important to be compressed in a lossy way. CBR traffic most easily handles such applications, since it is smooth and nonbursty.

• *Variable bit rate.* Variable bit rate (VBR) traffic may take the form of fixed-size packets being generated at irregular intervals or of variable-sized packets being generated at regular intervals. Voice and video sources are examples of sources that generate the two types of VBR traffic. An *on-off source* alternates between a period in which fixed-size packets arrive at regular intervals and an idle period. Voice traffic exhibits this behavior: talk spurts alternate with periods of silence. The output of a video source, which encounters different compression ratios for the same output quality level, results in variable-sized packets being generated at regular intervals.

Bursty traffic requires a large amount of buffer at the nodes. Also, traffic characteristics may change as packets flow through multiple hops in a network. Traffic that was smooth at the source may become bursty at an intermediate node as various traffic classes compete for the output links of the node. As an example, consider a situation in which two traffic classes C1 (CBR with low priority) and C2 (bursty traffic with high priority) compete for the same output link at a node. Though the C1 was originally smooth at its source, some of its packet transmission may be delayed because of the presence of packets of higher-priority traffic C2. Thus, the delaying of packets of C1 to accommodate C2 will make the previously smooth C1 bursty.

7.2.4   Traffic Models

A hard real-time application requires a specific quality of service (QoS) in terms of delay, delay jitter, and loss bounds from the network. The characteristics of the traffic the application generates must be known a priori to guarantee this QoS. However, this is not possible for VBR sources, since predicting the precise nature of future VBR transmissions is impossible. Instead, several models of VBR traffic have been proposed that are statistical in nature and that do not require precise knowledge of traffic characteristics.

Peak-Rate Model: Most hard real-time systems use the peak-rate model for traffic characterization. The parameters of this model, for a connection i, are minimum interarrival time (T_i) or maximum message rate ($1/T_i$), maximum message length (τ_i), and end-to-end delay bound (D_i). The bandwidth requirement for such a connection is τ_i/T_i. The peak-rate model is exact only for CBR traffic and overstates the bandwidth requirement for all VBR sources.

Linear Bounded Arrival Process Model: The linear bounded arrival process model uses an additional parameter, maximum burst size B_i. In this model, in any time interval t, the maximum number of arriving packets may not exceed $B_i + (t/T_i)$. This model can guarantee deterministic delay bounds.

7.2.5   Performance Requirements

Parameters such as maximum end-to-end delay, delay jitter, and maximum loss rate constitute an application's performance (QoS) requirements. Throughput guarantee is also important, but it is provided automatically by the traffic characterization, that is, the bandwidth requirement. The end-to-end delay is the most important parameter for many applications that have stringent real-time requirements.

Delay jitter is important for continuous media playback applications. For such applications, the ideal case would be to have constant delay (or zero delay jitter). If a network ensures bounded delay jitter, the destination of a transmission can calculate the amount of buffers required to achieve zero delay jitter. The smaller the delay jitter bound, the less buffer space needed. The amount of buffer space required can be determined from the peak data rate and delay jitter of the connection. For example, a single video source transmitting 30 frames per second, each containing 2 Mb of data, would require a 60 Mb buffer at the destination to eliminate delay jitter, if the delay jitter experienced by the connection is 1 second. A network can bound delay jitter by delaying packets, which require storage within the network. In network design, the trade-off between shared high-speed memory within the network and lower-speed dedicated memory at the destination must be considered to control delay jitter.

Message loss occurs when delays cause messages to be delivered after their deadline or because of buffer overflow. Deterministic service provides zero loss, whereas statistical service provides nonzero loss. With deterministic service, all packets meet their performance requirements even in the worst case. With statistical service, probabilistic bounds are provided instead of worst-case bounds, and the overall network utilization increases through statistical multiplexing gain.

7.3   Resource Management

7.3.1   Introduction to Traffic Management

Most multimedia applications consist of a heterogeneous mix of video, voice, and data with diverse QoS requirements. Supporting this heterogeneity in a cohesive manner within a network is a challenging task. This section presents the controls that must be incorporated in a network to manage the traffic generated by various applications. The degree of sharing of network resources and hence the utilization that can be achieved depend on the network's bandwidth allocation strategy. When the majority of the traffic the network carries is bursty (defined by a certain ratio of average to peak rate) in nature, it is advisable to adopt an allocation close to the average rate of the generated stream. However, such an approach may lead to *congestion*. Controlling congestion in a high-speed environment is a serious and challenging problem.

7.3.1.1 Congestion and Its Control   Most multimedia sources are bursty in nature. Even the naturally stream-based sources like voice and video may be rendered bursty by the compression and coding schemes employed in their transmission. Two factors that influence the policy a network should adopt for bandwidth allocation are link utilization and guarantees provided to the applications the network runs. Guarantees can easily be provided to an application if a network employs a peak-rate allocation. However, if the sources have high burstiness, peak-rate allocation may lead to gross underutilization of bandwidth. Average-rate allocation, on the other hand, improves the utilization because of gains achieved through statistical multiplexing. The drawback in this case is the possibility of congestion, with delay/loss of cells leading to deterioration in the quality as a consequence.

7.3.1.2 Classifying Congestion   Congestion can be broadly classified, based on its duration, as short-term, medium-term, and long-term. *Short-term congestion* persists, by its nature, for durations of the order of packet transmission times. If not immediately controlled, it can lead to congestion sustained over longer durations, resulting in objectionable levels of losses and delays. *Medium-term congestion* persists over durations of the order of propagation delays. Congestion lasting for durations of the order of call duration and beyond can be classified as *long-term congestion*. Controlling each of these congestion types requires a different mechanism.

7.3.1.3 Difficulties in Congestion Control at High Speeds   Two main factors make congestion control hard at high speeds:

• The switching technology, as of now, is not compatible with existing transmission speeds. As a result, protocol processing time can be a bottleneck at high speeds. Thus, the protocols at the switches should be simple and fast.

• Increases in the ratio of propagation delay to packet transmission delay are another factor that makes congestion control at high speeds difficult. This phenomenon is explained as follows:

Let C be the capacity of the network (in Mbps), b be the packet length (in bits), and L be the length of the network (in miles). These parameters can be combined to form a single network parameter, commonly denoted as a, which is the ratio of the latency of the channel (i.e., the time it takes energy to move from one end of the link to another) to the time it takes to pump one packet into the link [10]. It measures how many packets can be pumped into one end of the link before the first bit appears at the other end. It is defined as $a = 5LC/b$. The factor 5 appearing in the equation is simply the approximate number of microseconds it takes light to move one mile.

Consider the following example. In a typical case, assume two switching nodes are separated by 100 miles of cable (L); packet size is 1K bits (b). For a 1 Mbps (C) link, packet transmission time ($= b/C$) is 1 ms, whereas at 1 Gbps, packet transmission time becomes 1 μs. Since the propagation delay ($= 5L$) remains the same at 0.5 ms, the ratio of propagation time to transmission time has now increased thousandfold at 1 Gbps. That is, the value of a is 0.5 at 1Mbps and is 500 at 1Gbps. This means that before any congestion information can travel back to the source node, more than 500 packets have already been pumped into the link. Thus any of the techniques successfully employed for transmission at megabits speeds and below become totally ineffective at gigabits speeds, since any congestion information transmitted could become obsolete by the time it reaches the source node.

7.3.1.4 Approaches to Congestion Control

Reactive versus Proactive Control: *Reactive control* of congestion is based on the use of feedback information from the congested node to the source node for throttling the traffic flow. For the reasons stated above, such a scheme is ineffective at high speeds. The alternate strategy, *preventive control,* employs effective schemes at the network entry points and prevents the network from reaching disagreeable levels of congestion. Preventive congestion control schemes are applied at different levels: *call admission control, traffic policing,* and *packet scheduling.*

The main goal of resource management, guaranteed delivery of real-time messages, implies four main actions (figure 7.1):

1. *Call control* decides whether a given call can be admitted into the network. It has two components: *routing* and *call admission control.* The routing component aids in finding a route from the source to the destination. The call admission control tests and reserves resources during call establishment and renegotiation so that the traffic can flow according to the QoS specification. When the lifetime of a call is over, the call is torn down, which involves releasing the resources reserved for the call.

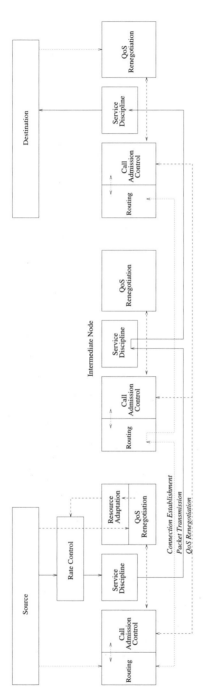

Figure 7.1
Framework for network resource management

2. *Rate control* ensures that the source does not violate the traffic (rate) contract to which it has agreed. Traffic violation occurs because of misbehaved users or inexact traffic characterization.

3. *Service discipline* allocates resources to the connections during data transfer, adhering to the reservations made during channel establishment. Three types of resources are allocated by a service discipline, namely, bandwidth, processing time (for deciding time of service), and buffer.

4. *Resource adaptation* monitors resource availability and adapts to resource changes during the ongoing real-time session through QoS renegotiation. This is particularly relevant in the context of multimedia communication, during which QoS parameters and associated resources can be changed. When such changes occur, renegotiation of QoS parameters begins. A renegotiation request can come either from the user, who wants to change the QoS, or from the network, due to overload and congestion.

7.3.2 Call Control

7.3.2.1 Routing during Real-Time Channel Establishment Before any real-time message can be transmitted, a real-time channel must be established that has the traffic characteristics and the performance requirements specified by the call. This involves selection of a (qualified) route for the channel that can satisfy its QoS requirements and traffic characteristics without compromising on the guarantees of the existing channels. That is, when a new request comes in, a set of call admission control conditions are tested at each node along the path from the sender to the receiver. If the call admission test is successful at a given node, the resources required by the call are reserved at that node. For multimedia traffic, the QoS negotiation might take place between the network and end systems.

Broadly speaking, there are two schemes for real-time channel establishment: *single-pass* and *two-pass* schemes [18]. A two-pass scheme [6] has two phases: the *reservation phase* (forward pass) and the *relaxation phase* (reverse pass). The forward pass proceeds from the source to the destination of the call, and the reverse pass proceeds in the opposite direction. A typical two-pass channel establishment scheme works as follows:

Reservation Phase

1. The initiator of the call sends traffic specification and QoS requirements in a reservation message (connection request).

2. The routing component selects the best link for the channel (neighbor node), based on the routing algorithm used, and then consults the call admission control module to check whether the call request can be admitted on the selected link.

3. If the call admission is not successful, the routing algorithm may select next-best link or reject the call.

4. If the call admission is successful, the resources requested by the call, such as bandwidth and buffers, are reserved, and the call request is passed on to the selected neighbor node.

5. Steps 2–4 are repeated until the destination of the call is reached or the call is rejected.

6. If the call is rejected at an intermediate node or by the destination, the resources reserved along the path up to that point are released.

Relaxation Phase

1. Once the forward pass is successful, the destination initiates the reverse pass.

2. During the reverse pass, the resources that were allocated excessively during the forward pass are released, so that these excess resources can be allocated to other calls.

Since the two-pass scheme reserves no more resources than are required by a particular call, a routing algorithm using the two-pass scheme always offers a higher average call acceptance rate than its single-pass counterpart. On the other hand, since the single-pass scheme has no relaxation phase, it offers a low average call setup time. In a two-pass scheme, the required resources must be reserved during the forward pass so that other calls cannot reserve the same resources during their forward passes. This averts the possibility of two or more calls confirming the same resource during their reverse passes.

7.3.2.2 Call Admission Control The purpose of call admission control is to determine which resources are required to provide the QoS requested by a particular connection, determine if these resources are available, and then reserve these resources if they are available. The resources that need to be reserved are mainly buffer space at each node and link bandwidth along the path from the sender to the receiver of the connection. The admission control algorithm consists of a set of tests, generally of three types:

• A *link bandwidth test* for throughput guarantees.

• A *spatial test* for buffer allocation, to provide delay jitter and reliability guarantees.

• A *scheduler saturation test,* which is necessary to avoid a situation in which it is impossible to meet deadline constraints. For example, suppose a node receives two packets at the same time from two different channels. Let their respective node service times be 4 and 3 and their respective node deadlines 6 and 6. There is no way to schedule the packets so that both meet their deadlines.

Usually different service disciplines require different admission control tests. A complete solution to managing real-time channels needs to specify both the service discipline and associated call admission control tests.

7.3.3 Rate Control

In a resource sharing packet switching network, the admission control and scheduling scheme by themselves are not sufficient to provide performance guarantees, because users may, inadvertently or otherwise, attempt to exceed the rates specified at the time of channel establishment. The primary aim of the rate control or traffic policer is to enforce the source traffic's compliance with the negotiated values of the characteristics throughout the life of the channel. It can also shape the input stream so that its characteristics are amenable to the scheduling mechanisms to provide the required QoS guarantees, in which case it is referred to as a traffic shaper. There is a subtle difference between enforcement and shaping functions. The former checks the input stream for conformance with the negotiated values, whereas the latter shapes it to be more agreeable to the scheduling policies. The rate controller performs the required regulation at the sending host. This prevents rate violation at the sending host and intermediate nodes and buffer overflow at the receivers. The leaky bucket algorithm [19], the jumping window scheme, and the shift register-based traffic shaper [16] are examples of traffic shapers.

7.3.3.1 Leaky Bucket   The leaky bucket (LB) algorithm implements a linear bounded arrival process (LBAP) by defining a bucket containing up to B_i tokens. LB for a stream i is characterized by two parameters: the bucket size (token buffer size) B_i, which decides the maximum burst size, and the token generation rate T_{ti}. The basic LB algorithm works as follows: The LB shaper consists of a token counter and a timer. The counter is incremented by one every T_{ti} units of time and can reach a maximum value of B_i. A packet of the stream is admitted into the network only if the token count is positive when it arrives. Otherwise, the packet is either discarded or buffered at the data buffer. Each time a packet is admitted, the counter is decremented by one. By this arrangement, an average rate of $1/T_{ti}$ is enforced on the admitted traffic. The maximum burst size is restricted to B_i.

Clearly, T_{ti} should be greater than the average arrival rate T_{ai} for stability and less than the peak arrival rate T_{pi} for maximizing bandwidth utilization. An input data buffer of size b_i permits statistical variations. An arriving packet finding the input buffer full is said to be a *violating packet* and can be dropped.

Figure 7.2 shows a generalized model of a leaky bucket traffic shaper in which a peak-rate limiting spacer is assumed to be an integral part. When a burst arrives at the input, even if enough tokens are present to permit admission, the packets are not instantaneously

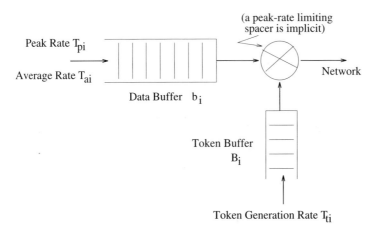

Figure 7.2
Generalized model of leaky bucket

admitted into the network. Successive packets are delayed by τ_i, the transmission time at negotiated peak rate $\tau_i = 1/T_{pi}$. This is referred to as leaky bucket with (peak-rate) policing (LBP). For the leaky bucket parameters defined above, the maximum burst size at the output is $\overline{B}_i = B_i/(1 - T_{ti}/T_{pi})$. This includes the new tokens that arrive during the transmission of the first B_i packets.

7.3.3.2 Jumping Window In the jumping window scheme, access to the network is regulated by limiting the number of cells (fixed-size packets) buffered for transmission within a fixed time interval to a maximum number N. A new interval starts at the end of the preceding interval. Since bursts of two consecutive windows can coincide, the worst-case burst size admitted into the network is $2N$. In a variation of this scheme, called triggered jumping window, the time windows are not consecutive, but rather are triggered by the first arriving cell.

7.3.3.3 Shift Register Traffic Shaper The shift register traffic shaper (SRTS) makes use of the temporal profile of the packet stream admitted by the traffic shaper over the immediate past N time slots, where a time slot τ refers to the reciprocal of the peak rate. This temporal history can be maintained by a shift register, with a bit 1 corresponding to every packet sent. The shift register is shifted once to the right every time slot τ. The N slots are viewed as three windows (figure 7.3): one window, W_1, which limits the maximum burst size; a second window, W_2, for long-term average policing, corresponding conceptually to the two LBP parameters; and a third window, W_3, for providing a vari-

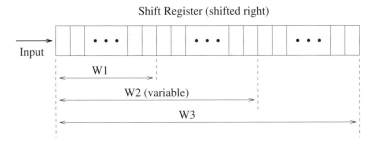

Figure 7.3
SRTS's view of shift register

able burstiness feature. A packet is admitted into the network only when the following holds:

$$(n_1 < \hat{n}_1) \wedge (n_2 < \hat{n}_2) \wedge (n_3 < \hat{n}_3),$$

where n_i refers to the number of bit 1s in the ith window W_i of size N_i, and $\hat{n}_i$ is the corresponding maximum count permitted. T_i denotes the time duration of window W_i, so that $T_i = \tau N_i$. Thus the bit contents of the shift register, at any instant, provide an image of the history of the packets sent. The SRTS scheme generates an $(\hat{n}_1, T_1; \hat{n}_2, T_2; \hat{n}_3, T_3)$ smooth traffic, which means that over any period of duration T_i, the number of packets $n(T_i) \leq \hat{n}_i$. By using window W_3 with a proper choice of window parameters, SRTS provides an adjustable burstiness feature while complying with the LB bounds over a predicted duration.

7.3.4 Service Discipline

Whereas a call admission control algorithm reserves resources when a call is established, a packet service discipline allocates resources, according to the reservation, during data transfer. Three types of resources are allocated by a service discipline [23]: (1) bandwidth (which packets get transmitted), (2) promptness (when these packets get transmitted), and (3) buffer space (which packets are discarded). These resources correspond to QoS parameters throughput, delay, and loss rate, respectively. The corresponding network mechanisms are *regulation, scheduling,* and *buffer management,* as shown in figure 7.4.

The end-to-end deadline of a channel is divided into per-node deadlines. The scheduler at each node should ensure that the node's packets are transmitted before their deadlines. As mentioned earlier, delay jitter can be controlled by having a buffer at the destination and intentionally delaying early-arriving packets at intermediate nodes. The scheduling

QoS parameter	network mechanism
Throughput	Traffic shaping
Delay and delay jitter	Scheduling
Loss	Buffer management

Figure 7.4
QoS parameters and network mechanisms

mechanism has to take into account this aspect also. Multimedia applications, especially, require efficient buffer management at the end systems to avoid traditional data copying.

7.3.5   Resource Adaptation

For the purpose of adaptation, resources are monitored at the end hosts as well as at the intermediate nodes during data transmission. This monitoring function continuously observes whether the processed QoS parameters for the transmission are exceeding their negotiated values. Resource adaptation is applicable for continuous media applications and is achieved by (1) notification to the parties involved in transmission of change and renegotiation of QoS parameters and (2) adaptation of resources to accommodate changes at the end hosts, the intermediate nodes, or both. A change in QoS can be initiated by either the sender or the receiver of a connection. If the sender requires a change in QoS, this may imply the need to adapt sender, intermediate nodes, and receiver. The necessary changes are incorporated subject to admission control.

7.3.6   Goals of Real-Time Communication Mechanisms

A real-time communication mechanism aims to provide the following:

• low delay and low delay jitter
• adaptability to dynamically changing network load and traffic conditions
• ability to integrate real-time and non-real-time services
• high effective bandwidth utilization
• high call acceptance rate, low call setup time, and low cost paths for channels
• scalability with increasing network size
• efficient packet processing and buffer management

7.3.7   Network Model

In the rest of this chapter, we make the following assumptions about the network with which we are dealing:

1. The nodes of the network are connected using an arbitrary topology.

2. The network provides guaranteed communication service, that is, predictive service is not considered.

3. The communication mechanism is of packet switching type.

4. The channel establishment uses a two-pass scheme.

7.3.8 Routing and Switching Tables

During channel establishment, routing is used (i.e., a routing table is consulted) in probing for a path for the channel, and a unique channel identifier is assigned to the channel. The assignment of identifiers to a channel is either distributed or centralized. In distributed assignment, the sequence of locally unique identifiers, along the path, defines the channel, whereas in centralized assignment, a globally unique identifier is assigned to each channel, and this value is the same at every node along the path. The distributed channel identifier scheme can be further classified into two subcases:

• Identifier space per node. In this scheme, all channels passing through any of the links at a given node use the same identifier space. When a new call arrives at or departs from a node, the node has to assign the next free identifier, which is taken from the identifier space of the node, to that channel.

• Identifier space per link of a node. In this scheme, every link of a node has its own separate identifier space. When a new call arrives or departs a node, the node has to assign the next free identifier for that channel from the identifier space of the link in which the call arrives or departs.

7.3.8.1 Switching Table   Each node maintains a switching table that stores routing information about the channels passing through the node. Once a channel has been established, an entry is made in the switching table of each node along the path of the call. If a distributed scheme is used for assigning identifiers, then the *Out Channel ID* of a channel at a node should be the same as the *In Channel ID* of its succeeding node for that channel, so that the sequence of locally unique channel identifiers results in a valid channel (path).

During the forward pass of a call establishment, the fields of switching tables, such as *In Link, In Channel ID,* and *Out Link,* that pertain to that call are filled at all the nodes along the path of the call. When an identifier-space-per-link scheme is used, a fourth field, *Out Channel ID,* can also be filled during the forward pass, because a node can determine the next available identifier on the link at its successor node, since all the channels to the successor node on this link pass through the current node. On the other hand, when an

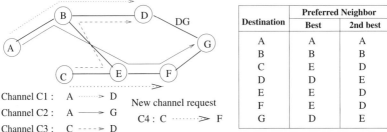

Channel C1 :   A ·······> D
Channel C2 :   A ———> G   New channel request
Channel C3 :   C ----> D   C4 : C ·······> F
(a) An arbitrary network topology

Destination	Preferred Neighbor	
	Best	2nd best
A	A	A
B	B	B
C	E	D
D	D	E
E	E	D
F	E	D
G	D	E

(b) Routing table for Node B

In Link	In CID	Out Link	Out CID
AB	1	BD	1
AB	2	BE	2
EB	3	BD	3

Switch table
for Node B

In Link	In CID	Out Link	Out CID
AB	1	BD	1
AB	2	BE	1
EB	1	BD	2

(c) Connection identifier (CID) per node scheme

(d) CID per link scheme

In Link	In CID	Out Link	Out CID
CC	1	CE	1
CC	2	CE	?

In Link	In CID	Out Link	Out CID
BE	2	EF	1
CE	1	EB	3
CE	3	EF	?

In Link	In CID	Out Link	Out CID
EF	1	FG	1
EF	2	FF	2

filled during reverse pass   filled during reverse pass

Node C   Node E   Node F
(e) Switch table updation (CID per node scheme) at nodes along the path of channel C4 during call establishment

Figure 7.5
Routing and switching tables

identifier-space-per-node scheme is employed, the entry *Out Channel ID* is filled during the reverse pass, because a node cannot know the available channel identifier for the *In Channel ID* in the succeeding node, since channels to/via the successor node can have different links associated with them. Once the call request reaches its destination, the destination can decide its *Out Channel ID* on its own. During the reverse pass, the *In Channel ID* of a node is copied to the *Out Channel ID* of its predecessor node in all the nodes along the path of the call. When the reverse pass reaches the source, the call is accepted, and the channel is identified as a sequence of locally unique identifiers.

Figure 7.5(a) shows an example of a network topology with three connections already established. The link between two nodes A and B is denoted as AB. We use the following convention for the fields in the switching table: If a node A is source of a call, then its

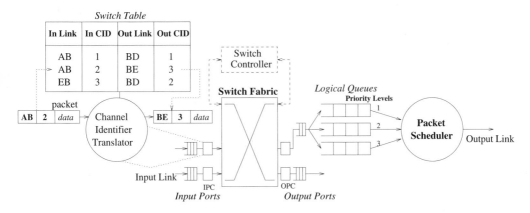

Figure 7.6
General architecture of a switching node

In Link is AA to signify the call originated locally. Similarly, if node B is destination of a call, then its *Out Link* is BB to signify that there is no outlink for the call. The routing table for node B is given in figure 7.5(b). The switching tables for node B with node and link identifier space are given in figures 7.5(c) and (d), respectively. The routing table uses shortest-path routing, and the switching table has entries for the three established connections given in figures 7.5(c) and (d), assuming initially there were no connections. Suppose a new connection request originates at node C, asking to establish a connection to node F. Assume the QoS of the call can be satisfied by the shortest-path route; that is, the path for the new call is $C \rightsquigarrow E \rightsquigarrow F$. Figure 7.5(e) depicts how switching table entries are filled for the new call ($C \rightsquigarrow F$) during the forward and reverse passes in an identifier-space-per-node scheme.

7.3.9 Processing at a Node

Each message carries the identifiers for its path during its transmission. The sequence of processing steps involved at each intermediate (switching) node during transmission is given below. Steps 1 and 3 are performed at the source and destination nodes. Typical processing in a node is shown in figure 7.6.

1. *Translation:* When locally unique channel identifiers are used, a virtual channel identifier (VCI) is translated from one to another.

2. *Switching:* The physical transportation of messages from the input link (port) to the desired output link (port) is referred to as switching. The output ports are logically divided into different priority levels corresponding to different guarantees. Each port has an associated port controller.

3. *Scheduling:* Each packet to be transmitted is enqueued into the output queue (priority level) of the link with which it is associated. The role of scheduling is to decide the transmission time of packets waiting in the output queue of each link. Typical node processing per output link is given in figure 7.6.

7.4   Switching Subsystem

The term *switching system* of the network refers to the functional unit in the network that interconnects external (network) links. The switching subsystem is responsible for receiving cells from external links and routing and transmitting them on appropriate external links. Within the switching subsystem, a *switching fabric* performs the actual routing function. Many switching fabrics are constructed by interconnecting a number of smaller building blocks, called *switching elements.*

Figure 7.6 shows the general architecture of a switching subsystem. Input port controllers (IPCs) and output port controllers (OPCs) are present at the respective ports. The IPC contains a VCI table that maps each input VCI to an output VCI, and an output port address. Before a given cell is released into the switching fabric, its input VCI is replaced with an output VCI, and an output port address is appended for self-routing. The main functions performed by different units of the switching subsystem are discussed below:

• *IPCs* typically provide buffering, cell processing, VCI translation, and cell duplication for multicasting and multiplexing traffics.

• *OPCs* typically provide buffering and demultiplexing.

• The *switching fabric* routes cells from input ports to output ports. It commonly deals with the following issues: (1) establishing paths between input and output ports within the fabric, (2) contention resolution for cells contending for the links or other internal resources of the switch, and (3) supporting multiple connections simultaneously between input and output ports.

Multistage interconnection network (MIN)–based switching fabrics are based on switching elements organized in stages. Switching fabrics in which interconnections are restricted to elements in adjacent stages are referred to as *regular;* otherwise they are said to be *irregular.*

• Generally, each *switching element* (SE) is built on a single integrated circuit (IC). Because of pin limitations, each IC has a fixed amount of I/O bandwidth. A 2×2 switching element operates in four ways (figure 7.7): (1) straight mode, (2) cross mode, (3) upper broadcast, and (4) lower broadcast. In straight mode, the cell from input I_k is intended for output O_k, for $k = 0, 1$. In cross mode, the cell from input I_k is intended for output O_{1-k},

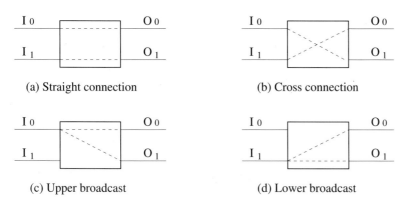

(a) Straight connection   (b) Cross connection

(c) Upper broadcast   (d) Lower broadcast

Figure 7.7
2×2 switching element with possible valid states

for $k = 0, 1$. In the upper (lower) broadcast, the cell from input I_0 (I_1) is intended for both outputs O_0 and O_1.

• The *switch controller* is also called the management and control processor. Its job is to communicate with controllers of the various ports involved and facilitate switch operation, administration, and management. The switch controller checks for the availability of cells at the inputs in every time slot.

7.4.1 Design Issues in Switching Systems

Some major design issues for a switching subsystem are outlined below:

Blocking versus nonblocking: Switching fabrics can be classified as blocking or non-blocking. In those that are blocking, blocking can take two forms: *Internal link blocking* occurs in cases where two cells contend for a particular link inside the switching fabric. *Output port blocking* occurs when two or more cells are contending for the same output port. To deal with output port blocking, queues are employed to buffer contending cells. There are a number of ways to reduce internal blocking:

• Place buffers in every SE.

• Add extra stages to the MIN and produce extra paths.

• Use deflection routing when extra stages are present in the MIN. *Deflection routing* is a scheme in which a cell, instead of being buffered at an intermediate SE, is intentionally misrouted based on certain heuristics but still reaches its destination, via a slightly longer path.

• Use a hand-shaking mechanism between stages or a back-pressure mechanism to delay the transfer of the blocked cell.

• Use multiple networks in parallel to provide multiple paths from any input to any output or multiple links for each switch connection.

• Install a distribution network in front of the switch to reduce or eliminate the possibility of internal link blocking. For example, in a batcher-banyan network, a sorting network is used in front of the shuffle exchange network to sort output port requests that do not cause internal link blocking from those that do.

• Recirculate cells that cause blocking (in switches with recirculating capability) and route them in the next cycle.

Buffering in SEs: Buffers can be employed at each SE to avoid internal link blocking. However, there are problems associated with buffering in SEs:

• It is difficult to estimate the exact buffer size necessary to eliminate internal link blocking.

• The complexity of the switch increases as the buffer size of the SE increases.

• Different types of buffer partitions are required for real-time and non-real-time traffic.

• Buffering in optical networks requires optical signal to electrical signal conversion to buffer the cells in electronic buffers and electrical to optical conversion to route the cells from the buffer.

Moreover, when traffic is heavy to a few output ports (hot spot traffic), the performance of a switch deteriorates rapidly because of a phenomenon called *tree saturation* [5], in which a tree of occupied buffers is rooted at the hot spot port, spans across stages, and has leaves at the input ports. The number of occupied buffers at the root of the tree is very large and decreases along the stages toward the input port. This causes buffer overflow at the SE, resulting in cell loss, thereby reducing the level of switch performance. Various schemes have been proposed to avoid tree saturation and to ensure that hot spot traffic can be supported with little degradation to uniform traffic that is equiprobably destined to other output ports.

Queueing Performance: The location of its queues is one of the critical factors in determining the performance of a switching fabric. There are three types of queueing schemes: (1) input queueing, (2) output queueing, and (3) shared queueing.

In *input queueing,* queues are employed at each input port of a switching fabric. If multiple cells destined to the same output arrive at the inputs of the switch at the same time slot, then the *switch controller* allows only one to pass through the switch in that time slot. The others wait in their respective input queues until the switch controller allows them to pass, one at a time, in subsequent time slots. Thus, if n cells arrive (at n different inputs) at a certain time, then they reach their destination in n consecutive time slots. So long as one of these cells stopped by the switch controller is waiting in an input queue for its turn to pass through the switch, it stops any other cells in its queue, even those destined for a different output that could have traveled to their destination without contention. This phenomenon is called head-of-line (HOL) blocking. As a result of HOL blocking, a switch can remain underloaded, resulting in throughput degradation. HOL blocking limits the theoretical maximum throughput for any nonblocking space switch operating in packet-switched mode that employs input queueing with random traffic to 58% of output queueing [15]. Various techniques such as switch expansion, windowing, and channel grouping have been proposed to reduce HOL blocking.

In *output queueing,* queues are employed at each output port of a switching fabric. Multiple cells destined to the same destination are allowed to pass to the output either serially, one after another, at different, shorter time slots within one time slot of the switch, or in parallel through parallel paths in that single time slot. The first of these methods of resolving output contention is based on the time division principle. If n cells are waiting to be routed to the same output, then the flow of cells within the switch fabric must be speeded up to n times the speed of arrival of cells to the switch fabric. That is, the internal link speed of the switch must be n times that of the external link speed. The second method of resolving output contention is based on the space-time principle. To route n cells to a given output, n parallel paths are provided, and these n cells travel through the switch in a single time slot. The switch controller takes the responsibility of allocating n cells to the n parallel paths. When all these n cells arrive at the output simultaneously, they are stored in n output buffers.

In both the input queueing and output queueing schemes, each input and output has dedicated queues (buffers) connected to it. This increases the amount of buffers required, and the buffers are also underutilized because the buffers are dedicated irrespective of the traffic demand. To improve upon this, in some switches, buffers are shared by all inputs or all outputs. However, this *shared queueing* requires a complex buffer management logic.

Compared to those with input queueing architectures, switching fabrics with output queueing generally show severe implementation problems. The two different queueing strategies may be mixed, in an attempt to couple the advantages peculiar to a single strategy adopted alone.

Routing: Cells may be routed within the switching fabric based on the results of an algorithm that is run to compute the routes. The time and space complexities of such algorithms are an important performance measure. There are two approaches for routing cells:

• *Self-Routing SEs.* When using self-routing SEs, only VCI translation has to be performed at the input of the switch fabric. After the translation, an internal header is appended to each cell before it enters the switch fabric. In a switch fabric with k stages, the internal header is subdivided into k subfields (k bits when 2×2 SEs are used). Subfield i contains the destination output port of the SE in stage i.

• *Controlled SEs.* When using this approach, the switch controller sets the position of each of the SEs based on the cells at the inputs of the SEs.

Multicasting: One important requirement of a modern switching fabric is the ability to support multicasting. Multicastable switches have the capability of sending cells from one input port to many output ports. Video conferencing is an example of an application that requires multicasting.

Scalability: Switching systems are required to grow in accordance with the needs of the applications. The design of a switching fabric should facilitate easy expansion.

Reliability: Switching systems must be continuously available.

Testability: It must be possible to test a switching system while it is in operation and locate failures.

7.4.2   A Taxonomy of Switching Fabrics

A number of switching fabrics have been proposed in the literature. The design for each has some merits and demerits related to performance, complexity, modularity, and cost. A unique taxonomy of switching architectures is difficult to develop, since different parameters can be used for classification. In general, the methodology for implementing the physical connection between input and output ports within a switching fabric can be based on either a time division principle or a space division principle.

In a time division approach, the use of physical resources is multiplexed among several input-output connections based on discrete time slots. A bus is an example of a physical resource that can accommodate time division multiplexing. A shared memory, which is the repository of the cells supplied by the input ports and removed by the output ports, can also implement connections based on time division. That is, input and output ports communicate through time-multiplexed use of the shared memory. Shared-memory switches support broadcasting and are less complex compared to MIN-based switches and crossbar switches. The main drawback of the shared-medium switches is that they can support only a limited number of ports.

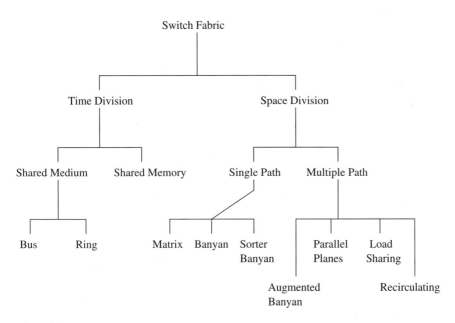

Figure 7.8
Taxonomy of switching fabrics

A taxonomy based on Newman's classification [14] is given in figure 7.8. Space division switches can also be classified based on several other parameters, such as

- the structure of their switching fabrics:
- Fabrics with a shared medium (ring, bus, etc.).
- Crossbar-based fabrics.
- Disjoint-path fabrics (trees, multiple rings, or buses).
- MINs.
- the type of service they provide internally (blocking or nonblocking).
- the location of their queues (input queueing, output queueing, or shared queueing).

7.4.2.1 Crossbar-Based Switches Crossbar-based switches are also called simply *crossbar switches.* In such a switch, there exist N^2 paths between N input and N output ports, configured such that there is a single contact point for each input-output port combination. The crossbar is the most straightforward nonblocking-single path architecture, but it is nevertheless highly complex. A self-routing crossbar architecture is not scalable, since its complexity (cost) grows quadratically as the number of ports increases.

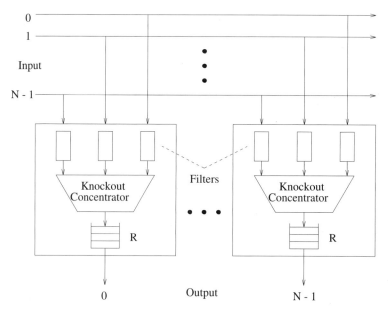

Figure 7.9
Knockout switch

An example of a crossbar switch is the knockout switch [20], shown in figure 7.9. The bus interfaced at input port i can transmit to output ports numbered 0 to $N - 1$. Each output port of the switch has a concentrator and N filters. The filters at output port i filter the cells off the buses that are destined for output port i. Because this filtering is based on each cell's destination address, the switch is self-routing. The concentrator at output port i with R buffers ($R < N$) implements an R out of N selection algorithm, similar to that of a knockout tournament, for selecting R cells for transmission out of the possible N arriving at that port. Hence, in the worst case $N - R$ cells are lost.

7.4.2.2 Multistage Switches Multistage switches are also referred to as multistage interconnection networks. A MIN has the following attractive features:

- It offers high throughput, because several cells can be switched in parallel.
- Its modular architecture permits scalability.
- It is suitable for VLSI implementation due to its modular design.
- It contains simple, self-routing SEs.
- It supports multicasting in a variety of ways.

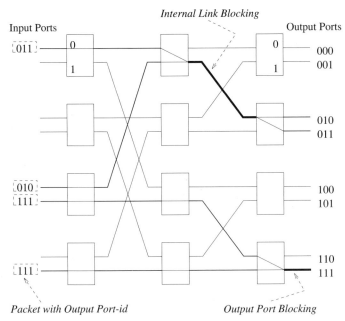

Packet with Output Port-id   *Output Port Blocking*

Packets destined for ports (011) and (010) cause internal link blocking

Packets destined for port (111) cause output port blocking

Figure 7.10
Multistage interconnection network

• It is fault-tolerant, because of the availability of multiple disjoint paths between input-output pairs.

The principal characteristics of MINs are the following: (1) they consist of $O \log N$ stages, with $N/2$ SEs per stage, and (2) the SEs are self-routing for cell movements from any input port to any output port.

Banyan networks were the early architectures that used simple SEs organized in multiple stages. Banyan networks are internally blocking networks. Some well-known switches belonging to the class of banyan networks are delta, shuffle exchange, baseline, omega, and generalized cube networks. These networks are topologically equivalent.

A Multistage Interconnection Network: Figure 7.10 shows an example of a MIN. It also illustrates the MIN's self-routing property, in that the output port addresses of cells govern the connections at the SEs for their routing. For example, if the output port address of a cell is 011, the cell should be routed to 0th output (top output) of an SE at stage 0, the

1th output (bottom output) of an SE at stages 1 and 2. The figure also shows internal link blocking and ouput port blocking.

7.5 Packet Service Disciplines

In this section, we discuss some important service disciplines that have been proposed for real-time message scheduling. Guaranteed service requires that a network protect users (channels) from two sources of variability:

1. Misbehaving users or inaccurate characterization of traffic can cause packets to be sent at a higher rate than the bandwidth allocated to them.

2. Network fluctuations may cause a higher instantaneous arrival rate at a node, even though the channel satisfies the bandwidth constraint at the source host.

The rate at the source host can be controlled by traffic policing schemes, as discussed earlier in the chapter. Network fluctuation should be controlled by the service discipline. Packet service disciplines are broadly classified into two categories:

• *Rate-based methods* translate the QoS a connection requests into a transmission rate or bandwidth. There is a predefined set of allowable transmission rates, which are assigned static priorities. The bandwidth allocated guarantees a fixed maximum delay for each packet in a given rate class. Service disciplines such as hierarchical round robin [23], stop-and-go [8], weighted fair queuing [4], virtual clock, and rate-controlled static priority belong to this category.

• *Scheduler-based methods* instead analyze the potential interactions among messages of different connections to determine if there is any possibility of a deadline's being missed. Priorities are then assigned based on deadlines. Earliest due date–delay (EDD-D) [6] and Earliest due date–jitter (EDD-J) are examples of scheduler-based methods.

Rate-based methods have the advantage of simple implementation, whereas scheduler-based methods allow bandwidth, delay, and delay jitter to be allocated independently.

Service disciplines can also be classified as either *work-conserving* or *non-work-conserving*. A scheduler with a work-conserving discipline never leaves a link idle when there is a packet to transmit. Earliest due date–delay, virtual clock, and fair queuing are examples of work-conserving disciplines. A scheduler with a non-work-conserving discipline assigns each packet an *eligibility time,* either implicitly or explicitly. Even when a link is idle, if no packets are eligible, none are transmitted. Hierarchical round robin, stop-and-go, and earliest due date–jitter are examples of non-work-conserving disciplines.

With work-conserving disciplines, the traffic pattern is distorted inside the network because of fluctuations in network load. On the other hand, in non-work-conserving disciplines, this distortion is implicitly controlled by delaying packets until their eligibility time.

At first glance, work conservation might seem obviously preferable, since it promises lower end-to-end delays for packets. However, methods that minimize jitter are always non-work-conserving.

A detailed comparison of various service disciplines can be found in [22, 23].

7.5.1   Rate-Based Methods

A rate-based service discipline provides a connection with a minimum service rate independent of the traffic characteristics of other connections. Such a discipline manages the following resources: bandwidth, service priority, and buffer space. In conjunction with appropriate admission policies, such a discipline enables a network to offer connections performance guarantees in terms of throughput, delay, delay jitter, and loss rate. Rate-based service disciplines will not serve packets at a higher rate than that specified in the service contract.

7.5.1.1   Hierarchical Round Robin   In the hierarchical round robin (HRR) scheme, there are number of levels, each with a fixed number of slots[1] serviced in round-robin fashion. A channel is allocated a given number of service slots at a selected level, and the scheduler cycles through the slots at each level. The time taken to service all the slots at a given level is called the *frame time* at that level. The total link bandwidth is partitioned among these levels. The key to HRR lies in its ability to give each level a constant share of the link's bandwidth. Higher levels get a lower amount of bandwidth than lower levels, so higher levels have greater frame times than lower levels. Since the scheduler always completes one round through its slots once every frame time, it can offer a maximum delay bound to the channels allocated to that level.

The frame time for level 1, which is the smallest of all the levels, is the basic cycle time. If there are n_1 slots in a level 1 frame, then b_1 slots are given away (allocated) to higher levels, and the remaining $(n_1 - b_1)$ slots are used for the level 1 connections. Similarly, level 2 has n_2 slots and frame time $FT_2 = (n_1/b_1).n_2$, because level 2 gets b_1 slots in every n_1 slot times, and it needs n_2 slots in all. Out of these n_2 slots, b_2 slots are given away to levels higher than 2, and so on. In general, the frame time at level i is the interval between serving a slot in successive frames (of level i) and is given by $FT_i = (n_1/b_1).(n_2/b_2) \ldots (n_{i-1}/b_{i-1}).n_i$. The bandwidth alloted for level i is $(n_i - b_i)/FT_i$. Thus, the scheme statically partitions bandwidth among levels by appropriately choosing n_i and b_i. A connection at level i gets a_j of the n_i slots and gets a bandwidth of a_j/FT_i cells/second. It will have to wait at most FT_i cell times before it is first serviced after it

---

1. A slot represents transmission of a fixed-size packet.

is enqueued for transmission. Since the smallest value for a_j is 1, the smallest level of bandwidth at level i is $1/FT_i$, which is the minimum granularity of bandwidth for that level. One-level HRR is a non-work-conserving round-robin service discipline.

Admission Control Test: Let T_{F_i} represent the period of the frame for connection i, α_j be the set of connections passing through link j, and τ_i be the maximum size of a message in connection i. The admission control test for determining whether to admit the $(n + 1)$th connection on a link is a simple bandwidth test:

$$\sum_{k \in \alpha_j} \tau_k/T_{F_k} \leq 1. \tag{7.1}$$

That is, the admission control test checks whether the sum of the utilization of all the channels passing through the link is less than or equal to one, where utilization of a channel is taken to be the ratio of its maximum message length to the period of its frame size.

Example: Consider a link having a total bandwidth of 4 Mbps, and the HRR scheme having three levels of slot allocation, as shown in the tables of figure 7.11. The schematic diagram and the schedule produced by the HRR scheme for this allocation are as given in the figure.

7.5.1.2   Stop-and-Go   The stop-and-go service discipline is similar to HRR in that it uses a multilevel framing strategy. It aims to preserve the smoothness property of traffic as it traverses the network. Time is divided into frames, which are periods of constant length. Stop-and-go defines *departing* and *arriving* frames for each link. At each node, the arriving frame of each incoming link is mapped onto the departing frame of the output link by introducing a constant delay δ, where $0 \leq \delta < T$. In each frame time, only packets that arrived at the node in the previous frame time are sent. Thus, an output link may be left idle even when there are packets in the node to be transmitted. Therefore, stop-and-go, like HRR, is a non-work-conserving service discipline. The stop-and-go uses the same admission control test as HRR.

7.5.1.3   Weighted Fair Queuing   Fair queuing (FQ) has a simple aim: If N channels share an output link, then each should get $1/N$ of the link's bandwidth, provided that if any channel uses less than its share, the slack is equally distributed among the other channels. This could be achieved by performing a byte-by-byte round-robin (BR) service among the channels. Since providing such a service is impractical, FQ emulates BR: Each packet is allocated a transmission time (time stamp), which is the time at which the packet would have been transmitted were the scheduler actually doing BR. Packets are then transmitted in the order of their time stamps, emulating BR. Weighted fair queuing (WFQ) is a variation of FQ in which weights are associated with channels corresponding to the number of bytes

level i	n_i	b_i	FT_i	slot bandwidth
1	4	1	4	1 Mbps
2	4	1	16	250 Kbps
3	2	0	32	125 Kbps

channel	bandwidth need	level assigned	no. of slots
C1	2 Mbps	1	2
C2	1 Mbps	1	1
C3	250 Kbps	2	1
C4	500 Kbps	2	2
C5	125 Kbps	3	1
C6	100 Kbps	3	1

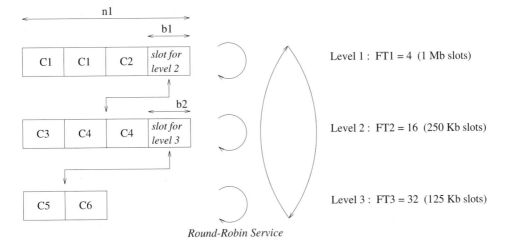

(a) HRR with slot allocation to 6 channels

C1	C1	C2	C3	C1	C1	C2	C4	C1	C1	C2	C4	C1	C1	C2	C5

(b) Schedule produced by HRR up to 16 slots

Figure 7.11
HRR scheduling scheme

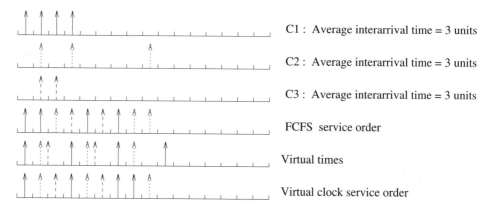

C1 : Average interarrival time = 3 units

C2 : Average interarrival time = 3 units

C3 : Average interarrival time = 3 units

FCFS service order

Virtual times

Virtual clock service order

Figure 7.12
Comparison of virtual clock and FCFS

of service a channel receives per round of BR service. Different fractions of the link's bandwidth are thus assigned to channels according to their weights.

7.5.1.4   Virtual Clock   Virtual clock (VC) emulates time division multiplexing (TDM). It allocates each packet a virtual transmission time: the time at which the packet would have been transmitted were the scheduler actually doing TDM. For example, if a particular source (channel) is to receive a service rate of 10 packets/second, incoming packets from that source are stamped with virtual service times 0.1 second apart. By sending packets in virtual time order, VC emulates TDM.

Figure 7.12 offers an example to illustrate the working of VC. In the example, three connections (C1, C2, and C3) share the same output link. All three connections have an average packet interarrival time of 3 units. Assume that the packets from all the connections are of the same size and that transmission of one packet takes one time unit. Hence, each connection reserves 33% of the link bandwidth, and packet delay at this link for these connections is 3 units from the time packets arrive. The actual packet arrival patterns of the three connections are shown in the figure. As can be seen, connection C1 transmits packets at a higher rate than specified. The fourth timeline in figure 7.12 shows the service order of packets when the first-come-first-served (FCFS) discipline is used. The misbehavior of C1 affects the network's performance with respect to C2; that is, the second packet of C2 is serviced one time unit after its delay bound. The fifth and sixth timelines show the virtual service time assignment and service order of packets using VC discipline, respectively. Since the VC algorithm assigns each packet a virtual transmission time based on the arrival pattern and reservation of the connection to which the packet belongs, well-behaving connections suffer no performance degradation because of other connections' misbehavior. In the example, although connection C1 is sending packets at a higher rate than specified, the VC algorithm ensures that each well-behaving source, in this case C2 and C3, is not affected, that is, that all the packets in all three connections are serviced before their deadlines.

7.5.2 Scheduler-Based Methods

An application specifies the end-to-end deadline (i.e., path deadline) for the messages in a connection. From this path deadline, the link deadline for each of the links in the path must be determined; that is, for each link, the feasibility of scheduling the new connection together with the existing connections must be checked.

7.5.2.1 Earliest Due Date–Delay

The earliest due date–delay (EDD-D) method was first proposed for computing the minimum acceptable link deadline for packets of a given connection [6]. In EDD-D, the scheduler sets a packet's deadline to the time at which it would have been sent had it been received according to the service contract, which is just the expected arrival time added to the link deadline at the node. For example, if a source assures the scheduler that it will send packets every 0.5 seconds, and the link deadline at a node is 1 second, then the kth packet from the source is assigned a deadline of $0.5k + 1$. This method is valid under the assumption that the sum of all message transmission times is less than the shortest interarrival time of any connection using the link. Depending on the types of delay bounds required for a particular connection, different types of channels can be defined. The EDD-D method supports deterministic, statistical, and best-effort channels. The schedulability test for this method includes testing the deterministic constraint, statistical constraint, scheduler saturation constraint, and buffer space constraint. The checking of these constraints varies depending on the type of channel requested for a connection. EDD-D supports the following types of real-time channels:

• *Deterministic channels* have absolute delay bounds, necessary for hard real-time communication.

• *Statistical channels* have bounds expressed in statistical terms; for instance, the probability that the delay of a particular packet is smaller than the given delay bound must be greater than some given value.

In EDD-D, three queues are maintained at each node corresponding to each of the channel types: (1) a deterministic queue, (2) a statistical queue, and (3) a best-effort queue. Messages are arranged in each of these queues in nondecreasing order of message deadlines at that link. When a scheduling decision is to be made at run time, the following sequence occurs:

1. If the deadline of the first message in the statistical queue is greater than the beginning time (link deadline minus service time) of the first message in the deterministic queue, then the first message of the deterministic queue is serviced.

2. Otherwise, the same test is carried out between the first message of the best-effort queue and the first message of the statistical queue. If the beginning time of the latter is lower, then the first message in the statistical queue is serviced.

3. Otherwise, the first message in the best-effort queue is serviced.

7.5.2.2 Earliest Due Date–Jitter   The earliest due date–jitter (EDD-J) discipline extends EDD-D to provide delay jitter bounds. After a given packet has been served at a node, it is stamped with the difference between its link deadline and its actual finish time at the node. A regulator at the entrance of the next node holds the packet for this duration before making it eligible to be scheduled. This provides minimum and maximum delay guarantees for each packet transmitted.

7.5.3 Work Conserving versus Non–Work-Conserving Methods

As noted above, service disciplines can also be classified as either work-conserving or non–work-conserving.

7.5.3.1 Work-Conserving Disciplines   In a work-conserving discipline, there is a state variable associated with each connection to monitor and enforce its traffic. As each packet from a connection arrives, the state variable is updated according to

• the reservation made for the connection when the connection was established or renegotiated,

• the traffic arrival history of the connection and/or other connections during the data transfer.

The packet is then assigned the value of the state variable for the connection to which it belongs. The assigned value is used as a priority index, and packets are served in increasing order of their priority index. The priority index calculation and update depend on the following issues:

• Whether the calculation is based on just the rate parameters or both the rate and delay parameters.

• Whether the update is based on system load–*independent* parameters or system load–*dependent* parameters. In EDD-D and VC, the update is based only on per-connection parameters but not on system load. On the other hand, in WFQ, the update is based on a notion of virtual time. The evolution of virtual time measures the progress of the system and depends on the system load.

7.5.3.2 Coupling between Bandwidth and Delay In EDD-D, two parameters are used to update the priority index: minimum packet interarrival time and node delay bound. Thus EDD-D can provide flexible delay and bandwidth allocation. In disciplines such as VC, WFQ, HRR, and stop-and-go, only the rate parameter is used. Although these disciplines can provide delay bounds, having only a rate parameter introduces the problem of coupling between delay bound and bandwidth. For a connection to get a low delay bound, a high bandwidth needs to be allocated for the channel that carries it. This will result in wastage of resources when a low-delay connection also has a low throughput.

The coupling between bandwidth and delay means that for a given bandwidth reserved for a particular connection at a given link, only one delay value is possible for that connection at that link. This in turn means that schemes that use only the rate parameter to update the priority index cannot guarantee a lower delay than that which is coupled with the connection's bandwidth reservation. The following example illustrates this point. Assume there are four channels sharing one output link, with each channel assigned one fourth of the link's bandwidth. The service time of a message for each channel is one time unit. In HRR and stop-and-go, the smallest possible frame time is 4—that is, the smallest delay bound for all four channels is 4—whereas a scheduler-based method such as the EDD-D can guarantee a delay bound of less than 4 for some of the channels. In HRR and stop-and-go, the coupling between bandwidth and delay implicitly deals with the scheduler saturation constraint; that is, no explicit check is required for this constraint.

7.5.4 Rate-Controlled Static Priority

Although the EDD-D has the advantage of providing flexibility in bandwidth and delay allocation, it is based on a sorted priority mechanism, which is difficult to implement. HRR and stop-and-go use framing strategy, which is simple to implement, instead of sorted priority, but such a strategy has the disadvantage of introducing a coupling between bandwidth and delay. The goal of rate-controlled static priority (RCSP) is to decouple bandwidth and delay without sacrificing implementation simplicity.

An RCSP scheme has two components (as shown in figure 7.13): a rate controller and a static priority scheduler. Conceptually, a rate controller consists of a set of regulators corresponding to each of the connections traversing the node; each regulator is responsible for shaping the input of its connection into the desired traffic pattern. When a packet arrives at the node, the regulator calculates an eligible time and assigns it to the packet. The packet is transmitted at its eligibility time. Different methods of calculating the eligibility time of a packet result in different types of regulators.

The static priority scheduler in an RCSP scheme uses a non-preemptive static priority policy: it always selects for transmission the packet at the head of the highest-priority queue that is not empty. The static priority scheduler assigns each connection a priority level, corresponding to a delay bound, during connection establishment. Multiple connections

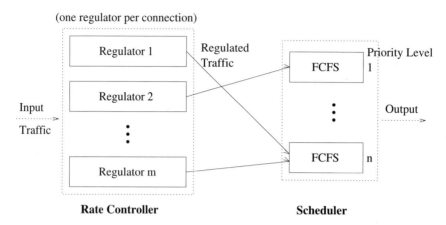

Figure 7.13
RCSP service discipline

can be assigned to the same priority level, and the packets of a priority level are served on an FCFS basis.

Through different combinations of regulators and schedulers, a general class of service disciplines can be realized, known as *rate-controlled service disciplines*. HRR and stop-and-go can be implemented with rate-controlled servers by selecting appropriate regulators and schedulers. EDD-J and RCSP are rate-controlled servers.

7.6 Summary

• Real-time applications require specific QoS, in terms of throughput, delay, delay jitter, and loss bounds, from the network on which they are implemented.

• A network can provide three types of service to the applications it carries, namely, guaranteed service, predictive service, and best-effort service.

• The main goal of resource management—guaranteed delivery of real-time messages—implies four main actions: call admission control, rate control, scheduling, and resource adaptation.

• Call admission control uses routing to probe a potential path for the call and performs an admission test at every node along the path. A channel for the call can be established in a single pass or in two passes. Single-pass schemes are fast, whereas two-pass schemes use resources efficiently.

• The primary aim of rate control is to enforce compliance of the characteristics of the source traffic with the negotiated values throughout the life of the channel.

• Scheduling allocates resources to connections at run time, adhering to the reservations made during connection establishment. Three types of resources are allocated: bandwidth, processing time, and buffer.

• Resource adaptation means monitoring the availability of resources and adapting to resource changes during an ongoing real-time session by renegotiating QoS.

• Channel identifier translation, switching, and scheduling are the three important functions performed at a switching node.

• In a switching fabric, two types of blocking can occur: internal link blocking and output port blocking. Buffering at SEs and queueing at the input/output of the switching fabric are among the many techniques employed to alleviate internal link blocking and output port blocking, respectively.

• Scheduling disciplines can be broadly classified into rate-based and scheduler-based. Rate-based methods have the advantage of simple implementation, whereas scheduler-based methods allow bandwidth, delay, and delay jitter to be allocated independently, thereby resulting in better schedulability.

• A service discipline is said to be work-conserving if it never leaves a link idle when there is a packet to transmit. Work conservation offers lower end-to-end delays for packets. Methods that minimize jitter are always non–work-conserving.

Exercises

1. What is the most important distinguishing feature of real-time communication when compared with traditional data communication?

2. Distinguish between hard and soft real-time communication applications.

3. Order *pure packet switching, pure circuit switching,* and *packet-oriented switching* in terms of the following two parameters:

(a) real-time guarantees on message delivery

(b) effective bandwidth utilization

4. Name two traffic models commonly used to statistically characterize VBR sources. List the parameters each model uses.

5. What two factors complicate congestion control in very-high-speed networks? What type of congestion control mechanisms are consequently unsuitable in such networks?

6. In a two-pass channel establishment scheme, why is it necessary to reserve (in fact, overreserve) resources in the forward pass and then require that these reservations be relaxed in the reverse pass?

7. What kinds of tests does a call admission control module perform at each node in the network?

8. What is meant by *deflection routing* in the context of switching subsystems? What type of switching problem does this technique help overcome?

9. What is HOL blocking? Compare HOL blocking with the tree saturation effect.

10. What two schemes are used for distributed channel identifier assignment? In which of these schemes can the *Out Channel ID* entry of the switching table not be filled in the forward pass (of channel establishment), and why not?

11. Distinguish between work-conserving and non–work-conserving service disciplines. Why are non–work-conserving disciplines useful?

12. Characterize each of the following service disciplines according to whether it is (i) rate-based or scheduler-based and (ii) work conserving or non–work-conserving:

(a) hierarchical round robin

(b) stop and go

(c) weighted fair queuing

(d) virtual clock

(e) earliest due date–delay

(f) earliest due date–jitter

(g) rate-controlled static priority

13. Consider the following scenario. Two nodes are connected by a 1,000-mile cable; the link bandwidth is 10 Mbps; and packet size is 2 Kbits. Compute the number of packets that will be in transit, at any time, on the cable when packets are sent continuously. Assume that light takes $5\mu sec$ to travel one mile. For this case, which of the congestion control schemes is better, proactive or reactive?

14. For the following cell routing, determine which ports at which cells arrive successfully in the example multistage network depicted in this chapter:

(a) Cell in input port i intended for output port $(7 - i)$. If there is an internal blocking between two cells, resolve using the following methods: (i) the cell intended for the lower indexed output port is dropped; (ii) the cell intended for the higher indexed output port is dropped.

(b) Cells in input ports are intended for output ports as follows: 0 to 3; 2 to 4; 3 to 5; 4 to 2; 5 to 4; and 6 to 1. Find the number of instances of internal link blocking and output port blocking. If there is an internal blocking between two cells, resolve using the following ways: (i) the cell intended for the lower indexed output port is dropped; (ii) the cell intended for the higher indexed output port is dropped.

(a)

channel	bandwidth need
C1	2 Mbps
C2	500 Kbps
C3	250 Kbps
C4	250 Kbps

(b)

channel	bandwidth need
C1	1.375 Mbps
C2	125 Kbps
C3	375 Kbps
C4	125 Kbps

Figure 7.14
Exercise 7.16 channel requests

(c) Cells in input ports are intended for output ports as follows. Some cells are intended for more than one output port (multicasting): 1 to 2 and 6; 2 to 5 and 7; 3 to 3; 4 to 0 and 1; 7 to 4. If there is an internal blocking between unicast and multicast cells, resolve using the following methods: (i) the unicast cell is dropped; (ii) the multicast cell is dropped.

15. Consider two connections C1 and C2 having average interarrival times of 5 and 2 units, respectively. For the following arrival pattern (times at which packets arrive), determine FCFS service order, virtual times, and virtual clock service order.

```
C1 :  1   2   3   4
C2 :      2       4
```

16. Consider a link having a total bandwidth of 3 Mbps and an HRR scheme having three levels of slot allocation with the following frame times: $FT1 = 3$ (three 1 Mb slots), $FT2 = 12$ (four 250 Kb slots), and $FT3 = 24$ (four 125 Kb slots). For the connections given in figure 7.14, show the slot assignments and the service order produced by the HRR scheme up to the time every slot is serviced at least once. (Assume that slots in a level are assigned to connections in ascending order of connection number.)

References

[1] H. Ahmadi and W. E. Denzel. "A survey of modern high-performance switching techniques." *IEEE JSAC,* vol. 7, no. 7, pp. 1091–1103, Sept. 1989.

[2] C. M. Aras, J. F. Kurose, D. S. Reeves, and H. Schulzrinne. "Real-time communication in packet-switched networks." *Proc. IEEE,* vol. 82, no. 1, pp. 122–139, Jan. 1994.

[3] A. Campbell, G. Coulson, and D. Hutchison. "A quality of service architecture." *Computer Communication Review,* vol. 24, no. 2, pp. 6–27, Apr. 1994.

[4] A. Demers, S. Keshav, and S. Shenker. "Analysis and simulation of fair queuing algorithm." In *Proc. ACM SIGCOMM,* pp. 1–12, 1989.

[5] D. M. Dias and Manoj Kumar. "Preventing congestion in multistage networks in the presence of hotspots." In *Proc. IEEE Intl. Conf. on Parallel Processing,* vol. 1, pp. 9–13, 1989.

[6] D. Ferrari and D. C. Verma. "A scheme for real-time channel establishment in wide-area networks." *IEEE JSAC,* vol. 8, no. 3, pp. 368–379, Apr. 1990.

[7] D. Ferrari. "Multimedia network protocols: Where are we?" *Multimedia Systems,* vol. 6, no. 4, pp. 299–304, 1996.

[8] S. J. Golestani. "A framing strategy for congestion management." *IEEE JSAC,* vol. 9, no. 7, pp. 1064–1077, Sept. 1991.

[9] D. D. Kandlur, K. G. Shin, and D. Ferrari. "Real-time communication in multihop networks." *IEEE Trans. Parallel and Distributed Systems,* vol. 5, no. 10, pp. 1044–1056, Oct. 1994.

[10] L. Kleinrock. "The latency/bandwidth tradeoff in gigabit networks." *IEEE Communications,* vol. 30, no. 4, pp. 36–40, Apr. 1992.

[11] K. Y. Lee, H. Yoon, and M. T. Liu. "Performance evaluation of a class of multipath packet switching interconnection networks." *Journal of Parallel and Distributed Computing,* vol. 3, no. 4, pp. 389–396, July 1992.

[12] V. O. K. Li and W. Liao. "Distributed multimedia systems." *Proc. IEEE,* vol. 85, no. 7, pp. 1063–1108, July 1997.

[13] K. Nahrstedt and R. Steinmetz. "Resource management in networked multimedia systems." *IEEE Computer,* vol. 28, no. 5, pp. 52–63, May 1995.

[14] P. Newman. "ATM technology for corporate network." *IEEE Communications,* vol. 30, no. 4, pp. 90–101, Apr. 1992.

[15] A. Pattavina. "Non-blocking architectures for ATM switching." *IEEE Communications,* vol. 31, no. 2, pp. 38–48, Feb. 1993.

[16] S. Radhakrishnan, S. V. Raghavan, and A. K. Agrawala. "A flexible traffic shaper for high speed networks: Design and comparative study with leaky bucket." *Computer Networks and ISDN Systems,* vol. 28, no. 4, pp. 453–469, Feb. 1996.

[17] S. Rampal, D. S. Reeves, and D. P. Agrawal. "An evaluation of routing and admission control algorithms for real-time traffic in packet-switched networks." In *Proc. High Performance Networking,* pp. 77–91, 1994.

[18] S. Shenker and L. Breslau. "Two issues in reservation establishment." In *Proc. ACM SIGCOMM,* pp. 14–26, 1995.

[19] J. S. Turner. "New trends in communication (or which way to the information age?)." *IEEE Communications,* vol. 24, no. 10, pp. 8–15, Oct. 1986.

[20] Y. S. Yeh, M. G. Hluchyj, and A. S. Acampora. "The knockout switch: A simple modular architecture for high performance packet switching." *IEEE JSAC,* vol. 5, no. 8, pp. 1274–1283, Oct. 1987.

[21] E. W. Zegura. "Architectures for ATM switching systems." *IEEE Communications,* vol. 31, no. 2, pp. 28–37, Feb. 1993.

[22] H. Zhang and S. Keshav. "Comparison of rate-based service disciplines." In *Proc. ACM SIGCOMM,* pp. 113–121, Sept. 1991.

[23] H. Zhang. "Service disciplines for guaranteed performance service in packet-switching networks." *Proc. IEEE,* vol. 83, no. 10, pp. 1374–1396, Oct. 1995.

8 Route Selection in Real-Time Wide Area Networks

Overview

In this chapter, we first present some well-known routing algorithms used in datagram networks. Next we present the QoS routing problem, goals of QoS routing algorithms, and performance metrics. We then describe different types of routing approaches and also present some known algorithms, along with a performance study of these algorithms, followed by a discussion of the delay-constrained routing problem in detail. Finally, we present several schemes for establishing dependable real-time channels in wide area networks.

8.1 Basic Routing Algorithms

In traditional datagram networks, since no circuits are established, each packet in a transmission carries the destination address for the transmission and consults the routing table at each intermediate node to reach the destination. The routing table can be constructed using a centralized algorithm (Dijkstra's algorithm is a classical example) or a distributed algorithm (the distance vector algorithm and the link state algorithm are the classical examples). Centralized algorithms cannot take into account the topological changes that can occur because of node and/or link failures and addition of new nodes and/or links, and hence are static. Distributed algorithms, which learn the topological changes and compute the routes based on the updated topology information, are more dynamic.

In circuit-switched networks, during real-time channel establishment, routing tables are consulted to find a path from a given source to a given destination, as discussed in the previous chapter. That is, the channel establishment algorithm relies on underlying distributed routing algorithms, such as the distance vector algorithm or the link state algorithm.

8.1.1 Dijkstra's Shortest-Path Algorithm

A communication network can be modeled as a graph in which the vertices and edges of the graph represent the nodes and links of the communication network. The cost of a communication link is modeled as the weight of its corresponding edge in the graph. Dijkstra's algorithm is centralized and requires the complete topology of the network (graph) with link (edge) weights to compute the shortest path from a given source node to all the other nodes in the network. The graph G is denoted as $G = (V, E)$, where V and E are the vertex and edge sets of the graph, respectively. The weight of the edge from vertex u to vertex v is denoted as $w(u, v)$ and must be nonnegative. The possible metrics for representing the weight of an edge are hop count (in which case $w(u, v) = 1$), bandwidth of the link, mean transmission delay, queueing delay on the link, and a combination of these. By changing the weight function, the algorithm can compute the "shortest" path according to any one of these metrics.

Dijkstra's algorithm maintains a set S of vertices whose final shortest paths from the source s have already been determined. The algorithm repeatedly selects the vertex $u \in V - S$ with the minimum shortest path estimate, inserts u into S, and "relaxes" all the edges leaving u. *Relaxation* refers to the technique the algorithm uses that repeatedly decreases the upper bound on the actual shortest path weight of each vertex until the upper bound equals the shortest path weight. Dijkstra's algorithm is formally given below:

Dijkstra(G, w, s)   G: graph, w: weights of the edges, s: source vertex
>   **begin**
>   Let $d[v]$ denote the weight of the shortest path found so far from s to v.
>   Let $path[v]$ denote the predecessor of v in the shortest path.
> $\forall v \in V \ d[v] = \infty, path[v] = \text{nil};$
> $d[s] = 0; S = \emptyset; T = V;$
>   **While** $(T \neq \emptyset)$ **do**
>>   Let u be a vertex in T for which $d[u]$ is minimum.
>> $T = T - \{u\}; \quad S = S \cup \{u\};$
>>   **For** each vertex v adjacent to u
>>>   **If** $(d[v] > d[u] + w(u, v))$ /* relaxation step */
>>>> $d[v] = d[u] + w(u, v);$
>>>> $path[v] = u;$

end.

By tracing back the $path[v]$, the sequence of vertices that form the shortest path from s to v can be obtained. The final value of $d[v]$ denotes the weight of the shortest path from s to v.

8.1.2   Distance Vector Routing

Distance vector routing, also referred to as "old ARPANET routing" or "Bellman-Ford routing," requires that each node maintain a vector containing the best known distance from itself to each possible destination and the link to be used to get there. In this type of routing, each node maintains a vector indexed by, and containing one entry for, each node in the network. The entry contains two parts: (1) the preferred outgoing link to use to reach that destination node and (2) an estimate of the "distance" (cost) to that destination node. The metric for distance can be hop count, delay, queue length of the path, or any other similar metric. As mentioned earlier, if the metric is hop count, the "distance" is just one hop. If it is queue length, the node simply examines each queue. If it is delay, it can be measured by sending special packets.

The distance vector routing algorithm works as follows:

1. Each node is assumed to know the "distance" to each of its neighbors.

2. Each node starts with a distance vector consisting of the value 0 for itself and the value infinity for every other destination.

3. Each node sends its distance vector to each of its neighbors whenever the distance information changes as well as when a link to a neighbor (that was down earlier) comes up.

4. Each node saves the most recently received distance vector from each of its neighbors.

5. Each node calculates its own distance vector, based on minimizing the cost to each destination, by examining the cost to that destination reported by each neighbor in turn and then adding the cost of the link to that neighbor.

6. The following events cause recalculation of the distance vector:

• Receipt of distance vector from a neighbor containing modified information.

• Failure of the link to a neighbor. In such a case, the existing distance vector from that neighbor is discarded before the distance vector is recalculated.

The main problems with distance vector routing are its slow convergence after a topological change and "count-to-infinity" problem, a situation in which nodes force each other to monotonically increase (update) their distance vectors. One popular technique used to speed up convergence of distance vectors is *split horizon*. However, split horizon does not solve the count-to-infinity problem in all cases.

8.1.3   Link State Routing

The link state routing algorithm works as follows:

1. Each node discovers its neighbors, learns its node-id, and measures the delay or cost of transmission to each of its neighbors.

2. It constructs a packet, known as a *link state packet,* that contains a list of node-ids of neighbors and cost of transmission to each of its neighbors.

3. It sends its link state packet to all the nodes in the network using flooding or some other means.

4. Each node now has the complete knowledge of the network topology, and each node computes the shortest path to every other node using Dijkstra or some other centralized routing algorithm.

Each node generates its link state packet periodically as well as any time it discovers that (1) it has a new neighbor, (2) the cost of the link to an existing neighbor has changed, or (3) a link to a neighbor has failed.

Link state routing is widely used in practice. For example, the open-shortest-path-first protocol (OSPF), which is increasingly being used in the Internet, uses a link state algorithm.

8.2   Routing during Real-Time Channel Establishment

8.2.1   Basic Results of the QoS Routing Problem

In a real-time network, at any point in time, many channel establishment requests are active whose objective is to find a qualified routing path from their respective sources to their destinations. Path selection within routing is typically formulated as a shortest-path optimization problem. The objective function for optimization can be any one of a variety of parameters, such as number of hops, cost, delay, or some other metric that corresponds to a numeric sum of the individual link parameters along a selected path [15]. Wang and Crowcroft [27] have studied the QoS routing problem, that is to find a path that satisfies one or more QoS requirements, and classified the metrics involved into additive, multiplicative, and concave metrics. It has been shown that the problem of finding a path subject to constraints on two or more additive and multiplicative metrics in any possible combination is NP-complete [5].

Efficient algorithms (Dijkstra and Bellman-Ford) exist for computing shortest paths in communication networks. However, within the context of satisfying diverse QoS requirements, the algorithms become more complex as constraints are introduced into the optimization problem. Such constraints typically fall into two categories: link constraints and path constraints [15]. A *link constraint* is a restriction on the use of links on a path (such as the constraint that the available capacity (such as bandwidth) on the links must be greater than or equal to that required by the call), whereas a *path constraint* is a bound on the combined (e.g., cumulative, multiplicative) value of a performance metric along a selected path (such as the restriction that the end-to-end delay offered along the path must not exceed what the call can tolerate). Path constraints make a routing problem intractable. For example, finding a path that satisfies two independent path constraints is NP-complete [5]. Therefore, heuristics are usually employed to solve the QoS routing problem.

8.2.2   Desirable Characteristics of QoS Routing Algorithms

For a QoS routing algorithm to perform well in practice, it is necessary to also take into account, apart from the optimization aspect of the routing, factors such as overall network performance, the possibility of out-of-date information in the routing tables, frequent changes in link parameters, and resource reservation during channel establishment.

We believe that routing algorithms intended to be used as route selection mechanisms for real-time channel establishment in wide area networks must possess the following characteristics:

1. They must be able to maximize the overall performance of the network without sacrificing the requirements of any particular call.

2. They must be designed to enable resource reservation to be built into the routing strategy [23].

3. They must be able to function with as little global state information as possible.

4. They must also be adaptive to changes in link parameters, such as link delay and available bandwidth.

5. They must be able to optimize on multiple constraints, as is required in the case of QoS routing [27].

8.2.3 Performance Metrics

In the context of real-time communication, traditional metrics such as average message delay and route distance of a single connection are meaningless, as they do not necessarily indicate anything about the timeliness of the receipt of messages and hence are inapplicable to connection-oriented real-time services.

For an accepted call-request R let us define the following functions:

- $accepted(R) = 1$.
- $cost(R) = $ cost of the path chosen for R.
- $setup(R) = $ number of vertices visited by the call setup packet.
- $dist(R) = $ length of the path (in terms of hop count) chosen for R.

For a call request R that is rejected, all functions return a value of 0. Let N be the total number of call-requests generated. The following metrics are appropriate for analyzing the performance of QoS routing algorithms and must be optimized in order to optimize the global performance of a real-time network:

- Average call acceptance rate (ACAR): the percentage of real-time channel establishment requests accepted:

$$ACAR = \frac{\sum_{i=1}^{N} accepted(R)}{N}.$$

• Average call setup time (ACST): the average time required to set up a real-time channel, measured in terms of number of vertices visited by the call setup packet:

$$ACST = \frac{\sum_{i=1}^{N} setup(R)}{\sum_{i=1}^{N} accepted(R)}.$$

• Average routing distance (ARD): the average hop count of the established channels:

$$ARD = \frac{\sum_{i=1}^{N} dist(R)}{\sum_{i=1}^{N} accepted(R)}.$$

• Average cost (AC): the average cost of the established channels:

$$AC = \frac{\sum_{i=1}^{N} cost(R)}{\sum_{i=1}^{N} accepted(R)}.$$

The first metric is very important, as it measures call throughput. The second metric is crucial in the context of real-time and interactive multimedia applications and load-balancing algorithms in distributed real-time systems, which require fast channel setup. The third metric is essential because a short route is less costly. The fourth metric is important because cost minimization is one of the key goals of the QoS routing algorithms.

8.3   Route Selection Approaches

There are two approaches to solving the route selection problem: centralized and distributed.

8.3.1   Centralized Route Selection Approach

A centralized route selection approach assumes the existence of a global network manager that maintains information about all the established real-time channels and the network topology and can thus select an appropriate route for each real-time channel request. In such a centralized approach, the network manager has to approve every real-time channel request. Although this approach is better than distributed approach in terms of selecting a qualified route by employing an efficient algorithm for network management, it suffers in terms of both performance and reliability due to the absence of precise network state information and the very nature of centralized control, respectively. Moreover, the centralized approach is not scalable.

8.3.2 Distributed Route Selection Approach

In contrast to the centralized approach, the distributed route selection approach offers better performance, is scalable, and is more reliable. Since the number of potential routes between a source and destination is very high, choosing a qualified route for a real-time channel is not an easy task. The objective of any routing algorithm is to find a qualified path with minimal operational overheads. A number of researchers have recently studied the distributed routing problem in the context of real-time channel establishment. Several heuristic routing algorithms have been proposed for the real-time channel establishment problem [10, 15, 24, 27]. The existing distributed routing algorithms fall into two major categories: flooding-based and preferred neighbor.

8.3.2.1 Flooding-Based Approach In a flooding-based approach, a node that is attempting to find a qualified route forwards a call setup packet to all (or some) of its neighbors except the node from which the packet has come. The flooding-based approach is superior in terms of ACST and ARD at the cost of ACAR. The lower ACST and ARD of the flooding approach is due to its nonbacktracking nature, since all potential paths are probed simultaneously, whereas its poor call acceptance stems from its excessive reservation of resources, such as bandwidth and buffers, along many paths from source to destination during the call setup.

A distributed scheme based on the flooding approach has been proposed in [24] for route selection during real-time channel establishment. In this approach, the number of messages used for establishing a call is at most $2K$, where K is the number of links in the network. This is very expensive and results in resources being reserved in many nodes, thereby reducing the ACAR.

Flooding-Based Fault-Tolerant Routing In another flooding-based approach for sending real-time packets from a sender to a receiver, multiple copies of a packet are sent to the same destination, each copy along a different path; that is, the paths by which the copies are sent are node disjoint [20]. This guards against a single packet being delayed beyond its deadline by other packets using part of the same path. It also protects against failures that cause some paths to be disconnected. The question is how many copies to send out. The more the copies sent, the greater the probability that it will reach its destination before its deadline. One might, therefore, want to send many copies for messages having tighter deadlines. However, if too many copies of a message are sent, other real-time packets with later deadlines may find it impossible to reach their destinations before their deadlines, although multiple copies of packets with tighter deadlines reach their destination on time. Therefore, sending too few copies as well as too many copies will result in poor performance: there is an optimal number of copies that need to be sent to ensure optimal performance. Given an arbitrary multihop network with nodes having local knowledge, however, it is impossible to determine this optimal number of copies of a packet to be sent.

8.3.2.2 Preferred Neighbor Approaches The preferred neighbor routing approach is fundamentally a backtracking-based route selection method. This framework describes a set of actions to be performed by each node whenever it receives a call setup or a call reject packet. When a node v receives a call setup packet, it forwards it along the first preferred link. (How the preferred links are determined is discussed in the next paragraph.) If the other end of this link sends back a reject packet, then node v attempts to forward the packet along the next preferred link, and so on, until either the call setup packet reaches its destination, indicating the call has been successfully set up, or it has tried a specified number of links. If all such attempts result in failure to find a successful link, then v sends a reject packet back to the node from which it received the call setup packet.

In a preferred neighbor approach, preferred neighbors are chosen based on a heuristic such as shortest path first (SPF) or lightly loaded link first (LLF). In comparison to flooding, the preferred neighbor approach offers higher ACAR at the cost of ACST and ARD. Its higher ACAR is due to reservation of resources along only one path as opposed to multiple paths in the flooding-based approach, and its poorer ACST and ARD stem from its backtracking nature (backtracking occurs when there is no qualified path from the current node to the destination through preferred neighbors of the current node).

There are two types of preferred neighbor heuristics: (1) local-/static-knowledge-based and (2) dynamic non-local-knowledge-based. Algorithms such as SPF and LLF are examples of the first type. The processing overhead associated with these heuristics is almost the same, since they use either local link information or relatively static global information. For example, the preferred neighbor table of LLF is based on local link information, whereas that of SPF is based on the relatively static topology of the network.

A distributed route selection algorithm based on the preferred neighbor approach has been proposed in [10]. Haung et al. studied the existing routing heuristics, such as SPF and LLF, and found that the SPF performs better in terms of ACAR and ARD under uniform traffic and more poorly when the call requests are focused on some hot (popular) nodes or links. On the other hand, the LLF tries to balance the load on each link by selecting the preferred neighbor nodes in a round-robin fashion. For unbalanced traffic, it indeed increases the ACAR, but under uniform traffic, it tries to balance the load on each preferred node. Even a slightly unbalanced load between two preferred nodes will probably cause the LLF to select a route with a longer distance. Even under light load, the LLF scheme still changes the chosen route dynamically, which is quite unnecessary.

Two-Level Shortest Path First Algorithm   To overcome the problems associated with the SPF and LLF heuristics, a routing algorithm, called the two-level shortest path first (TSPF) algorithm, has been proposed in [10]. This algorithm sorts the links of a node into a heavy group and a light group, based on a threshold value of load. The SPF heuristic is applied, first within the light group, and then within the heavy group. All three of these algorithms (SPF, LLF, and TSPF) are poor in terms of ACST, since they generate excessive backtracks under heavy loads.

8.3.3   Parallel Probing Approach

The algorithms discussed in the previous subsections are not aimed at improving multiple performance metrics simultaneously. They also do not perform well under different load conditions. This has motivated many researchers to try to come up with a routing approach whose objective is to improve all the metrics (ACAR, ACST, and ARD) simultaneously and cater to different load conditions. In this subsection, we will discuss one approach that attempts to satisfy this objective: the *parallel probing* approach.

The parallel probing approach, proposed in [17], combines the benefits of both the flooding and preferred neighbor approaches and also the benefits of the multiple preferred neighbor heuristics that it employs in a unified way. In this approach, we search for a qualified path by simultaneously probing at most k different paths using k different heuristics, one for each path. Since searching in parallel (for a qualified path) reduces the number of backtracks compared to sequential searching, the average call setup time is shorter in the case of parallel search, but this speed comes at the cost of reserving more resources. For example, when k paths are simultaneously searched through parallel probing, the amount of resources that are tentatively reserved (and thus are not available for other calls) is approximately k times those reserved when a single path is searched through sequential probing.

To remedy this excessive resource reservation without losing the fast call setup capability, parallel probing uses a concept called *intermediate destinations* (IDs), which are subsets of nodes along the least-cost path between the source and destination of a call. The least-cost metric can be expressed in terms of (minimum) number of hops or based on (least) load, or a combination of hop count and load, or some other measurement. When a call request arrives, the source node (ID_0) first decides the IDs for the call and then initiates probes for a qualified path to the first intermediate destination (ID_1) by sending probe packets (the ID list is appended to each probe packet) in parallel on k different paths determined by employing k different heuristics. The probe packet that first reaches ID_1 is considered to be the winner of the segment that originates at the source node and ends at ID_1. The subsequent probe packets corresponding to the same call reaching ID_1 are rejected, and the resources they have reserved are released immediately to the previous ID (i.e., the source node). Now the parallel probing starts all over again from ID_1 to ID_2 in a similar manner. This procedure is repeated until the destination is reached or timeout has occurred. The reverse pass follows the path used during the forward pass either for relaxing/confirming (when the call is accepted) or for releasing (when the call is rejected) the resources along the path. If the resources reserved at a node are not confirmed within a specified time interval, then the node automatically releases the resources reserved for that call.

When a probe packet is sent from the source node, it is assigned a unique identifier obtained by concatenating the node number with the local request counter and the heuristic identifier. The heuristic identifier indicates which heuristic a node uses to find its neighbor.

8.3.3.1   Node and Procedure-Types   To formally present the parallel probing approach, we first define some node types, then define some procedures that will be invoked when a node receives a probe packet. The nodes of the network, with respect to a call, are classified into four types:

• SOURCE. The source node of a call.

• DESTINATION. The destination node of a call.

• ID. An intermediate destination of the call. A call can have more than one ID, and the search for paths proceeds sequentially from one ID to another. The selection of IDs and the sequence in which the IDs are to be searched for is determined by the least-cost metric between the SOURCE and the DESTINATION of the call. Let $ID_0, ID_1, \ldots, ID_{n-1}, ID_n$ be the sequence of IDs of a call. Without loss of generality, ID_0 is the SOURCE and ID_n is the DESTINATION.

• IID. An intended intermediate destination of the call, which is an ID to which a route is currently being probed. ID_i is an IID iff ID_{i-1} was the previous IID and ID_{i+1} will be the next IID. Without loss of generality, SOURCE (ID_0) is the first IID and DESTINATION (ID_n) will be the last IID.

• SN. A simple node. Any node that is not a member of any of the above categories. These are nodes between IDs along the least-cost path between SOURCE and DESTINATION.

A *segment* is the path obtained by the parallel probing algorithm between two consecutive IDs of a call. The procedures executed by nodes during call establishment are classified into six categories: Reserve(), Forward(), Release(), and Backtrack() (the procedures executed during the forward pass) and Relax() and Reject() (the procedures executed during the reverse pass). The IDs of a given call are appended to each probe packet,

PROBE_PKT, at the source node of the call. Each probe packet also has a path field that captures the sequence of nodes that constitutes the current path.

• Reserve(N, *ID_j*, *PROBE_PKT*). Route the probe packet (PROBE_PKT) from node N to its preferred neighbor for reaching node *ID_j* based on a heuristic. This involves performing a call admission test on the best preferred link of node N, checking for the availability of bandwidth required by the call. If the call admission is successful, it returns "success," and the resources necessary for transmission are reserved; otherwise, it returns "failure." If the admission test fails on the best preferred link, the call admission test is performed on the next-best preferred link. This procedure is repeated until either the call admission is successful or a fixed number of tries has been made. The following algorithm summarizes the procedure:

> **Reserve**(N, *ID_j*, PROBE_PKT)
> **begin**
>   **Repeat**
>   **If** (call admission is successful)
>   Reserve bandwidth on the preferred link.
>   Send PROBE_PKT to the preferred neighbor.
>   **return**(success).
>   **else** Select the next preferred link.
>   **until** (maximum number of neighbors have been tried).
>   **return**(failure).
> **end.**

• Forward(*ID_i*, *IID*, *PROBE_PKT*). This procedure initiates parallel probes on k paths using k different heuristics. For each probe, it invokes the Reserve() procedure. If all probes fail the admission test, then a Release() procedure is invoked to release the resources reserved between *ID_i* and *ID_{i-1}*. The following algorithm summarizes the procedure:

> **Forward**(*ID_i*, *IID*, *PROBE_PKT*)
> **begin**
>   Let $H_1, H_2, \ldots, H_k$ be the k heuristics.
>   **For** $p = 1$ to k **do**
>   Select the *best* neighbor based on heuristic H_p.
>   status[p] = Reserve(*ID_i*, *IID*, *PROBE_PKT*).
>   **If** (none of status[p] is successful, $1 \leq p \leq k$) **then**
>   **If** (*ID_i* is SOURCE) **then** call is rejected.
>   **else** Release(*ID_i*, *ID_{i-1}*, PROBE_PKT).
> **end.**

- Release(ID_i, ID_{i-1}, *PROBE_PKT*). Release the resources along the path between intermediate destination ID_i and intermediate destination ID_{i-1} using the path stored in the PROBE_PKT.

- Backtrack(N, *PROBE_PKT*). Backtrack from node N to its predecessor (say $pred(N)$) in the routing path, which is stored in PROBE_PKT. This implicitly releases the resources reserved for the call from $pred(N)$ to N. Node N could be of type SN or ID. If $pred(N)$ is SOURCE, the PROBE_PKT is dropped.

- Relax(*DESTINATION*, *SOURCE*, *PROBE_PKT*). This procedure is invoked when the forward pass is successful. It relaxes the excess resources reserved for the call, such as bandwidth, buffers, and delay guarantee (delay is an additive metric), along the path, where the path is stored in PROBE_PKT, from DESTINATION to SOURCE of the call. If cycles are present in the path, they are also removed by releasing the resources reserved in the nodes that form the cycles.

- Reject(ID_i, *SOURCE*, *PROBE_PKT*). This procedure is invoked when it proves impossible to set up a particular channel. It releases the resources along the path, where the path is stored in PROBE_PKT, from node ID_i to the SOURCE of the call. ID_i is the last ID in the IDs list, meaning there is no remaining ID that can become an IID to which a probe can be initiated. As a special case, ID_i could be the DESTINATION of the call.

8.3.3.2 Parallel Probing Algorithm Figure 8.1 shows the pseudocode of the parallel probing algorithm executed when a call request arrives or a probe packet is received at a node. When a probe packet is received, depending on the node type, different case statements will be executed.

In parallel probing, at a node of type SN or ID, resources might be reserved for a call more than once as multiple probe packets pass through that node. If the call is successful and that node forms part of the qualified path, then the Relax() procedure will confirm only one of these reservations and the remaining reservations will be released either by Reject() or Release() procedures.

8.3.3.3 Properties of the Parallel Probing Approach The parallel probing approach possesses the following properties:

- Liveness. The use of IDs ensures the forward movement of probe packets toward the destination. This eliminates the possibility of a probe packet's getting stuck within a group of nodes that form a cycle.

- Adaptiveness. The different segments of a qualified path may very well have been selected by different heuristics employed (as shown in figure 8.2), depending on the load condition on a particular segment.

Parallel Probing(SOURCE, DESTINATION, k)
begin
   1. When a new call request arrives do the following.
      SOURCE: Assemble probe packet (PROBE_PKT) with intermediate
                  destinations $(ID_0, ID_1, \ldots, ID_{n-1}, ID_n)$,
                  without loss of generality, ID_0 is SOURCE and ID_n is DESTINATION.
     $IID = ID_1$; Forward(SOURCE, IID, PROBE_PKT). /* initiates parallel probing on k paths */
   2. When a probe packet arrives do the following.
     Switch (current node type) /* node type is with respect to the probe packet */
       case IID: Let the current node be ID_i. /* intended intermediate destination */
         If (PROBE_PKT is already seen by ID_i) **then**
            Release(ID_i, ID_{i-1}, PROBE_PKT). /* loser */
         else $IID = ID_{i+1}$; Forward(ID_i, IID, PROBE_PKT). /* winner packet - the
                first PROBE_PKT */
       case ID: Let the current node be ID_i. /* intermediate destination */
         If (IID is ID_k such that $i < (k - 1)$) **then** /* reached a past ID; cycle is encountered */
            Release(ID_i, ID_{k-1}, PROBE_PKT). /* cycle removal */
         else if (IID is ID_{i+1} and all the k probe packets have returned) **then** /* IID is not
                reachable */
            Delete ID_{i+1} from IDs list. /* this is to keep track of the actual IDs list */
            If (ID_i is the last element in the IDs list) **then**
                Reject(ID_i,SOURCE, PROBE_PKT). /* call is rejected. */
              else $IID = ID_{i+2}$; Forward(ID_i, IID, PROBE_PKT). /* parallel probe to new IID */
         else status = Reserve(ID_i, IID, PROBE_PKT). /* already known IID */
            If (status is failure) **then** Backtrack(ID_i, PROBE_PKT).
       case SN: Let the current node be N. /* simple node */
         status = Reserve(N, IID, PROBE_PKT). /* already known IID */
         If (status is failure) **then** Backtrack(N, PROBE_PKT).
       case DESTINATION:
         If (PROBE_PKT is already seen) **then** /* for loser packet */
            Release(DESTINATION, ID_{n-1}, PROBE_PKT).
         else if (call is acceptable) **then** /* for winner packet and call is acceptable */
            Analyze for cycles - mark the nodes in the path that form the cycles.
            Relax(DESTINATION, SOURCE, PROBE_PKT). /* call is accepted - reverse pass */
         else Reject(DESTINATION, SOURCE, PROBE_PKT). /* call is rejected - reverse pass */
end.

Figure 8.1
Parallel probing algorithm. From G. Manimaran, H. S. Rahul, and C. Siva Ram Murthy [17], in *IEEE/ACM Trans. Networking* 7 (5). © IEEE, 1999.

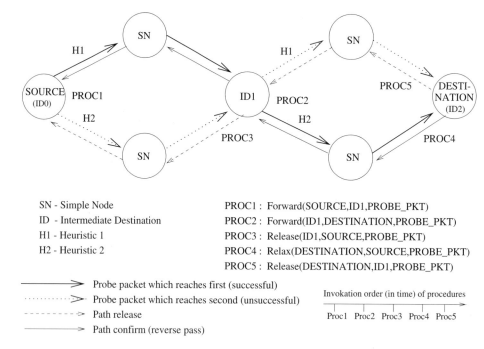

SN - Simple Node   PROC1 : Forward(SOURCE,ID1,PROBE_PKT)
ID - Intermediate Destination   PROC2 : Forward(ID1,DESTINATION,PROBE_PKT)
H1 - Heuristic 1   PROC3 : Release(ID1,SOURCE,PROBE_PKT)
H2 - Heuristic 2   PROC4 : Relax(DESTINATION,SOURCE,PROBE_PKT)
                                            PROC5 : Release(DESTINATION,ID1,PROBE_PKT)

————————————▷ Probe packet which reaches first (successful)
·············▷· Probe packet which reaches second (unsuccessful)   Invokation order (in time) of procedures
- - - - - - - ▷ Path release
————————————▷ Path confirm (reverse pass)   Proc1 Proc2 Proc3 Proc4 Proc5

Figure 8.2
Typical channel establishment by parallel probing. From G. Manimaran, H. S. Rahul, and C. Siva Ram Murthy
[17], in *IEEE/ACM Trans. Networking* 7 (5). © IEEE, 1999.

• Generality. The parallel probing approach reduces to the flooding approach if the k
heuristics selected for parallel probing are the same, and it reduces to the preferred neighbor
approach when the number of paths searched in parallel is one, that is, when $k = 1$.

• Cycle-free path. The qualified routing path produced by the parallel probing is cycle
free.

Theorem 1:   Any qualified routing path produced by the parallel probing is cycle free.

Proof: Two types of cycles are possible: (1) cycles involving SNs, that is, the cycle
originates and terminates at the same SN, and (2) cycles involving IDs, that is, the cycle
originates and terminates at the same ID.

Cycles of type (1) cannot exist in a path determined by the parallel probing algorithm, since the heuristics employed for parallel probes ensure cycle-freeness in each
segment of the path. Even if the heuristics employed allow cycles, during the reverse pass,
such cycles can be removed. Cycles of type (2) could arise in two ways, as discussed
below.

The first possibility arises when the IID is ID_k and the current node is ID_i, such that $i < (k - 1)$. This means that the probe packet has reached an ID that had become the IID in the past, which implies a cycle of the form $ID_0, ID_1, \ldots, ID_i, \ldots, ID_{k-1}, \ldots, ID_i$. The portion of the path from ID_{k-1} to ID_i has to be removed. The first step of case ID of the algorithm does exactly this.

The second possibility arises when the following sequence of events takes place: (1) The IID is ID_k and the current node is ID_i such that $i > k$; this means that a probe packet has reached an ID that will become an IID in the future. In such cases, the ID node forwards the probe packet just as it would if it were an SN node (the last **else** part of case ID of the algorithm in figure 8.1). (2) ID_i becomes the IID. The sequence of events (1) and (2) results in creation of a cycle of the form $ID_0, ID_1, \ldots, ID_i, \ldots, ID_k, \ldots, ID_i$. The portion of the path from ID_i to ID_k to ID_i has to be removed. Such cycles are removed during the reverse pass of the algorithm by either the Relax() procedure or the Reject() procedure.

Theorem 2: The parallel probing algorithm does not leave dangling resources in the network. *Dangling resources* are unusable resources that are reserved on some links (and nodes) such that they are neither part of any successfully established real-time channel nor part of any ongoing channel setup attempt.

Proof: To prove this, we identify the procedures that reserve and release resources and also the node types that execute these procedures. Resources are reserved by procedures Reserve() and Forward(), and either or both of these are executed by nodes of type SOURCE, IID, ID, and SN. Reserve() reserves resources on a single link, and Forward() reserves resources on k links. Resources are released by procedures Release() and Backtrack(), and either or both of these are executed by nodes of type IID, ID, SN, and DESTINATION. The forms of unnecessary resource reservations, which could result in dangling resources, and the proper mechanisms for releasing such resources, are listed below.

• Since the algorithm itself ensures the release of resources between an IID (say ID_i) and ID_{i-1} for all the nonfirst probe packets reaching the IID, executing Release() ensures there are no dangling resources between two consecutive IDs.

• When an ID, say ID_i, becomes the last element in the IDs list, Reject() releases the resources reserved from ID_i to SOURCE.

• The algorithm detects certain cycles involving IDs in the forward pass and removes the unnecessary resources in the cycles (refer to case ID of the algorithm in figure 8.1). Similarly, Relax() removes other cycles during the reverse pass.

• When Backtrack() takes place at an ID or SN, the resources reserved on a link are released.

Thus, all reserved resources are either used by the successful channels, or properly released, or are part of ongoing channel setup attempts.

Theorem 3: A call setup initiated at a node is either set up or rejected in a finite time.

Proof: A call setup is initiated by executing Forward() at the SOURCE node of the call. Since the algorithm has the liveness property—that is, forward movement of probe packets from one ID to another in the order $ID_0, ID_1, \ldots, ID_{n-1}, ID_n$, it completes the forward pass in a finite time. It is obvious that the reverse pass also takes finite time, executing either the Relax() (for successful setup) or the Reject() (for call rejection) procedure.

8.3.3.4 Example for Parallel Probing Figure 8.2 depicts how the parallel probing algorithm establishes a channel for $k = 2$. Note that the path established has two segments, the first segment having been selected by heuristic H1 and the second by heuristic H2. The sequence of events taking place in figure 8.2 is given below:

1. To start with, $IID = ID_1$. SOURCE executes procedure Forward(SOURCE, IID, PROBE_PKT). This involves sending two probe packets, one using heuristic H1 (on the upper link) and the other using heuristic H2 (on the lower link).

2. The probe packet corresponding to heuristic H1 reaches ID_1 (the current IID) first. (This is the winner packet in segment 1.)

3. Now, $IID = DESTINATION$. ID_1 executes procedure Forward(ID_1, DESTINATION, PROBE_PKT). This involves sending two more probe packets, one using H1 (on the upper link) and the other using H2 (on the lower link).

4. Heuristic H2's first probe packet, which was sent from SOURCE, reaches ID_1. (This is the loser packet in segment 1.)

5. ID_1 executes procedure Release(ID_1, SOURCE, PROBE_PKT). This immediately releases the resources in the segment between SOURCE and ID_1 obtained using heuristic H2.

6. DESTINATION (which is the current IID) receives heuristic H2's second probe packet, which was sent from ID_1. (This is the winner packet in segment 2.)

7. DESTINATION accepts the call and executes procedure Relax(DESTINATION, SOURCE, PROBE_PKT). This confirms the channel from DESTINATION to SOURCE.

8. DESTINATION receives heuristic H1's second probe packet, which was sent from ID_1. (This is the loser packet in segment 2.)

9. DESTINATION executes procedure Release(DESTINATION, ID_1, PROBE_PKT). This releases the resources in the segment between ID_1 and DESTINATION obtained using heuristic H1.

8.4   Simulation Studies

In this section, we discuss the simulation studies presented in [17] for evaluating the performance of the parallel probing approach in terms of average call acceptance rate, average call setup time, and average route distance for a wide range of traffic and QoS parameters for different network topologies. Before presenting the results, we describe the simulation model and the parameters used in the simulation.

8.4.1   Simulation Model

To study the effectiveness of the parallel probing approach, in terms of all three metrics, its performance is compared with that of the flooding algorithm [24] and the TSPF algorithm [10]. Since the objective of any routing algorithm is to find a qualified path with minimal operational overheads, local-/static-knowledge-based heuristics for parallel probes are chosen. The number (k) of parallel paths searched simultaneously by the parallel probing approach is taken as two, and the heuristics employed in the search are SPF and LLF.

The IDs for the parallel probing approach are chosen based on the shortest path between the source and destination of the call. For example, let the length of the shortest path be n and the number of IDs be m, excluding source and destination. Then the ID_i of a call is the $(i * \frac{n}{m+1})$th node in the shortest path. In the simulation, the flooding algorithm sends a message to all its neighbors except the node from which the packet has come. The call admission test used, at each node, is the admission test of HRR scheduling algorithm described in the previous chapter. HRR is a rate-based scheduling discipline with a simple admission test: to decide whether to admit a new channel on a link, it checks whether the sum of the utilization (the utilization of a channel is the ratio of its maximum message length to the period of its frame size) of all the channels passing through the link (including the new channel) is less than or equal to one.

Three different network topologies have been considered for evaluating the performance of the different route selection algorithms. For performance study in a wide area network, the ARPA network shown in figure 8.3 (21 nodes, 26 links) has been taken as a representative topology. In the simulation, the delay and bandwidth of the links of the networks are taken to be 1 and 100, respectively. To obtain the desired performance metrics, for each simulation run, 5,000 call requests are generated. Each point in the simulation curves is an average of several runs, resulting in a confidence level of 95%. The simulation parameters are given in figure 8.4. Call requests for the simulation are generated according to the following two distributions:

1. Uniform distribution. The source-destination pair of a call is uniformly chosen from the node set.

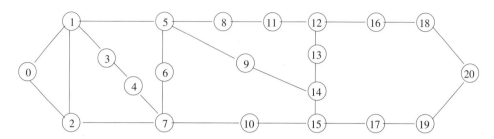

Figure 8.3
ARPA network (21 nodes, 26 links)

parameter	explanation	value taken when	
		varied	fixed
λ	call arrival rate	0.6, 0.7, . . . , 1.0	[0.5, 0.65]
del-min	minimum end-to-end delay of a call	–	10
del-max	maximum end-to-end delay of a call	10, 20, . . . , 50	20
bw-min	minimum bandwidth of a call	–	2
bw-max	maximum bandwidth of a call	2, 4, . . . , 12	4
dur-min	minimum duration of a call	–	200
dur-max	maximum duration of a call	200, 400, . . . , 1200	400
num-ID	number of intermediate destinations excluding source and destination	0, 1, 2, . . . , 5	2
hp-pair	% of hot-pair communication	10, 20, . . . , 60	0
stime	maximum call setup time	3, 4, . . . , 7	–

Figure 8.4
Simulation parameters. From G. Manimaran, H. S. Rahul, and C. Siva Ram Murthy [17], in *IEEE/ACM Trans. Networking* 7 (5). © IEEE, 1999.

2. Hot communication pair distribution. $p\%$ of all call requests are set to a particular hot (popular) source and destination pair; the other calls follow uniform distribution.

The other parameters of a call are generated as follows:

• The duration, bandwidth, and end-to-end delay requirements of a call are uniformly distributed between their respective minimum and maximum values.

• The interarrival times of call establishment requests follow exponential distribution with mean $1/\lambda$ for each node.

For studies in figures 8.5–8.9 and figure 8.11, there is no hot communication pair, and for studies in figures 8.5–8.10, the number of intermediate destinations used by the parallel probing approach is taken as two. To review, the main objective here is to devise a route selection approach that attempts to improve all three performance metrics simultaneously, since all are important in a real-time network, and also to adapt to different load conditions. To this effect, the experiments are so designed to study the effect of different QoS and traffic parameters for both uniform and hot-pair (nonuniform) communication patterns. Here, we present the results for the ARPA network topology. The simulation results plotted in figures 8.5–8.11 are those for this network.

8.4.2   Simulation Results

From figures 8.5(a)–8.10(a), it can be observed that the parallel probing approach offers higher ACAR than the other two algorithms for all the parameters varied. This is due to lower call setup overhead (in terms of resource reservation while probing for paths), because of the use of intermediate destinations and the high adaptiveness of parallel probing in terms of using multiple heuristics for path probing; that is, it allows a routing path to have different segments selected by different heuristics, whereas the flooding algorithm suffers because of tentative reservation of resources on multiple paths simultaneously, which increases the blocking of new calls. On the other hand, the TSPF suffers because of its less adaptiveness, but is still better than the flooding.

From figures 8.5(b,c)–8.10(b,c), it can be seen that flooding offers lower ACST and ARD than the other two algorithms because it probes for paths simultaneously on all links of a node. Also, note that the ACST and ARD for flooding are the same because it does not generate backtracking. The ACST and ARD of the parallel probing approach are very close to those of flooding and better than those of TSPF because of the controls on backtracking in parallel probing.

8.4.2.1   Effect of Call Traffic Characteristics   The effect of traffic characteristics of a call, namely, call arrival rate, call setup time, and call duration, are depicted in figures 8.5, 8.6, and 8.7, respectively.

As figure 8.5(a) shows, the ACAR decreases under all three algorithms for increasing values of call arrival rate. More calls arrive at higher loads, which in turn consume more resources, increasing the number of calls that are dropped. That is, at higher loads, more and more calls attempt to use the fixed available resources. Also, it can be observed that the ACST and ARD increase with the increases in load. At higher loads, finding a qualified path involves more of a search in the network, as most of the resources are already in use by the existing channels.

Figure 8.6 shows the effect of varying call setup time. An increase in call setup time introduces a trade-off between an improvement in ACAR due to the increased number of

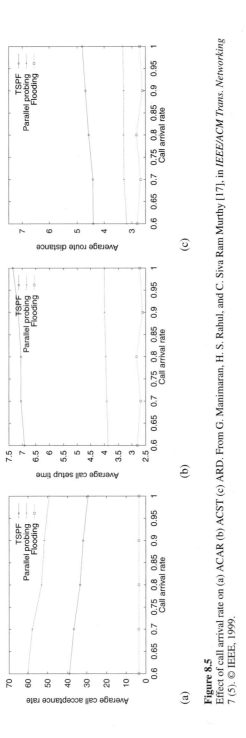

Figure 8.5
Effect of call arrival rate on (a) ACAR (b) ACST (c) ARD. From G. Manimaran, H. S. Rahul, and C. Siva Ram Murthy [17], in *IEEE/ACM Trans. Networking*
7 (5). © IEEE, 1999.

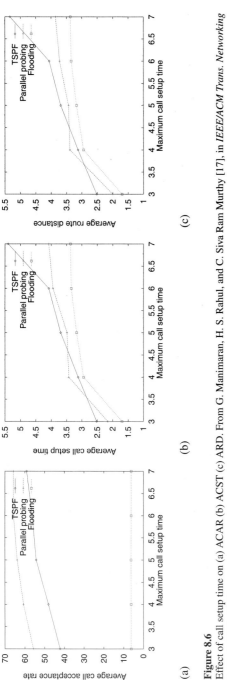

Figure 8.6
Effect of call setup time on (a) ACAR (b) ACST (c) ARD. From G. Manimaran, H. S. Rahul, and C. Siva Ram Murthy [17], in *IEEE/ACM Trans. Networking* 7 (5). © IEEE, 1999.

backtracks and a deterioration in ACAR due to excess resource reservation for a longer time. From figure 8.6(a), we can see that as the call setup time increases, the ACAR improves for all three algorithms (though the amount of improvement is not very significant for flooding), because the route selection algorithms are allowed to probe for channels for a longer time (more backtracking), which increases the chances of establishing a channel. Note that the ACAR curve corresponding to flooding is almost flat, since the flooding algorithm does not involve backtracking. Also note that as the call setup time increases, the ARD increases for all three algorithms, again because the algorithms are allowed to probe for paths for longer times, resulting in longer paths.

ACAR deteriorates when the ratio of call duration to call setup time is significantly lower. In the experiments, a large value, approximately 100 ($\approx 300/3.5$), is chosen for this ratio, and hence the gain obtained through the increase in backtracking more than offsets the deterioration.

From figure 8.7(a), it can be observed that the ACAR decreases with increasing call duration. For higher values of call duration, the currently active calls block resources (rendering them unavailable for the new calls) for longer durations. From figures 8.7(b) and (c), we see that increasing call duration increases the call setup time for parallel probing and TSPF because of blocking of resources. The call setup time of flooding increases very little because of its flooding (and hence no-backtracking) nature.

8.4.2.2   Effect of Call QoS Requirements   The effect of QoS requirements of a call, namely, bandwidth and end-to-end delay requirements, are depicted in figures 8.8 and 8.9, respectively. From Figure 8.8(a), we can see that the ACAR offered by all the three algorithms decreases for increasing values of bandwidth requirement. The reserving of more bandwidth for currently active calls results in more blocking of new calls. Also, for the same reason, the ACST and ARD increase with increasing bandwidth requirements.

The effect of varying the end-to-end delay constraint imposed by a call is shown in figure 8.9. As the end-to-end delay increases, the ACAR also increases, because the chances of meeting the delay constraint of a call are higher when the end-to-end delay is large; that is, the nodes along the path of a call can assign a higher node deadline (delay) for the messages of the call. The ACST metric decreases with increasing end-to-end delay for the same reason.

8.4.2.3   Effect of Hot Pair Communication   For this study, nodes 3 and 14 of the ARPA network (figure 8.3) are chosen as the hot communication pair (HCP). From figure 8.10, we can see that the ACAR decreases and the ACST and ARD increase with increasing hot pair communication percentage. In all three algorithms, an increase in hot communication saturates the paths between the HCP nodes after resources have been reserved for a certain number of calls, and hence subsequent calls are rejected until some of the resources are released through call tear down.

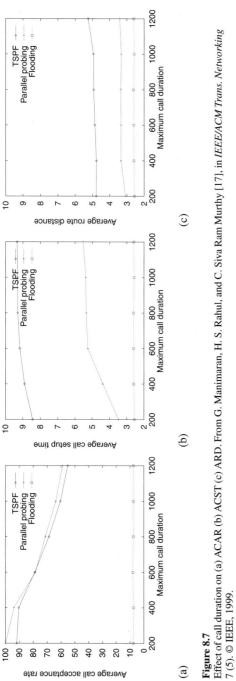

Figure 8.7
Effect of call duration on (a) ACAR (b) ACST (c) ARD. From G. Manimaran, H. S. Rahul, and C. Siva Ram Murthy [17], in *IEEE/ACM Trans. Networking* 7 (5). © IEEE, 1999.

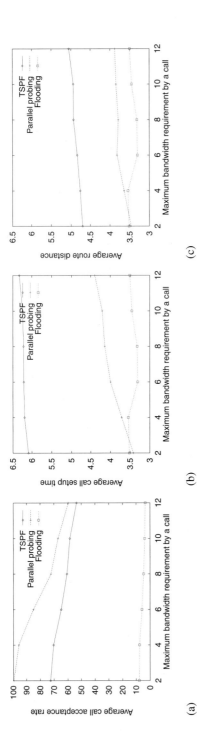

(a)

(b)

(c)

Figure 8.8
Effect of maximum bandwidth requirement of a call on (a) ACAR (b) ACST (c) ARD. From G. Manimaran, H. S. Rahul, and C. Siva Ram Murthy [17], in *IEEE/ACM Trans. Networking 7* (5). © IEEE, 1999.

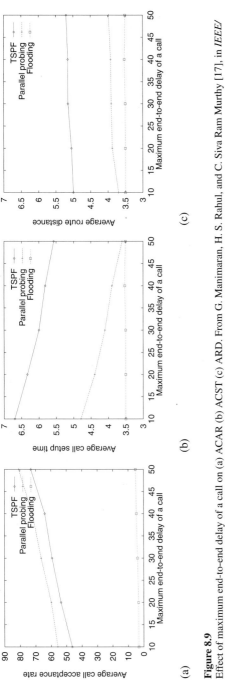

Figure 8.9
Effect of maximum end-to-end delay of a call on (a) ACAR (b) ACST (c) ARD. From G. Manimaran, H. S. Rahul, and C. Siva Ram Murthy [17], in *IEEE/ACM Trans. Networking 7 (5)*. © IEEE, 1999.

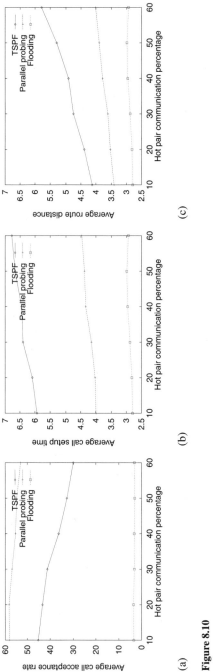

(a)

(b)

(c)

Figure 8.10
Effect of hot pair communication on (a) ACAR (b) ACST (c) ARD. From G. Manimaran, H. S. Rahul, and C. Siva Ram Murthy [17], in *IEEE/ACM Trans. Networking* 7 (5). © IEEE, 1999.

In conclusion, the parallel probing approach offers a higher call acceptance rate than that of the TSPF and flooding, and its setup time and routing distance are close to that of the flooding. Parallel probing is thus better than flooding and TSPF in improving all the three metrics simultaneously for different simulated load conditions.

8.4.2.4   Effect of Number of Intermediate Destinations   The effect of the number of IDs used in the parallel probing approach is depicted in figure 8.11. For this figure, 0%, 20%, and 40% HCP is considered, and nodes 3 and 14 of the ARPA network are chosen as the HCP.

Note that parallel probing introduces the concept of routing to IDs specifically to control excessive reservation of resources on parallel paths. The choice of the number of IDs is crucial in determining the overall performance of the network. When the number of IDs is very low, excessive resource reservations along the path still occur, which in turn reduces the ACAR. As a special case, when *num-ID* is 0, parallel probing reduces to k-path flooding, which reserves resources on k paths from a source up to the destination (in the worst case) during the forward pass. On the other hand, when the number of IDs is very large, the routing path is dictated by the least-cost metric used to identify the IDs. As a special case, when *num-ID* is equal to the length of the least-cost path, parallel probing reduces to the least-cost path heuristic.

The proper choice of *num-ID* depends on the topology of the network. When the network topology is dense, a higher value of *num-ID* is preferable to reduce the excessive reservation of resources by probe packets that arises because of the existence of a greater number of disjoint paths between any given source-destination pair. Any reasonable value of *num-ID* should be much less than the diameter of the network. From figure 8.11 (for ARPA), we can see that the overall peak performance (simultaneously considering all three metrics) occurs when the number of IDs (*num-ID*) is one.

Similarly, the choice of k is also crucial in determining the network's overall performance. When the network's topology is sparse, a lower value of k is preferable, because a higher value of k will cause the probe packets to visit many common nodes, reserving resources multiple times in such nodes, thereby reducing ACAR. In parallel probing, apart from the performance point of view, extra processing overhead comes in the form of sending k probe packets at every ID as opposed to one probe packet in conventional preferred neighbor approaches such as SPF, LLF, and TSPF. This extra processing overhead is much lower, however, as the number of IDs is much less than the diameter of the network.

8.5   Distributed Delay-Constrained Routing Algorithms

One of the problems studied in this class of constrained optimization problems is the least-cost delay-constrained routing problem [22]. Delay constraint is a very common

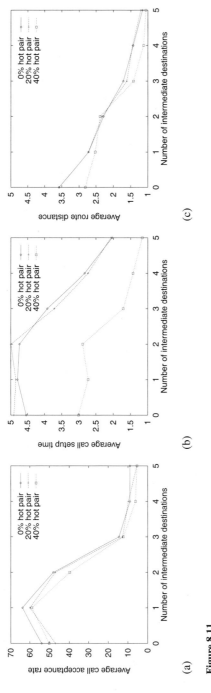

Figure 8.11
Effect of number of intermediate destinations on (a) ACAR (b) ACST (c) ARD. From G. Manimaran, H. S. Rahul, and C. Siva Ram Murthy [17], in *IEEE/ACM Trans. Networking* 7 (5). © IEEE, 1999.

requirement of many real-time applications. Cost minimization captures the need to distribute network resources efficiently among the various calls. The cost of a link is intended
as an abstraction that could, in practice, be mapped to a variety of link parameters, such as
the number of calls using the link and the reciprocal of available bandwidth.

8.5.1 Network Model

For the purpose of studying the least-cost delay-constrained routing problem, the network
is modeled as an undirected graph $G = (V, E)$, where V is the set of nodes and E is the set
of interconnecting links. We associate the following four functions with each link $e \in E$:

Delay function	$D : E \rightarrow R^+$
Cost function	$C : E \rightarrow R^+$
Total Bandwidth function	$TB: E \rightarrow R^+$
Available Bandwidth function	$AB: E \rightarrow R^+$

A path $P = (v_0, v_1, v_2, \cdots, v_n)$ in this network has two associated characteristics:

$$\text{Cost } C(P) = \sum_{i=0}^{n-1} C(v_i, v_{i+1}).$$

$$\text{Delay } D(P) = \sum_{i=0}^{n-1} D(v_i, v_{i+1}).$$

In the case of the *static network model,* it is assumed that for each $e \in E$, $C(e)$, $D(e)$,
and $TB(e)$ are fixed, and $AB(e)$ varies depending on the usage of the link. In the *dynamic
network model,* $C(e)$ and $D(e)$ are also allowed to vary. When the parameters $C(e)$ and
$D(e)$ of a particular link e change, it is assumed that this change is known to the nodes
attached to e immediately, even though the updating of tables in remote nodes (to reflect
these changes) may be delayed. This is a reasonable assumption to make, since nodes can
be expected to monitor the state of their adjacent links and register changes in the link
parameters immediately. Propagation of this information either directly (using link state
packets) or indirectly (by executing the distributed Bellman-Ford algorithm) to other nodes
will generally be delayed.

8.5.2 Problem Formulation

We model a channel establishment request (also referred to as a call) in the network
described above as a 5-tuple:

$R = (id, s, d, B, \Delta),$

where id is the call request identification number, $s \in V$ is the source node for the call, $d \in V$ is the destination node for the call, B is the bandwidth requirement, and Δ is the delay constraint to be satisfied. Let P_{sd} denote the set of all paths of the form $P = (s = v_0, v_1, v_2, \cdots, v_n = d)$ between source s and destination d that satisfy the following two conditions:

$AB(e) \geq B, \forall e = (v_i, v_{i+1}), 0 \leq i \leq n - 1.$

$D(P) \leq \Delta.$

The least-cost delay-constrained routing problem can now be formulated as

Find $P' \in P_{sd}$ such that $C(P') = \min\{C(P) : P \in P_{sd}\}$.

8.5.3 Delay-Constrained Unicast Routing Algorithm

A delay-constrained unicast routing (DCUR) algorithm, proposed recently in [22] for solving the least-cost delay-constrained routing problem, uses entries in the cost and distance vector tables maintained at each node to decide on the next node to which a given routing packet is to be passed. In the algorithm, every node initially attempts to forward the packet to the next node along the least-cost path to the destination. However, if the least delay from the next node to the destination is such that the delay constraint is violated, then the node attempts to forward the packet to the next hop along the least-delay path to the destination. Each node therefore makes a choice only between the next node on the least-cost path and the next node on the least-delay path to the destination. The algorithm, by restricting the choice to these two nodes, fails to consider links that could potentially offer a better overall cost-delay performance. In addition, because of its reliance on cost and distance vector tables, the algorithm is dependent on the accuracy of these tables. For dynamic networks whose link parameters vary frequently, this accuracy cannot be guaranteed.

8.5.4 Sriram et al.'s Algorithm

Sriram et al. [25] present a framework for describing preferred neighbor routing algorithms and propose three heuristics for the least-cost delay-constrained routing problem. To implement the proposed heuristics in conjunction with the preferred-link routing approach, each node in the network is equipped with two data structures, namely, a *history buffer* and a *preferred link table*.

8.5.4.1 Data Structures at Each Node

History Buffer   The history buffer (HB) at each node v contains one entry for every call for which v has received a call setup packet. Each entry contains a pair of elements $(packet, tried)$, where $packet$ is the call setup packet received by this node and $tried$ is the number of preferred neighbor links on which v has tried to forward the request. Therefore, the HB at a node v contains the complete status information for every call that v has handled. The entry corresponding to a particular call is removed when that call is either accepted or rejected.

Preferred Link Table   The structure of the preferred link table (PLT) to be maintained at each node depends on the nature of the heuristic function employed to construct the table. For the purpose of describing the structure of the PLT, we classify all heuristic functions as one of two major types, namely, destination-specific heuristics and call-specific heuristics.

Destination-specific heuristics are those whose computation is specific to each destination. If two different call requests arriving at a given node have the same destination nodes, then under a destination-specific heuristic, the two calls will share an identical list of preferred links. Each node v in the network is equipped with a PLT that contains one row for every destination. Each row contains the preferred links for that particular destination ordered in terms of decreasing preference. The maximum number of entries per row is denoted by κ. Obviously κ is upper-bounded by the maximum degree (i.e., the number of neighbors) of any node in the network. The preference for a link will be determined based on the value of a heuristic function computed for each (link, destination) pair.

Call-specific heuristics are those whose computation depends on the particular parameters carried by a given call setup packet arriving at the node. Under a call-specific heuristic, the list of preferred links is thus computed individually for each call request. As a result, the ordering of the preferred links in the path will be call-specific instead of simply destination-specific. For such heuristics, the number of rows in the PLT varies dynamically depending on the number of calls the node is currently handling. The table entries corresponding to a particular call are removed when that call is accepted or rejected.

8.5.4.2   Tests before Forwarding

Before forwarding any packet along a link, each node conducts three tests on the link parameters. The link is used for forwarding the packet only if all the tests are successful. The tests are described below.

Let $R = (id, s, d, B, \Delta)$ be a call request, and let P be a call request packet arriving at a node v. Let $P.path$ denote the path taken by the packet up to this point and $P.delay$ denote the cumulative delay along this path. Before forwarding the packet along link $l = (v, v')$, node v conducts the following three tests:

Bandwidth test. Verify that $AB(l) \geq B$.

Delay test. Verify that $P.delay + D(l) \leq \Delta$.

Loop test. Verify that v' is not a node in $P.path$.

8.5.4.3   Heuristic Functions

In this section, we describe heuristics [25] used to load the PLT tables at each node in the network. We also describe the computation to be performed in and the intuitive reason governing the choice of each heuristic. In describing the heuristics, we will use the following notation:

- $LDELAY(x, d)$ = the least delay from node x to node d in the network.
- $LCOST(x, d)$ = the cost of the least-cost path from node x to node d.
- $LDNHOP(x, d)$ = the first link on the least-delay path from x to d.
- $LCNHOP(x, d)$ = the first link on the least-cost path from x to d.

These values are assumed to be available at each node as a result of executing a distributed distance vector algorithm like the Bellman-Ford algorithm.

Residual Delay Maximizing Heuristic: The residual delay maximizing (RDM) heuristic is a call-specific heuristic. Let a call setup packet P belonging to call request $R = (id, s, d, B, \Delta)$ arrive at node v. For each link $l = (v, x)$ at v, let $RDM(l, R)$ denote the value of the heuristic for link l corresponding to call request R. Then we define

$$RDM(l, R) = \frac{C(l)}{\Delta - P.delay - D(l) - LDELAY(x, d)},$$

where $C(l)$ and $D(l)$ denote the cost and delay, respectively, of link l. If, in the calculation of the function, a particular link l produces a negative denominator, then that link is not included in the preferred list. The links are arranged in the preferred list in increasing order of their RDM values, so that the links with lower RDM values are given greater preference. The intuitive idea underlying this function is to maximize the residual delay (i.e., the delay available for setting up the rest of the path) at the same time minimizing the cost of the link chosen. A similar idea of residual delay has also been used by Kompella et al. [14] in their multicast routing algorithm.

Cost-Delay Product Heuristic: The cost-delay product (CDP) heuristic is a destination-specific heuristic. We define the cost-delay product, corresponding to the destination d, of a link $l = (v, x)$ to be

$$CDP(l) = C(l) \star (D(l) + LDELAY(x, d)),$$

where $C(l)$ is the cost of the link and $D(l)$ its delay. To load the PLT entries corresponding to the destination d, the following steps are performed:

- The links adjacent to v are arranged in increasing order of their CDP values, and the first κ links are chosen.
- If this chosen set does not contain $LCNHOP(v, d)$, then $LCNHOP(v, d)$ is placed as the first preferred link, and the last link in the set originally chosen is dropped.

- If now the set does not contain $LDNHOP(v, d)$, then $LDNHOP(v, d)$ is used to replace the last preferred link in the chosen set.

This final set of links is used to populate the PLT entry for destination d.

Partition-Based Ordering Heuristic: The partition-based ordering (PBO) heuristic is a destination-independent and call-independent heuristic. Let $avg(v)$ denote the average cost of all the links adjacent to v. The links adjacent to a node v are partitioned into two sets *below* and *above*, where

$below(v) = \{l : C(l) <= avg(v)\}.$

$above(v) = \{l : C(l) > avg(v)\}.$

The links in the two sets are then separately sorted in increasing order of their delay values. A new list is then created, containing the sorted *below* set, followed by the sorted *above* set. The first κ links from this new list are chosen and used to populate the table (which in this case reduces to a single-row table).

In all three of the above heuristics, ties between two links are resolved by giving preference to the link with larger available bandwidth.

8.5.4.4 Example of Delay-Constrained Routing   In this section, we describe how the DCUR algorithm handles a set of five call requests in a small five-node network. We then illustrate how Sriram's algorithm handles the same requests using the RDM heuristic. The five-node network is shown in figure 8.12. Each edge of the network is labeled with an ordered pair representing the (cost,delay) values of the link. Each edge is assumed to have a total bandwidth of 30 units. Consider the five call requests given in figure 8.13, which occur one after another in the specified order. Figure 8.14 shows the least-cost and least-delay paths between every pair of vertices in figure 8.12.

8.5.4.5 Route Selection by the DCUR and RDM Algorithms   In the following description of the steps executed by both the algorithms, we will use the notations $LDNHOP(x, d)$, $LCNHOP(x, d)$, $LDELAY(x, d)$, and $LCOST(x, d)$, defined previously. We will also use $D(a \rightarrow b)$ and $C(a \rightarrow b)$ to denote the delay and cost of the link connecting vertices a and b.

Routes Chosen by the DCUR Heuristic

1. Call 1. (source $= 1$; destination $= 3$; $\Delta = 6$)

   At node 1:

- Attempt along the least-cost path using the link $LCNHOP(1, 3) = (1 \rightarrow 2)$.

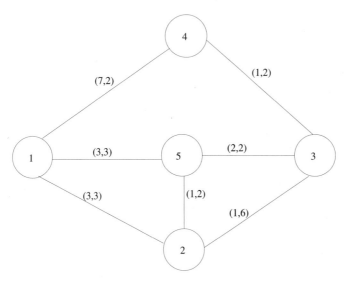

Figure 8.12
Network with (cost,delay)

call id	source	dest.	bandwidth	Δ
1	1	3	10	6
2	2	4	10	7
3	2	4	10	6
4	2	4	10	6
5	2	4	10	7

Figure 8.13
Set of call requests

- Calculate minimum possible delay if $(1 \rightarrow 2)$ is chosen.

$D(1 \rightarrow 2) + LDELAY(2, 3) = 3 + 4 = 7.$

- Since $7 > \Delta$ and $LDELAY(1, 3) < \Delta$, node 1 chooses $LDNHOP(1, 3) = (1 \rightarrow 4)$.

- Forward packet to node 4.

At node 4:

- Receive a packet P from node 1 with $P.delay = D(1 \rightarrow 4) = 2$.

- Attempt along the least-cost path, $LCNHOP(4, 3) = (4 \rightarrow 3)$.

vertex pair	least-cost path	least cost	least-delay path	least delay
(1, 2)	$1 \rightarrow 2$	3	$1 \rightarrow 2$	3
(1, 3)	$1 \rightarrow 2 \rightarrow 3$	4	$1 \rightarrow 4 \rightarrow 3$	4
(1, 4)	$1 \rightarrow 2 \rightarrow 3 \rightarrow 4$	5	$1 \rightarrow 4$	2
(1, 5)	$1 \rightarrow 5$	3	$1 \rightarrow 5$	3
(2, 3)	$2 \rightarrow 3$	1	$2 \rightarrow 5 \rightarrow 3$	4
(2, 4)	$2 \rightarrow 3 \rightarrow 4$	2	$2 \rightarrow 1 \rightarrow 4$	5
(2, 5)	$2 \rightarrow 5$	1	$2 \rightarrow 5$	2
(3, 4)	$3 \rightarrow 4$	1	$3 \rightarrow 4$	2
(3, 5)	$3 \rightarrow 5$	2	$3 \rightarrow 5$	2
(4, 5)	$4 \rightarrow 3 \rightarrow 5$	3	$4 \rightarrow 3 \rightarrow 5$	4

Figure 8.14
Least-cost and least-delay paths between pairs of vertices in figure 8.12

- Since $P.delay + D(4 \rightarrow 3) < \Delta$, forward packet to node 3, which is also the destination. Hence the selected route is $1 \rightarrow 4 \rightarrow 3$; cost $= 8$.

2. Call 2. (source $= 2$; destination $= 4$; $\Delta = 7$)
The algorithm proceeds as in the previous call.
The route that is chosen is $2 \rightarrow 1 \rightarrow 4$; cost $= 10$.

3. Calls 3, 4, and 5. Calls 3, 4, and 5 all use the pair of vertices (2, 4) as the source-destination pair. This set of calls was chosen to illustrate how the algorithms deal with hot pair communication, wherein a large number of calls are generated for a given (source,destination) pair. The DCUR algorithm will choose the path $2 \rightarrow 1 \rightarrow 4$ for each of these calls, as each call has a delay constraint less than 8 (which is the delay along the least-cost path between 2 and 4). However, after call 3 is accepted, link (1, 4) will have no available bandwidth, as it is supporting calls 1, 2, and 3, each of which requires 10 units. Therefore, the DCUR algorithm will reject calls 4 and 5.

Routes Chosen by the RDM Heuristic

1. Call 1. (source $= 1$; destination $= 3$; $\Delta = 6$)

   At node 1: The RDM value is computed for each of the three links adjacent to node 1:
- For link $(1 \rightarrow 2)$: $RDM(1 \rightarrow 2) = \frac{3}{6-0-3-4} < 0$; skipped because it fails delay test.
- For link $(1 \rightarrow 5)$: $RDM(1 \rightarrow 5) = \frac{3}{6-0-3-2} = 3$.
- For link $(1 \rightarrow 4)$: $RDM(1 \rightarrow 4) = \frac{7}{6-0-2-2} = 3.5$.

The lowest value is for link $(1 \to 5)$, hence the packet is forwarded to node 5 via link $(1 \to 5)$.

At node 5: Here again the RDM values are computed for the three links adjacent to node 5:

- For link $(5 \to 1)$: skipped because it fails loop test.
- For link $(5 \to 2)$: RDM$(5 \to 2) = \frac{1}{6-3-2-4} < 0$; skipped because it fails delay test.
- For link $(5 \to 3)$: RDM$(5 \to 3) = \frac{2}{6-3-2-0} = 2$.

Hence the packet is forwarded to node 3 via link $(5 \to 3)$.
The selected route is $1 \to 5 \to 3$; cost $= 5$.

2. Call 2. (source $= 2$; destination $= 4$; $\Delta = 7$)

At node 2:

- For link $(2 \to 1)$: RDM$(2 \to 1) = \frac{3}{7-0-3-2} = 1.5$.
- For link $(2 \to 5)$: RDM$(2 \to 5) = \frac{1}{7-0-2-4} = 1$.
- For link $(2 \to 3)$: RDM$(2 \to 3) = \frac{1}{7-0-6-2} < 0$; skipped because it fails delay test.

Hence the packet is forwarded to node 5 via link $(2 \to 5)$.

At node 5:

- For link $(5 \to 2)$: RDM$(5 \to 2) = \frac{2}{7-2-2-5} < 0$; skipped because it fails delay test.
- For link $(5 \to 1)$: RDM$(5 \to 1) = \frac{3}{7-2-3-2} = \infty$.
- For link $(5 \to 3)$: RDM$(5 \to 3) = \frac{2}{7-2-2-2} = 2$.

Hence the packet is forwarded to node 3 via link $(5 \to 3)$.

At node 3:

- For link $(3 \to 2)$: skipped because it fails loop test.
- For link $(3 \to 5)$: skipped because it fails loop test.
- For link $(3 \to 4)$: RDM$(3 \to 4) = \frac{1}{7-4-2-0} = 1$.

Hence the packet is forwarded to node 4, which is the destination.
The chosen route is $2 \to 5 \to 3 \to 4$; cost $= 4$.

3. Calls 3, 4, and 5. RDM will route call 3 along the path $2 \to 5 \to 3 \to 4$ similar to call 2. Link $(5, 3)$ will now be saturated, as it is used by calls 1, 2, and 3. When call 4 arrives, RDM will choose $(2, 5)$ and forward the packet to node 5. At 5, link $(5, 3)$ will fail the bandwidth test, and link $(5, 1)$ will fail the delay test. Therefore RDM will backtrack to node 2. The link $(2, 1)$ will be the next preferred link at node 1, and the path $2 \to 1 \to 4$ will be selected. The path chosen for call 5 is $2 \to 5 \to 1 \to 4$. Hence all the calls will be

call number	DCUR performance	RDM performance
1	Accepted; Cost $= 8$	Accepted; Cost $= 5$
2	Accepted; Cost $= 10$	Accepted; Cost $= 4$
3	Accepted; Cost $= 10$	Accepted; Cost $= 4$
4	Rejected	Accepted; Cost $= 10$
5	Rejected	Accepted; Cost $= 10$

Figure 8.15
Call acceptance performance of the DCUR and RDM algorithms

accepted. In fact, RDM will be able to accomodate yet another call between $(2, 4)$ with the same bandwidth requirement.

Comments on the Performance   Figure 8.15 summarizes the performance of the two algorithms in the above example. The example clearly illustrates where the preferred neighbor approach using the RDM heuristic scores over the DCUR algorithm. In the case of calls 1 and 2, the DCUR algorithm, at each node, attempted to forward the packet via the least-cost route. However, since the delay constraint was not satisfied, it finally chose only the least-delay route between the source and destination. The RDM algorithm, however, was able to find a route in both cases that was neither the least-cost nor the least-delay route but satisfied the delay constraint without excessive cost. Calls 3, 4, and 5 illustrate that because of its ability to search for alternate paths, the RDM algorithm is able to distribute the hot pair communication load between nodes 2 and 4 among different routes, resulting in a greater level of call acceptance.

8.6   Dependable Real-Time Channels

Real-time channels (virtual circuits) provide QoS guarantees as long as traffic sources obey their traffic specifications and there are no component (link and/or node) failures.[†] Traffic is usually regulated through traffic shaping at the source nodes, as discussed in the previous chapter. Component failures are handled by either rerouting the channel around the faulty components or by employing redundant channels.

   Providing fault tolerance to real-time channels has become a problem of growing importance for the following reasons:

• Because of the nature of some real-time applications, the packets carried by such real-time channels have criticality.

[†] In this chapter, faults and failures are used interchangeably.

- Since real-time networks carry a large volume of data, an outage for even a small interval of time will result in the loss of a large volume of data, which will in turn affect a large user community.

This growing importance of fault tolerance motivates the need for a *survivable network,* a network that has the capability of detecting and recovering from failures. Survivable networks can be broadly classified into protection-based and restoration-based networks. In *protection-based networks,* dedicated protection mechanisms are provided to cope with failures. Such networks use a *forward recovery approach.* In *restoration-based* networks, when a failure occurs, an attempt is made to acquire the resources necessary to restore the channel. These networks use a *detection and recovery* approach.

A survivable network might have the following desirable properties: (1) fast and efficient detection of failures, (2) fast restoration, (3) full restoration (the state of the network after a failure should be the same as before the failure), (4) minimum impact of failure on the existing channels, and (5) minimal cost.

8.6.1   Forward Recovery Approaches

Forward recovery approaches are an example of a protection mechanism in which multiple copies of a packet (or enough redundant information to recover from the loss of a packet) are sent simultaneously over disjoint paths to mask the effect of failures. Such approaches have the advantage of transparently handling faults without service disruption. However, they incur extra cost in terms of the extra bandwidth used to achieve fault tolerance.

8.6.2   Traffic Dispersion

Traffic dispersion is a mechanism by which traffic from a source node is dispersed along multiple paths to a destination, each of which is called a *subchannel.* Each subchannel guarantees the same amount of bandwidth, and the sum of the subchannel bandwidths is equal to the bandwidth of the channel. Since the bandwidth requested by each subchannel is very low compared to the channel bandwidth, the chances of establishing many small-bandwidth subchannels is very high compared to the chance of establishing a single high-bandwidth channel, thereby improving the call acceptance rate.

When dispersity routing[1] is combined with a forward recovery approach, extra subchannels are used for fault tolerance purposes, and the paths of the subchannels are disjoint

---

1. Note that pure traffic dispersion is not a fault-tolerant approach.

so that faults can be tolerated. The dispersity-based forward recovery approach, called the (N, K, S) system [3], is formally stated as follows:

• *Dispersity(N)*. A channel is split into N subchannels. A packet is split into N subpackets, and all subpackets are sent in parallel, one per subchannel.

• *Redundancy($N - K$)*. $N - K$ subchannels carry redundant information to achieve fault recovery. A certain number of subpackets can be corrupted or lost without affecting the recipient's ability to decode the packet. The number of subpackets that can be corrupted without affecting decodability depends on N, K, and the error-correcting code used. It can be no larger than $N - K$.

• *Disjointness(S)*. S is the maximum number of subchannels of a connection that can share a given link. When it becomes impossible to determine enough disjoint paths to meet the dispersity requirements, sharing of links by subchannels proves very useful in improving the call acceptance rate.

A channel with attributes (N, K, S) can tolerate up to $\lfloor \frac{N-K}{S} \rfloor$ faults transparently, if maximum distance separable codes are used [3]. An (N, K, S) system uses approximately N/K times the bandwidth required by an equivalent non-fault-tolerant channel.

8.6.3   Hot versus Cold Standby

The redundant subchannels of a dispersity system can be operated in hot or cold standby mode. In the case of hot standby, extra subchannels carry forward error correction (FEC) information during normal operation. In cold standby, extra subchannels are used only in the event of a failure.

The dispersity-based forward recovery approach with hot standby has the following advantages:

• Failures can be overcome transparently through FEC.

• Load on any particular path is smaller, which results in a better call acceptance rate (performance).

• Failure only partly affects the transmission capacity of a particular channel.

• Dispersity helps to even out the effects of bursts in traffic.

• Bandwidth splitting helps increase performance, especially when the network is heavily loaded.

• The path disjointness constraint becomes significant as N becomes larger and approaches the number of disjoint paths available.

8.7   Detection and Recovery Approaches

When a failure occurs in a restoration-based network, an attempt is made to acquire the resources, such as bandwidth and buffers, necessary to restore the channel with minimal disruption in service. Such networks use a *detection and recovery* approach, which is useful if occasional packet losses due to transient failures are tolerable and restoration is initiated only when a permanent failure is detected. This approach is also cost-effective.

In a datagram network, any necessary rerouting occurs at the packet level, whereas in a virtual-circuit-switched network, packet-level rerouting is unnecessary because all the packets traveling on a particular channel use a fixed path. Rerouting in virtual-circuit-switched networks can take place at two levels: the link level and the circuit level. In a *link-level* scheme,[2] all the circuits currently passing through the failed link are rerouted onto a nonfaulty link. In a *circuit-level* scheme, in contrast, each circuit is rerouted independently, possibly on different links. The link-level scheme offers a lower restoration time compared to the circuit-level scheme; however, the circuit-level scheme has a better chance than the link-level scheme of successfully rerouting the circuits.

In ATM networks, in addition to circuit-level and link-level rerouting, the rerouting can also be done at the virtual path (VP) level. At the VP (circuit) level, the network is restored after failure by rerouting the traffic from the failed VPs (circuits) to alternate VPs (circuits), as in [13] ([19]). VP-level rerouting offers the benefits of both the other schemes. It is also possible to devise an adaptive scheme that selects any of these schemes for use depending on the nature of failures. In ATM networks, survivability can also be achieved at the link level by employing multiple links, as in [12].

Detection and recovery approaches can be further classified into two categories: (1) reactive methods and (2) spare resource reservation methods.

8.7.1   Reactive Methods

In reactive methods, a new real-time channel is established when a fault is detected. This approach has low overhead in the absence of failures, but requires more restoration time when there is a failure. It also does not guarantee successful restoration for two reasons: (1) It may encounter a resource shortage during any recovery attempt, and (2) simultaneous recovery attempts may result in contention for resources.

---

2. If a node fails, all the links connected to it are also assumed to have failed.

8.7.2   Spare Resource Reservation Methods

Spare resource reservation methods avoid/minimize resource shortage during recovery by reserving a priori spare resources to be used in times of failure. These reserved spare resources can be used in two ways:

• *Local detouring.* Spare resources in the vicinity of a failed network component can be used to reroute failed channels. This has the drawback that resource usage becomes inefficient after failure recovery.

• *End-to-end detouring.* Establishing end-to-end backup channels with reserved spare resources avoids the drawback of inefficient resource usage after failure recovery encountered in local detouring and overcomes both the disadvantages of the reactive methods. The end-to-end detouring scheme is also known as the *primary-backup channel* scheme.

8.7.2.1   Primary-Backup Channel Scheme   A real-time channel is said to be *dependable* (D-connection) if it consists of one primary and one or more backup channels acting as cold standby. Each backup channel has the same bandwidth as its corresponding primary channel. A backup channel is activated on the failure of any network component in the primary channel. The two main issues here are (1) establishment of backup channel(s), before a failure, which involves selecting route(s) for the backup channel(s) (backup route selection) and assigning bandwidth to the backup channel(s) (spare resource allocation), and (2) failure detection and backup activation. D-connections are set up and torn down dynamically. The aim of any primary-backup channel scheme is to establish dependable channels that minimize spare resource reservation, thereby improving the call acceptance rate.

Backup Route Selection   The problem of optimal routing of backup channels to optimize spare resource allocation is known to be NP-complete. Therefore, heuristic cost functions and least-cost routing are used for setting up paths for backup channels. A cost function that takes *backup multiplexing* into account yields a better performance than non-backup multiplexing but requires information regarding the routing path of all the primary channels in the entire network to evaluate the cost function. Therefore, backup route selection is centralized and is usually done at the source node [8].

Spare Resource Allocation with Backup Multiplexing   Spare resource allocation with backup multiplexing is a resource-sharing technique used in the primary-backup channel scheme wherein, on each link, only a very small fraction of the resources, such as bandwidth, are allocated for all backup channels using that link. Such a link is then said to be *multiplexed.* Typically, the bandwidth assigned to the backup channels on a multiplexed link is the maximum among the bandwidth requirements of all the backup channels multi-plexed onto it. If these bandwidths are equal, the bandwidth allocated will be the same as the bandwidth required by any one of the backup channels. Two or more backup channels on a link can be multiplexed under the following conditions:

• The paths of the corresponding primary channels must be disjoint.

• At most one of the corresponding primary channels can fail at any given point in time.

Two types of backup multiplexing are possible:

1. *Deterministic multiplexing with resource aggregation.* This type of multiplexing adopts a deterministic failure model and calculates the exact amount of spare resources required to handle all possible cases under that model. Spare resource calculation differs depend-ing on the failure model chosen (single/double failure, link/node/both, etc.). Deterministic multiplexing is useful only when resource reservation is completely interchangeable among channels (as in rate-based scheduling algorithms in which bandwidth and delay are cou-pled) [9].

2. *Probabilistic multiplexing.* This type of multiplexing is used to cope with nondetermin-istic failure models, which assume that each network component fails at a particular rate. Backup channels are multiplexed using a modified admission test depending on the prob-ability of their simultaneous activation. A probabilistic multiplexing scheme can also be used for deterministic failure models. Unlike deterministic multiplexing, probabilistic mul-tiplexing is applicable to both rate-based and scheduler-based scheduling algorithms [9].

8.8   Work on Establishing Dependable Real-Time Channels

Dispersity routing coupled with error correction coding schemes, as reported in [3], is an example of a forward recovery approach to failure protection. Even though this approach has the advantage of handling failures without service disruption, it is too expensive for certain applications like multimedia communication, in which occasional packet losses are tolerable. If infrequent packet losses due to transient failures are tolerable, the detection and recovery approach, which detects and recovers from permanent failures, is more attractive and cost-effective. The methods proposed in [1, 2, 8, 13, 18, 29] are examples of the detection and recovery approach.

   The method described in [2] requires that all failures be broadcast to the entire network. It allocates no resources in advance for the channel(s), resulting in greater restoration time but lesser resource overhead in the absence of failures. The approach proposed in [29] provides guaranteed failure recovery under a single-failure model. In this method, additional resources are reserved in the vicinity of each real-time channel, and packets are locally detoured around failed components using the reserved resources. This method guarantees faster restoration but requires more resource overhead. The primary-backup scheme with backup multiplexing reported in [8] has the advantage of offering flexible fault tolerance level (in terms of number of backup channels) for each real-time channel and establishing channels dynamically. Backup multiplexing is used to minimize the spare resources reserved.

The approaches proposed in [1, 13, 18] are VP restoration methods in ATM networks based on the backup VP concept. In backup VP–based schemes, the routes for backup VPs are assigned off-line, based on the assumption of a fixed traffic demand, whereas bandwidth for the backup VPs is assigned either off-line or on-line (i.e., after a failure has occurred). Most of these schemes use on-line bandwidth assignment and therefore come under the category of detection and recovery approach. In these schemes, the fault tolerance level of each connection cannot be controlled individually.

8.8.1   An Integrated Approach to Establishing Dependable Real-Time Channels

In this section, we describe a fault-tolerant real-time channel establishment scheme for dynamically establishing D-connections, with control over the fault tolerance level of each D-channel, which provides both soft and hard real-time guarantees for message communication in multihop real-time networks. This involves route selection and bandwidth assignment for both primary and backup channels.

Supporting both hard and soft real-time communication with fault tolerance is a very common requirement of many real-world applications. Real-time channels with hard guarantees cannot tolerate loss of even a single packet, whereas real-time channels with soft guarantees can tolerate an occasional loss of a packet. Hard real-time communication is supported by deterministic channels, which guarantee absolute delay bound, whereas soft real-time communication is supported by statistical channels, in which the delay bounds are expressed in statistical terms: for instance, the probability that the delay of a message is less than the given delay bound must be greater than some given value.

Forward recovery approaches are inefficient for statistical channels because they establish backup channels in hot standby mode, which is unnecessary for statistical channels and leads to a lower call acceptance rate. Similarly, detection and recovery approaches are unsuitable for deterministic channels, since they do not provide nonzero restoration time, resulting in loss of packets, which is unacceptable in deterministic channels. This motivates the need for integrating forward error recovery approaches and detection and recovery approaches in a single fault-tolerant channel establishment scheme.

To realize this objective, Sriram et al. [26] recently proposed a scheme (we call it the *integrated scheme*) that combines the bandwidth splitting and FEC advantages of the dispersity-based forward recovery approach with the efficient spare resource allocation achieved through backup multiplexing in the detection and recovery approach. In the integrated scheme, the backup subchannels operate in cold standby mode to make multiplexing possible and the FEC subchannels operate in hot standby mode.

8.8.1.1 Description of the Integrated Scheme The integrated scheme is characterized by a 3-tuple (N_m, N_{fec}, N_b), where

• N_m denotes the number of *message subchannels* (without redundancy). This means that a given packet is split into N_m subpackets and transmitted in parallel on these N_m subchannels.

• N_{fec} denotes the number of (redundant) *FEC subchannels*. N_{fec} is a function of both the dispersity level (N_m) and the fault model (i.e., whether single/multiple simultaneous failures must be handled). In the case of the single-failure model, it can be shown that for successful error recovery, N_m and N_{fec} must obey the inequality $(N_m + N_{fec} + 1) \leq 2^{N_{fec}}$. This restriction places a lower bound on the value of N_{fec} for a given value of N_m. For example, $N_m = 2$ gives a value of $N_{fec} = 3$. Error-correcting codes that achieve this lower bound for all values of N_m are known.

• N_b denotes the number of *backup subchannels*. The method used to calculate the number of backup subchannels is discussed below.

In the integrated scheme, the message and FEC subchannels together are referred to as *primary subchannels*. The bandwidth allocated for each subchannel (referred to as *subchannel bandwidth*), whether primary or backup, is $\frac{1}{N_m}$th of the total bandwidth specified by the channel establishment request.

8.8.1.2 Choice of N_b The choice of N_b in the integrated scheme depends on two factors:

• the nature of the fault model used to characterize permanent faults

• whether the redundancy, usually used only to counter transient failures, is also used to overcome permanent faults.

For example, consider a certain system capable of handling one transient fault through the use of FEC subchannels. Suppose the double-link failure model is used for permanent faults. If a single permanent fault occurs in one of the primary subchannels of a connection in this system, a backup subchannel can be used to counter this failure, and the system can continue to enjoy single transient failure recovery. Now suppose another permanent fault occurs in one of the primary subchannels. There are two possible ways of countering this fault:

• Use the system's inherent FEC capability to overcome the fault and instead of another backup subchannel. This will mean that the system will no longer be capable of overcoming transient failures.

• To retain the capacity for transient failure recovery, use another backup subchannel to overcome this second permanent fault.

Clearly, depending on the importance of recovering from transient failures (which the application will dictate), the number of backup subchannels could be either equal to, or less than, the maximum number of permanent faults the fault model allows. This gives the system added flexibility and can be used to choose efficiently the number of multiplexed backup subchannels. Note that in the pure primary-backup scheme [8] (without redundancy), the number of backup channels is equal to the maximum number of permanent faults the fault model allows.

8.8.1.3 Formal Presentation of Integrated Scheme

An integrated D-channel request C is characterized in the integrated scheme by $((N_m, B, IS\_FEC), N_{PF}, N_{TF})$. We present below a pseudocode for channel setup (Channel_Setup()) and run time event handling of the integrated scheme. The D-channel is established with a given level of fault tolerance and forward error correction capability. These parameters are specified by the application and are negotiable. Channel setup is successful if the resource requirements of both the primary and backup channels can be satisfied. Otherwise, it is rejected. An established D-channel encounters many events, such as the occurrence of faults and subsequent recovery. Handling of these events is described below in Run_Time_Event_Handling().

Channel_Setup($C : (N_m, B, IS\_FEC), N_{PF}, N_{TF}$) /* Integrated D-channel request. */
    N_m: Number of primary subchannels, B: total bandwidth of the channel.
    IS_FEC: Boolean variable; true if no FEC channels are to be used for overcoming permanent
        faults, false otherwise.
    N_{PF}: Number of permanent faults to be tolerated by the D-channel.
    N_{TF}: Number of transient faults to be tolerated by the D-channel.
begin
    Calculate $N_{fec} = g(N_m, N_{TF})$ /* g(): coding scheme used for FEC. */
    If (IS_FEC is true) $N_b = N_{PF}$ **else** $N_b = N_{PF} - N_{TF}$.
    Establish ($N_m + N_{fec}$) disjoint paths each having a bandwidth of B/N_m.

Find paths for the N_b subchannels.

For each link l of each backup subchannel

    If (single link fault-tolerance) **Spare_Resource_Single_Link**(l)

    else (double link fault-tolerance) **Spare_Resource_Double_Link**(l)

    Reserve bandwidth b_l for link l

end.

Run_Time_Event_Handling(D-channel C) /* event handling in the integrated scheme. */

begin

    NPF = 0;   /* NPF: counter maintaining the number of permanent faults encountered. */

    While (true) **do**

        Switch(*event*)

        begin

            case *event* = TRANSIENT_FAULT:

                Forward error recovery at the destination node.

            case *event* = PERMANENT_FAULT:

                NPF = NPF + 1;

                If ($NPF \leq N_b$) activate a backup subchannel.

            case *event* = LINK_RESTORED:

                Reactivate corresponding primary channel;

                Deactivate one of the backup channels in use.

                NPF = NPF − 1;

        end

end.

8.8.1.4   **Backup Multiplexing in the Integrated Scheme**   The integrated scheme uses the backup multiplexing technique of [8] to reduce the amount of spare resources reserved for the backup subchannels. Backup multiplexing is based on the idea that it is possible to determine whether two backup channels will simultaneously be brought into action. Given the routes of the primary channels, if it can be shown that, under a given fault model, two particular backup channels will never be activated together, then the two can share the bandwidth on their common links. In the integrated scheme, a modified version of the backup multiplexing algorithm proposed in [8] is used to calculate the amount of spare resources to be allocated for the backup subchannels of the various connections. The algorithms used to calculate the required spare resources in the case of single-link and double-link failure models are given below.

The algorithms presented adopt a deterministic failure model [8] and calculate an amount of spare resources that is just enough to handle all possible cases under the assumed failure model. Whenever a backup subchannel is to be established, the appropriate algorithm has to be run on all links of the backup path. For each link l of the backup path, the first and second algorithms presented below calculate the required spare bandwidth b_l for single-link or double-link fault tolerance, respectively.

Spare_Resource_Single_Link(Link l) /* single link fault-tolerance. */
begin
    For each link $i, i \neq l$
        For each connection c whose backup subchannel uses l
            If c has a primary subchannel using i
                $b_{i,l} = b_{i,l} + B/N_m$
    $b_l = max\{b_{i,l}\}, \forall i \neq l$ /* b_l: spare bandwidth at link l. */
end.

Spare_Resource_Double_Link(Link l) /* double link fault-tolerance. */
begin
    For each link $i, i \neq l$
        For each connection c whose backup subchannel uses l
            If c has a primary subchannel using i
                $b_{i,l} = b_{i,l} + B/N_m$
    For each pair of links i and $j, i \neq j, i \neq l, j \neq l$
        For each connection c whose second backup subchannel uses l
            If (c has two different primary subchannels using links i and j) **or**
                /* this term is due to traffic dispersion */
                (c has a primary subchannel using i and first backup subchannel using j)
                $b_{i,j,l} = b_{i,j,l} + B/N_m$
    $b_l = max\{b_{i,l} + b_{i,j,l}\}, \forall i \neq l, \forall j \neq l$
end.

8.8.2 Advantages of Integrated Scheme

The integrated scheme adapts well to applications having either hard or soft real-time communication requirements or both. It improves the call acceptance rate significantly, for a given degree of fault tolerance, because of its efficient resource allocation mechanisms, such as bandwidth splitting (by traffic dispersion) and backup multiplexing. Moreover, the integrated scheme has the flexibility of being able to be reduced to either of the two basic approaches by suitable choice of N_m, N_{fec}, and N_b. For example, when $N_b = 0$, the integrated scheme reduces to the dispersity-based forward error recovery approach. Similarly, when $N_m = 1$ and $N_{fec} = 0$, it reduces to the primary-backup channel approach.

8.8.3 Applications of Dependable Real-Time Channels

The integrated D-channel scheme can satisfy the communication requirements of many real-world problems. For example, the air defense system and air traffic control system (ATCS), both of which are inherently distributed, are two important applications of the scheme. These applications involve both hard and soft real-time communication, with fault tolerance requirements, between different nodes of the system. In this section, we briefly describe the applicability of the integrated scheme for the ATCS.

The ATCS (described in chapter 12) is organized around three types of facilities (namely, centers, TRACONs, and airport towers) along with the associated radar and weather-sensing equipment. The information exchanged between various facilities in the ATCS falls into two major categories:

• Exchange of critical information takes place during hand-off and track coordination between adjacent facilities. This communication has hard deadlines and must be made fault-tolerant. This communication requirement can be satisfied by establishing dependable real-time channels with deterministic guarantees between each pair of adjacent facilities. To handle failures of interfacility links, it is necessary to establish D-channels between every pair of adjacent nodes. The primary channel for each node pair is established via one of the shortest (based on hop count) paths connecting the two facilities. The primary and backup channels are established so that they are disjoint.

• Exchange of less-critical information between various facilities might include weather information, registered flight plans, and so forth. This communication is less critical and also less frequent compared to the previous case. This communication requirement can be satisfied by establishing dependable real-time channels, with statistical guarantees, between relevant nodes.

8.9 Summary

• In traditional datagram networks, each packet in a transmission is routed by consulting the routing table at each intermediate node until the packet reaches its destination. Routing tables are constructed using algorithms such as Dijkstra's algorithm, the distance vector algorithm, and the link state algorithm.

• In real-time networks, a real-time channel is established satisfying the QoS requirements of a call request before actual transmission of packets begins.

• The constraints associated with the QoS routing problem typically fall into two categories: link constraints and path constraints. Path constraints make a routing problem intractable.

- A route selection algorithm aims at improving average call acceptance rate and reducing average call setup time and routing distance.
- Route selection during channel establishment can be centralized or distributed. The distributed approach can be broadly classified into flooding-based and preferred neighbor–based approaches.
- The flooding approach offers better ACST and ARD but has poorer ACAR than SPF and LLF. SPF offers better performance (ACAR, ACST, ARD) for uniform traffic, whereas LLF performs better for non-uniform traffic.
- The parallel probing approach attempts to improve all three performance metrics simultaneously for different traffic conditions by combining the benefits of the preferred neighbor and flooding-based approaches.
- The least-cost delay-constrained routing problem is an important constrained optimization problem. The heuristics presented in [22] and [25], employing the preferred neighbor approach, are some known solutions to this problem.
- A dependable real-time channel consists of one primary and one or more backup channels acting as cold standby. A backup channel is activated on failure of any network component in the primary channel. Two main issues here are (1) establishment of backup channel(s), before a failure, which involves selecting route(s) for the backup channel(s) (backup route selection) and assigning bandwidth to the backup channel(s) (spare resource allocation), and (2) failure detection and backup activation.

Exercises

1. Compare distance vector and link state routing algorithms with respect to

(a) adaptiveness

(b) computational cost at routing nodes

(c) efficient multiple-constraint optimization.

Give reasons for your comparisons.

2. The distance vector routing algorithm for a single-constraint optimization problem can be summarized by the equation

$$C_{\min}(x, y) = \min_{v \in N(x)}\{C(x, v) + C_{\min}(v, y)\},$$

where $N(x)$ denotes the set of neighbors of x, $C(x, v)$ is the cost of link (x, v), and $C_{\min}(x, y)$ is the cost of the least-cost path between x and y. Assuming that all link delays and delay constraints are integers, extend the above equation to obtain a dynamic programming formulation of the delay-constrained least-cost routing problem (i.e., derive an expression for $C_\Delta(x, y)$, which is the lowest cost of any path connecting x and y with a delay less than Δ). If Δ is a bounded integer, what will be the time complexity of the dynamic program (polynomial, exponential, logarithmic, etc.)?

3. Consider the following metrics: delay, delay jitter, cost, available bandwidth, and transmission probability($= 1 -$ packet loss probability).

(a) Classify these metrics into additive, multiplicative, and concave metrics.

(b) Considering all possible pairs from among these metrics, list those pairs that would *not* give rise to an NP-complete problem.

(c) Classify these metrics into path/link constraints.

4. List five important characteristics required for QoS routing algorithms used in wide area networks.

5. Compare the flooding and preferred neighbor approaches with respect to ACAR, ACST, and ARD. Give reasons for your comparisons.

6. What is meant by *liveness* and *adaptiveness* of a routing algorithm? How does the parallel probing approach guarantee liveness?

7. Characterize LLF, SPF, TSPF, RDM, CDP, and PBO as call/destination-specific/ independent heuristics.

8. What is the meaning of the terms *hot spot node* and *hot pair communication*? Why is the performance of routing algorithms influenced by the presence of hot spots and hot pairs?

9. The flooding approach, if left uncontrolled, will lead to a packet explosion within the network. Suggest three methods to control this explosion. How do you think the time-to-live entry (in IP packets) can prove useful in this regard?

10. The network shown in figure 8.16 employs distance vector routing, using delay as the optimization metric. The links are labeled in the figure with integer values representing their delays. Suppose C gets the following vectors:

• From B: $(5, 0, 8, 12, 6, 2, 4)$

• From D: $(16, 12, 6, 0, 9, 10, 6)$

• From G: $(7, 6, 3, 9, 3, 4, 0)$

Compute the distance vector for node C.

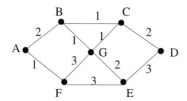

Figure 8.16
Exercise 8.10 example network

11. For which of the three heuristics defined in section 8.5.4.3 is the delay test redundant (i.e., any link chosen by that heuristic automatically satisfies the delay test)?

12. Explain the importance of κ, the maximum number of preferred links, in the algorithm described in section 8.5.4. How do you think κ influences the metrics ACAR, ACST, ARD, and AC? How can knowledge of the average network degree help in choosing a value for κ?

13. With reference to the network model of section 8.5.1, let the delay of a link (x, y) be denoted by $D(x, y)$ and the cost by $C(x, y)$. The least-cost delay-constrained routing problem can be experimentally studied under two simulation conditions:

• Case 1. $C(x, y) = (1 + \omega)D(x, y)$, where ω is a random number between 0 and 1.

• Case 2. $C(x, y) = D_{\max} - D(x, y)$, where $D_{\max}$ denotes the maximum delay in any link of the network.

Which of the above two cases will pose a tougher delay-constrained routing problem? Which of the two algorithms presented for dealing with this problem, DCUR or RDM, do you think, will adapt better to the tougher case? Why?

14. The following problem is based on the network used in question 10. Assume that a route has to be set up between nodes A and D using the parallel probing algorithm. Let G be the only ID involved. At each stage, the parallel probing algorithm employs two heuristics, SPF and LLF. The paths chosen by these heuristics at each stage are given below:

• Stage 1 (A to G). SPF chooses ABG, LLF chooses AFEG.

• Stage 2 (G to D). SPF chooses GED, LLF chooses GBCD.

Construct a timing diagram that depicts the sequence of events (procedure invocations) during the route selection. Assume that all the routing activities at the nodes are performed instantaneously so that the delay probe packets experience is dictated solely by the delays along the network links. For each event, indicate the source, the destination, and the type of procedure.

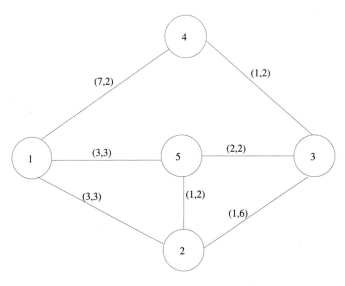

Figure 8.17
Exercise 8.15 example network

15. With reference to figure 8.17, answer the following questions:

(a) If the *CDP* heuristic is used for routing to destination node 4, what will be the relevant *PLT* entries at nodes 2, 5, and 3?

(b) If the *PBO* heuristic is used for routing to node 4, what will be the PLT entries at nodes 2, 5, and 3?

(c) Consider a unicast channel establishment request with source node 2, destination node 4, and delay constraint $\Delta = 7$. What will be the routes constructed by the *CDP* and the *PBO* heuristics? (Use the answers to the previous two subquestions.)

References

[1] J. Anderson, B. Doshi, S. Dravida, and P. Harshavadhana. "Fast restoration of ATM networks." *IEEE JSAC,* vol. 12, no. 1, pp. 128–138, Jan. 1994.

[2] A. Banerjea, C. Parris, and D. Ferrari. "Recovering guaranteed performance service connections from single and multiple faults." Technical report no. TR-93-066, Univ. of California, Berkeley, 1993.

[3] A. Banerjea. "Simulation study of the capacity effects of dispersity routing for fault-tolerant real-time channels." In *Proc. ACM SIGCOMM,* pp. 194–205, 1996.

[4] M. Boari, A. Corradi, and C. Stefanelli. "Adaptive routing for dynamic applications in massively parallel architectures." *IEEE Parallel & Distributed Technology,* pp. 61–74, Spring 1995.

[5] M. R. Garey and D. S. Johnson. *Computers and Intractability: A Guide to the Theory of NP-Completeness.* W.H. Freeman, San Francisco, 1979.

[6] E. Gustafsson and G. Karlsson. "A literature survey on traffic dispersion." *IEEE Network,* pp. 28–36, Mar./Apr. 1997.

[7] S. Han and K. G. Shin. "Efficient spare-resource allocation for fast restoration of real-time channels from network component failures." In *Proc. ACM SIGCOMM,* 1997.

[8] S. Han and K. G. Shin. "A primary-backup channel approach to dependable real-time communication in multihop networks." *IEEE Trans. Computers,* vol. 47, no. 1, pp. 46–61, Jan. 1998.

[9] S. Han and K. G. Shin. "Experimental evaluation of failure-detection schemes in real-time communication networks." In *Proc. IEEE Fault-Tolerant Computing Symp.,* 1998.

[10] N. Haung, C. Wu, and Y. Wu. "Some routing problems on broadband ISDN." *Computer Networks and ISDN Systems,* vol. 27, no. 1, pp. 101–116, 1994.

[11] J. Jaffe. "Algorithms for finding paths with multiple constraints." *Networks,* vol. 14, no. 1, pp. 95–116, Spring 1984.

[12] Y. Kajiyama, N. Tokura, and K. Kikuchi. "An ATM VP-based self-healing ring." *IEEE JSAC,* vol. 12, no. 1, pp. 171–178, Jan. 1994.

[13] R. Kawamura, K. Sato, and I. Tokizawa. "Self-healing ATM networks based on virtual path concept." *IEEE JSAC,* vol. 12, no. 1, pp. 120–127, Jan. 1994.

[14] V. P. Kompella, J. C. Pasquale, and G. C. Polyzos. "Multicast routing for multimedia communication." *IEEE/ACM Trans. Networking,* vol. 1, no. 3, pp. 286–292, June 1993.

[15] W. C. Lee, M. G. Hluchyi, and P. A. Humblet. "Routing subject to quality of service constraints in integrated communication networks." *IEEE Network,* July/Aug. 1995.

[16] J. Y. Leung, T. W. Tam, C. S. Wong, and G. H. Young. "Routing messages with release time and deadline constraints." *Journal of Parallel and Distributed Computing,* vol. 31, no. 1, pp. 65–76, 1995.

[17] G. Manimaran, H. S. Rahul, and C. Siva Ram Murthy. "A new distributed route selection approach for channel establishment in real-time networks." *IEEE/ACM Trans. Networking,* vol. 7, no. 5, pp. 698–709, Oct. 1999.

[18] K. Murakami and H. Sim. "Near-optimal virtual path routing for survivable ATM networks." In *Proc. IEEE INFOCOM,* pp. 208–215, 1994.

[19] E. Oki, N. Yamanka, and F. Pitcho. "Multiple-availability-level ATM network architecture." *IEEE Communications,* vol. 33, no. 9, pp. 80–88, Sept. 1995.

[20] P. Ramanathan and K. G. Shin. "Delivery of time-critical messages using a multiple copy approach." *ACM Trans. Computer Systems,* vol. 10, no. 2, pp. 144–166, May 1992.

[21] S. Rampal, D. S. Reeves, and D. P. Agrawal. "An evaluation of routing and admission control algorithms for real-time traffic in packet-switched networks." In *Proc. High Performance Networking,* pp. 77–91, 1994.

[22] H. F. Salama, D. S. Reeves, and Y. Viniotis. "A distributed algorithm for delay-constrained unicast routing." In *Proc. IEEE INFOCOM,* 1997.

[23] S. Shenker and L. Breslau. "Two issues in reservation establishment." In *Proc. ACM SIGCOMM,* pp. 14–26, 1995.

[24] K. G. Shin and C. Chou. "A distributed route-selection scheme for establishing real-time channels." In *Proc. High Performance Networking,* pp. 319–330, 1995.

[25] R. Sriram, G. Manimaran, and C. Siva Ram Murthy. "Preferred link based delay-constrained least cost routing in wide area networks." *Computer Communications,* vol. 21, no. 8, pp. 1655–1669, Dec. 1998.

[26] R. Sriram, G. Manimaran, and C. Siva Ram Murthy. "An integrated scheme for establishing dependable real-time channels in multihop networks." In *Proc. IEEE Intl. Conf. on Computer Communications and Networks,* pp. 528–533, Boston, 1999.

[27] Z. Wang and J. Crowcroft. "Quality-of-service routing for supporting multimedia applications." *IEEE JSAC,* vol. 14, no. 7, pp. 1228–1234, Sept. 1996.

[28] B. M. Waxman. "Routing of multipoint connections." *IEEE JSAC,* vol. 6, no. 9, pp. 1617–1622, Dec. 1988.

[29] Q. Zheng and K. G. Shin. "Fault-tolerant real-time communication in distributed computing systems." In *Proc. IEEE Fault-Tolerant Computing Symp.,* pp. 86–93, 1992.

9 Multicasting in Real-Time Networks

Overview

In this chapter, we discuss the most important issues in the design of a multicast communication system, with special emphasis on multimedia multicasting. We begin by discussing some fundamental concepts in the multicast communication paradigm. We then discuss some characteristics of multimedia applications that have special relevance to multicasting. Next, we present an architectural framework for characterizing multicast sessions and identify four key components of this architecture. These four components constitute the subject matter of discussion for the succeeding sections. Finally, we discuss how multimedia multicasting is currently being supported on the Internet.

9.1   Introduction

One way communication can be characterized is by the number of receivers targeted by a particular sender. Traditional communication models have been one-to-one, or *unicast,* and one-to-all, or *broadcast.* Between these two extremes lies *multicast,* which refers to the targeting of a data stream to a select set of receivers. The multicast communication model is consequently a generalization of both the other models. This model is used to characterize the communication patterns in a wide spectrum of applications such as replicated databases, command and control systems, distributed games, audio/video conferencing, and distributed interactive simulation. The following is a list of some common applications that make use of multicast communication:

• *Multimedia.* A number of users "tune in" to a video or audio transmission from a multimedia source station.

• *Teleconferencing.* A group of workstations form a multicast group so that a transmission from any member is received by all other group members.

• *Databases.* All copies of a replicated file or database are updated at the same time.

• *Distributed computation.* Intermediate results are sent to all participants in a distributed computation.

• *Real-time workgroups.* Files, graphics, and messages are exchanged among active group members in real time.

A number of multimedia group applications[1] also make extensive use of the multicast communication paradigm. In fact, the proliferation of multimedia applications associated

---

1. Multimedia group applications are those that produce multiple time-correlated delay-sensitive streams of continuous media.

with new high-speed networks is driving the need for reliable group communication mechanisms and protocols. A number of interesting issues arise out of the interaction between multicast communication and networked multimedia systems. Special-case solutions are needed that exploit the unique characteristics of multimedia streams to achieve efficient multicasting. In particular, the problem at hand is characterized by three important features:

• Data must be sent to multiple destinations whose configuration changes with time.

• The volume of data is large and requires high bandwidth.

• The value of the data is sensitive to delay.

9.1.1   Multicast Fundamentals

The difference between multicasting and separately unicasting data to several destinations is best captured by the host group model. A *host group* is a set of network entities sharing a common identifying multicast address, all receiving any data packets addressed to this multicast address by senders that may or may not be members of the same group and have no knowledge of the group's membership. This definition, proposed by Deering and Cheriton, implies that, from the sender's point of view, this model reduces the multicast service interface to a unicast one. The definition also allows the group's behavior to be unrestricted in multiple dimensions: groups may have local (LAN) or global (WAN) membership, be transient or persistent in time, and have constant or varying membership. Consequently, we have the following types of multicast (or host) groups:

• *Pervasive groups* have members on most of the links or subnets in a network, whereas *sparse groups* have members only on a small number of widely separated links.

• *Open groups* are those in which the sender of data need not be a member of the group, whereas *closed groups* allow only members to send to the group.

• *Permanent groups* exist forever, or at least for a significantly longer duration than *transient groups.*

• Membership in *static groups* remains constant over time, whereas *dynamic groups* allow members to join/leave the group.

The multicast communication paradigm poses two unique issues that are not relevant in traditional point-to-point communication systems and that make many traditional point-to-point solutions inextensible to the multicast environment:

• *Receiver control.* A point-to-point (unicast) session consists of two participants, one of which is usually the server/sender/initiator, and the other, the client/receiver/slave. Connection establishment/tear down, flow control, and error recovery are driven from one end (usually the sender end). In a dynamic multicast session, any participant may join/leave the group at any time. Each participant can also have different QoS requirements and expect personalized flow control. Hence, traditional source-driven solutions used in the point-to-point environment will not be able to accommodate the requirements of a multicast session. Clearly, receiver-controlled techniques are a must.

• *Heterogeneity management.* Group communication systems have to deal with a much higher degree of *heterogeneity* than that in point-to-point communication systems. In the latter, protocol mechanisms merely had to deal with network heterogeneity (in WANs), wherein different portions of a network are composed of different kinds of switches and links with varying capabilities. Multicasting, however, aggravates heterogeneity problems, as simple paths turn into trees, and, in addition to switches and links, hosts within a group can also differ. Thus, in the multicast environment, the twin issues of *host heterogeneity* and *network heterogeneity* need to be addressed.

9.1.2 Characteristics of Multimedia Applications

In this section, we highlight those characteristics of multimedia applications that have special relevance to multicasting. For each such characteristic, we indicate which aspects of multicast communication that characteristic affects.

In a distributed multimedia communication system, data of discrete and continuous media are transmitted, and information exchange takes place. Typically, transmitted information is divided into individual units (packets) and subsequently sent from one system component to another. A sequence of such individual packets is called a *data stream.* Packets can carry data of either continuous (or time-dependent) or discrete (or time-independent) media, thereby giving rise to continuous media and discrete media data streams, respectively. An example of a continuous media data stream is the transmission of speech in a telephone system. The retrieval of a document from a database can be seen as setting up a discrete media data stream.

9.1.2.1 Delay Sensitivity
Many audio/video applications are *interactive,* in the sense that data reception is interleaved with playback of the associated media streams, rather than playback strictly following data reception. This implies a requirement for the provision of *bounded delays* between sender and receiver, which influences issues such as multicast routing, feedback-based congestion control, and resource reservation.

9.1.2.2 Synchronization
Continuous media transmission requires the following kinds of synchronization (the first two synchronization requirements are common to both unicast and group communication, whereas the third requirement is unique to applications involving group communication):

• *Intramedia synchronization.* For most continuous media streams, information must be presented at regular intervals to avoid distracting the human user. This implies an upper bound on delay jitter.

• *Intermedia synchronization.* Different media components (such as audio and video) of a single composite *wide stream* must be delivered at their destination in synchrony. Usually, intermedia synchronization requirements are quite stringent and more critical than the other two synchronization requirements. For example, the audio and video of a person speaking (lip synchronization) must be presented within 80 ms of each other to be unnoticeable.

• *Interreceiver synchronization.* Some group applications impose an upper bound on the *delay variance.*[2] This is important for applications that require all group members to function in a synchronous manner (for example, to execute a distributed computation).

These three synchronization requirements influence multicast communication issues such as routing and traffic control.

9.1.2.3 Coding and Compression   Digitization of audio and video streams has opened up the possibility of employing coding and compression techniques to minimize bandwidth requirements for transmission. However, because of lack of standardization, several representational formats (i.e., different coding schemes) for each media type can coexist. This requires translation services (traditionally handled by the presentation layer) at one or more of the following points: the transmitter, the receiver, and the network. In unicasting, this translation can be accomplished effectively at either the transmitter or the receiver (since at most two different formats are involved in any unicast session). In contrast, with multicasting, each receiver could have a different receiving format. Consequently, sender-based translation would require duplicated streams for each receiver, which precludes link sharing over common paths. Hence, translation at the receiver is the most economical and scalable approach.

One particular type of coding technique, *hierarchical coding* (also referred to as *layered* or *subband coding*), has special relevance to multicast communication. This coding technique splits a continuous media signal into components of varying importance. The original signal may be reconstructed by aggregating all the components, but even a proper subset of these components can approximate it well. Efficient multicasting can be achieved through use of this technique by allowing different receivers to choose different subsets of the original signal's components based on their requirements and available resources. The use of hierarchical coding permits extremely efficient solutions to a num-

---

2. Delay variance is the maximum time difference in the receipt of a given packet by two different members of a multicast group.

ber of multicast communication issues, such as routing, congestion control, and resource reservation. These special-case solutions are discussed in the relevant sections of this chapter.

9.2   An Architectural Framework for Multicast Communication

A network architecture that aims to provide complete support for multicast communication is burdened with the task of managing the multicast sessions it carries in a manner transparent to the users (applications). This goal of transparent multicast service imposes specific requirements on the network implementation. To understand the different services that such a network must provide, we now discuss the various stages and events in the life cycle of a multicast session. This helps us identify the different components required in a multicast-capable network architecture. Each component is then discussed individually in the succeeding sections.

Consider the sample multicast session depicted in figure 9.1, consisting of a source, two receivers, and two intermediate nodes. The sequence of events relevant to this multicast session is as follows:

1. The first step in the initiation of a multicast session is the creation of a multicast group. Normally, groups come in two different types: either they are groups that are known to all network nodes and have a predefined, well-known group ID (multicast address), or they are groups created for a specific purpose and known only to the relevant nodes in the network. In the first case the session requires no explicit group creation, and the source can merely use the well-known multicast address. In the second case, the source contacts the *group manager,* which is responsible for managing multicast addresses and preventing address clashes, and makes a request for a new unique group ID (message *Request GID* in figure 9.1). The group manager, based on a certain group addressing mechanism, will return a unique multicast address to the source. Depending on the implementation, either the source or the group manager could be responsible for conveying this address to other multicast group members. A group manager can be implemented either as a central network-wide authority or as a distributed group manager process running in all the network nodes. Section 9.3 discusses a number of these group addressing and management issues.

2. The next step in the multicast session is the construction of a multicast distribution tree. For this, the source contacts the *routing module* (*Create Route* message in figure 9.1) and makes a request for route construction. Along with this request, the source includes information (such as the required minimum bandwidth and the acceptable source-receiver

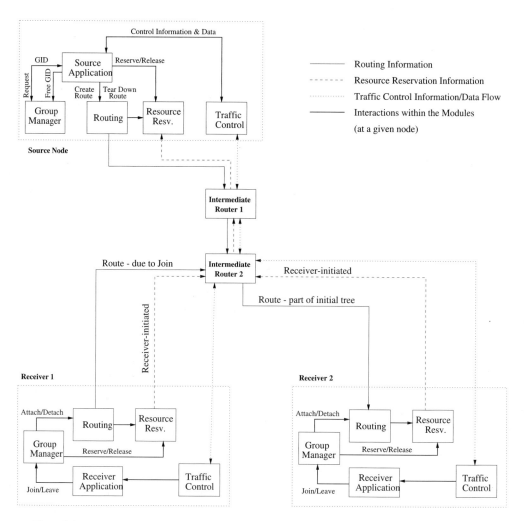

Figure 9.1
Architectural framework for multicast communication

delay) that the routing module can use to construct a suitable multicast tree. The routing module then makes use of a suitable tree construction algorithm to construct a tree spanning the source of the multicast and all the other multicast group members.

3. Next comes resource reservation (which could take place either in conjunction with the routing phase or immediately afterward). The source contacts the *resource reservation module,* passing on detailed information regarding its QoS requirements and its traffic flow specification. Based on this information, the resource reservation module computes the amount of resources that need to be reserved for the session on the various tree links. Using the path information available from the routing phase, the reservation module then reserves the necessary resources along the chosen tree.[3]

4. Once the above three phases have been successfully completed, data transmission can begin. During data transmission, two different kinds of run time events in particular can affect the transmission.

• *Group membership changes.* Since membership in some groups is dynamic, a network must be able to track current membership during a session's lifetime. Tracking is needed both to start forwarding data to new group members and to stop the wasteful transmission of packets to destinations that have left the group. When a node wishes to join a multicast session, it sends a *Join* message to the group manager module, which in turn sends an *Attach* message to the routing module (refer to figure 9.1). The routing module then constructs a path attaching this new node to some point in the existing multicast tree. (In the figure, *Receiver 2* attaches to the tree at *Intermediate Router 2.* Hence, the routing message from *Receiver 2* to *Intermediate Router 2* is directed from the former to the latter.) The resource reservation module then reserves the necessary resources (depending on the receivers' reception requirements) on this attachment path. *Leave* requests are also handled similarly, through interaction between the application, the group manager, routing, and resource reservation modules, and the intermediate routers.

• *Transmission problems.* Problems that arise during transmission could include events such as swamped receivers (necessitating flow control), overloaded intermediate nodes (necessitating congestion control), or faulty packet transmissions (necessitating error control). The *traffic control module,* working in conjunction with the schedulers at the receivers and the intermediate nodes (shown in figure 9.1), is responsible for performing the

---

3. Resource reservation schemes normally fall into one of two categories (discussed later): source-initiated two-pass schemes or receiver-initiated single-pass schemes. In figure 9.1, we have depicted a receiver-initiated scheme, with the reservation messages traveling up the tree from the receivers toward the source.

necessary control activities to overcome any transmission problems that arise during the session.

5. At some point in time, when the session's useful lifetime has elapsed, the source initiates the session destruction procedures. It first contacts the resource reservation module (message *Release* in figure 9.1) and requests that all the resources (bandwidth, buffer space, etc.) allocated to the session be released. It then sends a *Tear Down Route* message to the routing module, asking it to flush all the session-specific routing table entries. Finally, the source sends a *Free GID* message to the group manager, thereby releasing the group ID (GID) that was assigned to it at the beginning of the session.

Based on the above discussion, it should be apparent that there are four major components in any multicast-capable network architecture:

• Group addressing (discussed in section 9.3)

• Routing (discussed in section 9.4)

• Resource reservation (discussed in section 9.5)

• Traffic control (discussed in section 9.6)

9.3   Group Addressing

Group addressing refers to the unique identification of a multicast group based on a given address. Both groups and addresses have associated lifetimes. In section 9.1.1, we distinguished between permanent and transient groups based on their relative lifetimes. Similarly, group addresses are classified as either *static* or *dynamic,* depending on whether they are assigned permanently to a given group or assigned to different groups at different instants of time. The most obvious matching between groups and addresses is to assign static addresses to permanent groups and dynamic addresses to transient groups. Note that assignment of static addresses to transient groups could result in insecure communication (wherein nonmembers receive messages meant for a certain group) whereas assignment of dynamic addresses to permanent groups merely causes unnecessary communication overhead.

   Group addressing schemes can be broadly divided into two categories depending on whether or not the application has the authority to select the group address (figure 9.2). A number of multicast address assignment protocols (in each category) have been proposed, such as central server [12], trial and error or random selection [58], Heidelberg multicast address protocol [58], multicast group authority [7], and distributed multicast address management [42]. Some current network layer protocols, such as Internet protocol (IP)

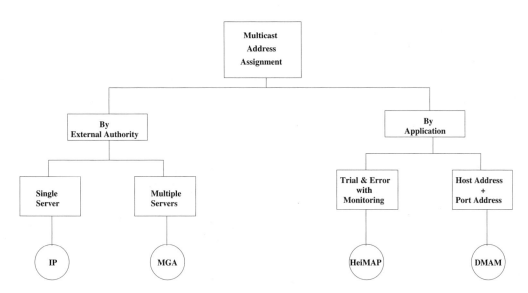

Figure 9.2
Classification of multicast address assignment protocols

and Internet stream protocol–version 2 (ST-II) also support special multicast addresses. In the following sections, we discuss the various schemes for multicast address assignment and analyze their relative advantages and drawbacks.

9.3.1   Desirable Features of a Multicast Address Assignment Scheme

Any efficient multicast address assignment scheme should have at least the following features:

• *Large address space.* With a diverse variety of applications requiring the use of multicast communication services, it is quite likely that a large number of group applications will be simultaneously running on any given network. Hence, schemes supporting a large number of addresses are required.

• *Secure communication.* A group is identified by an address at the IP (network layer) level that is later mapped to the data link layer addresses of individual hosts. It is important to ensure that a unique mapping exists between addresses at these two levels, so that nonmember hosts do not receive multicast messages meant for a certain group.

• *Fault tolerance.* Some of the existing schemes, such as central server, depend on a central authority to assign multicast addresses. This makes the address assignment scheme susceptible to a single point of failure. Consequently, resilience to failure of the address manager is an important requirement of any address assignment scheme.

• *Management of group dynamics.* Good address assignment schemes are required to manage the dynamics of group membership efficiently and with an aim to minimizing *join latency.*[4]

9.3.2   IP Multicast: Central Server

The multicast extensions to IP call for a special class of addresses, called *class D addresses* [12], to be reserved for multicast communication. The class D addresses (begin with 1110 and are in the range 224.0.0.0 to 239.255.255.255) may be assigned by the Internet Assigned Numbers Authority for permanent or temporary use. The creator of a multicast group contacts the central server (CS) and requests a multicast address (MCA). The CS assigns an MCA for the group and communicates this to the creator and to the other group members. Although this scheme guarantees consistency in address allocation, it suffers from lack of fault tolerance because of the presence of the central server.

9.3.3   Trial and Error or Random Selection

To eliminate the central server, a trial-and-error scheme has been proposed in [58] for selecting a free class D address. In this scheme, the creator of a group picks up a random address from the class D address space and broadcasts a SET message to all the hosts in the network. If the address is already in use, then hosts using that address send a REJECT message in response. If one or more reject messages are received, the creator sends a RESET message to all its members and repeats the process using a new randomly generated address. If no REJECT messages are received within a prescribed timeout period, then the chosen address is adopted as the multicast address of the group. Although the scheme performs satisfactorily in LAN environments, it is unsuitable for WANs because of the higher probability of simultaneous address allocation (this is a consequence of larger end-to-end delays) and high overhead for broadcast of the SET messages [42].

9.3.4   Heidelberg Multicast Address Protocol

The Heidelberg multicast address protocol (HeiMAP) [58] uses a modified trial-and-error scheme for multicast address assignment. In this scheme, all hosts monitor and store the multicast addresses currently in use. A creator of a group is therefore able to choose a random class D address that, to the best of its knowledge, is not being used by any other

---

4. Join latency is defined as the time gap between when a new group member decides to join a group and when it actually starts to receive packets addressed to that group.

group. The scheme is expected to reduce (in comparison with simple trial and error) the number of iterations required to obtain a successful address assignment.

9.3.5 Multicast Group Authority

In the multicast group authority (MGA) scheme [7], all multicast addresses are managed by a hierarchy of nodes (called MGA nodes) with a centralized controller at the root of the hierarchy. Initially, the entire multicast address space is in the hands of the root. Requests from applications for addresses are forwarded to the nearest MGA node, which results in a block of addresses being assigned to that node. The application then receives one of the addresses from this block. The size of the block is dependent on the position of the MGA node in the hierarchy. If an MGA node runs out of addresses to distribute, it requests more addresses from its parent node in the hierarchy. Depending on whether the parent node has free addresses to pass on, and if not, whether the nodes above it in the hierarchy do, this request may progressively travel up the hierarchy right up to the root. When the root runs out of addresses, it makes a request to the child nodes for reclamation of unused addresses. This request propagates down to the leaves of the hierarchy, with unused addresses being returned to the address pool. When an application completes, its address is returned to the nearest MGA node, which retains it until it is requested by its parent or needed by another application. The scheme manages the address space very efficiently because of the address reclamation feature. However, it does not specify the number of MGA nodes, the number of levels in the hierarchy, the selection of MGA nodes, and the process by which an application contacts the nearest MGA node.

9.3.6 Distributed Multicast Address Management

The distributed multicast address management (DMAM) scheme [42] uses the concept of an *extended multicast address* (a four-byte multicast address along with a two-byte virtual port number) for fully distributed address management. A multicast address manager (MAM) present on each host is responsible for creating extended multicast addresses using the host's four-byte multicast address. The disadvantage of this scheme is that it requires modification of the routers to take into account the virtual port numbers. Besides that, it mixes virtual port numbers, which are transport layer entities, with routing, which is a network layer issue. The scheme also requires modifications to the kernel code (in the routers) and address size modifications (six bytes instead of four) to the routing protocols and tables.

9.3.7 Multicast Address Resolution Server

The multicast address resolution server (MARS) scheme proposes a mechanism for mapping a high-level group address to a point-to-multipoint virtual circuit (VC) in ATM networks. It is therefore not actually an addressing scheme but more a mapping scheme based on an extension to the ATM address resolution protocol (ARP) server [33]. A MARS keeps extended tables of mappings of layer 3 group addresses and a list of ATM interfaces representing group members. A point-to-multipoint VC is maintained between the MARS and all ATM hosts desiring multicast support to provide asynchronous notification of group membership changes. This eliminates the need for the source of a multicast to manage dynamic group membership changes.

9.4   Multicast Routing

The basic means of conserving resources via multicasting is sharing: Instead of transmitting packets from a sender to each receiver separately, we can arrange for routes that share some links to carry each packet only once. Multicast route determination is traditionally formulated as a problem relating to tree construction. There are three reasons for adopting the tree structure:

• The source needs to transmit only a single packet down the multicast tree.

• The tree structure allows parallel transmission to the various destination nodes.

• The tree structure minimizes data replication, since the packet is replicated by routers only at branch points in the tree.

In this section, we provide a comprehensive discussion of multicast routing, with special emphasis on QoS routing (essential for multimedia communication). We begin by listing some technical challenges to multicast routing. We then develop the theoretical framework underlying multicast routing and also a system for classifying multicast routing algorithms. Based on this classification system, we take up specific important examples of each type and discuss the core ideas in those algorithms. We examine the influence of group dynamics on multicast routing and emphasize the inherent trade-offs involved in designing algorithms for such applications. Finally, we conclude the section by briefly discussing some proposals for multicast routing in ATM networks.

9.4.1   Technical Challenges to Multicast Routing

To provide a complete view of the goals of an efficient and practical routing scheme, we list below the technical challenges to multimedia multicast routing:

• The network load should be minimized. Within the problem of optimizing network resources, there are two subproblems: avoiding loops and avoiding traffic concentration on any one link or subnetwork.

• Basic support for reliable transmission must be provided. Ideally, route changes should have no side effects on the way data is delivered to group members that remain in the group. Link failure should not increase transmission delay or decrease resource availability. Too high a rate of change of routes could degrade higher level reliability.

• The routing algorithm should be able to design optimal routes, taking into consideration different cost functions (available resource, bandwidth, number of links, node connectivity) and QoS constraints (end-to-end delay, delay variance, packet loss rate). If designing an optimal route is a complex problem, maintaining route optimality after changes in the group and network will be much more complex. The requirement is therefore to find a good compromise between the efficiency of the route and the dynamics of the group.

• The amount of state information stored in the routers should be minimized. For some types of switches and intermediate routers, this becomes an important problem, as otherwise, delivery to a large group becomes infeasible.

• Integration of routing mechanisms with admission control and resource reservation techniques is required for the development of effective call establishment protocols.

9.4.2 Network Model and Notations

All notations and conventions used in this chapter are based on the network model defined in the previous chapter. However, to deal with trees, we need the following additional notations. A tree $T = (V_T, E_T)$ that is a subgraph of $G = (V, E)$ has an associated cost defined as

$$C(T) = \sum_{e \in E_T} C(e).$$

Given a path P and two nodes v_1 and v_2 belonging to this path, the portion of P connecting these two nodes is denoted by $Sub_P(v_1, v_2)$. $D_P(v_1, v_2)$ and $C_P(v_1, v_2)$ denote, respectively, the delay and cost of this portion of P. Similarly, given a tree T and two nodes v_1 and v_2 belonging to this tree, $P_T(v_1, v_2)$ denotes the path between v_1 and v_2 in this tree. The delay and cost of this path are then denoted respectively as $D_T(v_1, v_2)$ and $C_T(v_1, v_2)$.

9.4.3 Classification of Multicast Routing Algorithms

Multicast routing algorithms can be classified along four different dimensions (refer to figure 9.3):

• *The approach followed.* In section 9.4.4, we discuss three main approaches to multicast routing. Depending on its approach, we characterize a multicast routing algorithm as a *source-based, center-based,* or *Steiner-based* algorithm.

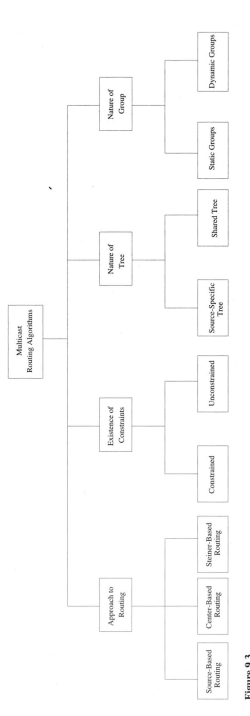

Figure 9.3
Classification of multicast routing algorithms

- *The existence of constraints.* A multicast routing algorithm can be designed either to accommodate one or more QoS requirements (which is essential for multimedia applications) or merely to optimize a certain metric (such as cost or delay). We distinguish between such algorithms by prefixing their name with either *constrained* or *unconstrained,* as the case may be.
- *Nature of the tree.* Multicast routing algorithms can be designed either to construct one tree for every (source,group) pair or to construct a shared tree for a group to be used by all senders transmitting to that group. We label the two types of algorithms as *source-specific* algorithms and *shared-tree* algorithms, respectively.
- *Nature of the group.* Routing algorithms can either be designed to accommodate membership changes, as in a *dynamic* multicast group, or assume a *static* group configuration. These two types of algorithms are characterized by prefixing their description with the words *dynamic* or *static,* respectively.

In the following sections, we present brief descriptions of various types of algorithms, indicating their properties by means of a 4-tuple. For example, (*Steiner-based, constrained, source-specific, static*) denotes a multicast routing algorithm that follows the Steiner tree approach to construct QoS-constrained source-specific multicast trees for routing to static multicast groups.

9.4.4   Theoretical Background: General Approaches to Multicast Routing

A few basic algorithms form the backbone for the development of effective multicast routing protocols. The initial development of multicast routing began with the need for *selective broadcast* [59]. One of the most simple approaches to broadcasting is *flooding,* discussed in Chapter 8. A refinement of the flooding algorithm that attempts to overcome its inefficient link utilization is the *spanning tree algorithm* proposed by Pearlman for extended LANs [41]. From these modest beginnings, there has been a lot of research into more efficient methods for multicast routing.

From the existing literature, three fundamental approaches to multicast routing can be identified [18]:

- Source-based routing approach
- Center-based tree approach
- Steiner tree approach

In the following sections, we highlight the unique characteristics of each of these approaches, cite examples, and assess their relative strengths and weaknesses.

9.4.4.1   Source-Based Routing Approach   This approach is essentially based on the reverse path forwarding (RPF) algorithm proposed by Dalal and Metcalfe in [10]. It involves the computation of an implicit spanning tree per source node that is usually the shortest-delay tree. The RPF algorithm is optimized for dense receiver distribution (*pervasive groups* of section 9.1.1) and can be implemented in a distributed fashion with local recovery. It has seen widespread use through its employment in IP multicast (distance vector multicast routing protocol [11], protocol-independent multicast [15]).

RPF designs a directed tree rooted at the source of a group and spanning all the group members. The main advantage of the RPF approach is that it requires no resources in addition to the classical unicast distance vector routing tables. The core idea in the RPF approach is the following:

A node forwards a certain multicast packet from source S iff the packet arrives at the node via the shortest path from the router back to S (i.e., the reverse path). The node forwards the packet on all incident links except the one on which the packet arrived.

The pure RPF algorithm is designed for broadcast and does not take group membership into account. Consequently, source-based routing approaches employ RPF in conjunction with *pruning techniques.* The pruning idea complements the basic RPF approach by recording group membership and forwarding a packet on a certain link only if a group member is known to exist downstream from that link. The recorded group membership entries are controlled by a timer and periodically flushed, thus clearing all the *prune* messages. The next packet that arrives causes a flooding that once more triggers *prune* messages from the relevant downstream nodes.

Advantages: The RPF algorithm computes an implicit spanning tree that is minimal in terms of delay characteristics. It is optimized for dense receiver distribution (i.e., pervasive groups) and can be implemented in a distributed fashion with local recovery. Moreover, it does not require any resources in addition to the classic unicast routing tables.

Disadvantages: The following are the key disadvantages of the source-based routing approach:

• The RPF algorithm was designed for broadcasting rather than multicasting. Hence, most source-based routing algorithms are efficient only for pervasive groups.

• The pruning variant of the RPF algorithm requires each node to maintain one unit of state information per source per group. This is quite acceptable if the number of sources per group is low. If the number of sources and/or number of groups grows too large, memory could be saturated in the intermediate routers.

However, despite these disadvantages, the source-based routing approach is the most commonly used approach because of its simplicity and ability to work with just unicast routing tables.

9.4.4.2 Center-Based Tree Approach   The center-based tree approach is a recently proposed routing scheme considered to be ideal for multiple-sender/multiple-recipient communication. The unifying feature of this class of algorithms is that they identify a *center node* for each multicast group and construct a distribution tree rooted at this center and spanning all the group members. Multicast packets from senders who are not members of the group are forwarded toward the center node until they reach some node of the distribution tree. From that point onward, the nature of the distribution tree dictates the forwarding of the packets to the group members.

The center-based tree approach accommodates both closed and open groups and uses a single shared tree for the entire group. The core-based tree (CBT) algorithm [1] and sparse-mode protocol-independent multicast (PIM) [15] are two commonly used algorithms based on this approach.

Advantages: The main advantages of the center-based tree approach are as follows:

• It is a totally receiver-based approach and consequently adapts well to dynamic multicast groups.

• It is suitable for sparsely distributed receivers, unlike the source-based routing approach.

• It has the advantage over RPF of requiring only one state information item per group, irrespective of the number of sources transmitting to that group (since it uses a shared tree).

Disadvantages: The center-based tree approach suffers from two important weaknesses:

• Optimal center location is an NP-complete problem and usually requires complete network topology and exact group membership details. A number of heuristics have been proposed for center location, as discussed below.

• Since all the source nodes use the same distribution tree to transmit packets to a certain group, traffic concentration in and around the center node can become extremely high. This leads to excessive congestion on the links of the distribution tree.

Heuristics for Center Location: Since the choice of the center node is the most important factor in determining the quality of a distribution tree, much work has been done on proposing heuristics for optimal center location. A comprehensive discussion of such heuristics can be found in [56]. Here, we discuss only some of the most important proposals for center location:

- *Optimal center-based tree (OCBT).* As a reference for comparison to other approaches, the optimal center-based tree is chosen by calculating the potential cost of the tree when rooted at each network node and choosing to locate the tree at the node that gives the lowest maximum delay among all those with minimum cost. Clearly, this is too expensive and hence not a practical solution.

- *Random source-specific tree (RSST).* The center in this approach is chosen randomly among the senders and does not change with changes in group membership. The PIM [15] and CBT [1] algorithms use a variation of RSST wherein the first source of the group is chosen as the center.

- *Minimum shortest-path tree (MSPT).* This approach requires calculating the potential costs for trees rooted at each group member and choosing the member with the lowest cost. Wei and Estrin [62] have shown that the MSPT approach performs almost as well as OCBT. Wall [59] has shown that, for each source, such a tree has a delay bound of three times that of a source-based tree rooted at the source node.[5]

- *Minimum-centered tree (MCT).* This algorithm picks the node with the lowest maximum distance (in terms of hop count) to any group member.

- *Average-centered tree (ACT).* This algorithm chooses the node with the lowest average distance to all the group members.

- *Diameter-centered tree (DCT).* This algorithm picks the node which lies at the midpoint of the lowest maximum diameter, defined as the sum of the distances to the two nodes farthest away.

The majority of the heuristics proposed above are centralized and require complete knowledge of network topology and link state information in order to select a good center node for constructing a good multicast tree. A few distributed heuristics have also been proposed in [56].

9.4.4.3   Steiner Tree Approach   The Steiner tree approach models the multicast tree construction problem in terms of the *graph-theoretic NP-complete Steiner problem* [25, 65], which is formally stated as follows:

Given a graph $G = (V, E)$, a cost function $C : E \rightarrow R^+$, and a set of nodes $D \subseteq V$, find a subgraph $H = (V_H, E_H)$ of G such that $V_H \supseteq D$ and the cost $C(H)$ (equal to the sum of the costs of the edges in E_H) is minimized.

Algorithms that come under this category focus on overall tree cost minimization. In other words, instead of concentrating on minimizing individual source-receiver path parameters,

---

5. A topologically centered tree has a delay bound two times that of a source-specific tree for each source.

the Steiner approach attempts to construct trees with minimum total cost. It is the most popular approach in the research community, and a majority of the proposals for multicast routing belong to this category. Introduction of QoS requirements into the Steiner problem results in the *constrained Steiner tree problem,* used to model multicast algorithms for multimedia applications.

Unconstrained Steiner Heuristics: A number of centralized algorithms that construct low-cost multicast routes, such as those in [9, 27, 44, and 60], are based on approximation algorithms for Steiner tree construction. We discuss two popular and near-optimal heuristics of this type, the Kou-Markowsky-Berman (KMB) heuristic [31] and the Takashami-Matsuyama (TM) heuristic [55], in the succeeding sections. To construct trees for video distribution, the Steiner problem has been modified in [35] to include nonconstant link costs. Here, link cost is assumed to be an increasing function of bandwidth and link length and is independent of the utilization or availability of the link. The idea of *destination biasing* is employed in [50], along with the greedy strategies of shortest-path trees and minimal-spanning trees, to construct low-cost unconstrained multicast trees. Some of the approximation algorithms produce solutions that are provably within twice the cost of the optimal solution and run in polynomial time, usually ranging between $O(n^3)$ and $O(n^4)$, where n is the number of nodes in the network. However, for these algorithms to be implemented as a working protocol, distributed heuristics are required. To address this problem, in [2], distributed SPH (shortest-path heuristic) and K-SPH (Kruskal-type SPH) heuristics have been described that deal with the construction of unconstrained Steiner trees.

Constrained Steiner Heuristics: To address the requirement of multimedia applications that have specific QoS requirements, the constrained Steiner tree problem (CSTP) was first proposed in [29].[6] In the most common version of the CSTP, the QoS constraint is a delay constraint.[7]

In the rest of this section, we discuss algorithms for the static and dynamic versions of both the constrained and unconstrained Steiner tree problems.

9.4.5   Unconstrained Static Steiner Heuristics

In this section, we will discuss two important unconstrained static Steiner heuristics that can be used to construct source-specific trees for multicast routing.

---

6. Even though [29] includes only delay constraints, we use "CSTP" to refer to all Steiner problems that take one or more QoS constraints into account.

7. This assumption implies that a specified upper bound on the source-receiver delay has to be satisfied for each receiver.

9.4.5.1 The KMB Heuristic

The KMB algorithm (considered to be the most optimal among all static Steiner heuristics) works through a sequence of five steps. Consider a graph $G = (V, E)$ and a set of multicast group members D. The KMB algorithm has the following five steps:

1. Starting from the graph G, construct a *closure graph* on D, denoted by G'. (G' is a complete graph on D such that the cost of an edge (u, v) in G' is equal to the cost of the least-cost path between u and v in G.)

2. Construct a minimal-spanning tree T' of G'.

3. Replace the edges of T' with the corresponding least-cost paths in G to get a subgraph G''.

4. Construct the minimal-spanning tree T'' of G''.

5. Prune the branches of T'' that contain no multicast group members to get the resultant solution tree.

The KMB algorithm is taken as the baseline algorithm in comparing and assessing the cost efficiency of other Steiner-based multicast routing algorithms.

9.4.5.2 The TM Heuristic

The TM heuristic is an extremely simple heuristic for iterative construction of near-optimal static Steiner trees. The heuristic requires merely that, at each stage/iteration of tree construction, the receiver that is added has the least-cost path between itself and the rest of the tree. The TM heuristic is sometimes also referred to as the minimum-cost-path heuristic (MCPH).

9.4.6 Delay-Constrained Static Steiner Heuristics

In this section, we discuss three heuristics for constructing delay-constrained source-rooted multicast trees for static multicast groups. As before, we begin with a formal problem definition.

9.4.6.1 Problem Definition

We model a multicast tree establishment request (also referred to as a multicast call request) in a network $G = (V, E)$ as a 4-tuple:

$$C = (s, R, B, \Delta),$$

where $s \in V$ is the source node for the call, $R = \{d_1, d_2, \ldots, d_m\} \subset V$ is the set of receiver nodes for the call, B is the bandwidth requirement for the call, and Δ is the delay constraint to be satisfied for each (source,receiver) pair. Given such a call C on the network $G = (V, E)$, we define a bandwidth- and delay-constrained spanning tree to be a tree $T = (V_T, E_T)$ rooted at s and satisfying the following conditions:

$V_T \subseteq V$ and $E_T \subseteq E$;

$s \in V_T$ and $R \subseteq V_T$;

$D_T(s, v) < \Delta, \quad \forall v \in R$;

$AB(e) > B, \quad \forall e \in E_T$, where $AB(e)$ is the available bandwidth in edge e.

Let $S(C)$ denote the set of all such spanning trees corresponding to call C. The problem can now be formulated as:

Find a spanning tree T_S such that cost, $C(T_S) = \min(C(T) : T \in S(C))$.

Such a tree is a bandwidth- and delay-constrained Steiner Tree (BDCST).

9.4.6.2 Kompella-Pasquale-Polyzos Heuristics   In [29], Kompella et al. describe two centralized heuristic algorithms (adapted from the KMB algorithm [31]) for the delay-constrained static multicast tree construction problem. Both assume that a given source has all the information (network topology, link delays, and link costs) necessary to construct the required tree. The algorithms have a common initial stage that involves the computation of a closure graph on the source node and the set of receiver nodes. However, the two algorithms use different heuristic functions to construct a spanning tree of the closure graph, which then yields the required multicast tree. Distributed versions of these two algorithms are presented in [30].

Closure Graph Computation: As in the KMB algorithm, the two heuristics of [29] compute a closure graph spanning the nodes of the set $K = \{s \cup R\}$. The closure graph is constructed as follows. The *least-cost feasible path* between two nodes u and v is defined as the least-cost path connecting them such that the delay along the path is less than Δ. We let $P_C(u, v)$ and $P_D(u, v)$ denote, respectively, the cost and delay of such a least-cost feasible path. Then the closure graph on set K is a complete graph on K such that the cost of the (u, v) edge is $P_C(u, v)$ and the delay is $P_D(u, v)$.

Spanning-Tree Construction: To construct a spanning tree of the closure graph, Kompella et. al [29] propose a greedy approach. At each stage, an edge is added to a partially constructed tree by choosing the one that minimizes a specified heuristic function. Two such heuristic functions have been described in [29]:

$$f_{CD}(v, w) = \frac{C(v, w)}{\Delta - (D(s, v) + D(v, w))};$$

$$f_C(v, w) = C(v, w);$$

where $C(v, w)$ is the cost of the edge (v, w), $D(v, w)$ is its delay, and $D(s, v)$ is the delay from the source s to v in the partially constructed spanning tree. The denominator of the f_{CD} heuristic represents the residual delay[8] at node w if the edge (v, w) is used to extend the tree. Hence, f_{CD} tries to simultaneously minimize the cost of the edge (v, w) and maximize the resultant residual delay. On the other hand, the f_C heuristic is purely cost-based.

The centralized algorithms proposed in [29] are unsuitable for larger networks, as the process of maintaining consistent network information at every node becomes prohibitively expensive. The distributed versions of these algorithms [30] avoid this problem by using only local information at each node. However, because the algorithms construct the tree by adding only one edge at a time, the amount of time required to actually set up the tree could be very large, especially for sparse, widely distributed multicast groups, in which the multicast tree could include a large number of links. This large setup time also means that if we attempt to include resource reservation along with the tree construction process, then resources (such as link bandwidth) might be reserved for a long time before they are actually needed. This results in poor network utilization, decreased overall throughput, and lower call acceptance rates. Another disadvantage of the algorithms is that they provide for no tunable parameters, which could be used to effect a compromise between the optimality of the tree and the time required to set it up.

In the next section, we describe two algorithms for delay-constrained low-cost multicast routing that overcome the disadvantages described above. The two algorithms assume the existence of a unicast routing strategy that constructs low-cost delay-bounded loop-free paths between a given pair of nodes.

9.4.6.3   Algorithm A1   In algorithm A1, two distinct phases can be identified. The first phase is distributed, provided the underlying unicast routing strategy is distributed. The second phase is a centralized computation to be performed at the source node.

Phase 1:   The first phase involves the construction of delay-constrained least-cost paths between the source and every destination using the unicast routing strategy. At the end of this phase of the algorithm, the source node has a set of $m(= |R|)$ paths, $(P_1, P_2, \ldots, P_m)$, with the following properties:

- Path P_i connects source node s to the ith destination node d_i.

- $\forall\, i,\ 1 \leq i \leq m,$ delay $D(P_i) < \Delta$ (delay constraint).

- Every edge in each of the m paths has an available bandwidth greater than the minimum requirement B.

---

8. The residual delay is the amount of delay still available for extending the tree without violating the delay constraint.

Phase 2: This phase constructs a multicast routing tree rooted at the source, using the *m* paths produced at the end of the first phase. Starting with an empty tree, the construction proceeds by adding one new source-destination path at a time (at each stage) to an existing tree. *Each time an existing tree is augmented by adding another path, loops have to be removed in such a way that the resulting structure produced is connected, and none of the delay constraints are violated.* Algorithm A1 accomplishes this by defining a *cut* operation on augmented trees that is able to remove loops without compromising on the delay requirements. The details are discussed in [53].

9.4.6.4 Algorithm A2

Algorithm A2 is a purely distributed algorithm, provided the unicast routing strategy is distributed. In this algorithm, as in algorithm A1, the multicast tree is constructed by adding one destination node at a time to the tree. In algorithm A1, this addition was purely computational, and all the decisions were made at the source node as part of phase 2. However, in algorithm A2, the destination nodes make the decision about how to attach to the existing tree, from a set of options provided by the nodes of the already existing tree.

To attach a new destination node to a partially constructed multicast tree, the following steps are performed:

1. From a select set of nodes (chosen based on a priority function) in the existing tree, the algorithm constructs delay-constrained least-cost paths (using a unicast routing strategy) to the new destination node.

2. When the destination node receives the unicast path setup packets generated in the previous step, it applies a selection function (based on the delay and cost properties of the path) to each unicast path.

3. The destination node then determines the path that has minimum selection function value and uses that path to attach itself to the existing tree.

Details about the priority function, the selection function, and the mechanism for loop-avoidance in this algorithm are provided in [53].

9.4.7 Unconstrained Dynamic Steiner Heuristics

In this section, we discuss some Steiner-based routing algorithms designed to accommodate dynamic multicast groups. The problem of updating a multicast tree to accommodate addition (join) or deletion (leave) of nodes (members) to the multicast group is known as the *on-line/dynamic multicast problem* in networks. The graph-theoretic version of this problem, known as the *on-line Steiner problem in networks,* is NP-complete [22] and has been addressed in [26] and [63]. In the extreme case, the on-line multicast problem can be solved as a sequence of static multicast problems, by rebuilding the tree at each stage using a static Steiner heuristic. However, this approach is too expensive and is unsuitable for ongoing real-time multicast sessions, which cannot tolerate the disturbances caused by excessive changes in the multicast tree after each addition or deletion.

Consequently, any algorithm for on-line updating of multicast trees must take into account two important and possibly contradictory goals. On the one hand, the cost of the multicast tree after each update should be kept as small as possible. This might require repeated reconfiguration of the tree after each update operation to remove unwanted high-cost edges from the tree. On the other hand, real-time multicast sessions cannot tolerate frequent large changes to the multicast tree as packets are constantly in flight within the tree. Therefore, a balance needs to be struck between cost reduction and minimization of the number of changes to the tree.

The on-line multicast problem was first presented by Waxman [60] and has since been addressed in [3, 26, 28, 63]. Waxman, in the first paper, divides on-line heuristics into two categories: those that allow reconfiguration (or rearrangement) of the tree and those that do not. The latter case allows no rearrangement of existing routes as new nodes are added to or removed from a group; that is, neither addition of edges during node removal nor deletion of edges during node addition is allowed. Imase and Waxman in [26] have investigated bounds for both kinds of heuristics. Considering only addition of members, they have shown that the lower bound for the *cost competitiveness* (defined as the ratio of cost of a multicast tree to that of an optimal tree for the same set of members) of any nonrearrangeable heuristic is

$$1 + \frac{1}{2} \lfloor \log_2(n-1) \rfloor,$$

where n is the number of members that have been added to the group up to that point. Imase and Waxman have also shown that no such finite bound exists if deletions are also considered. A rearrangeable heuristic, on the other hand, can have a finite bound for *cost competitiveness* taking into consideration both addition and deletion of nodes. In the following sections, we will discuss some important heuristics for the unconstrained dynamic Steiner problem.

9.4.7.1 GREEDY Algorithm A simple nonrearrangeable heuristic known as the GREEDY algorithm was proposed by Waxman in [60] with an aim to minimizing the perturbation to the existing tree when nodes are added or deleted. To add a node u to an existing multicast group, the closest node v already in the tree is chosen, and u is attached to v via the least-cost path. For a delete request, if the node being removed is a leaf node, then the branch of the tree supporting only that node is pruned. For the case of nonleaf nodes, no action is taken.

9.4.7.2 Edge-Bounded Algorithm The edge-bounded algorithm (EBA) [26] is a re-arrangeable heuristic. It works by enforcing an upper bound on the distance between nodes in a tree after each update operation. EBA works on the basis of distance graphs.[9] EBA is also parameterized by a value σ that decides the upper bound that the algorithm is trying to enforce. It is shown in [26] that the cost of the tree produced by EBA is at most 4σ times that of an optimal Steiner tree for the same group.

9.4.7.3 GSDM Algorithm The geographic spread dynamic multicast (GSDM) algo-rithm, proposed in [28], is a rearrangeable heuristic based on the notion of the *geographic spread* of a tree. Geographic spread is defined as follows. Given a graph $G = (V, E)$ and a subset $U \subseteq V$, the geographic spread (GS) of the set U, in the static case when tree T' spans U, is defined as the inverse sum of the minimum distance from a vertex v to a vertex in T', over all vertices $v \in V$, that is,

$$GS(U, V, E) = [\sum_{v \in V} \min_{u \in T'} \{distance(v, u)\}]^{-1}.$$

The principle behind the GSDM algorithm is to attempt local optimization when a re-ceiver node is added to the multicast group, but at the same time take into account the GS of the multicast tree from a global viewpoint, thereby making sure the whole network benefits in the long term. The greater the GS in the multicast tree, the more likely it will be that a new receiver node to be added is close to an existing node in the multicast tree, and this will therefore improve the local optimization, which in turn reduces the cost of the multicast tree. Deletions to a tree are handled as in GREEDY. For addition of mem-bers to an existing tree, GSDM identifies three key nodes in the tree as follows: Let A be the node that is to be added to the multicast group. Let B be the current multicast group member closest to A. Let C and D be the two nearest nodes to A that are neighbors on either side of B in the current tree. Then the three key nodes involved in the attachment of A are B, C, and D. GSDM compares the cost of four possible types of connections involving A, B, C, and D. The type of connection that minimizes the cost (if there is a tie, it is resolved in favor of the type that results in greater geographic spread) is then chosen.

9.4.7.4 ARIES Heuristic The recently proposed ARIES heuristic [3] aims to combine the computational simplicity of the GREEDY algorithm with the better competitiveness possible using a rearrangeable heuristic. The ARIES algorithm works by monitoring the accumulated damage to a multicast tree within local regions of the tree as members are

---

9. A distance graph is a complete graph on the same set of nodes as the original graph with the cost of edge (i, j) equal to the cost of the shortest path between i and j in the original graph.

added to or deleted from the group. When the damage to a particular region of the tree exceeds a threshold, then a simple rearrangement heuristic is used to recreate the tree.

9.4.7.5 Virtual Trunk Dynamic Multicast Algorithm   The nonrearrangeable virtual trunk dynamic multicast (VTDM) algorithm proposed in [34] is based on the following principle: In the dynamic multicast routing problem, if a static multicast algorithm is applied to reconstruct the tree for each request to add or delete, some nodes and links may be frequently used. If a dynamic multicast routing algorithm can use these same nodes and links, then it can conceivably construct low-cost trees matching the cost performance of the static multicast algorithm. To identify the nodes and links involved, the authors define the notion of a virtual trunk (VT), which is a tree of the underlying network. The nodes of the VT are determined using a weight function[10] that associates a positive real number with each node. The VT for a given connection is constructed by applying the KMB algorithm [31] to a selected set of nodes. It is then used as a template for modifying the tree in response to changes in group membership. New nodes are attached to the multicast tree by determining the least-cost path connecting the node to the VT. Node deletions are handled as in GREEDY.

9.4.8   Delay-Constrained Dynamic Steiner Heuristics

We refer to the delay-constrained version of the on-line multicast problem as the constrained on-line multicast (COLM) problem. Until recently, very little work had been done toward simultaneously addressing the twin issues of dynamic membership and delay constraint satisfaction. In the following sections, we formally state the COLM problem and discuss two recently proposed heuristics for solving it.

9.4.8.1   Problem Formulation   Successive updates to a multicast group are modeled here as a *request vector* $R = \{r_1, r_2, \ldots, r_n\}$ consisting of a sequence of n requests. Each request r_i is either of the form (v, add) (indicating the addition of v to the multicast group) or of the form $(v, remove)$ (indicating removal of v from the existing group), for some $v \in V$. S_i denotes the set of nodes that belong to the multicast group after satisfying requests $r_1, r_2, \ldots, r_i$ and is defined as

$$S_i = \{v | (v, add) = r_j, \text{ for some } j, 1 \leq j \leq i, \text{ and } (v, remove) \neq r_k, \text{ for all } k, 1 \leq k \leq i\}.$$

Two versions of the COLM problem are possible. The first version, referred to as *COLM-UC,* is the uniformly constrained on-line multicast problem, in which all members

---

10. The weight of a node is defined to be the number of shortest paths (between any two nodes of the network) passing through that node.

of the multicast group have identical delay constraints. The second version, referred to as *COLM-IC,* is the individually constrained on-line multicast problem, in which each member of the multicast group has its own delay constraint relative to the source. The model here applies to multicasting of multimedia information (such as video or audio multicasts) in which each receiver can subscribe to and receive a different quality of service.

An instance of COLM-IC on the network $G = (V, E)$ can be modeled as a 3-tuple (s, R, Δ), where s is the source node, relative to which all delay-constraints are measured; $R = \{r_1, r_2, \ldots, r_n\}$ is the *request vector* consisting of a sequence of n updates; and Δ: $\bigcup_{i=1}^{n} S_i \to R^+$ is a function that maps each multicast group member to its delay constraint. The objective of the COLM-IC problem is to determine a sequence of multicast trees $T_1, T_2, \ldots, T_n$ such that for each T_i, $1 \le i \le n$, the following are true:

- T_i spans the set $s \cup S_i$.

- $D_{T_i}(s, v) < \Delta(v)$, for each $v \in S_i$.

- Cost $C(T_i)$ is the minimum among all possible trees satisfying the above two conditions.

COLM-UC can be specified as a special case of the above formulation in which group members have the same delay constraint. In the case of COLM-UC, Δ can be thought of as a positive real number (rather than a function) representing this common delay constraint.

9.4.8.2   Lagrangian Relaxation-Based Algorithm   The Lagrangian relaxation-based algorithm (LRA) proposed in [24] handles deletion of nodes by merely pruning unnecessary branches from the tree (as in GREEDY). The problem of adding a new node to a multicast tree is reduced, through a suitable modification, to the problem of determining a delay-constrained minimum-cost path between the new node and the source. This modified problem is then solved using a heuristic based on the Lagrangian relaxation method frequently used to solve NP-hard problems.

9.4.8.3   Sriram et al.'s Algorithm   To achieve a balance between cost reduction and tree change minimization, Bauer and Varma [3] have suggested the technique (ARIES) of allowing the quality of a tree to degrade because of member additions/deletions up to a fixed threshold. Any further degradation results in a rearrangement of a portion of the tree using a simple static Steiner heuristic. In the algorithm proposed in [54], Sriram et al. adopt this idea of having the damage to a tree accumulate until rearrangement is triggered based on a threshold value for the deterioration being reached. However, since the algorithm has to deal with a constrained multicast tree, Sriram et al. employ a rearrangement technique that takes the delay constraints of the multicast group members into account.

In [54], a new technique is used for determining the point at which a rearrangement needs to be triggered. In ARIES, damage to any region of a tree is measured simply by counting the number of newly added or recently deleted nodes in that region. When this number exceeds a specified threshold, rearrangement is triggered. However, this measure does not take into account the contribution a particular region makes to the rest of the tree. By "contribution" of a region, we mean the number of multicast group members connected to the source through that region. In Sriram et al.'s method, even if a region of a tree has degraded to a certain extent (using ARIES's measure), as long as it is serving a large number of multicast members, it should not be disturbed; that is, rearrangement of a tree must be initiated only when a region of the tree that is serving only a small number of multicast members contributes considerably to the cost of the tree. A technique is proposed in [54] for having rearrangement triggered based on monitoring the usefulness of a region, rather than the damage done to it, and triggering a rearrangement when the usefulness falls below a threshold. The authors formalize this intuitive concept of *usefulness* through a mathematical definition of the *quality factor* of a region. Note that for applications that absolutely cannot tolerate any change in an existing multicast tree, the algorithm in [54] can be reduced to a nonrearrangeable algorithm by setting the usefulness threshold to 0.

This algorithm assumes the presence of a unicast algorithm for constructing delay-constrained least-cost paths between pairs of nodes.

9.4.9   Multicast Routing in the ATM Environment

The notion of point-to-multipoint VC was initially introduced in the ATM user-network interface (UNI) specification to handle audio conferencing applications. In the current standards for ATM, multicast group address abstraction does not exist. Hence, the source needs to be aware of all its group members at any given point of time. A partial solution to this problem is the MARS mapping scheme discussed in section 9.3.7. However, there is as yet no mechanism for receiver-controlled group membership in ATM networks. Groups of multicast-capable ATM interfaces are grouped into what are known as *clusters*. Two models have been proposed for multicast communication in such clusters:

• In the multicast VC mesh, a point-to-multipoint VC originates from each sender to all members of the multicast group. If a member joins or leaves, the VC needs to be updated. In addition, the ATM interface must terminate one VC for each active source in the cluster.

• In the multicast server (MCS) model, a server is chosen within each cluster and designated as the MCS. Each source establishes a point-to-point VC to the MCS, which in turn establishes a point-to-multipoint VC to the multicast group members. During the data transmission phase, the MCS is responsible for reassembling messages arriving on all incoming point-to-point VCs and forwarding them to the receivers.

Both the above solutions have some disadvantages. The VC mesh solution might initially seem preferable since it avoids the traffic concentration in and around the MCS that results in the MCS model. Data transmission delays are also likely to be lower, as the MCS approach requires reassembly of data packets. However, the MCS approach allows better control of group dynamics and enables sources to transmit to dynamic groups without worrying about group management.

9.5   Resource Reservation

Resource reservation is complex to set up in a multicast environment. A direct extension of point-to-point reservation techniques to the multicast environment does not yield efficient and scalable solutions. In this section, we examine the need for resource reservation and describe some general approaches to achieve it in the multicast paradigm. In section 9.7, we describe a popular resource reservation protocol used on the Internet, called RSVP.

Resource reservation is necessary for a network to provide service and performance guarantees to multimedia applications. The exact nature of reservations required depends on both the service guarantees and the approach taken toward satisfying them [32]. In general, resource reservation mechanisms can be viewed as a special case of switch state establishment techniques [66]. These mechanisms are employed during connection establishment, along with admission control. An alternative to reserving resources for an indefinite period of time during connection establishment is to have the applications make *advance* reservations for a future connection with a given lifetime [21]. This allows more sessions to be admitted with a given lifetime and also permits graceful negative responses to reservation requests.

The first component of resource reservation schemes is a specification model for flow characteristics. Then, an appropriate protocol (like RSVP) is required to communicate these specifications to receivers and to reserve resources on the transmission path so that the requested service parameters can be supported. Simple unicast approaches to resource reservations are generally either *source-initiated* or *receiver-initiated with/without advertisements*. In the following sections, we describe both of these approaches and discuss the changes necessary to extend them to the multicast case.

9.5.1   Source-Initiated Two-Pass Scheme for Unicast Communication

The source-initiated approach uses a two-pass scheme, with overallocations in the first pass and relaxations in the second, so that after the second pass end-to-end service is efficiently mapped to local reservations. A setup message containing the flow specification is sent toward destinations, with the intermediate nodes (switches) committing adequate resources for the connection, if available. Resources are normally overallocated early on along the path of the message, so that even if switches encountered farther along the path are short of resources, the connection can still be set up. After the setup message reaches the destination node, a response message is returned on the reverse path, allowing the intermediate switches to relax commitments if possible. The disadvantage with this scheme is that it wastes overallocated resources and other reservation attempts may be blocked until reservations are relaxed (which may take a long time in the case of multicast, as described below).

9.5.1.1 Multicasting For the above method to work in multicasting, there must be a way for senders to notify receivers of their properties, so that appropriate resource reservations can be made. In a perfectly homogeneous environment, reservations will be made once on each outgoing link of a node for all downstream receivers. However, receiver and network heterogeneity prohibits use of such a simple scheme, since each receiver and path may be able, or willing, to commit different amounts of resources. A direct extension of the two-pass scheme is to allocate resources as before, during the message's first trip down the tree, and then have all receivers send back their relaxation (or rejection) messages upstream. Each switch that acts as a junction will only propagate toward the source, the most restrictive relaxation among all those received. However, since paths from such junctions toward receivers may have committed more resources than are now needed, additional passes will be required for convergence. To handle dynamic groups without constant source intervention, this model can be augmented with receiver-initiated reservations that propagate toward an already established distribution tree [4]. The main disadvantage of this approach is that because of large convergence times (because of the additional passes) the overallocated resources remain locked up for a long time, resulting in the blocking of other reservation attempts.

9.5.2 Receiver-Initiated One-Pass Scheme for Unicast Communication

In the receiver-initiated approach, there is only a single pass, so only local reservations can be specified, and these result in an end-to-end service whose characteristics cannot be predicted in advance. As a result, depending on local decisions, the resources reserved through these end-to-end reservations may be either inadequate or superfluous. A solution to this problem is to use *advertisements* [51] in reserving resources. In this approach, source-initiated messages gather information about local links, without reserving resources, as they travel toward the receiver. The receiver can then decide how local reservation along the path would affect end-to-end services and then use the receiver-initiated approach to reserve appropriate per-link resources. Since the exact services and resources available at each link are included in the information gathered in the first pass, receivers can compose heterogeneous local services and link specific reservations to build enhanced end-to-end paths.

9.5.2.1 Multicasting A receiver-initiated approach to multicast resource reservation (used in RSVP [66]) proceeds as follows. Resource reservations are abandoned during a sender's multicast setup message, and reservations are based instead on the modified specifications with which receivers respond to the setup message. Again, resource reservations are merged at junction points of the multicast tree, but since the (now upstream) requests are expected to be heterogeneous, each junction reserves adequate resources for the most demanding receivers and reuses them to support the less demanding ones. Though efficient aggregation of resources in this approach is still a research issue, the approach has the potential to support both heterogeneous requests and resource conservation, possibly without overcommitting resources at any stage. This overcomes the disadvantage of the scheme discussed in the previous section. Since the mechanism for reserving resources converges in one, rather than multiple, passes, the reservation state in the switches can be periodically refreshed, turning the fixed *hard state* of a static connection into an adaptive *soft state* suitable for environments that are dynamic [66] (due to membership changes or routing modifications). In general, receiver-initiated resource reservation schemes converge faster, provide better support for heterogeneous QoS requirements, and scale well to dynamic multicast groups.

9.5.3 Other Issues in Resource Reservation

The interaction of routing and resource reservation (and therefore admission control) further complicates issues in the design of practical reservation mechanisms for multicast environments. Even in the simple case of static groups, success in building a multicast tree depends on the adequacy of resources on each switch. Ideally, the aim is to construct a tree using switches that pass the admissibility test, thus favoring the sender-initiated resource reservation approach. On the other hand, to prevent a particular construction from failing due to overallocation, receiver-initiated reservations are preferable (because of their faster convergence). In that case, however, the tree constructed by the routing algorithm may be inadequate to support the reservations, resulting in the rejection of a session that could, in principle, be successfully set up. The problem becomes more complicated still when applied to dynamic groups.

9.6 Multicast Traffic Control

Traffic control refers to a collection of dynamic control techniques for dealing with flow, error, and congestion control that become necessary to respond to run time events such as overloaded switches, transmission errors, failed links/switches, and overloaded receivers.

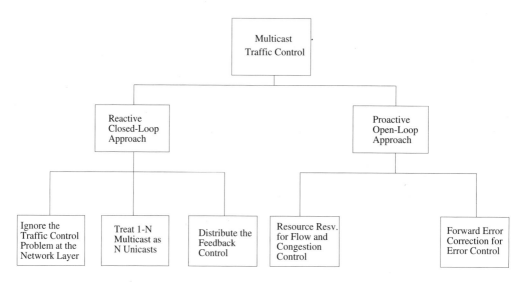

Figure 9.4
Approaches to multicast traffic control

Error control ensures that packets transmitted by a sender are received correctly at the other end of the connecton. Otherwise, packets may be received corrupted (detected by error-detection schemes) or may be lost (detected by missing packet sequence numbers). *Flow control* ensures that a sender does not swamp any receiver with data that cannot be consumed in time: a problem of insufficient resources at the receiver end. *Congestion control* deals again with the problem of insufficient resources, but this time on the network switches between sender and receiver. In this case, the lack of resources leads to the dropping of some packets by the overloaded network switches. Flow control is clearly an end-to-end issue that must be handled above the network layer, whereas error and congestion control depend on network status and can either be handled at the network layer (transparent to applications) or be addressed at the higher layers on an end-to-end basis.

There have essentially been two basic approaches to unicast traffic control:

• The proactive open-loop reservation-based approach (employed in real-time networks)

• The reactive closed-loop feedback-based approach (usually employed in networks carrying non-real-time traffic)

Both approaches have been extended to the multicast communication paradigm (refer to figure 9.4), as discussed in section 9.6.1 (reservation-based multicast traffic control) and section 9.6.2 (feedback-based control).

9.6.1   Open-Loop Reservation-Based Multicast Traffic Control

The reservation-based approach to multicast traffic control attempts to avoid having to deal with flow and congestion control by employing a combination of admission control and advance resource reservation. This ensures that there are no temporary resource shortages at either the receiver or the intermediate nodes and that they are all able to support a particular sender's data rate throughout the lifetime of that sender's connection. Error control is achieved using forward error correction (FEC) techniques. This kind of preventive action helps eliminate any reliance on feedback and all its associated scalability problems.

Multimedia multicasting imposes certain special restrictions that will make many scalable feedback approaches inapplicable. Consequently, the reservation-based approach in conjunction with FEC is the preferred choice for such applications. Of these two mechanisms, FEC is simpler to implement and imposes no requirements on the intermediate switching nodes. Resource reservation, however, is more complicated and requires specialized mechanisms (section 9.5). The next two sections will discuss how the special features of multimedia streams make the use of open-loop techniques not only essential, but also efficient.

9.6.1.1   Error Control   There are a number of reasons for using FEC-based techniques for error control in multimedia multicasting:

• Given the inability of most multimedia applications to tolerate critical errors, FEC schemes are quite appropriate and efficient (of course, the level of redundancy can be increased as needed).

• Traditional error control schemes based on automatic repeat requests (ARQs), which retransmit corrupted packets according to receiver-generated feedback, result in excessive delay in receiving the packet. There is no point in retransmitting a corrupted packet if the deadline for the delivery of the packet has also passed. Since ARQ schemes introduce additional delay and delay jitter into the media stream, they are not viable for most continuous-media applications.

• By making use of the special properties of media streams, it is possible to avoid using feedback and retransmissions to control error rates by employing *error concealment techniques* (such as computing a likely value for missing pieces of data through interpolation from neighboring values). For example, video frames can be coded in *intraframe* mode, in which spatial redundancy alone is exploited, or in *interframe* mode, in which temporal redundancy is also exploited. Using both techniques increases the compression ratio, but lost packets, while causing hot spot problems on one frame in intraframe mode, create longer-term problems in interframe mode. To achieve a trade-off between compression efficiency and error control, it is possible to essentially use interframe mode while periodically transmitting intraframe-encoded frames. These periodic special frames act as regeneration (or resynchronization) points to minimize problems due to lost packets.

• Hierarchical encoding of media streams provides the necessary flexibility to employ prioritized error control techniques. Different components of a stream can be transmitted with different levels of redundancy, reflecting their relative importance in the reconstruction of the complete signal at the destination node. The net effect is added reliability for important media components with only a moderate increase in transmission bandwidth.

9.6.1.2   Flow and Congestion Control   Preventive open-loop methods based on advance resource reservations are most suitable for flow and congestion control in multimedia multicast applications. Resource reservations not only are most appropriate for continuous media streams but also allow the effective employment of hierarchical (layered) coding with separate reservations per layer, to accommodate heterogeneous receivers.

Most resource reservation schemes are based on protocols that use feedback to determine and allocate resources. However, since resource reservation takes place in these schemes only once, before the start of actual information flow (rather than multiple times during the information flow, as in traditional dynamic feedback control mechanisms) the control overhead may be acceptable. It is important to note that resources must be reserved in such schemes on a per-stream basis (and if hierarchically encoded, on a per-layer basis), according to the characteristics of the relevant media. A communication abstraction promoting open-loop traffic control and providing a service analogous to that of a television broadcast channel is the *multimedia multicast channel* proposed in [39].

Effective open-loop congestion control can be exercised in high-speed networks by selectively dropping high-resolution contents without source or receiver involvement and with limited signal-quality degradation, which is localized to the subtree downstream from the congestion path.

9.6.2   Closed-Loop Feedback-Based Multicast Traffic Control

The closed-loop feedback-based approach to traffic control depends on periodic status/control information sent to the sender from the receivers and other intermediate nodes. The sender uses this control information to regulate and control the characteristics of the generated data stream in response to receiver- and network-triggered events. For error control, the receiver of corrupted packets or packets that have not arrived within a certain time interval asks the sender to resend them. For flow control, a receiver may ask a sender to either increase or decrease its transmission rate, depending on the receiver's current ability to consume packets. For congestion control, one or more congested intermediate nodes inform the sender of their inability to support the sender's current data rate.

Closed-loop feedback-based techniques do not scale well to multicast communication. This is especially true for multimedia multicasting, wherein the special requirements of multimedia communication preclude the employment of delay-intensive feedback-based schemes.

9.6.2.1   Problems with Multicast Feedback Control   A direct extension of feedback-based unicast traffic control schemes to the multicast paradigm suffers from the following problems:

Feedback Implosion: When each member of a multicast group, in response to a particular sender's transmission, sends all the control information that any unicast receiver would have, that sender is likely to be swamped by control information. More seriously, control information sent by two different receivers could conflict.

Conflict between Per-Receiver Control and Host-Group Model: Many traffic control mechanisms are receiver-dependent. For example, a certain transmission rate suitable for a majority of the receivers of the transmission could swamp one particularly slow receiver. Hence, an efficient scheme would require the sender to treat that receiver in a specific manner without reducing the transmission rate to the other receivers.[11] However, this would violate the host-group model, wherein a sender should deal with a multicast group as a whole. Similarly, a certain packet could be received successfully by all receivers except one (which either does not receive the packet or receives a corrupted packet). Once again, an efficient scheme would require the sender to selectively retransmit the packet only to that receiver. However, the host-group model dictates that the sender either retransmit to all receivers (waste of resources) or ignore the error altogether. Clearly, there is a conflict between efficient per-receiver traffic control mechanisms and simplicity of the source interface (as dictated by the host-group model).

9.6.2.2   Proposed Solutions   There have been a number of attempts to develop scalable feedback control schemes (some of which are discussed in section 9.6.2.3) that overcome the problems set forth above. These schemes fall into three major categories:

1. *Ignore the problem.* The simplest solution is to ignore the traffic control problem at the network level and provide best-effort service. Delegating the resolution of transmission problems to the higher layers may be an adequate solution in many cases, since they may have additional information regarding application requirements and thus can implement more appropriate mechanisms.

---

11. An inefficient solution could of course reduce the transmission rate for all receivers to that which is acceptable to the slowest among them.

2. *Treat 1 to N multicast as N unicasts.* A second solution sacrifices the host-group model's simplicity by maintaining per-receiver state information during multicasts. A sender transmits one multicast packet but then acts as if it has sent N packets to N receivers, maintaining state information about each one of them. After multicasting a packet, the sender waits until a stable state is reached before multicasting the next packet. In terms of flow control, this slows down the sender enough so as not to swamp the slowest receiver. In terms of error control, this means taking corrective actions based on the most problematic receiver, forcing all the others to be delayed. If one or more receivers are unable to reach a stable state even after a number of retransmissions, they may have to be removed from the multicast group. Retransmissions may be multicast when many receivers lose the initial packet or unicast when only a few do. To avoid feedback implosion, all schemes of this type use *negative acknowledgments;* that is, recipients send responses only when problems occur, rather than confirming packets that are received correctly.

This solution does not scale well to large groups (even for very reliable links and rare congestion and flow control problems), as the source is required to act as the command center and store complete state information. Also, the scheme forces the connection's performance to be determined by the lowest common denominator: the slowest receiver, the most error-prone link, or the most congested path.

3. *Distribute the feedback control mechanism.* A third solution is to distribute the feedback control mechanism over the nodes of the multicast tree. Control is then *hierarchical,* as dictated by the multicast tree. A given receiver's feedback need not propagate all the way back to the sender. When an intermediate node receives the feedback, it takes corrective action itself or propagates a summary message (based on all the feedback messages it has received) recursively up the tree. In this case, feedback implosion in terms of number of messages is avoided, but the problem of conflicting reports remains. The solution attempts to localize feedback and corrective actions to the part of a tree containing problems. A potential benefit is that receivers that have paths to the sender that do not go through nodes currently reacting to problems achieve better performance. Also, the distribution of the feedback control mechanisms relieves the sender of the burden of having to deal with individual receivers. However, a very important disadvantage of this solution is that it demands more from intermediate tree nodes. For extremely complex control mechanisms, the increase in the cost of the intermediate switching nodes may be unacceptable.

A nonhierarchical approach to distributed feedback control, targeted to recovery of lost messages, is to let all receivers and senders cooperate in handling losses. When receivers discover a message loss, they multicast a retransmission request, and *anyone* that has that message can multicast it again. To avoid feedback implosion, these requests are sent after a fixed delay based on a particular receiver's distance from the source of the message. The idea behind this scheme is that most retransmission requests will never be sent because the first few multicasts will be received before the remaining receivers' fixed delay has elapsed.

9.6.2.3 A Survey of Proposals for Multicast Feedback Control   In this section, we survey some proposals for multicast feedback control. The next section takes up one such important proposal, receiver-driven layered multicast, and discusses its features in detail.

A scalable feedback control mechanism that can be used to estimate network conditions without creating feedback implosion problems has been proposed in [5]. The mechanism first estimates the number of receivers in a group, then determines the average quality of signal reception (the averaging technique is dependent on the nature of the application and the media stream) using probabilistic techniques. This method has been used in applications for senders to detect congestion problems and adapt their output rates and error redundancy levels.

Scalable feedback control can be further enhanced by splitting receivers into groups according to their respective reception status (congestion control) and capabilities (flow control). The data can then be tailored to suit a particular group's characteristics. This avoids the problems created by very fast/slow receivers dragging the entire group toward one extreme [8].

Shacham [49] has proposed a scheme for rate adaptation (flow control) and error control to specifically deal with the issue of host heterogeneity. The scheme is based on layered transmission (hierarchical coding) and compression and computes fixed optimal routes for a certain assumed traffic mix. However, it employs reactive, rather than pro-active, error control techniques.

A discrete scaling mechanism has been proposed in the Heidelberg transport system [16] that uses a receiver-oriented scheme for adapting to delivered bandwidth. In this scheme, receivers open and close multicast connections to adapt to changes in bandwidth.

Deering [12] first suggested the use of layered transmission with IP multicast, wherein layers are individually mapped onto multicast groups. This idea is extended, along with an adaptation protocol, in the receiver-driven layered multicast scheme, which is discussed in the following section.

Feedback schemes proposed for multicast traffic in ATM networks involve a mixture of end-to-end and network-based techniques. In the ATM ABR (available bit rate) service, resource management cells convey explicit feedback information to sources; on a multipoint call, these feedback messages are accumulated, and the worst case rate is forwarded to the source.

9.6.2.4 Receiver-Driven Layered Multicast   One of the most efficient schemes for multicast traffic control dealing specifically with flow and congestion control (which

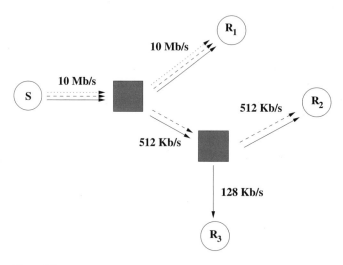

Figure 9.5
End-to-end adaptation

the authors refer to collectively as "rate adaptation") is receiver-driven layered multicast (RLM) [36].

Traditional source-based rate adaptation performs poorly in a heterogeneous multicast environment because there is no single target rate to adapt to (because of the conflicting bandwidth requirements of receivers). Hence, to overcome heterogeneity issues, the burden of rate adaptation has to be moved from the source to the receivers. One approach to receiver-driven adaptation is to combine a layered (hierarchical) source coding with a layered transmission system. Because subsets of layers are selectively forwardable at constrained network links, each user receives the best-quality signal that the network can deliver. The RLM scheme proposes that this selective forwarding be carried out using multiple IP-multicast groups (one per layer) in which each receiver specifies its level of subscription by joining a subset of the groups. Receivers adapt to congestion by adding or dropping layers (i.e., joining or leaving multicast groups). Hence, no explicit signaling between the source and the receivers or the receivers and the intermediate routers is needed.

For example, consider figure 9.5. Suppose source S is transmitting three layers of video information to receivers R_1, R_2, and R_3. Here, R_1 subscribes to all three layers and receives the full 10 Mbps transmission rate. If either R_2 or R_3 subscribes to all three layers, the 512 Kbps link becomes congested, and packets are dropped. Both receivers react to this congestion by dropping layer 3. Finally, because of a slow 128 Kbps connecting link, R_3

drops the second layer, too. Clearly, each layer defines its own multicast distribution tree whose configuration varies, depending on the congestion in the network.

Receivers search for an optimal subscription level by using a search-based scheme modeled on transmission control protocol's slow-start algorithm. To conduct this search, receivers must determine whether a certain subscription level is over the optimum or below the optimum. Oversubscription leads to congestion and can be detected through loss of packets transmitted. For detecting undersubscription, the RLM scheme requires receivers to conduct *join experiments,* wherein they attempt to subscribe to the next higher level. If such an attempt causes congestion, the receiver quickly drops the offending layer. On the other hand, if the experiment is successful, the subscription remains, and signal quality to that receiver improves.

Frequent join experiments cause transient congestion that can have an impact on the quality of the desired signal. To minimize the number of these experiments, the RLM scheme uses an *exponential-backoff linear-increase* scheme similar to the TCP slow-start algorithm. The increase in membership as a multicast session progresses can affect the frequency of join experiments. To overcome the effect of this factor, RLM employs a *shared-learning algorithm,* wherein receivers advertise their intention to conduct a certain join experiment. Other receivers are therefore able to perceive (because of the congestion that they themselves experience) whether a certain join experiment is successful or not. If it is unsuccessful, the other receivers do not attempt to repeat the same experiment in the near future. The learning algorithm is conservative, in that other receivers remember only failed experiments and not successful ones.

The RLM protocol is currently the most extensively used scheme for rate adaptation in multimedia multicast communication over best-effort networks (such as the Internet). Simulation results cited in [36] indicate that the protocol is extremely efficient (with respect to overhead) in detecting and managing congestion control without any of the problems highlighted in section 9.6.2.1.

9.7 Multicasting in the Internet

The Internet, though lacking support for many of the features discussed in the previous sections, has been extensively used as a test bed for algorithms and protocols supporting multimedia multicasting. Continuous growth of Internet applications that require communication among groups of processes or simultaneous dissemination of data to different destinations has led to considerable interest in multicast communication over the Internet. These applications span audio/video multicast [20], distributed whiteboards, image communications, electronic mail, and network news. In this section, we provide a

functionality	protocol(s)/mechanisms
Group Addressing	IP Class D Addresses
Group Management	IGMP
Multicast Routing	DVMRP, PIM, MOSPF, CBT
Resource Reservation	RSVP, ST-II
Transport Protocol	RTP
Transport Control Protocol	RTCP
Session Advertisement	SDP
Reliable Communication	TMTP, LBRM, SRM

Figure 9.6
Internet protocols for multimedia multicasting

brief overview of some important multimedia multicast protocols used in (or proposed for) the Internet. Figure 9.6 lists some of these protocols, grouping them based on their functionality.

With respect to the protocols listed in figure 9.6, the issue of group addressing using IP class D addresses has already been discussed as part of the central server technique in section 9.3.2. The rest of this section deals individually with the remaining protocols listed in the figure.

9.7.1   Internet Group Management Protocol

The group management protocol associated with the Internet is Internet group management protocol (IGMP) [12]. It is used to report host-group memberships to neighboring multicast routers. IGMP supports the host-group model (refer to section 9.1.1), with receivers explicitly joining a group denoted by multicast addresses. Multicast-aware routers periodically multicast, on a well-known address, membership queries on their LANs and gather replies from interested hosts to discover which groups have members present in their area. Routing algorithms such as distance vector multicast routing protocol use this information for selective pruning of multicast trees. IGMP also makes extensive use of the TTL (time-to-live) entry in IP packets to control how far/near the actual receivers are to the sender.

IGMP has gone through various stages of evolution and undergone a number of revisions during its existence. Initially, host members joined just by advertising on local subnets. This caused the multicast routers on those subnets (or LANs) to make an appropriate entry in their routing tables. Hosts left groups by not sending such periodic advertisement messages, thus causing the routing table entries to time-out. IGMP v2 added a mechanism for *low-latency leave,* allowing a more prompt pruning of a routing tree when no members of a particular group were present on that tree's subnet. IGMP v3 adds a further enhancement referred to as *selective source reception* that makes it possible to target traffic from senders of a particular group to reach only certain receivers of that group (as opposed to traffic from all senders automatically reaching all receivers). Receivers also can now send information to the multicast routers of only *desired sources,* which the routing algorithms then use to optimize on bandwidth (through source pruning).

9.7.2   Internet Routing Protocols

In this section, we discuss the routing protocols most commonly used in the Internet (specifically, in the multicast backbone (MBone) network).

9.7.2.1   Distance Vector Multicast Routing Protocol   Distance vector multicast routing protocol (DVMRP) [11] is characterized by the 4-tuple (*source-based, unconstrained, source-specific, dynamic*). In this protocol, multicast routers exchange reverse-path distances [10] to build a delivery tree, rooted at the source, for each group. Once the delivery tree is built, reverse path forwarding [10] is used to decide whether or not a packet should be forwarded to another node. Superfluous datagram copies are avoided through a one-step look-ahead (i.e., by examining a child's reverse path node to its source). The scope of multicast delivery is limited using the TTL capability of Internet datagrams.

The rapid growth of the MBone necessitated the revision of DVMRP to include hierarchy [57]. The authors of [57] propose organizing the MBone in regions having address-independent identifiers. A two-level routing hierarchy is proposed: intraregion multicast routing, for which routers may run any protocol they wish, and interregion multicast between boundary routers using DVMRP.

9.7.2.2   Multicast Open Shortest Path First   Unlike DVMRP, which is based on distance-vector routing, multicast open shortest-path-first (MOSPF) [37] is a multicast routing protocol based on OSPF v2, which takes advantage of the link state database. It is characterized by the 4-tuple (*source-based, unconstrained, source-specific, static*). MOSPF allows routers to build efficient source-based shortest-path trees without flooding even the first datagram of a group transmission. Link efficiency is therefore higher than in DVMRP. However, MOSPF requires heavy computation for each multicast (source,group) combination and is suitable only for small networks or subnets (possibly within a region of the proposed hierarchical DVMRP).

9.7.2.3   Protocol-Independent Multicast   The previous two protocols, though good enough for the limited purpose of the multicast backbone, do not scale well to the global Internet. To extend multicast support to wide area groups, protocol-independent multicast (PIM) [15] has been proposed. PIM operates in two modes, *sparse* or *dense,* depending on

the distribution of a particular group across a network. PIM-DM (dense mode) is essentially the same as DVMRP, except that the unicast routes are exported directly from the existing unicast routing tables. PIM-DM is characterized by the same 4-tuple as DVMRP.

PIM-SM (sparse mode) uses a center-based approach wherein explicit join messages are sent by receivers to rendezvous points to meet new sources. When a new multicast group is introduced to a network that uses PIM-SM, a node in the network called a *rendezvous point* (RP) (determined using the RSST center location algorithm described in section 9.4.4.2) is assigned to the group. Each multicast group member then sends a join message to the RP via the shortest path. These join messages build a directed tree rooted at RP that can be used to deliver packets to all current group members. As a session progresses, PIM-SM allows a receiver to switch from shared-tree to source-based delivery using a simple mechanism. PIM-SM is characterized by the 4-tuple (*center-based, unconstrained, shared, dynamic*).

9.7.3 Reservation Protocol

Reservation protocol (RSVP) is designed to enable senders, receivers, and routers of communication sessions (both unicast and multicast) to communicate with each other to set up the necessary router state to support guaranteed services. It attempts to accommodate heterogeneous receivers across the Internet and can run on top of IP v4 or IP v6. The use of *soft-state* and *receiver-initiated resource reservations* are some of the novel features of this reservation protocol. More importantly, RSVP is general enough to be considered a protocol for *switch state* establishment [66].

Figure 9.7 summarizes the RSVP protocol architecture. Admission control determines if a given router/link has sufficient resources to satisfy the QoS requirements for existing connections. Policy control determines if a particular user that is attempting to reserve resources has administrative permission to do so. If both check out, the RSVP daemon sets parameters in the packet classifier, which determines the QoS for each packet, and the packet scheduler, which orders packet transmissions; otherwise, the reservation request is denied [6].

9.7.3.1 Message Exchanges in RSVP   RSVP uses two kinds of messages to reserve resources: *Path* and *Resv.* Prior to transmitting, each data source sends a *Path* message, which contains a flow specification (*flowspec*), to the destination multicast address. The *Path* message establishes the routing state in the intermediate nodes as it travels from the source to the receivers along a distribution tree specified by the underlying routing protocol. Each router that receives a *Path* message makes suitable entries in its routing tables, including information such as sender ID, *flowspec,* and multicast address. As a result, not only are the receivers of a given transmission informed of the flow specification of the data traffic, but the intermediate nodes also obtain the *Path* state information.

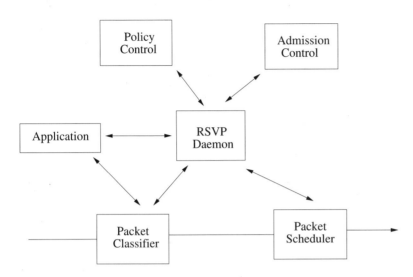

Figure 9.7
RSVP architecture

Based on information received via the *Path* messages and from higher-layer protocols, each receiver can determine its QoS requirements and initiate a *Resv* message to reserve specific resources for the transmission. The *Resv* message travels in the opposite direction from the *Path* message; that is, it travels up the distribution tree. Multiple receivers may send *Resv* messages toward the same data source. These *Resv* messages are merged as they travel up the multicast tree, and only the merged *Resv* is forwarded toward the source (refer to section 9.5.2). This receiver-initiated resource reservation scheme is considered one of the key features of the RSVP design and enables it to handle heterogeneous receivers easily.

Besides these two key message types, RSVP also uses some auxiliary messages, like *PathTear* and *ResvErr.* Figure 9.8 summarizes these types and indicates their direction of propagation.

9.7.3.2   Use of Soft State   Another key feature of RSVP is its use of soft state. According to the authors of [66] soft state is defined as *"a state maintained at the network switches which, when lost, will be automatically reinstalled by RSVP soon thereafter."* Routing and reservation entries in RSVP are controlled by a timer. Once the timer associated with a particular routing entry expires, that entry is flushed from the routing table. Consequently, RSVP expects senders and receivers to periodically resend their *Path* and *Resv* messages, respectively, to reset the timers. RSVP's use of soft state enables it to easily

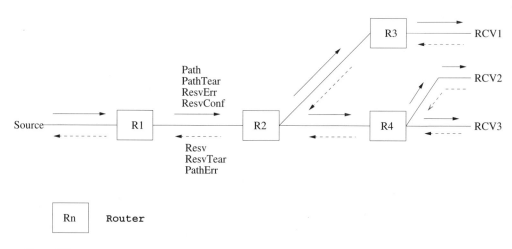

Figure 9.8
Message exchanges in RSVP

accommodate membership changes and adapt to route modifications. Members can leave a group by merely refraining from sending the periodic *Resv* messages that reserve resources for receiving that group's transmission. Similarly, a new member can join a group simply by sending a *Resv* message toward the distribution tree, resulting in the creation of a new routing entry in the relevant routers. When the routing protocol causes a route modification, a sender sends its postmodification *Path* messages via the new route. Hence, the next set of *Resv* messages from the receivers will follow this new route toward the source. Consequently, the required resources get reserved along the new route, whereas the original reservations are released, once their timers run out. In effect, soft state has enabled the resource reservations to follow route changes easily without requiring any explicit intervention from either the source or the receivers.

9.7.3.3 Reservation Styles in RSVP RSVP supports three kinds of reservation styles. Two factors decide the nature of a reservation style: whether the reservation is *distinct* (each sender has its own RSVP flow) or *shared* (the same RSVP flow can be used by multiple senders) and whether the reservation is *explicit sender* (the reservation is made only for the senders explicitly listed in the *Resv* message) or *wildcard sender* (the reservation is made for any sender). These possibilities give rise to the following reservation styles:[12]

---

12. Note that wildcard sender combined with distinct reservation does not make sense.

- *Fixed filter* provides explicit sender selection along with distinct reservations. This style is suitable for applications like video conferencing, in which each video stream has its own RSVP flow.

- *Wildcard filter* provides wildcard sender selection along with shared reservations. It is used by extremely high-bandwidth applications to reduce network load through efficient resource aggregation.

- *Shared explicit filter* combines explicit sender selection with shared reservations. It is identical to wildcard filter except in that it provides better security (because of the explicit sender specification).

9.7.3.4   Advantages of RSVP   The following are the major advantages of the RSVP scheme:

- RSVP accommodates unicast, one-to-many multicast, and many-to-many multicast easily and efficiently.

- Through the receiver-driven model and the use of reservation filters, it allows calls to allocate resources efficiently.

- It uses soft state to adapt to group membership changes and route modifications.

- Its packet format is quite straightforward, and the operations it specifies are computationally simple. Hence, it allows low-cost implementation in end systems and routers.

9.7.4   Real-Time Protocol

The Internet has traditionally used the IP, which provides connectionless, datagram-based, best-effort delivery, for network-layer service. Reliability is provided at the transport layer by using either transmission control protocol (TCP) or user datagram protocol (UDP). TCP provides error-free byte streams and uses a windowing scheme for flow and congestion control. However, these very characteristics have made TCP unsuitable for real-time multimedia applications, for two reasons in particular:

- The reliability and flow control mechanisms used in TCP are designed for point-to-point or unicast communication. Their extension to multicast communication suffers from the problems outlined in section 9.6.2.1. Consequently, TCP does not really lend itself to multicast communication.

- The traffic control techniques used in TCP do not take the characteristics of continuous-media streams into account. For example, the occasional loss of an audio packet is acceptable to most applications, whereas a delay in retransmission (which is TCP's error-recovery mechanism) is usually unacceptable.

The unsuitability of TCP for continuous-media applications has motivated the development of real-time protocol (RTP) [48], a new end-to-end transport protocol for the transmission of real-time continuous-media data. RTP is intended to be used in conjunction with reservation models (like RSVP) that act at the network layer. It provides support for timing information, packet sequence numbers, option specification, source identification, and encryption. It provides no additional error control or sequencing mechanism. Applications can use the above basic framework and adapt it to their own requirements by adding any necessary loss detection (making use of the sequence numbers) and intermedia and intramedia synchronization (making use of the timing information) mechanisms. In effect, RTP is a deliberately incomplete protocol framework, making it easily malleable for applications.

RTP requires all receivers to periodically multicast session packets containing the nodes' identity, reception reports, packet losses, interarrival delay variations, and synchronization information. All receivers hear these periodic reports, and adaptive senders use them for feedback control. RTP has been found to be suitable for use on top of UDP/IP or ST-II [17].

9.7.5   Real-Time Control Protocol

Real-time control protocol (RTCP) is a companion protocol to RTP. It is intended to be used to exchange QoS and failure information between applications in end systems. It can be used to gather feedback from receivers that is tailored to suit an application's requirements for traffic control. Applications transporting multimedia information on the Internet are expected to use RTP for transport control and RTCP for scalable feedback control (refer to section 9.6.2.3), along with other application-specific FEC schemes.

9.7.6   Session Directory Protocol

Session directory protocol (SDP) [23] provides a mechanism by means of which applications can learn what streams are currently in the network. SDP describes these streams in enough detail to allow end hosts to launch suitable applications that use the streams. For example, the *sd* (*session directory*) program in the multicast backbone uses SDP to provide users with a list of ongoing multicast sessions. Users are thus able to launch applications and join sessions at the click of a button.

9.7.7   The Multicast Backbone

The development and employment of the multicast backbone network began in March 1992, when the first audiocast on the Internet took place from the Internet Engineering Task Force (IETF) meeting in San Diego. Since then, the immense popularity of the multicast backbone (MBone) has motivated the development of a number of unique mechanisms and

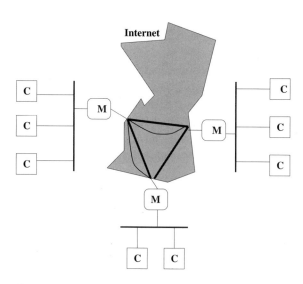

Figure 9.9
MBone topology: islands, tunnels

protocols tailored to suit its characteristics and overcome the drawbacks of the Internet. In the rest of this section, we discuss the structure of the MBone network, list the protocols employed on the MBone [20], and expand on some issues involving the MBone that have yet to be satisfactorily resolved.

9.7.7.1 Structure of the MBone Network The MBone is a virtual network running on *top* of the Internet. It is composed of multicast-capable *islands* interconnected by unicast *tunnels*. Each island has internal support for multicasting and has one host (hereafter referred to as the *M-host*) running the *mrouted* multicast routing daemon. A tunnel connecting two islands runs from the M-host of one to the M-host of the other.

Figure 9.9 depicts three islands of the MBone. Each island consists of a local network connecting a number of client hosts (labeled C in the figure) and one host running the *mrouted* daemon (labeled M). Thick tunnels are primary feeds between islands, with thin tunnels acting as backups.

Basically, a multicast packet is sent from a client (group member), which puts out the packet on the local subnet. The packet is picked up by the M-host for that subnet, which then consults its routing tables to determine the tunnels onto which it will place the packet. The M-hosts at the other end of the tunnels pick up the packet and check if there are one or more clients on their local subnet who have subscribed to that multicast group. If so, the M-hosts put the packet on their local subnet to be picked up by interested clients. Whether or not they put the packet on the subnet, the M-hosts also examine their routing tables and forward the packet on to other tunnels, if needed.

9.7.7.2 Tunnels in MBone When multicast packets are sent through interisland tunnels, they have to be *repacked.* Two mechanisms have been used to accomplish this. The first mechanism uses the loose source and record route (LSRR) option provided by the IP packet structure. In this mechanism, the *mrouted* daemon modifies a datagram coming from a client by appending to it an IP LSRR option on which the multicast group address is placed. The IP destination address is set to the (unicast) address of the *mrouted* host on the other end of the tunnel. The IP address is used during intratunnel forwarding, whereas the multicast address is used by the M-hosts to index into their routing tables. The second mechanism for repacking multicast packets is *encapsulation.* In this method, the original multicast datagram is put into the data area of a standard IP packet, which is then addressed to the receiving M-host. The intermediate hosts in the tunnels merely use the unicast IP address of the M-host for intratunnel forwarding, whereas the receiving M-host strips out the IP header and reclaims the original multicast datagram.

Each tunnel in the MBone has two associated characteristics: a *metric* and a *threshold.* The metric specifies a routing cost that is used by the DVMRP routing protocol for computing distance vectors. The threshold of a tunnel is defined as the minimum remaining TTL that a multicast datagram must possess to be forwarded via that tunnel. When sent to the network by a client, each multicast datagram is assigned a specific TTL. For each M-host the packet passes, its TTL is reduced by 1. If a packet's remaining TTL is lower than the threshold of a certain tunnel that DVMRP wants to send the packet onto, the packet is dropped. This mechanism can be used to limit the scope of a multicast transmission.

9.7.7.3 Pruning in MBone Initially, MBone did not employ any pruning of multicast trees; that is, all multicast datagrams were sent to all M-hosts in the MBone network as long as no threshold limits were violated in such a transmission. Pruning was employed only in the leaf subnets, where the local *mrouted* daemon put a datagram onto the local network only when one or more clients belonging to the particular group were slated to receive that datagram. In effect, *truncated broadcast* was being executed on the MBone network. Later, with the growth in the size of the MBone, scalability problems forced MBone routers to employ a more sophisticated pruning mechanism.

Pruning as implemented in the MBone network today works as follows: If an *mrouted* daemon gets a multicast packet for which it has no receiving clients or tunnels to forward to, it not only drops the packet but also sends a signal upstream indicating that it wants no further packets stamped with the group address of the packet it has just rejected. The upstream *mrouted* daemon notices this and stops sending packets with that address to the downstream host. If later, a client on a downstream M-host joins the group, the M-host sends a signal upstream indicating that it now wants packets bearing that group address. Pruning information is flushed regularly, and truncated broadcast will then be carried out for some time before pruning takes over once again.

9.7.7.4   Protocols Used in MBone   All traffic in the MBone uses the UDP rather than TCP (for the reasons outlined in section 9.7.4). On top of UDP, most MBone applications use RTP (along with the companion protocol RTCP) as their transport protocol. Group addressing is based on class D IP addresses, whereas IGMP is used for group management. Most MBone applications use 8KHz pulse code modulation (PCM) with 8-bit resolution (effectively generating 64kbps) for audio transfer and Consulative Committee of International Telephone and Telegraph (CCITT) H.261 standard for video transfer.

9.7.7.5   Problems with MBone   Despite its immense popularity and usage, the MBone network suffers from a number of inherent problems that have yet to be completely resolved. Eriksson, in [20], has listed the following as the most critical problems in the current MBone system:

• Most places in the MBone network are incapable of handling more than one MBone session at a time. The main limiting factor in a majority of these places is bandwidth, though some also lack the necessary computing power in the end systems and multicast routers.

• Since MBone uses UDP for transmission, many MBone sessions adversely affect other non-MBone TCP traffic. Consider, for example, an audio stream from an MBone session sending audio packets on a fully loaded Internet link that is already supporting a number of TCP connections. When the UDP audio traffic arrives on the link, congestion occurs, resulting in the loss of a number of packets. The TCP congestion control mechanism immediately steps in and backs off transmission. Effectively, many TCP connections then stop using the link for some time (or slow down their transmission rate on that link), giving up their bandwidth to the UDP audio stream. Consequently, the MBone session survives as a "courtesy" of TCP.

• The MBone scope control mechanism depends on the correct choice of TTL values by the end system applications that source the multicast packets. Since many applications allow users to control this value, a simple mistyped TTL value could result in flooding, with multicast packets reaching unnecessary portions of the network (before pruning can set in).

• The MBone does not yet have a fine-grained resource allocation mechanism that can achieve equitable distribution of network bandwidth between various MBone sessions as well as between MBone traffic and non-MBone traffic.

• Many *mrouted* daemons on the MBone suffer problems due to excessive tunnel fan out; that is, these daemons are forced to deal with a number of downstream islands. Many of these hosts lack the necessary CPU cycles to handle such a fan out, affecting the MBone traffic in all the downstream islands.

• Lastly, many hosts and routers in the Internet do not yet handle multicast traffic properly. They frequently generate a number of Internet control message protocol packets flooding large portions of the MBone.

Despite these problems, the tremendous rate of increase in the usage of the MBone has continued unabated since its inception in 1992.

9.8   Summary

• The proliferation of multimedia applications associated with new high-speed networks is driving the need for reliable group communication mechanisms and protocols.

• The main goal of multimedia multicasting is to transport high volumes of delay-sensitive data to multiple destinations.

• A multicast-capable network architecture has four key components: group addressing and management, routing, resource reservation, and traffic control.

• A number of group addressing schemes ranging from fully centralized central server schemes to completely distributed addressing schemes have been proposed for multicast communication.

• Group addressing schemes must be able to generate a large number of addresses, provide for secure communication, be fault-tolerant, and be able to manage dynamic multicast groups.

• QoS multicast routing involves the construction of a tree spanning all the members of a group as well as the sender(s) and capable of meeting the QoS requirements of the applications.

• Multicast routing algorithms fall into three major categories: source-based, center-based, and Steiner tree. The first two categories are more suitable for datagram environments, whereas the Steiner tree algorithms are more suitable for virtual-circuit networks.

• Resource reservation along a multicast tree can be handled in two ways: through either a source-initiated two-pass approach or a receiver-initiated single-pass scheme. The receiver-initiated approach is better suited to handle heterogeneous receivers and has better convergence.

• Traffic control for multicast communication poses two important problems not present in unicast communication: feedback implosion and host heterogeneity. Open-loop reservation-based schemes for traffic control are generally more suitable for multimedia multicasting than closed-loop feedback-based schemes.

• A number of protocols have been proposed for providing support for multimedia multicasting in the Internet. The MBone network serves as the primary test bed for validating and improving these Internet protocols.

Exercises

1. What are the three key features of the multimedia multicasting problem?

2. What is the host-group model? How does this model define the service interface that a source (of multicast messages) can expect to receive from the network?

3. Classify multicast groups based on the following parameters:

(a) physical distribution of group members

(b) restriction on the possible sources to a multicast group

(c) lifetime of the group

(d) temporal nature of group membership

4. Give two reasons why managing both network and host heterogeneity is tougher in multicast communication than in simple point-to-point communication.

5. How does the HeiMAP group addressing protocol improve on the performance of the trial-and-error scheme? Why are both these schemes unsuitable for use in WAN environments?

6. List four desirable features of an efficient multicast address assignment scheme. Which of these features does the central server scheme not possess?

7. What is the rationale behind formulating multicast route determination problems as tree construction problems?

8. Name the three different approaches to multicast route construction. Which of these approaches are suitable for connection-oriented virtual circuit networks and which are more suited to datagram Internet-like networks? Give reasons for your choices.

9. Discuss the main idea behind the center-based tree approach to multicast routing. Name two practical multicast routing algorithms that employ this approach.

10. For multimedia multicasting, what is the need for resource reservation? Name the two basic approaches to resource reservation in this context. Which of these approaches does the RSVP protocol employ?

11. What are the two basic approaches to unicast traffic control? Which of these two approaches scales better to the multicast paradigm?

12. Discuss the key features of the RLM scheme for multicast traffic control. In this scheme, how do receivers determine an optimal subscription level that maximizes their signal quality subject to the resource constraints?

13. List the multicast routing protocols most commonly employed in the Internet. Characterize each of these algorithms using the 4-tuple system developed in section 9.4.

14. Define *soft state* in the context of RSVP. Why have the RSVP designers chosen to use soft state in the intermediate nodes of a connection?

15. Describe the two techniques used to forward packets through interisland tunnels in the MBone network.

References

[1] T. Ballardie, P. Francis, and J. Crowcroft. "Core-based trees (CBT): An architecture for scalable inter-domain multicast routing." In *Proc. ACM SIGCOMM,* pp. 85–95, 1993.

[2] F. Bauer and A. Varma. "Distributed algorithms for multicast path setup in data networks." *IEEE/ACM Trans. Networking,* vol. 4, no. 2, pp. 181–191, Apr. 1996.

[3] F. Bauer and A. Varma. "ARIES: A rearrangeable inexpensive edge-based on-line Steiner algorithm." *IEEE JSAC,* vol. 15, no. 3, pp. 382–397, Apr. 1997.

[4] R. Bettati et al. "Connection establishment for multi-party real-time communication." In *Proc. Intl. Workshop on Network and Operating System Support for Digital Audio and Video,* pp. 255–265, 1995.

[5] J. C. Bolot, T. Turletti, and I. Wakeman. "Scalable feedback control for multicast video distribution in the Internet." In *Proc. ACM SIGCOMM,* pp. 58–67, 1994.

[6] R. Braden, L. Zhang, S. Berson, S. Herzog, and S. Jamin. "Resource reservation protocol (RSVP)—Version 1 functional specification." *Internet RFC,* Aug. 1996.

[7] R. Braudes and S. Zabele. "Requirements for multicast protocols." *Internet RFC 1458,* May 1993.

[8] S. Y. Cheungm, M. H. Ammar, and X. Li. "On the use of destination set grouping to improve fairness in multicast video distribution." In *Proc. IEEE INFOCOM,* pp. 123–129, 1996.

[9] C. H. Chow. "On multicast path finding algorithms." In *Proc. IEEE INFOCOM,* pp. 1274–1283, 1991.

[10] Y. K. Dalal and R. M. Metcalfe. "Reverse path forwarding of broadcast packets." *Communications of the ACM,* vol. 21, no. 12, pp. 1040–1048, Dec. 1978.

[11] S. Deering, C. Partridge, and D. Waitzmann. "Distance vector multicast routing protocol." *Internet RFC 1075,* Nov. 1988.

[12] S. Deering. "Host extensions for IP multicasting." *Internet RFC 1112,* Aug. 1989.

[13] S. Deering and D. R. Cheriton. "Multicast routing in datagram internetworks and extended LANs." *ACM Trans. Computer Systems,* vol. 8, no. 2, pp. 85–110, May 1990.

[14] S. Deering. "Multicast routing in a datagram internetwork." Ph.D. diss., Stanford University, Stanford, Calif., 1991.

[15] S. Deering et al. "The PIM architecture for wide-area multicast routing." *IEEE/ACM Trans. Networking,* vol. 4, no. 2, pp. 153–162, Apr. 1996.

[16] L. Delgrossi et al. "Media scaling for audiovisual communication with the Heidelberg transport system." In *Proc. ACM Multimedia,* pp. 99–104, 1993.

[17] L. Delgrossi and L. Berger. "Internet stream protocol—Version 2 protocol specification." *Internet RFC 1819,* Aug. 1995.

[18] C. Diot, W. Dabbous, and J. Crowcroft. "Multipoint communications: A survey of protocols, functions and mechanisms." *IEEE JSAC,* vol. 15, no. 3, pp. 277–290, Apr. 1997.

[19] M. Doar and I. Leslie. "How bad is naive multicast routing." In *Proc. IEEE INFOCOM,* pp. 82–89, 1993.

[20] H. Eriksson. "MBone: The multicast backbone." *Communications of the ACM,* vol. 37, no. 8, pp. 54–60, Aug. 1994.

[21] D. Ferrari, A. Gupta, and G. Ventre. "Distributed advance reservation of real-time connections." *Multimedia Systems,* vol. 5, no. 3, pp. 187–198, 1997.

[22] M. R. Garey and D. S. Johnson. *Computers and Intractability: A Guide to the Theory of NP-Completeness.* W.H. Freeman, San Francisco, 1979.

[23] M. Hardly and V. Jacobson. "SDP: Session Directory Protocol." Internet draft, Multipart Multicast Session Working Group, 1995.

[24] S. Hong, H. Lee, and B. H. Park. "An efficient multicast routing algorithm for delay-sensitive applications with dynamic membership." In *Proc. IEEE INFOCOM,* pp. 1433–1440, 1998.

[25] F. Hwang and D. Richards. "Steiner tree problems." *Networks,* vol. 22, no. 1, pp. 55–89, Jan. 1992.

[26] M. Imase and B. Waxman. "Dynamic Steiner tree problems." *SIAM J. Disc. Math.,* vol. 4, no. 3, pp. 369–384, Aug. 1991.

[27] B. K. Kadaba and J. M. Jaffe. "Routing to multiple destinations in computer networks." *IEEE Trans. Communications,* vol. 31, no. 3, pp. 343–351, Mar. 1983.

[28] J. Kadirire and G. Knight. "Comparison of dynamic multicast routing algorithms for wide-area packet switched (asynchronous transfer mode) networks." In *Proc. IEEE INFOCOM,* pp. 212–219, Apr. 1995.

[29] V. P. Kompella, J. C. Pasquale, and G. C. Polyzos. "Multicast routing for multimedia communication." *IEEE/ACM Trans. Networking,* vol. 1, no. 3, pp. 286–292, June 1993.

[30] V. P. Kompella, J. C. Pasquale, and G. C. Polyzos. "Two distributed algorithms for the constrained Steiner tree problem." In *Proc. Comput. Commun. Networking,* June 1993.

[31] L. Kou, G. Markowsky, and L. Berman. "A fast algorithm for Steiner trees." *Acta Informatica,* vol. 15, no. 2, pp. 141–145, 1981.

[32] J. Kurose. "Open issues and challenges in providing QoS guarantees in high-speed networks." *Computer Communication Review,* vol. 23, no. 1, pp. 6–15, Jan. 1993.

[33] M. Laubach. "Classical IP and ARP over ATM." *Internet RFC 1577,* Jan. 1994.

[34] H. Lin and S. Lai. "VTDM—A dynamic multicast routing algorithm." In *Proc. IEEE INFOCOM,* pp. 1426–1432, 1998.

[35] N.F. Maxemchuck. "Video distribution on multicast networks." *IEEE JSAC,* vol. 15, no. 3, pp. 357–372, Apr. 1997.

[36] S. McCanne and V. Jacobson. "Receiver-driven layered multicast." In *Proc. ACM SIGCOMM,* pp. 117–130, Sept. 1996.

[37] J. Moy. "Multicast routing extensions for OSPF." *Communications of the ACM,* vol. 37, no. 8, pp. 61–66, Aug. 1994.

[38] C. A. Noronha and F. A. Tobagi. "Optimum routing of multicast streams." In *Proc. IEEE INFOCOM,* pp. 865–873, June 1994.

[39] J. C. Pasquale, G. C. Polyzos, E. W. Anderson, and V. P. Kompella. "The multimedia multicast channel." *Internetworking: Res. & Exp.,* vol. 5, no. 4, pp. 151–162, 1994.

[40] J. C. Pasquale, G. C. Polyzos, and G. Xylomenos. "The multimedia multicasting problem." *Multimedia Systems,* vol. 6, no. 1, pp. 43–59, 1998.

[41] R. Perlman. *Interconnection in Bridges and Routers.* Professional Computing Series, Addison-Wesley, Reading, MA, 1992.

[42] S. Pejhan, A. Eleftheriadis, and D. Anastassiou. "Distributed multicast address management in the global Internet." *IEEE JSAC,* vol. 13, no. 8, pp. 1445–1456, Oct. 1995.

[43] S. Ramanathan. "Multicast tree generation in networks with asymmetric links." *IEEE/ACM Trans. Networking,* vol. 4, no. 4, pp. 558–568, Aug. 1996.

[44] V. J. Rayward-Smith and A. Clare. "On finding Steiner vertices." *Networks,* vol. 16, no. 3, pp. 283–294, 1986.

[45] G. N. Rouskas and I. Baldine. "Multicast routing with end-to-end delay and delay variation constraints." *IEEE JSAC,* vol. 15, no. 3, pp. 346–355, Apr. 1997.

[46] H. F. Salama, D. S. Reeves, and Y. Viniotis. "Evaluation of multicast routing algorithms for real-time communication on high-speed networks." *IEEE JSAC,* vol. 15, no. 3, pp. 332–345, Apr. 1997.

[47] H. F. Salama, D. S. Reeves, and Y. Viniotis. "A distributed algorithm for delay-constrained unicast routing." In *Proc. IEEE INFOCOM,* 1997.

[48] H. Schulzrinne, S. Casner, R. Frederick, and V. Jacobson. "RTP: A transport protocol for real-time applications." *Internet RFC 1889,* Jan. 1996.

[49] N. Shacham. "Multipoint communication by hierarchically encoded data." In *Proc. IEEE INFOCOM,* pp. 2107–2114, 1992.

[50] A. Shaikh and K. Shin. "Destination driven routing for low-cost multicast." *IEEE JSAC,* vol. 15, no. 3, pp. 373–381, Apr. 1997.

[51] S. Shenker and L. Breslau. "Two issues in reservation establishment." *Computer Communication Review,* vol. 25, no. 4, pp. 14–26, 1995.

[52] R. Sriram, G. Manimaran, and C. Siva Ram Murthy. "Preferred link based delay-constrained least cost routing in wide area networks." *Computer Communications,* vol. 21, no. 8, pp. 1655–1669, Dec. 1998.

[53] R. Sriram, G. Manimaran, and C. Siva Ram Murthy. "Algorithms for delay-constrained low-cost multicast tree construction." *Computer Communications,* vol. 21, no. 8, pp. 1693–1706, Dec. 1998.

[54] R. Sriram, G. Manimaran, and C. Siva Ram Murthy. "A rearrangeable algorithm for the construction of delay-constrained dynamic multicast trees." *IEEE/ACM Trans. Networking,* vol. 7, no. 4, pp. 514–529, Aug. 1999.

[55] H. Takashami and A. Matsuyama. "An approximate solution for the Steiner problem in graphs." *Intl. J. Math. Educ. in Sci. and Technol.,* vol. 14, no. 1, pp. 15–23, 1983.

[56] D. G. Thaler and C. V. Ravishankar. "Distributed center location algorithms." *IEEE JSAC,* vol. 15, no. 3, pp. 291–303, Apr. 1997.

[57] A. Thyagarajan and S. Deering. "Hierarchical distance-vector multicast routing for the MBone." In *Proc. ACM SIGCOMM,* pp. 60–66, Sept. 1995.

[58] B. Twachtmann and R. G. Herrtwich. "Multicast in the Heidelberg transport system." Technical report no. 43.9306, IBM European Networking Center, Heidelberg, Germany, 1994.

[59] D. W. Wall. "Mechanisms for broadcast and selective broadcast." Ph.D. diss., Dept. of Electrical Engineering, Stanford University, 1980.

[60] B. M. Waxman. "Routing of multipoint connections." *IEEE JSAC,* vol. 6, no. 9, pp. 1617–1622, Dec. 1988.

[61] B. M. Waxman. "Performance evaluation of multipoint routing algorithm." In *Proc. IEEE INFOCOM,* pp. 980–986, 1993.

[62] L. Wei and D. Estrin. "The tradeoffs of multicast trees and algorithms." In *Proc. Intl. Conf. Computer Commun. Networks,* pp. 12–14, Sept. 1994.

[63] J. Westbrook and D. Yan. "Greedy algorithms for the on-line Steiner tree and generalized Steiner problems." In *Proc. Workshop on Algorithms and Data Structures,* pp. 621–633, Aug. 1993.

[64] R. Widyono. "The design and evaluation of routing algorithms for real-time channels." Technical report no. ICSI TR-94-024, Intl. Computer Science Institute, University of California at Berkeley, June 1994.

[65] P. Winter. "Steiner problem in networks: A survey." *Networks,* vol. 17, no. 2, pp. 129–167, 1987.

[66] L. Zhang, S. Deering, D. Estrin, S. Shenker, and D. Zappala. "RSVP: A new resource reservation protocol." *IEEE Network,* vol. 7, no. 5, pp. 8–18, Sept. 1993.

10 Real-Time Communication in Multiple Access Networks

Overview

In this chapter, we discuss real-time communication in a local area network, specifically, a multiple access network. First, we identify the relevant issues and then describe a model to support real-time communication in multiple access networks. Next, we present a classification of real-time communication protocols. We also describe several well-known algorithms under each of these classes in detail. Finally, we discuss real-time communication in a switched local area network.

10.1 Introduction

Many real-time applications, such as command and control systems, image processing and transmission, industrial process control, and automated manufacturing, are implemented as distributed real-time systems. Distributed systems are employed in these applications not only because of the nature of the applications themselves but also because of their potential to offer high performance, reliability, better resource sharing, and scalability. The key to success in using distributed systems for these applications is the timely execution of computational tasks that usually reside on different nodes and often communicate with one another to accomplish a common goal. Ensuring the timely execution of tasks in such systems necessitates ensuring the timely delivery of messages among communicating tasks. In a real-time system, each message has an explicit deadline before which it must be delivered to the destination; otherwise, it is considered to be lost.

In this chapter, we specifically address the issue of support for real-time communication in multiple access networks. The nodes in a multiple access network are connected by means of a common medium through which the communication among nodes takes place. If two or more nodes transmit simultaneously, the transmissions will collide, with the result that none of the transmissions is successful.

Figure 10.1 shows a typical multiple access network. Local area multiple access networks typically have a geographical expanse of a few kilometers. They are one of the most common types of networks used to support distributed real-time applications.

To meet their deadlines, real-time messages must be properly scheduled for transmission. Scheduling in multiple access networks is the responsibility of a medium access control (MAC) protocol, which arbitrates access to the shared medium and determines which message to transmit at any given time [17].

In real-time communication, parameters such as time constraint (deadline), message loss, and offered load are interrelated. For a fixed value of any one of these parameters, a trade-off exists among the other two [13]:

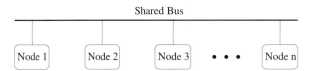

Figure 10.1
Multiple access network

- For a fixed traffic load, the larger the imposed message deadline, the smaller the message loss.

- For a fixed message loss, the larger the offered traffic load, the larger the deadline needed to realize this fixed loss.

- For a fixed deadline, the larger the offered traffic load, the larger the message loss.

10.1.1   Message Classification

As mentioned in chapter 5, real-time messages can be classified into two categories:

- *Periodic messages.* With periodic messages (also known as *synchronous messages*), communication among periodic tasks is periodic. Each periodic message is characterized by its period and message length (number of packets/slot).

- *Aperiodic messages.* The arrival pattern of aperiodic messages (also known as asynchronous messages) is stochastic, in contrast to the deterministic arrival nature of periodic messages. The characteristics of aperiodic messages, like those of aperiodic tasks, are known to the node only when they arrive. Each aperiodic message has its own deadline and message length.

10.1.2   Differences between Bus and Processor Scheduling

Distributed scheduling for a bus (channel) in multiple access networks is fundamentally different from the centralized approach used for processor scheduling. Because of the distributed nature of MAC protocols, substantial overhead is incurred for obtaining global state information in multiple access networks. Because of this overhead, the optimality results for centralized scheduling do not always hold for distributed scheduling. An overhead that is too high may nullify any benefit obtained by using a good centralized algorithm. Three important issues distinguish the bus scheduling problem from the processor scheduling problem [14]: task preemption, priority-level granularity, and buffering.

10.1.2.1   Task Preemption   In processor scheduling, it may be reasonable to assume that a particular task can be preempted at any time and resumed later at the point of preemption. This assumption is invalid in the bus scheduling context, because any message transmission on the bus that is preempted must be retransmitted in its entirety. Preemption is not an issue in slotted channels if the service time (length) and deadlines of messages are integer number of slots, and message transmission is synchronized to slot boundaries.

10.1.2.2 Granularity of Priority Levels In processor scheduling, it is reasonable to assume that there are a sufficient number of priority levels to assign distinct priorities to each task. This is not the case in the bus scheduling context. Resolving each contention for the channel takes at least one round trip of the bus, incurring the associated propagation delay. Consequently, a bus protocol allows messages to contend for slots with a limited number of distinct priority levels. Messages may contend at one fixed level or may be allowed to change their priority over time as a function of their deadline; however, the choice of priority levels is limited to a smaller set, compared with the essentially infinite set for processor scheduling. This could result in two messages contending for transmission at the same priority level even though one would have gotten higher priority than the other if more priority levels were available. Since ties in priority level are resolved arbitrarily, this can result in *priority inversion,* a situation in which a message to which an optimal algorithm would have assigned a higher priority than another message is instead assigned a lower priority and vice versa. In other words, the message with the higher intrinsic priority does not win contention for the transmission slot, because it is forced to contend at the same level as a message of inherently lower priority and loses at the tie-breaking stage.

10.1.2.3 Buffering Problems Two buffering issues are unique to bus scheduling: (1) shortening the deadline of a message and (2) assigning priority to a message. The bus's scheduling algorithm may determine the deadline (criticality) of a message depending on the availability of buffer to store the message, and this may be shorter than the task's inherent deadline. If only one buffer is available, for example, then the message has to be sent before a second message arrives, even if this is before the message's actual deadline. When additional buffer is available, on the other hand, the message's deadline need not be shortened.

Generally, scheduling algorithms for buses associate a priority with each message. Once a message is assigned the highest priority, it is assumed that the message is sent in consecutive slots until the entire message is sent or until a higher-priority message appears. A bus interface unit typically performs the message dispatching and receiving functions. Unfortunately, this arrangement may be difficult to implement. A simple solution to the problem has been proposed, called *packet pacing.* Consider a periodic message consisting of n packets[1] that must be sent within a deadline of p slots. If the message is of the highest

---

1. A packet in the context of bus scheduling is a unit of transmission sent on a slot.

priority, these messages are sent in the first n consecutive slots, which could cause buffering problems. The basic idea of packet pacing is to divide the message into n single-packet (slot) messages. Thus, one packet is sent every p/n slots. That is, the message length and deadline of each of these single packet messages are 1 and n/p, respectively. For example, a five-packet message with a period of 100 would be treated as five single packet messages with a period of 20 slots each. This smooths out the transmission and minimizes the buffering problem. *Pacing loss* occurs in the packet pacing scheme, however, when p/n is not an integer because the deadline needs to be rounded down to the next integer in order to ensure that the deadline is met.

10.2   Real-Time MAC Protocols: Issues and Strategies

A MAC protocol can be thought of consisting of two processes, an *access arbitration process* and a *transmission control process*. The access arbitration process decides *when* a particular node should transmit, and the channel access rights are passed at that point to that node. The transmission control process decides *for how long* a particular node should continue to transmit. The choice of access arbitration process is important, because it affects performance metrics such as throughput, message delay, and fairness.

A transmission control process may allow a given node to send a single message or multiple messages before it transfers control to another node. In general, there are two types of transmission control process: static and dynamic. In the *static* case, the amount of time that a node may continue to send messages over the channel is fixed at design time. In the *dynamic* case, the amount of time a node is allowed to send is determined at run time. The transmission control process thus plays a critical role in meeting the deadlines of messages. Each node must be guaranteed a certain minimum send time to send messages and control information. On the other hand, giving a node an overly large send time is not desirable, as the sending node then monopolizes channel for a long duration, blocking the transmission of messages from other nodes, possibly violating the deadlines of these messages. Therefore, any medium access protocol should have appropriate arbitration and transmission control processes depending on the real-time traffic requirements of the application.

10.2.1   Design Issues of Real-Time MAC Protocols

The design considerations for non-real-time LAN protocols are fairness (maximize), average message delay (minimize), and bandwidth utilization (maximize). In a real-time context, however, these metrics are of secondary importance. The most important metric in a real-time context is the *schedulability* of the network, and improving schedulability means increasing the number of messages whose deadlines are met. A real-time MAC protocol should possess the following properties:

• *Predictability.* The worst-case channel access time for a node must be guaranteed, which allows the protocol to predict whether a message can be transmitted before its deadline. Such a guarantee ensures that if a message is accepted for transmission, it will be successfully transmitted.

• *Timing correctness.* To satisfy the time constraints of real-time messages, the network's access arbitration process must choose correctly the next node to gain access to the channel.

• *Overhead.* In distributed (network) environment, nodes usually have little knowledge about messages waiting for transmission in other nodes. Consequently, the access arbitration logic often makes decisions based on obsolete information about other nodes. To overcome this problem, the access arbitration process may attempt to gather information about other nodes in the network. However, the extra overhead incurred in gathering such information results in lower effective channel utilization.

• *Utilization.* The fraction of the channel capacity utilized for useful message transmission should be maximized. In other words, the protocol overhead should be minimized.

• *Fairness.* The amount of bandwidth allocated to a given node should be independent of its position in the network, and the protocol should have control over it.

• *Stability under transient overload.* The utilization of a network should not decrease when the network is overloaded. Also, in an overloaded network, messages should be prioritized based on their criticality.

10.2.2   Message Delays

An understanding of the channel access delays experienced by messages helps in designing a real-time medium access protocol. A message sent by the upper layer of a sending node may typically experience any of the following delays in reaching the upper layer of the receiving node:

1. Processing and queuing delays in the upper layers of the sending node.

2. Message queuing delay in the MAC layer of the sending node. This is the time the message takes to gain access to the communication medium after being queued.

3. Message transmission delay, which is the time the message takes to be transmitted on the communication medium.

4. Propagation delay.

5. Message queuing delay in the MAC layer of the receiving node.

6. Processing and queuing delays in the upper layers of the receiving node.

Message transmission delay and propagation delay are beyond the control of any protocol. A real-time MAC protocol should try to minimize message queuing delay. The message queuing delay at a receiving node depends on how quickly the node responds to the message arrival and how efficiently it avoids message collision.

10.2.3   Strategies for Service Guarantees

Real-time LAN protocols adopt the following three strategies for providing service guarantees:

• *Static guarantees.* In this strategy, an attempt is made to guarantee the transmission of a message before its deadline at design time. This ensures predictability, meaning that once a message is accepted for transmission, it is guaranteed to meet its timing constraints. The static guarantees strategy is applicable only to periodic messages, whose characteristics are known a priori.

• *Dynamic guarantees.* This is similar to the static guarantees strategy, except that the guarantee is given at run time (on message arrival) rather than at design time. The dynamic guarantees strategy is applicable to aperiodic messages, whose characteristics are not known a priori. It is more flexible and adaptive than the static guarantees approach.

• *Best effort.* In this strategy, the network tries to meet the timing constraints of messages, but no guarantees are given that it will be able to do so. This strategy can be used for soft real-time applications in which the consequences of missing deadlines are not severe. It offers better bandwidth utilization than the previous two.

10.2.4   Inadequacies of Traditional LAN Protocols for Real-Time Communication

The most popular non-real-time LAN protocols, such as 802.3 (Ethernet), 802.4 (token bus), and 802.5 (token ring), are inadequate for supporting real-time communication. The specific inadequacies of each of these protocols are discussed here in turn.

Though the Ethernet protocol has some desirable properties for real-time communication, such as simplicity and robustness, it cannot be used for real-time communication requiring guarantees because of certain limitations. Consider the principle behind the Ethernet protocol. The protocol adopts a binary exponential back-off waiting strategy for collision resolution. It relies on the assumption that the probability of two or more nodes trying to transmit at the same time decreases with time. Because of the inherently nondeterministic nature of this type of collision resolution, the Ethernet protocol cannot give a worst-case time bound for collision resolution, which implies that *predictability* of message transmission cannot be achieved. Further, it is impossible to achieve fairness in the access arbitration process, as any node can access the channel at any instant. This leads to problems of priority inversion, as explained earlier.

In the token bus protocol, a token is passed from node to node of the network, and the node with the token at any given point is the only one eligible to transmit messages at that point. A node passes the token to its successor node after transmission of its message is complete or the timer expires. The protocol supports four levels of priority. For each priority class, some guaranteed bandwidth is allocated prior to network operation. All real-time messages have to be mapped onto these four levels. This leads to priority inversion. The protocol is also prone to failure due to token loss. Since the protocol stresses transmission control, it must maintain a number of timers and states for enabling transmission at various prioritized levels, leading to a complex run time state.

In the token ring protocol, the nodes of a network are connected in a ring. To be eligible to transmit messages at any given point, a node must have a token, given to it by the ring. After transmission of a message, the node releases the token back to the ring, which can then pass it on to another node. Global priority is implemented using a priority field in the token. A node currently transmitting can reserve the next transmission slot by writing its priority in the reservation field. A node can reserve consecutive slots only up to a maximum period of *token holding time* that is set prior to network operation. The number of priority levels is fixed, and all the timing constraints of the messages are mapped onto these fixed number of levels, thus making the protocol not well-suited for real-time communication. Moreover, schedulability analysis is not possible, since messages arrive dynamically and are scheduled on dynamic priority basis.

10.2.5   Real-Time Communication with Periodic Messages

To be able to guarantee transmission of synchronous messages, a protocol must exhibit the following properties [17]:

• *Synchronous message utilization.* If the sum of the utilization[2] of all the messages in a periodic message set is less than some achievable bound according to a given protocol, then that message set is schedulable by that protocol. The protocol determines the specific utilization bound.

• *Robustness.* The protocol must be robust in the face of changes to the characteristics of periodic message streams carried by a given system. A small change in these characteristics should not affect the overall schedulability of the system.

• *Limited propagation of timing faults.* If messages in a particular periodic stream arrive more frequently than specified or are longer than specified, then that periodic stream violates its specifications. A violation may cause message deadlines in that stream to be missed. Such a violation of specifications should not affect the other streams in the

---

2. The utilization of a message is the ratio of its length to its period.

network; the messages of other streams should still meet their deadlines even if those in the stream committing the violation do not.

• *Asynchronous message handling.* In practice, many complex distributed real-time systems need to handle both periodic and aperiodic messages. The protocol for such systems should have the capability of supporting both of these message types. Even if the aperiodic messages the system must handle have no timing constraints, they need to be ensured a minimum throughput to avoid problems such as buffer overflow.

• *Run time overhead.* The run time overhead of a protocol includes the time the access arbitration process spends arbitrating access to the communication medium. A protocol with a low run time overhead is preferred.

The RMS algorithm (discussed in chapter 2) can be used to schedule periodic messages in a bus. Because of the distributed nature of the bus network, the RMS algorithm can only be approximated; it cannot be exactly implemented. Also, using the RMS algorithm with a priority-driven protocol requires global priority arbitration each time a packet is sent. This may result in priority inversion, as discussed in section 10.1.2. Moreover, in the RMS algorithm, a higher-priority message can preempt a lower priority message at an arbitrary point in time. As discussed in section 10.1.2, this is difficult to implement in bus scheduling.

10.2.6   Real-Time Communication with Aperiodic Messages

A guarantee strategy should be used for asynchronous messages whenever it is essential that the messages meet their deadlines. If the maximum message arrival rate (minimum interarrival time between messages) of asynchronous messages is known at design time, then messages may be guaranteed at that time by allocating sufficient bandwidth to them. If this information is not known at the time the system is designed, a message must be guaranteed soon after its arrival in the system, before the actual transmission of the message begins. A decision is made as to whether a given message is to be admitted into the system based on an *admission test,* and this leaves enough time for the application to take some recovery actions if the message fails the admission test. In other words, the time at which an admission test is performed decides the time available for any necessary recovery action. In section 10.5.3, we discuss some dynamic guarantee strategies that perform admission tests. Protocols that attempt to guarantee aperiodic messages can follow three basic approaches [17]:

1. *Periodic server.* In this approach, the protocol maintains a periodic server for each source of aperiodic messages. The maximum arrival rate of the aperiodic messages decides the period of this server. The server is activated at regular intervals for a fixed number of

slots in which aperiodic messages, if any, that have arrived since the end of the last interval from the aperiodic source with which the periodic server is associated can be transmitted. If there are no messages to be transmitted in a given activation of a server, the channel slots allotted for that activation are wasted, resulting in poor channel utilization. On the other hand, this protocol involves minimal overhead.

2. *Conservative estimation.* The basic idea behind this approach is as follows: When a new message arrives at a node, the node checks the deadline of the message. If the deadline is greater than or equal to the node's worst-case channel access time plus the message length, the transmission of the message is guaranteed; otherwise it is not. Deterministic collision resolution protocols, discussed in section 10.3.3, belong to this category. The advantage of the conservative approach is that it has relatively little overhead, since no extra (control) messages are sent. This is offset, however, by the poor schedulability offered by protocols belonging to this category because they assume the worst-case scenario at all times.

3. *Dynamic reservation.* The basic idea behind this approach is to dynamically reserve future access to the channel. When a new message M arrives at a node n, the node attempts to reserve an interval of time to transmit M by broadcasting a special control message. The control message informs other nodes that a given interval of time is reserved for use by node n. The control message itself has a deadline, corresponding to the deadline of the message it is attempting to guarantee. If the control message cannot be sent by its deadline, then message M is not guaranteed.

10.3   Real-Time LAN Protocols

Medium access protocols in multiple access networks fall into one of two categories, (1) *controlled access protocols* and (2) *contention-based protocols.* Controlled access protocols reserve channel bandwidth for each node, and nodes receive service in round-robin fashion. Contention-based protocols allow nodes to access the channel on a message-by-message basis, without no concept of connection between source and destination that allows transmission of multiple messages from the source to the destination in consecutive or non-consecutive time slots.

10.3.1   Controlled Access Protocols

Controlled access protocols can be further classified as either preallocating (PA) or demand-adaptive (DA). Whereas the PA protocols allocate a channel to each node statically before run time, the DA protocols attempt to do so dynamically at run time based on the demand of each node.

10.3.1.1 Time Division Multiple Access Protocol In the time division multiple access (TDMA) protocol, the channel is slotted, and slots are assigned before run time to each node in the network. Each node then attempts to transmit its message in its pre-assigned slot. When messages are periodic, assigning slots statically is feasible, as the transmission characteristics of the messages are known a priori. Thus, pure TDMA protocol has the potential to guarantee timely delivery of periodic messages. However, it cannot handle aperiodic messages, because nodes are allowed to transmit messages only during their fixed slots and thus cannot accommodate messages that arrive on a schedule that is not fixed. Also, the static allocation of bandwidth in this protocol can lead to the channel remaining idle when nodes have no messages to transmit in the reserved slots.

10.3.1.2 Demand-Adaptive Protocols DA protocols are either reservation-based or token-based. In reservation-based protocols, such as the broadcast recognition multiple access (BRAM) and the mini-slotted alternating priorities (MSAP) protocols, every transmission phase is preceded by a reservation phase. The time delay between successive transmissions by a node is bounded by the maximum length of the reservation plus transmission cycles. The token-passing mechanism in BRAM and MSAP is implicit (as opposed to explicit, as in token-based protocols). In implicit token-passing protocols, a token circulates among nodes in a predetermined order. If a node does not have a message waiting for transmission when it receives the token, then after a brief waiting time, the next node gets the token implicitly. This prevents nodes that do not have messages to send from wasting token holding time.

Though reservation-based protocols do not waste channel bandwidth through static allocation, as in pure TDMA protocols, any improvement in performance gained through eliminating this waste is offset by an increased overhead due to transmission of control information, such as reservation slots, and delays incurred through token rotation.

In a token-based protocol, a token message is circulated among the nodes in a network in such a way that only one node possesses the token message at any point in time. Only the node having the token has the right to transmit a message.

One prominent token-based protocol is fiber-distributed data interface [28]. This protocol uses a target token rotation time (TTRT), high-priority token holding time (for synchronous packets), and token holding time (THT). Although we can ensure a good distribution of bandwidth in this protocol by appropriately varying the high-priority token holding time, FDDI nevertheless has two inherent disadvantages that can affect real-time traffic. First, the requirement that the TTRTs be identical for all nodes seriously limits the use of FDDI in handling heterogeneous real-time traffic. If a particular node requires a very small TTRT, then network utilization may be severely reduced, as the token must then be rotated in a very short interval, which wastes bandwidth on token passing. Also, FDDI cannot change the TTRT and the high-priority THT on-line, and this is especially problematic when the real-time load fluctuates dynamically as new real-time messages are admitted and old ones are dropped. In fact, most timed-token protocols suffer from the above limitations. The FDDI protocol is discussed in detail in section 10.6.

10.3.2   Contention-Based Protocols

Contention-based protocols assume a broadcast medium. Carrier sense multiple access (CSMA), with or without collision detection (CD), is an example of a contention-based protocol. In CSMA protocols, nodes sense the channel and transmit on that channel only when they detect that it is idle. Since there is no coordination between nodes, multiple nodes may attempt to transmit simultaneously, resulting in collisions. When a collision occurs, the transmitting nodes, which observe the channel continuously, abort their transmission and retransmit at a later time. Since every node decides for itself when to transmit a message, CSMA, like all contention-based protocols, is a distributed algorithm.

We now discuss some protocols that incorporate a priority mechanism into the CSMA protocol. Though there is still no explicit coordination between nodes in these protocols, the nodes do see a consistent time if their clocks are synchronized, and they observe the same channel except for slight differences that exist due to propagation delays. Priority-based protocols exploit this common information. Suppose a node has a set of messages to transmit. It has to decide when these messages can be transmitted on the channel. It has the following information: (1) the state of the channel, (2) the priorities of the messages waiting for transmission, and (3) the time according to the synchronized clock. It has no knowledge about the priorities of messages waiting in other nodes. The protocol must use the aforementioned information to decide whether or not to attempt message transmission at any given point. We discuss contention-based real-time MAC protocols further in the subsequent portion of this chapter.

10.3.2.1   Virtual Time CSMA Protocols   Virtual-time CSMA (VTCSMA) protocols [35] compute the priority of a message based on virtual or real time and certain other parameters, such as message deadline, message laxity,[3] and message length. In these protocols, each node has two clocks. One clock gives the real time and the other gives the virtual time. The real clock (RC) and virtual clock (VC) at a node are synchronized with the corresponding clocks at all the other nodes. When a channel is busy, the VC for

---

3. A message's laxity is the maximum time that message transmission can be delayed and still allow the message to meet its deadline.

that channel stops running. When the channel is again idle, the VC is reset as given in equation (10.3) and runs at a rate $\eta > 1$. For example, $\eta = 2$ means that VC runs twice as fast as the RC when the channel is idle.

Each message M to be transmitted is associated with a parameter called *virtual time to start transmission, VS_M*. When the VC time is greater than or equal to VS_M, M is eligible for transmission. A message is sent only when its VS_M is less than or equal to the time on the VC. Letting the virtual clock run along the arrival time of messages implements first-come-first-served (FCFS) policy, along the deadline axis implements earlier-deadline-first (EDF) and least-laxity-first (LLF) policies, and along the message length axis implements shortest-message-first (SMF) policy. The laxity of a message indicates its urgency and is equal to $D_M - T_M - current\ time - propagation\ delay$ for a message M. A message with negative laxity is assumed to be lost. When a message M arrives at a node, its VS_M is set as follows, depending on the policy used.

$$VS_M = \begin{cases} A_M, & \text{for realizing FCFS policy,} \\ D_M, & \text{for realizing EDF policy,} \\ L_M, & \text{for realizing LLF policy,} \\ T_M, & \text{for realizing SMF policy,} \end{cases} \tag{10.1}$$

where A_M, D_M, L_M, and T_M are the arrival time, deadline, laxity, and transmission time of message M, respectively.

When a node senses the channel is idle and the node has an eligible message, it transmits the message. If the message collides with another message, each node involved in the collision either retransmits its message immediately, with probability p_i, or modifies the VS_M of its message, with probability $(1 - p)$, to a random number drawn from an interval (A,B), where

$$(A, B) = \begin{cases} (VC, L_M), & \text{for FCFS policy;} \\ (RC, D_M), & \text{for EDF policy;} \\ (RC, L_M), & \text{for LLF policy;} \\ (0, T_M), & \text{for SMF policy.} \end{cases} \tag{10.2}$$

When the channel switches from busy state to idle state, the VC is initialized as follows:

$$VC = \begin{cases} no\ change, & \text{for FCFS policy;} \\ RC, & \text{for EDF and LLF policies;} \\ 0, & \text{for SMF policy.} \end{cases} \tag{10.3}$$

Among the four VTCSMA protocols, virtual EDF and virtual LLF have been found to offer better schedulability than the other two.

While (true) **do**
 1. **If** (new message M arrives) initialize VS_M as per Equation (10.1);
 2. **If** (channel is busy) $RC \leftarrow RC + 1$; continue;
 3. Initialize VC as per equation (10.3); /* channel transition from busy to idle */
 4. **Repeat**
  a. Discard the messages having negative laxities;
  b. $RC \leftarrow RC + 1$;
  c. $VC \leftarrow VC + \eta$;
  until ($\exists M$ such that $VS_M \leq VC$ or the channel becomes busy)
 5. **If** (channel is busy) continue;
 6. Transmit M;
 7. **If** (collision occurs)
  • Retransmit immediately with probability p, or
   modify VS_M as per equation (10.2) with probability $(1 - p)$;
 8. continue;

Figure 10.2
VTCSMA algorithm

node	RC at arrival	D_M	L_M	RC at transmission
1	0	28	12	6
2	12	38	22	22
3	16	52	36	38
4	20	68	52	45
5	20	68	52	45

Figure 10.3
VTCSMA-L Transmission status table for $\eta = 2$, transmission time $= 16$ (RC: real clock; L_M: laxity of message, relative to current time)

 The VTCSMA protocol relies on a probabilistic approach for resolving collision and hence cannot guarantee worst-case channel access delay. Also, under this protocol, the real clock at all nodes must be fairly synchronized to achieve consistent systemwide scheduling decisions. The VTCSMA protocol at each node works as shown in figure 10.2.
 Figure 10.3 illustrates the VTCSMA-L protocol (L stands for LLF). The figure shows the transmission status under the protocol of messages arriving at different nodes. Initially, the channel is idle. Transmission begins when RC is 6, which, at $\eta = 2$, corresponds to the VC being 12. Since $VC = L_M$ for node 1, M_1 is transmitted. Since each message has a transmission time of 16, this sets RC to 22 $(16 + 6)$. Since VC now is reset to this

value, $VC = L_M$ for node 2, and M_2 can be transmitted immediately. When M_3 is ready for transmission, at time 36, transmission of M_2 is not yet completed, and this results in M_3 being dropped entirely. After transmission of M_2, the VC is reset to time 38 to correspond to the RC at that point. After RC advances to time 45, which corresponds to the VC being 52, both M_4 and M_5 are ready for transmission. Both messages simultaneously contend for the channel, resulting in collision. Then VTCSMA-L allows M_5 (say) to be transmitted immediately with a probability p_i and modifies the virtual sending time of M_4 to be a random value drawn from the interval (RC, latest sending time) which in this case is (45, 52). Let us assume that the value chosen is 47, two RC units away from the current RC time of 45. When RC reaches 47, the virtual clock reads 56 (52 + 2 ∗ (time elapsed on RC = 2)), and M_4 will be dropped, since the channel is busy for transmitting M_5.

10.3.2.2 The Preemption-Based CSMA Protocol   The preemption-based CSMA (PBCSMA) protocol prioritizes newly arriving messages based on message laxity [29]. This protocol offers an advantage over VTCSMA in that it gives a critical message the right to access the channel regardless of whether the channel is currently busy or idle. This preemptive nature of the protocol makes it an improvement over the VTCSMA in terms of the number of messages transmitted. This protocol adopts a probabilistic approach to collision resolution similar to that of the VTCSMA protocols. Priority granularity is restricted to two levels. The working of the protocol is as follows:

• A message is characterized as critical if its laxity is less than a predefined threshold; otherwise it is classified as noncritical.

• Transmission of a critical message begins with the broadcast of a notifier.

• When a new message arrives and the channel is idle, the message is sent.

• When a new message arrives and is classified as critical and the channel is busy, if the message currently being transmitted is not critical, it is preempted to allow the newly arriving critical message to be sent.

• Transmission of a noncritical message from a node is not possible as long as the channel is busy. Nor is a noncritical message sent right after the channel becomes idle. The node waits for one slot, and if the channel remains idle, it sends the message.

• If it collides with another message on the channel, a noncritical message is suspended for the duration of a slot, and if that slot is not occupied by a critical message, the noncritical message is retransmitted with some probability p_i.

• If a critical message collides with another message on the channel, it is retransmitted immediately with probability p_i.

10.3.3   Deterministic Collision Resolution Protocols

As mentioned earlier, the traditional CSMA/CD protocol is unsuitable for real-time communication because of the probabilistic nature of its collision resolution. CSMA/CD-based networks involved in real-time communication must therefore modify their procedures to resolve collisions in a deterministic manner, to ensure predictability. Many researchers have extended the CSMA protocol to provide such deterministic collision resolution (DCR), thereby guaranteeing worst-case channel access delay. In DCR-based protocols, collisions are resolved by imposing an order among nodes when two or more nodes try to transmit messages simultaneously over the channel. The CSMA/CD-DCR protocol [15], preorder CSMA/CD-DCR (CSMA/CD-DCRP) [30], and the waiting room protocol [20] are examples of DCR protocols.

10.3.3.1   Waiting Room Protocol   The DCR-based waiting room protocol [20] guarantees worst-case channel access delay. It is based on the establishment of a logical waiting room for messages to be transmitted. Channel access under the WR protocol proceeds in *rounds*. Only messages that are at the head of the send queue in each node at the end of a particular round are transmitted in the following round. At the beginning of each round of access, the message waiting at the front of the send queue of each node in the network enters the waiting room. As it moves from the send queue to the waiting room, each message is encoded with a *prelude* followed by the actual message. The prelude contains the channel access arbitration information, which the node uses to determine whether it is that node's turn to send a message. Once inside the waiting room, a message is transmitted only when it gets its turn. The remaining messages in the send queue are considered, in the order in which they arrived, only after all the messages in the waiting room have been transmitted and the waiting room becomes empty.

One implementation of WR protocol, based on the *binary countdown* protocol [27], is described below [20]. Channel access is synchronized in this implementation, in that every node attempts to access the channel only when the previous transmission is completed. A node first transmits a prelude, and if found eligible, it transmits the actual message. A listen-while-talk device is needed at each node to determine eligibility: when a node notices that a higher-order bit position that is 0 in the prelude of its own message has been set to 1 in the message of some other node, it considers itself ineligible to transmit and stops further transmission. At the end of transmission of a message, all nodes attempt to transmit the first messages in their send queue. The prelude sent by each node before every message has a status bit and the priority of the node. The status bit is set to 1 if the message is in the waiting room, otherwise it is 0. Each node's priority is static and is assigned during system design. The WR protocol is implemented as follows:

- If the status bit of at least one of the messages is 1, the node with the highest-priority message with status bit 1 transmits its actual message; all other nodes stop transmitting. Thus, the message that has the highest priority and that is already in the waiting room gets transmitted.

- If the status bit of all messages is 0, the highest-priority message gets transmitted; all other nodes stop transmission and set to 1 the status bit of the first messages in their send queue, logically signifying that the message is entering the waiting room. Thus, if the waiting room is empty, all waiting messages enter the waiting room, and the highest-priority message gets transmitted.

Assume N nodes are connected to a bus-based system. The worst-case channel access delay for messages depending on their position in the queues is computed as follows:

- *Message already inside the waiting room.* The worst-case channel access delay for messages already in the waiting room occurs for the message from the node with the lowest priority when messages generated by all other nodes are also in the waiting room. If there are N nodes in the network, this delay is $(N-1) \times (T_m + A_m)$, where T_m and A_m are transmission time per message and arbitration overhead per message, respectively.

- *Message in front of the send queue.* For this case, the worst-case delay occurs for the message that is in front of the send queue of the lowest-priority node. The worst-case delay occurs when the lowest-priority message arrives an instant later than the messages in front of all $N-1$ other nodes' send queues enter the waiting room. So this message misses its chance of entering the waiting room in the current round. It must wait to enter the waiting room, along with $N-1$ other messages from the other nodes, in the next round, and because it is from the node with the lowest priority, it will be the last message in that round to transmit. The time elapsed, in the worst case, before this message gets transmitted is $2 \times (N-1) \times (T_m + A_m)$.

- *pth message in a send queue.* The pth message in a send queue is the one that has $(p-1)$ messages ahead of it. For this case, the worst-case channel access delay (which applies to the pth message in the send queue of the node with the lowest priority) is no more than $(((p-1) \times N) + (2 \times (N-1))) \times (T_m + A_m)$.

10.3.3.2 CSMA-Based DCR Protocols CSMA-based DCR protocols attempt to use the efficient CSMA protocol for transmission of messages without collision. When collision occurs, these protocols switch to a collision resolution (CR) mode, in which collisions are resolved in a deterministic manner. The DCR protocols work under the following assumptions:

- A population of N nodes share the channel.
- The channel propagation delay is τ time units (in reality τ corresponds to the maximum round-trip propagation delay).
- The channel is slotted, and the slot length is τ time units.
- Carrier sensing is instantaneous. Each node is capable of detecting an idle slot, a successful transmission, and a collision. All nodes abort transmission immediately after detecting collision. A collision lasts for only τ units of time.
- The channel can transmit only one message at any given time. Two or more messages sent concurrently over the channel result in a collision.
- Each packet is of constant length requiring k time units for transmission. Each message may consist of several packets. (For the rest of this discussion, we assume that each message consists of a single packet.)
- Each time it receives the right to transmit, each node is allowed to transmit only message at a time.

Definitions:

- *Epoch.* The time elapsed from the time of collision detection to the time of completion of collision resolution. The length of an epoch includes the time spent in resolving the collision and the time spent in transmitting all the messages that collided.
- *Channel access time.* The time elapsed from the time when a message is ready to be transmitted to the time at which transmission of that message actually starts. The maximum channel access time is the worst-case channel access time.
- *Search sequence.* The sequence of node numbers according to which a binary tree is traversed, conforming to a binary tree traversal algorithm. (For example, the preorder traversal algorithm produces the following search sequence when the binary tree in figure 10.5 is traversed: 1, 2, 4, 8, 16, 17, 9, and so on.)

10.3.3.3 Preorder DCR Protocol   The underlying principle of the preorder DCR protocol (DCR-P) is to resolve collisions in a deterministic way. In DCR-P, all nodes in a network are mapped onto vertices of a unique binary (UB) tree: a binary tree that has the height of its leaf vertices differing by at most 1. When vertices are added to a UB tree, they are added from the leftmost position first.

A node in a LAN (network) is mapped onto a vertex or set of vertices in a UB tree by assigning to the node one or more indices called *node indices*. A node's indices correspond to the positions of that node in the binary tree for the network. The positions of a node in the tree in turn determine the message transmission slots assigned to it in the event of a collision. Multiple indices are assigned to a node to give higher priority to that node. If the characteristics of messages arriving at a particular node are known a priori, a vertex on the UB tree can be assigned to that node, depending on the criticality and periodicity of the messages. It is the designer's responsibility to assign node indices to the various nodes of the network. The protocol works as follows:

- A node senses the channel.
- If the channel is idle, the node transmits a message.
- If no collision occurs, the transmission is successful.
- If a collision is detected, message transmission is aborted, and all nodes enter collision resolution mode.
- Each node that has a message to transmit then waits until its turn, according to the priority assigned to the node at the design stage, as described above, and transmits the message.

In the event of a message collision, the UB tree is traversed in preorder to resolve the collision, as discussed below.

Preorder Tree Traversal: Preorder tree traversal is a well-known binary tree traversal method. Preorder traversal is recursively defined as follows:

- Visit the tree's root node.
- Traverse the left subtree in preorder.
- Traverse the right subtree in preorder.

An example of preorder tree traversal is given in section 10.3.3.2 as part of the definition of search sequence.

Adapting Preorder Traversal to Collision Resolution: The preorder traversal algorithm is tailored to network scheduling as follows:

- The slot following a collision is reserved for the root node of the tree, T_x, for transmission of a message (equivalently, visiting the root node).
- The next slot is reserved for the left subtree. All nodes in the left subtree (of T_x) are eligible to transmit in this slot.
- The algorithm stops traversing the left subtree in preorder, upon successful transmission of messages from every node in that subtree that has a message ready to transmit or if the slot remains idle (indicating the left subtree has no more messages ready to transmit).
- The right subtree is then traversed in preorder.
- The algorithm continues to traverse the tree in preorder until the collision is resolved.

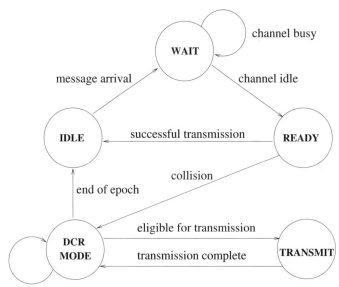

Figure 10.4
State diagram of DCR protocol

The state diagram of DCR protocol is given in figure 10.4. Example 1 explains how the DCR-P algorithm works.

Example 1:   Consider a subtree (T_7) rooted at node 7 of the tree shown in figure 10.5 (ignore for the moment the labels adjacent to and at the top of the vertices). Subtree T_7 has root node 7 and descendants 14, 28, 29, 15, 30, and 31. Assume that the algorithm is traversing the subtree T_7. There are three possibilities:

1. The slot assigned to subtree T_7 for transmission may go idle, implying no node in subtree T_7 has a message ready for transmission.

2. The slot may be used for message transmission by only one of the nodes of the subtree T_7, implying that only one node has a message ready.

3. If the algorithm experiences a collision in the slot assigned to the subtree T_7, transmission stops, and the following slot is reserved for node 7 to transmit a message. Node 7 transmits a message, if it has one, or this slot may go idle if node 7 has no message ready. The next slot is assigned to the first node on the left subtree, T_{14}. The first node on the right subtree, T_{15}, is given a chance to transmit only after the entire left subtree (i.e., the subtree rooted at T_{14}) has been traversed in preorder.

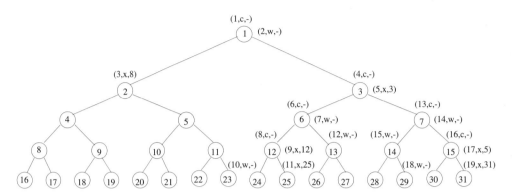

Figure 10.5
Working of the DCR-P protocol

Example 2: Consider a network consisting of 31 nodes, each of which is assigned a distinct node index (1 to 31) as shown in the binary tree in figure 10.5. Let us assume that the nodes contending for a given channel at time t are 3, 8, 12, 15, 25, and 31. The DCR-P protocol proceeds to resolve the resulting collisions as shown in figure 10.6. In figure 10.5, the parenthetical labels associated with the vertices of the tree show the way the collision resolution proceeds. The three-element label (i, j, k) associated with each subtree and vertex represents the channel status at each step when the collision is being resolved: i represents the slot number, j represents the channel status, and k the node index if a message is transmitted. A label at the top of a vertex denotes the status of the channel in the slot assigned to that subtree. A label to the right of a vertex represents the status of the channel in the slot assigned to the vertex. Thus, all six contending messages are successfully transmitted at the end of the epoch, which consists of six message transmissions, seven idle slots, and six collisions. As the number of nodes with messages ready for transmission increases, the length of any resulting epoch increases.

After the current epoch has been started, transmission of newly arrived messages in a particular node in the current epoch depends on the node index assigned to that node. If collision resolution is underway and the current vertex being searched is i and a message arrives at a node with node index j, two possibilities exist regarding transmission of that message:

• If the node index j appears later than i in the preorder search sequence, node index j has yet to be searched, and the message can be transmitted in the current epoch. The current node index being searched (i) and the node index of the arrived message (j) are said to be *in the same tree* if the messages in both nodes are scheduled in the same epoch.

	1	2	3	4	5	6	7	8	9	10	11	12	13	14	15	16	17	18	19		- slot number
	C	W	X	C	X	C	W	C	X	W	X	W	C	W	W	C	X	W	X		- channel status
	*	1	8		3		6		12	24	25	13		7	14		15	30	31		- node address

an epoch

* - first collision is detected

C - contention

X - successful transmission

W - idle slot

Figure 10.6
Channel status for the DCR-P protocol

• If the node index j appears earlier than the node index currently being searched (i) in the preorder search sequence, the node index j has already been searched in the current epoch, and the newly arrived message cannot be transmitted in the current epoch (as the algorithm searches the nodes strictly in the forward direction, according to the preorder search sequence). Transmission of the message is possible only in the next epoch. The current node index being searched (i) and the node index of the arrived message (j) are said to be *in adjacent trees* if messages from the two nodes are scheduled in consecutive epochs.

Therefore, any message that arrives during collision resolution can either be in the same tree or an adjacent tree with respect to the node currently being searched. The worst-case channel access delay occurs when all nodes have messages to send in a given epoch. Under such a situation, collision occurs for every contention slot.

10.3.3.4   Preorder Deadline-Based Protocol   Though the DCR-P protocol provides a bound on worst-case channel access delay, its schedulability is poor because it does not take into account the deadlines of the messages that need to be transmitted. The preorder deadline-based (DOD-P) protocol, a modification of the DCR-P protocol, uses a deadline-driven scheduling policy [15]. Since multiple access protocols and uniprocessor scheduling algorithms have similar design objectives, a good dynamic scheduling policy used in task scheduling, such as minimum laxity first (MLF) policy, can be adopted for network scheduling.

If MLF policy is adopted, messages at each node are queued according to minimum laxity first. For a good approximation of centralized MLF policy in a network (distributed), the concept of message class is now introduced. The *message class* is an index, computed on-line and assigned to each message, of the laxity of that message. All messages with deadlines $D + \delta$ (i.e., messages whose deadlines are fairly equal) are assigned to the same message class. In other words, more than one message (from different nodes or from the same node) can belong to the same message class. Numbering of the classes starts from 1. Only a small number of classes are considered for scheduling at any one time to minimize run time scheduling overheads. The number of classes considered for scheduling at one time is fixed and is denoted as F, and F is thus the number of laxity equivalence classes considered for scheduling at a given time. Messages belonging to classes 1 to F are said to be *eligible messages*. All the nodes with eligible messages at any given time can transmit at that time. The message classes of eligible messages form a binary tree, called a *time tree*, similar to the UB tree used in the DCR-P protocol. The maximum number of nodes in the time tree is the same as the maximum number of message classes considered for scheduling, that is, F. Proper scheduling of messages of each class closely approximates that of the centralized MLF policy.

Message Class Computation: Message class is computed whenever a *reference event* occurs. These reference events are

1. Initial collision. A collision detected before the nodes enter into an epoch, which initiates a time tree search.

2. Completion of static tree search. Searching for a time tree search node results in a collision if more than one message belongs to a particular message class. In this case, collision is resolved by initiating a static tree search. The *static tree* is the binary tree formed with node indices of the class, which is the same tree used in DCR-P. Completion of the static tree search is the second reference event.

Each node keeps track of the time at which one of the reference events occurs (the *reference time*). Message class is then computed with respect to the current reference time. This implies that the clock must be synchronized at all nodes. The DOD-P protocol assumes that all clocks are fairly synchronized and that clock skew does not affect message class computation. For computing message class, a time interval c, called the laxity equivalence class, is defined, where c covers the messages having comparable laxities. All messages whose laxities fall in the interval between t (current reference time) and $(t + c)$ (the first equivalence class) are placed in the same message class. The next message class is given to the messages whose laxities fall within $(t + c)$ and $(t + 2c)$, and so on until all messages have been placed in the appropriate class.

For a given value of F, a large value for c has two major implications: (1) Even the messages with larger laxities are considered for scheduling that otherwise would not be considered, and (2) messages with large laxity differences may be grouped into the same class. The latter may cause each class to contain more than one message, which may result in priority inversion. Therefore, a perfect MLF policy cannot be closely approximated by choosing a large value of c. If a very small value of c is chosen, on the other hand, the nodes may withhold the transmission of messages though the channel is idle, as the computed message classes are not in the range 1 to F.

The message class (m_{index}) is computed as follows:

$$m_{index} = \max\{1, \lceil (E - t)/c \rfloor\} + m^*_{index} \tag{10.4}$$

where E is the absolute deadline, t is the current reference time, c is the laxity equivalence class, m^*_{index} is the last message class searched, and the operator $\lceil \rfloor$ denotes the rounding operation to the nearest integer. Message class as computed using equation 10.4 is a linear mapping from message laxities to message classes. For example, if the preorder search sequence of a time tree with seven nodes is 1, 2, 4, 5, 3, 6, 7, the message classes 1, 2, 3, 4, 5, 6, and 7, respectively, would get mapped onto those nodes.

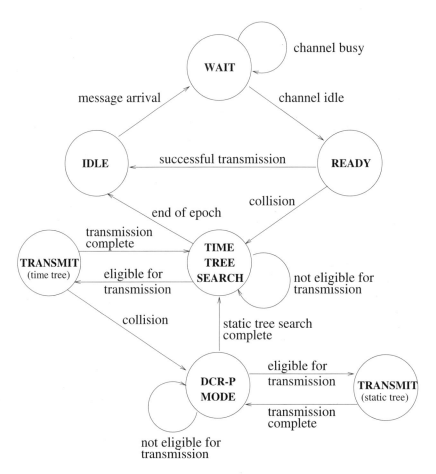

Figure 10.7
State diagram of DOD-P protocol

The DOD-P algorithm differs from the DCR-P algorithm in the way it handles and resolves collisions. The DOD-P algorithm resolves collisions in two steps. Initial collision initiates a time tree search. In a time tree search, if a particular transmission is successful, the algorithm proceeds to search the next node (in preorder) in the time tree. If a collision occurs while the algorithm is searching a time tree node, a static tree search is initiated. These two steps are repeated until all the nodes in the time tree are searched. As mentioned earlier, message class is computed (1) after the initial collision and (2) at the completion of a static tree search. The value of m^*_{index} in equation 10.4 for the first case (i.e., after initial collision) is 0. Figure 10.7 shows the state diagram of the DOD-P protocol.

Example 3: Consider a 31-node network and static tree (figure 10.5) identical to that in Example 2. Let the height of the corresponding time tree be 1; hence, the number of time tree nodes is 3, corresponding to (message) equivalence classes 1 to 3. The *i*th message class maps onto the *i*th element in the preorder search sequence of the time tree. Assume the nodes (with messages) that contend for a particular channel at time *t* are 3, 8, 12, 15, 25, and 31. Let the message class computed for corresponding messages be 2, 2, 3, 1, 4, and 6. The DOD-P algorithm proceeds as follows: (1) initial collision occurs; (2) collision resolution starts with a time tree search. First node 15 (message class 1) transmits its message. Then message class 2 is searched. In this slot, there is a collision, because nodes 3 and 8 have the same message class. A static tree search is then initiated to resolve the collision, and the collision between nodes 3 and 8 is resolved as in DCR-P protocol. After the static search tree is completed, message classes are recomputed, and any further collisions are resolved in a similar manner. Note that nodes 25 and 31 do not participate in the first collision, since their message classes are not in the range 1 to 3. After message class recomputation, those new message classes in the range 1 to 3 are eligible to contend for the channel.

10.4   DCR-Based Protocols for Multipacket Messages

Several applications demand transmission of time-constrained messages composed of more than one packet to be transmitted by a particular deadline. If the DCR protocol were simply extended to transmit multipacket messages, the system's performance (in terms of number of messages guaranteed) would be poor, as a consequence of its allowing only one packet of a message to be transmitted in a given epoch. A large message would require several epochs for transmission, which would lead to a majority of the messages being dropped and would reduce the system's level of performance.

   These limitations were the motivations for developing reservation-based protocols for messages with multiple packets. In the rest of this section, we present reservation-based protocols that use *notifiers* to reserve the channel for multiple message transmissions. The DCR transmission policy is modified in these protocols by splitting channel access into periods of *notification* and *transmission*. Before transmitting a message, node *i* transmits a notifier indicating the number of service slots (length) required by its message (C_i) and its deadline (D_i).

10.4.1   Modified DCR Protocol

The first protocol considered here is an extended version of the DCR protocol (known as the modified DCR protocol, or MDCR) based on notifiers supporting transmission of multipacket messages. A static mapping of nodes in the LAN to vertices of a binary tree is done as discussed in section 10.3.3.3. The MDCR algorithm at any given node proceeds as follows:

1. Node i senses the channel and, if it finds the channel idle, attempts to transmit the notifier (C_i, D_i) of a message it wishes to transmit.

2. If no collision occurs, and the message notifier is transmitted successfully, node i begins transmission of the message, provided the message has non-negative laxity; otherwise, the message is dropped. During transmission of the message, no other node tries to transmit over the channel (i.e., they observe the channel at step 1 of the sequence and find it is occupied).

3. If notifier transmission fails, all nodes enter the collision resolution mode, as in DCR.

4. In the collision resolution mode, the collision resolution tree is traversed in preorder. During tree traversal, each node, when its turn is reached, transmits a notifier for its message (if any) and then actually transmits the message if the message has non-negative laxity; otherwise, the message is dropped.

Though MDCR allows transmission of multipacket messages, it suffers from some limitations. The protocol's main drawback is that it transmits messages strictly based on the initial mapping of nodes of the LAN to the vertices of the collision resolution tree, thus enforcing a static priority order among nodes. Thus, MDCR can allow messages with larger laxity (smaller priorities) to get transmission rights before more critical messages with smaller laxities (higher priorities), because of the static order of tree traversal. This could lead to an implicit priority inversion, in which a higher-priority message gets lower priority and vice versa.

10.4.2   Laxity-Based DCR Protocol

To overcome the limitations of MDCR, laxity-based DCR (LDCR) protocol, which dynamically assigns priorities to messages based on laxity (higher priorities are assigned to messages having smaller laxities) and also allows multipacket message transmission, has been proposed. The laxity (L_i) of message m_i at time t is defined as the maximum amount of time by which the transmission of a message can be delayed and still meet its deadline:

$$L_i = D_i - C_i - t,$$

where C_i and D_i are the service time and deadline of message m_i, respectively, and t is the current time.

The LDCR protocol works based on a notion of *message deferment,* in which a message with higher laxity is deferred to allow messages with lower laxities to be transmitted, thus preventing the potential priority inversion that could be encountered in the MDCR scheme. In LDCR, the static mapping of nodes of the LAN to the vertices of the collision resolution (CR) tree is similar to that in DCR-P, as discussed in section 10.3.3.3. The manner in which this mapping is accomplished is left to the designer. The CR tree is traversed in preorder; that is, when a collision occurs, the next three slots are reserved for the root, the left subtree, and the right subtree, respectively. Each node maintains a queue of messages sorted in increasing order of laxity. In the actual implementation, the queues are maintained as a *delta list* [6] for efficient storage of messages, since this involves minimal overhead in updating the associated laxity. In a delta list–based message queue, the laxity of a message is stored relative to the laxity of its predecessor in the queue. Thus updating the delta list as time progresses involves minimal overhead, as only the laxity of the message at the head of the queue is modified. When a new message arrives, it is inserted at appropriate position, a laxity is assigned to it with respect to its predecessor in the queue, and the laxity of its successor message in the queue is modified. Messages with negative laxity are removed from the queue.

The LDCR protocol consists of three phases: contention mode, CR mode, and LLF mode, which are described below. The combination of CR mode and LLF mode defines an epoch in the LDCR protocol, in contrast to the DCR and MDCR protocols, wherein an epoch is defined by the CR mode alone.

1. *Contention mode (when channel is idle).*

(a) Each node examines the message at the head of its queue. If the laxity of the message is negative, the message is dropped.

(b) Otherwise, it attempts to transmit a notifier for the message.

(c) If the notifier transmission is successful, the message is transmitted.

(d) If a collision occurs during notifier transmission, all nodes enter into CR mode and the CR tree is traversed in preorder.

2. *Collision resolution mode.*

(a) When a node n_i gets its turn in the CR mode, it transmits its notifier. Thus every other node is informed of the message requirements of node n_i.

(b) If the laxity of a message (the first message in the queue of n_i) is less than a specified threshold (but nonnegative), then the message is transmitted; otherwise the message is deferred, and preorder traversal continues. If two or more messages have laxity less than or equal to the threshold value, preference in transmission is given to the message with the shorter service time. This minimizes the time that the channel is blocked, thereby improving the chances of successful transmission for subsequent messages.

(c) After the CR tree has been completely traversed, if some deferred messages remain to be transmitted, the protocol enters the LLF mode.

3. *LLF mode.* In LLF mode, all deferred messages are transmitted, based on the laxity order of messages among nodes. This phase is required to allow those messages that have arrived in the current epoch to be transmitted before the next epoch. By doing this, the overhead due to collision between messages of two different epochs is eliminated.

4. Once the first message at all nodes has been either transmitted or dropped, the next epoch begins.

Note that the importance of threshold in step 2(b) was reflected in the discussion of the DOD-P protocol, whereby the choice of c is a critical design decision made depending on the characteristics of the real-time traffic to be supported.

10.4.2.1   Illustrative Examples   Figure 10.8 illustrates the greater effectiveness of the LDCR over the MDCR. The example considers a LAN with four nodes. The first entry (at time 0) in the tables of figure 10.8 is the initial status of the queue at each node (each node has a single message to transmit). The numbers in parentheses give the (number of slots, deadline) for each message. For example, node N_1 has a message having deadline of 17 and requiring 5 slots for transmission. In this example, the preorder search sequence is N_1, N_2, N_3, and N_4, and it is assumed that the notifier transmission takes one time slot and that the service times and deadlines of messages are multiples of a time slot.

Let us first trace a few steps in the MDCR protocol's processing of this example. At time 1, all nodes attempt to transmit their notifier, which results in collision; thus all nodes enter the CR mode. At time 2, N_1 (the root of the CR tree) transmits its notifier, then proceeds to transmit its message from time slot 3 onward for 5 time slots. Thus all other nodes back off for a period of 5 slots. Even though this message has a very large laxity (10) compared to the laxities of other messages, it is still transmitted first. As a result of this, some nodes end up having negative laxities by the time they get their turn to transmit. By time 8, for example, two nodes in the left subtree (N_2 and N_3) must drop their messages, as their laxities become negative at the end of slot 4 and 7, respectively. At time 9, the node in the right subtree (N_4) transmits its notifier successfully and transmits its message successfully before its deadline.

The behavior of the LDCR protocol is similar to that of MDCR up to time 2, that is, after transmission of the notifier of the message at N_1. After transmission of the notifier, the LDCR computes the laxity for this message and finds that the laxity is greater than the threshold (which the designer has set to 1); hence it defers transmission of the message. At time slot 4, N_2 transmits its notifier, and the LDCR finds that the laxity of the message is zero; hence the message is transmitted immediately. The protocol proceeds in this manner.

From the above example, it can be noted that the LDCR protocol transmits all the messages successfully, whereas the MDCR protocol can transmit only 50% of the messages. The key aspect that contributes to the improved performance in LDCR is the deferment of the message at N_1, which has a large laxity. This allows the more critical messages at N_2, N_3, and N_4 to be transmitted before their deadlines.

time	N_1	N_2	N_3	N_4
0	(5, 17)	(2, 6)	(2, 9)	(2, 12)
1	C	C	C	C
2	N(5, 17)			
3	X(5, 17)			
4	X(5, 17)	D(2, 6)		
5	X(5, 17)			
7	X(5, 17)		D(2, 9)	
8		I	I	
9				N(2, 12)
10				X(2, 12)
11				

time	N_1	N_2	N_3	N_4
0	(5, 17)	(2, 6)	(2, 9)	(2, 12)
1	C	C	C	C
2	N(5, 17)			
3	defer $(L_1 = 9)$	C	C	
4	$(L_1 = 8)$	N(2, 6)		
5	$(L_1 = 7)$	X(2, 6)		
7	$(L_1 = 5)$		N(2, 9)	
8			X(2, 9)	
10	$(L_1 = 2)$			N(2, 12)
11				X(2, 12)
12	LLF-$(L_1 = 0)$: X(5, 17)			
17				

Figure 10.8
The working of the MDCR and LDCR protocols (C: collision; N: notifier; X: transmit; L: laxity counter; D: drop; I: idle)

10.4.3 DCR-Based Dynamic Planning-Based Protocol

The MDCR and LDCR protocols for multipacket messages are of a best-effort nature, since they perform no admission test for guaranteeing the transmission of messages. In a dynamic real-time system, in the absence of a priori knowledge of message arrival rates and patterns, it is impossible to guarantee the timely delivery of all of the messages that arrive. Many hard real-time applications, however, require *predictability* of message transmission, meaning that once a message is admitted into the system, it is always transmitted before its deadline. This requirement has motivated the development of planning-based protocols for guaranteeing the transmission of messages on-line.

In a dynamic planning-based protocol, when a message arrives at a node, the message scheduler at the node dynamically determines the feasibility of scheduling the new message without jeopardizing the guarantees that have been provided for the previously scheduled messages. Thus, for predictable message transmission, a schedulability analysis (also known as a *message admission test*) must be conducted before transmission of a particular message is begun. If the message passes the admission test, the required number of channel slots are reserved for the message. The planning-based approach allows this type of admission control and results in a reservation-based system. In this section, we describe a dynamic planning-based protocol that is a variant of the LDCR protocol, namely, the guarantee-based LDCR protocol.

10.4.3.1 The Guarantee-Based LDCR Protocol The guarantee-based LDCR (LDCR-G) protocol is based on the best-effort LDCR protocol, which was described above. The operation of LDCR-G is identical to that of the LDCR protocol apart from the LDCR-G's admission policy for new messages. The LDCR-G protocol admits a message based on an estimate of the worst-case message service time and ensures successful transmission of all messages it admits. The semantics of this protocol are as follows: Messages are admitted based on an estimate of worst-case message service time, and their transmission is guaranteed if their service times do not exceed this estimate.

The key aspect of the admission test in LDCR-G is that it computes the worst-case channel access delay incurred before a newly arrived message can be transmitted. If this delay, denoted as *WCT,* allows the message to be transmitted before its deadline, then the message is admitted into the system; otherwise the message is dropped. For achieving this predictability in message transmission, the protocol computes the *WCT* it might take a node to access the channel before it begins transmission of the newly arrived message. *WCT* is computed in the manner described below. The important terms used in the test are:

- *Queue:* list of messages, in the order of arrival, to be transmitted in subsequent epochs

- M_{est}: worst-case service time estimate for any message in the system

- N: number of nodes

- *Rank:* position of message in the queue
- *Pos_tree*: position of node in the tree
- *N_col*: maximum number of collisions in the tree traversal
- *Time_for_Not*: time for notifier transmission
- *t*: current time

The LDCR-G computes the *WCT* of each arriving message as follows:

- All messages are to be transmitted in epochs. The time slots used for transmission of all messages prior to the epoch in which the new message is to be transmitted is computed. The number of such epochs is captured by the rank term k. This time is $(M_{est} + Time\_for\_Not) * (N * (k - 1))$.

- Next, the time elapsed due to transmission of messages at nodes before the current node in the preorder traversal of the CR tree in the kth epoch is computed: $(M_{est} + Time\_for\_Not) * (Pos\_tree - 1)$.

- Last, the overhead due to collision is computed: $N\_col * k$. Note that the overhead for notifier transmission is accounted for in the previous two computations.

- Combining these times, the *WCT* is given by

$$WCT_j^k = (M_{est} + Time\_for\_Not) * (N * (k - 1) + Pos\_tree - 1) + N\_col * k. \qquad (10.5)$$

The admission test for a message having rank k that arrives at node j at time t is then

$$WCT_j^k + C_j^k \leq D_j^k - t. \qquad (10.6)$$

There is a trade-off in this protocol between performance and the strictness of the admission test. A larger value for M_{est} implies a more pessimistic estimate of *WCT*, which results in lower performance. Thus the value of M_{est} should be carefully chosen depending on the requirements of each particular application. The proof of the protocol's correctness is as follows.

Lemma: If a message passes the admission test and its service time is less than or equal to the worst-case service time (M_{est}), then the protocol guarantees the successful transmission of the message.

Proof: The proof is achieved by contradiction. Assume that a message passes the admission test, and its service time is less than or equal to M_{est}. Invalidation of this guarantee can occur only if the *WCT* of the message (which is computed using M_{est}) increases subsequently. But the *WCT* of the message can increase only if the service time of any other admitted message exceeds M_{est}. Clearly, this contradicts the assumption that all the admitted messages have service times less than or equal to M_{est}. Hence the lemma is proved.

10.4.3.2 Generalization of LDCR-G Protocol In many real-time applications in which guarantees are given to messages, applications must be given sufficient time to recover if messages they generate fail the admission test; that is, the admission decision for a message is made at or before a certain amount of time (recovery period) before its deadline, and the protocol guarantees that all admitted messages will be transmitted successfully. An admission test for giving guarantees should be performed when $L_i \geq RP$ for some message i, where RP is called the *recovery period;* that is, a message is either guaranteed or rejected before its laxity becomes less than the recovery period. This allows the application to take recovery action if the message is rejected. From the semantics of LDCR and LDCR-G protocols, it can be seen that they are different instances of the same general protocol, as described below.

• In the generalized protocol, when RP = 0, a guarantee needs to be given only when laxity is equal to zero. This means that a message will not be rejected until its $L_i = 0$. This reduces to the best-effort LDCR protocol.

• In the generalized protocol, when the RP of a message is set to be its initial laxity (laxity on arrival), the protocol should perform the admission test on arrival of the message. If the message passes the admission test, it is guaranteed to be sent; otherwise it is rejected. This represents the semantics of the LDCR-G protocol.

10.5   Real-Time Communication with Periodic and Aperiodic Messages

In many real-time applications, such as air traffic control and multimedia, periodic messages arrive dynamically. To support real-time communication with performance guarantees in such applications, real-time channels[†] need to be established dynamically with the specified traffic characteristics and QoS requirements for the periodic messages [11].

10.5.1   Properties of Real-Time MAC Protocol

The following properties are desirable in a real-time MAC protocol. Such a protocol should (1) support real-time channel establishment, (2) provide a bounded response time to channel establishment requests, (3) support scheduling of aperiodic messages along with periodic messages, and (4) be distributed in nature.

1. *Real-time channel establishment.* To provide guaranteed real-time communication, a protocol needs to establish real-time channels for the periodic messages (or message stream) of an application. A real-time channel is established by reserving the necessary

---

[†] In this section, *channel* refers to a logical connection as opposed to the shared physical link assumed in the previous sections.

resources according to the specified traffic characteristics of the periodic message, if the admission of this connection does not jeopardize the guarantees given to the messages already admitted. The protocol should have an associated admission test that is to be performed before admitting any periodic message.

2. *Bounded response time.* In many real-time applications, such as air traffic control and multimedia, since requests for channel establishment for periodic messages arrive dynamically, one cannot predict a priori whether messages will meet their deadlines. Therefore, in the context of scheduling dynamically arriving message streams, predictability means that once a periodic message stream is admitted (i.e., a real-time channel is established for the stream), all deadlines of messages corresponding to this real-time channel will be met. The protocol should provide a bounded response time to a channel establishment request (i.e, the time taken to determine acceptance/rejection of a message stream should be bounded) so that some alternate recovery action can be initiated in case the request is rejected.

3. *Integrated scheduling of periodic and aperiodic messages.* Besides the periodic messages, which require hard real-time guarantees, the protocol should also support scheduling of aperiodic messages, which may have soft deadlines or no deadlines at all.

4. *Distributed nature.* Since a given channel is shared by a number of nodes in multiple access networks, the nodes need to cooperate and coordinate with one another for (1) transmitting channel establishment requests, (2) admission test and resource reservation, and (3) transmission of messages so that all messages meet their deadlines. These functions can be performed in either a centralized or a distributed manner. Centralized schemes are prone to single-point failure, wherein the failure of the central node (scheduler) paralyzes the entire system. Also, centralized schemes incur substantial overhead through the process for giving channel access rights to the nodes. Therefore, a distributed scheme is preferred wherein every node participates in decision making in a decentralized manner. All nodes need to have global state information if the required functions are to be performed in a distributed manner.

10.5.2   Centralized Protocol for Multiple Access Bus Networks

A guarantee-based protocol for scheduling of periodic messages in multiple access bus networks has been proposed in [5]. It is a centralized protocol and is suitable for networks that have a centralized control unit, called the link control unit (LCU), for controlling access to the shared link (e.g., field bus), as shown in figure 10.9. The LCU is responsible for token allocation and resource reservation (admission control) for real-time channels sharing the link. The LCU sends high-priority (i.e., real-time) and normal (i.e., non-real-time) tokens to all nodes on the link according to their needs and principles of fairness. An expiration time parameter is associated with each token sent. The node must return any token it receives before the token expires.

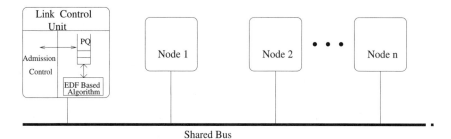

Figure 10.9
Multiple access bus network with LCU

10.5.2.1 LCU Scheduling Algorithm

1. When a channel establishment request for a periodic message M_i with message transmission time t_i and period p_i arrives at a particular node, the node's LCU tries to reserve link capacity by performing the admission test

$$\sum_i \frac{t_i + overhead_i}{p_i} \leq 1,$$

where the index i runs over all the admitted real-time channels and the current request. The main part of the overhead in the equation is determined by the token passing time.

2. If the admission test is satisfied, the LCU reserves the required link capacity, updates information about existing real-time channels (that is, it adds the current request to the periodic queue, PQ) and sends a confirmation message to the requesting node. Otherwise, the LCU sends a rejection message to the requesting node.

3. The LCU then follows an EDF [16]-based algorithm for allocating tokens to the real-time channels (message stream requests in PQ) such that each real-time channel gets to transmit on the link for t_i time in every time period p_i.

4. When there is no real-time message ready for transmission, the LCU issues a non-real-time token whose expiration time is set to the beginning of the next scheduled activity (when a real-time message is ready for transmission), and this token circulates among all the nodes on the network.

10.5.2.2 Node Scheduling Algorithm

1. If a node receives a real-time token, it transmits messages over the specified real-time channel[4] until message transmission is over or the token expires, whichever is earlier.

---

4. A node can establish multiple real-time channels.

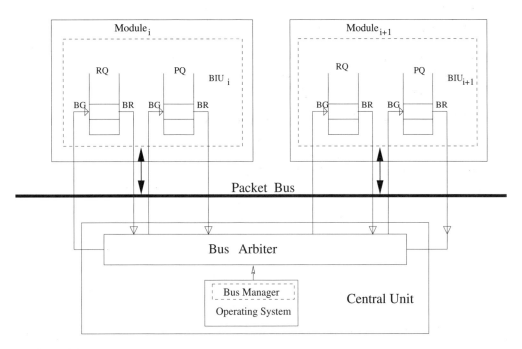

Figure 10.10
Bus arbitration—backplane bus of workstation

2. If a node receives a non-real-time token, it transmits non-real-time messages until the token expires or circulates the non-real-time token among other nodes, if it completes the transmission of its non-real-time messages before the token expires.

Since this scheme requires no complex scheduling algorithm at the node, it can be implemented on a node with low computing capability. Though it supports non-real-time messages, it provides no explicit support for aperiodic real-time messages. It also suffers from the disadvantages of a centralized protocol, namely, token overhead for link access control and vulnerability of the centralized control unit.

10.5.3   Scheduling Algorithm for Backplane Bus

An algorithm for centralized scheduling of periodic and aperiodic messages has also been proposed for the backplane bus of a workstation [12]. A multimedia workstation consists of a number of hardware modules, such as a network interface module, a storage module, a video display module, and an image processing module, connected by a packet bus, as shown in figure 10.10. Every module has a bus interface unit (BIU) that connects it to the packet bus. The output buffer of the BIU consists of two parts: a periodic queue (PQ) and an aperiodic queue (RQ). Each queue has its own bus request (BR) and bus grant (BG) signals that the BIU uses for arbitration. A bus arbiter (BA) resolves any contention among the units for the packet bus. The BA periodically executes a service algorithm with a period of N time slots (a time slot τ is the time taken to transmit one packet), called the *bus service cycle time,* which is much larger than the period of any periodic message.

10.5.3.1 Admission Test   With each message stream it presents for transmission, an application passes message stream parameters, message size M_i and period T_i, to the *bus manager,* an operating system daemon executing in the central unit. The bus manager computes c_i, the number of slots that need to be reserved for this message in each service cycle. The message stream is admitted if the following condition holds:

$$c_i + Q \leq N - \alpha,$$

where c_i is the smallest integer that satisfies

$$M_i \leq c_i(\lceil T_i/(N*\tau)\rceil - 2),$$

Q is the number of time slots in a cycle reserved for periodic messages already admitted, and α denotes the number of slots dedicated for random (aperiodic) messages. α is a system parameter that should be changed only when a change in the fraction of bandwidth allocated to periodic traffic is desired.

If the stream is admitted, Q is incremented by c_i. On termination of the message stream M_i, Q is decremented by c_i. After any change in Q, its value is written in register Q in the BA. PQs and RQs contend for the bus whenever they have messages to transmit. The BA is responsible for resolving such contentions. Two counters, n and q, in the BA are initialized at the beginning of every service cycle with the values of registers N and Q, respectively. The value of counter n denotes the remaining number of slots in a given service cycle, and counter q denotes the number of slots allotted to message streams that have not yet been used by message streams during the current service cycle.

10.5.3.2 BA Scheduling Algorithm   The BA does its job in every time slot according to the following rules:

1. If $n > q$, it grants the bus to an RQ, if any RQ is requesting it; otherwise, it grants the bus to a PQ, if any PQ is requesting it.

2. If $n \leq q$, it grants the bus to a PQ, if any PQ is requesting it; otherwise, it grants the bus to an RQ, if any RQ is requesting it.

3. It decrements q each time it grants the bus to a PQ.

4. It decrements n. If $n = 0$, it reloads counter n from register N and counter q from register Q.

In this scheduling scheme, aperiodic traffic tends to remain in high priority most of the time without jeopardizing the guarantees of the periodic messages. Also, the service policy has a simple realization. However, this scheme cannot be used directly for multiple access bus networks for the following reasons:

1. In multiple access bus networks, periodic traffic arrives at each node independently, unlike in the backplane bus, where it is centralized.

2. There are no control lines to convey bus request and bus grant information.

3. There is no central bus arbiter that performs access arbitration based on the channel reservations of the admitted requests.

Hence this scheduling algorithm cannot be used as such for multiple access networks, in which global state information (control messages) needs to be collected using the same shared bus that is used for message transmission.

10.5.4   Distributed Protocols for Integrated Scheduling of Periodic and Aperiodic Messages

In [1], two protocols, the earliest-deadline-first (EDF) protocol and the BUS protocol, have been proposed for dynamic real-time channel establishment with support for scheduling of aperiodic (asynchronous) messages in multiple access bus networks. The protocols are distributed in nature, with each node executing the same algorithm. The protocols alternate between two phases:

• Reservation phase. During this phase, resources are reserved (i.e., real-time channels are established) for channel establishment requests (periodic messages) that pass the admission test.

• Transmission phase. During this phase, the nodes transmit messages on the real-time channels so as to guarantee the deadlines of all the admitted messages.

10.5.4.1   Components of the Protocols   The protocols have the following components:

• Request server (RS). This is a periodic server used for collecting periodic and aperiodic message requests and for providing a bounded response time to channel establishment requests. During the activation of the RS, in the reservation phase, nodes transmit message notifiers that contain information such as type of request (periodic/aperiodic), service time, period/deadline, and the node number of the message source. One slot in the channel is required for transmission of each message notifier. Since all nodes monitor the channel and the channel is a broadcast medium, all nodes get to know about the message traffic at the other nodes through these message notifiers. The preorder DCR protocol discussed in section 10.3.3.3 is used for transmitting message notifiers. This protocol is an efficient protocol, wherein when the load is light (say, only one message request is ready in the entire network), then only one slot is used for the RS and the remaining slots can be used for transmission of messages. When the load is heavy, on the other hand, collisions are resolved deterministically to bound the worst-case channel access delay, giving every node a chance to broadcast at least one message notifier in one RS period. The server concept has been borrowed from the task-scheduling algorithms that use an aperiodic server [8] for executing aperiodic tasks (discussed in section 2.3.3).

• Aperiodic server (AS). This is also a periodic server used for servicing aperiodic messages. The service provided may be either guaranteed service, for which the guarantee-based DCR protocol [23] can be used, or may be a best-effort service. In the best-effort service category, the service policy can be either fairness-oriented, in which the AS bandwidth is equally shared by all the contending nodes, or aimed at maximizing the throughput of aperiodic messages. The percentage of bandwidth reserved for aperiodic traffic is application dependent; that is, the service time and period of the server can be fixed based on the requirements of the application.

• Run-time scheduling. The run-time scheduling algorithms for the EDF and BUS protocols are based on the EDF algorithm [16] and backplane bus scheduling algorithm [12] (discussed in section 10.5.3), respectively. These algorithms are used during the transmission phase of the protocols.

• Admission tests. An admission test is associated with each protocol for admission control of real-time channel establishment requests.

In these protocols, the RS handles real-time channel establishment and bounded response time requirements. Integrated scheduling of periodic and aperiodic messages is supported by employing AS. The protocols are distributed in nature, thus satisfying all the desirable properties of a real-time MAC protocol.

10.5.4.2 Description of the Protocols An application running on the nodes of a network generates periodic and aperiodic messages in each node. Each node maintains two queues (local) for storing the local periodic (LPQ) and aperiodic (LRQ) message notifiers, as shown in figure 10.11. A message notifier must be broadcast before the transmission of the corresponding message. Each node also maintains two global queues, an aperiodic queue (GRQ) for storing the aperiodic message notifiers that have been broadcast successfully on the bus, and a periodic queue (GPQ) for storing the notifiers of admitted real-time channels (periodic messages). The RS and AS notifiers are placed in the GPQ of each node. The requests in the LPQ are maintained in order of arrival time of the message requests, and the requests in the LRQ are maintained in ascending order of deadline of the message requests. In the GPQ and GRQ, the message notifiers are also maintained

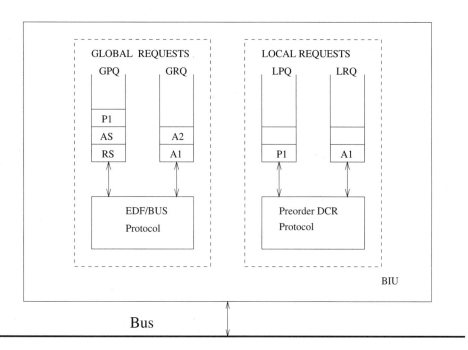

Figure 10.11
Node in multiple access network

in ascending order of deadline. In the EDF and BUS protocols, access rights to real-time channels are given for, say, *n* slots, based on the EDF/BUS run-time scheduling algorithm. Each node executes the following protocol once it has been granted access to a real-time channel:

Protocol(*RTchannel,n*) /* *RTchannel* specifies the channel that has access rights for *n* slots */
   1. **If** *RTchannel* = RS,
      Repeat steps (a)–(c) until a slot goes idle or RS service time is exhausted.
      (a) Transmit message notifiers from the local queues with priority to LPQ over LRQ as per the preorder DCR protocol.
      (b) **If** notifier transmission is successful and the notifier is for an aperiodic message then insert the notifier in the GRQ.
      (c) **else** if notifier transmission is successful and the notifier is for a periodic message then
         i. *result* = Admit(notifier) /* Perform admission test using the EDF/BUS protocol admission test */
         ii. **If** *result* = *success* then
            A. Insert the notifier in GPQ.

B. Reserve resources for this real-time channel and update link utilization information.

iii. **else** reject the request.

2. **If** *RTchannel* = AS, grant link access rights to messages in GRQ based on predetermined aperiodic message service policy/protocol.

3. **If** *RTchannel* = P_i, /* real-time channel *i* */ grant link access rights to the node that is the source of the real-time channel P_i.

When a node wishes to tear down a real-time channel, it transmits a channel termination request as the last message on that channel. All nodes then update their GPQ and link utilization information accordingly.

When none of the periodic messages is using the link (no message is ready in the GPQ), then aperiodic messages (if any) are serviced. In the event the GRQ is also empty (i.e., when the system load is light), the RS is activated, resulting in a much lower average response time to channel establishment requests compared to the RS period. It can be noted that when the system load is light, these protocols behave like a contention-based protocol, since RS follows a CSMA/CD-based DCR protocol. When the system load is heavy, the channel is granted to admitted requests without any collisions based on the EDF/BUS policy. Thus the protocols adapt well to the system load.

10.5.5   Comparison of the Protocols

10.5.5.1   Schedulability of Periodic Messages   The EDF protocol offers higher schedulability than the BUS protocol, because the admission test of the BUS protocol slightly overallocates bandwidth to periodic messages, and as a result of this overallocation, fewer real-time channels can be established. However, at run time, this overallocated channel bandwidth is made available for servicing aperiodic messages. The EDF protocol, which does not engage in this overallocation, can admit a higher number of periodic messages than the BUS protocol.

10.5.5.2   Response Time to Aperiodic Messages   The BUS scheduling scheme gives fast response to aperiodic messages without jeopardizing the guarantees given to admitted periodic messages. Aperiodic messages (if any) are serviced when there are no periodic messages to be transmitted by activating the AS for idle channel duration. Idle slots are uniformly distributed in the BUS protocol, since the service cycle time is much less than the deadline of aperiodic messages, resulting in better channel utilization for aperiodic messages. In the EDF protocol, besides the absence of overallocated bandwidth to be made available for aperiodic messages, occurrence of idle channel instances, when there are no periodic messages to be transmitted, is not uniform (i.e., the idle channel bandwidth is made available in bursts), and hence aperiodic messages cannot utilize the idle channel bandwidth efficiently.

10.5.5.3   Granularity of AS   In EDF protocol, though the idle channel time cannot be distributed uniformly, the AS time can be made available uniformly by changing the granularity of the AS, that is, by dividing the period and service time by the same constant factor. For example, a server with a service time of 4 units and a period of 10 units can be transformed into a server with a service time of 2 units and a period of 5 units. Similarly, the granularity of the RS can be reduced to improve response to message requests.

Example 4:   Consider a multiple access bus network with slot time τ equal to 5 microseconds. The bus service cycle N is 100 slots, that is, 500 microseconds. Let 10% of the bandwidth (10 slots) be reserved for the AS and 1% (1 slot) for the RS. Let all periodic message requests have a maximum service time (assumed to be the same for all requests) M_i of 73 slots (365 microseconds) with period P_i equal to 940 slots (4700 microseconds).

BUS Protocol

The number of slots required per cycle in the BUS protocol for a periodic request is 10 (i.e., $73 \leq 10 * (\lceil 4700/500 \rceil - 2)$). Since the number of slots available for periodic requests per service cycle is $89 = (100 - 10 - 1)$, a maximum of 8 real-time channels can be established simultaneously. Let us compute the overallocation of bandwidth for a message stream that has 20 instances. In $(4700 * 20)$ time duration, which equals 188 cycles (i.e., $940 * 20 = 18,800$ slots), 1,880 slots will be reserved for the periodic message stream, of which only 1,460 (i.e., $20 * 73$) will be used for periodic message transmission. The remaining 420 (i.e., $1880 - 1460$) overallocated slots are made available for aperiodic message transmission besides the 1,880 slots reserved for AS.

EDF Protocol

The channel utilization of each periodic request is $73/940 = 0.0777$, and hence 11 real-time channels can be simultaneously established with total periodic utilization equal to 0.8547 (less than the maximum of 0.89 permissible).

From this example, we can see that the EDF protocol (11 real-time channels) has a higher schedulability than the BUS protocol (8 real-time channels). In the BUS protocol, the extra 420 slots will be uniformly made available for servicing aperiodic messages and hence will result in higher channel utilization for aperiodic messages.

10.6   Fiber-Distributed Data Interface

Fiber-distributed data interface (FDDI) is an American National Standards Institute (ANSI) standard [7] for a 100 Mbps fiber optic token ring network. The FDDI cabling consists of

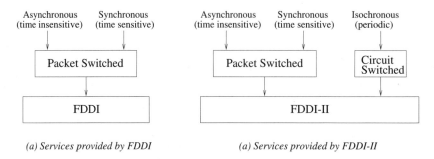

(a) Services provided by FDDI   (a) Services provided by FDDI-II

Figure 10.12
Services provided by FDDI and FDDI-II

two fiber rings, one transmitting clockwise and the other transmitting counterclockwise. It uses a *timed token* access method to share the medium among nodes (stations). In a token rotation medium access protocol, nodes are connected to form a ring. The basic FDDI MAC protocol works as follows: To transmit data, (1) a node must first acquire the *token,* a special type of frame used to grant permission to a node to transmit its data, (2) it then transmits its frame (packet), and (3) it then puts a new token back onto the ring as soon as it finishes its transmission. All messages move around the ring and are repeated by each node through which they pass. A node that reads its own address as the destination of a packet copies the packet and passes it to the next node in the ring. When the frame reaches the source node, it is removed from the ring. The time it takes for a token to traverse an idle ring is called the *walk time,* denoted as W_T. The access method in FDDI differs from the traditional token access method in that each node accurately measures the time taken by a token to rotate around the ring and uses it to determine the usability of the token.

Old LAN protocols such as Ethernet (IEEE 802.3) and token ring (IEEE 802.5) support only asynchronous (time-insensitive and generally throughput-sensitive) traffic. FDDI supports synchronous (time-sensitive) traffic in addition to asynchronous traffic, as shown in figure 10.12(a). Under the FDDI protocol, nodes on the network choose a target token rotation time (TTRT). Each node is allocated a *synchronous capacity,* the maximum amount of time a particular node is permitted to transmit in synchronous mode each time it receives the token. Each node's synchronous capacity is restricted to a preallocated fraction of $(TTRT - W_T)$, such that the cumulative synchronous capacity of the entire network is bounded by $(TTRT - W_T)$.

When a node receives a token, it first transmits its synchronous traffic for an amount of time bounded by its synchronous capacity. Then it transmits asynchronous traffic only if the time that has elapsed since the previous token's departure from the same node is less than TTRT. This protocol forces the token to rotate at a speed such that the maximum time between two consecutive token visits is bounded by $2 * TTRT$. In a network that uses only synchronous mode transmission, the time between consecutive token arrivals is bounded by one TTRT.

The FDDI MAC protocol uses three timers. The *token holding timer* determines how long a node may continue to transmit once it has acquired a token. This timer prevents a node from hogging the ring forever. The *token rotation timer* is restarted every time the token is seen. If this timer expires, it means that the token has not been sighted for too long an interval. In that case, the token has probably been lost, so the token recovery procedure is initiated. The *valid transmission timer* is used to time out and recover from certain transient ring errors. FDDI has a priority algorithm by which, for each token pass, it determines the message priority class that has access right to the channel. If the token is ahead of schedule, all priorities may transmit during that pass, but if it is behind the schedule, only the highest ones may transmit.

An important feature of FDDI that is also reflected in its name is its distributed nature. An attempt has been made to make all channel access algorithms in FDDI distributed in the sense that the control of the ring in the algorithms is not centralized. When any component fails, other components can reorganize and continue to function. This includes fault recovery, clock synchronization, token initialization, and topology control [10].

FDDI is a good candidate for mission-critical real-time applications, not only because of its high bandwidth, but also because of its dual-ring architecture. The bounded token rotation time provides the necessary condition to guarantee hard real-time deadlines, whereas the dual-ring architecture allows the maintenance of continuous real-time service under some failure conditions. Several civilian and military networks have adopted FDDI as their backbone network.

Although the synchronous traffic service provided by FDDI guarantees a bounded delay, the duration of the delay can vary. For example, with a TTRT value of 165 milliseconds on a ring with 10 microsecond latency, a node will get opportunities to transmit the synchronous traffic every 10 microseconds at zero load. Under a heavy load, it may occasionally have to wait as long as 330 microseconds. This type of variation may not suit many constant-bit-rate telecommunication applications that require strict periodic access. For example, in a 64 kbps voice conversation, one byte is received every 125 microseconds. Such circuit-switched traffic cannot be supported on FDDI. If an application needs guaranteed transmission of n bytes every T microseconds, or some integral multiples of T microseconds, the application is said to require *isochronous service*.

FDDI-II provides support for isochronous service in addition to the asynchronous and synchronous services provided by FDDI, as shown in figure 10.12(b). Like FDDI, FDDI-II runs at 100 Mbps. FDDI-II nodes can run in FDDI or basic mode. In the basic mode on FDDI-II, synchronous and asynchronous traffic is transmitted in a manner identical to that on FDDI: that is, isochronous service is not available in the basic mode. FDDI mode, however, supports all the three services. If all the nodes on a particular ring are FDDI-II nodes, then the ring can switch to hybrid mode, in which isochronous service is provided in addition to basic services. However, if there is even one node on the ring that is not an FDDI-II node, the ring cannot switch to the hybrid mode and must keep running in the basic mode. The main drawback to the FDDI network is that even if one or two nodes require isochronous service, hardware on all nodes on the ring must be upgraded to FDDI-II [10].

To service isochronous requests, FDDI-II uses a periodic transmission policy in which transmission opportunities are repeated every 125 microseconds. At this interval, a special frame called a *cycle* is generated. At 100 Mbps, 1,562.5 bytes can be transmitted in 125 microseconds. Of these, 1,560 bytes are used for the cycle and 2.5 bytes are used as the intercycle gap. At any given instant, the ring may contain several cycles. The bytes of the cycles are preallocated to various connections on the ring. These bytes are reserved for a particular connection in the sense that if the node owning that connection does not use it, other nodes cannot use it, and the bytes are left unused.

Most multimedia applications, such as video conferencing, real-time video, and entertainment video, can be supported by FDDI, since the required time guarantee is a few tens of milliseconds. This guarantee can easily be met with synchronous service and a small TTRT. Since the TTRT cannot be less than the ring latency, FDDI cannot support applications requiring delay bounds less than twice the ring latency. Similarly, applications requiring strict periodic access require FDDI-II.

10.7   Real-Time Switched LAN

The proliferation of real-time multimedia applications such as video conferencing and video on demand has increased the need for bandwidth in networks tremendously. The real-time LAN is unable to cope with the current demand for bandwidth. A solution to this problem is the extended or switched LAN (SLAN).

10.7.1   Overview

In an SLAN, nodes are connected through a local bus to form a *LAN segment*. Several LAN segments are interconnected by a switch that relays messages between different

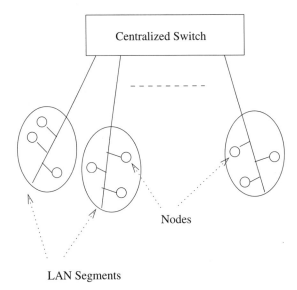

Figure 10.13
Switched LAN topology

LAN segments (figure 10.13). By reducing the number of nodes using a particular LAN, increased bandwidth can be offered to applications running on the SLAN. However, solving the problem of inadequate bandwidth is not sufficient. Since these applications are of a real-time nature, protocols are required for guaranteeing message transmission over the SLAN before the associated deadlines.

The switch or remote bridge in an SLAN is an electronic device that connects the different LAN segments and forwards packets from a node in one LAN segment to a node in another segment. By dedicating links between the switch and different nodes, we can reduce channel contention as well as the load on a particular link and consequently offer more bandwidth for applications that utilize that link. Further, every node is able to choose a link to the switch depending on its bandwidth requirements.

10.7.2   Switch Architecture and Design

The architecture of the switch can be centralized, distributed, or a hybrid of the two [32]. The centralized architecture has a single main CPU (MCPU) that handles all packets coming from every LAN segment (MAC port), as shown in figure 10.14. The distributed architecture requires a processor (MCPU) with buffer space for every MAC port, and the processors are interconnected using a cross-bar switch. Each MAC port has DMA

High-Bandwidth Bus

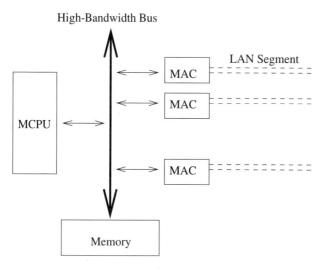

Figure 10.14
Centralized switch architecture

capability to read/write the main memory of the MCPU. The MCPU forwards packets. The tasks performed by the MCPU in real-time are buffer management, bridging, and execution of the 802.1d spanning tree protocol [9].

To understand the working of an SLAN, let us trace the flow of a packet that arrives at the switch from a LAN segment and is destined for the same/another LAN segment (figure 10.15). The MAC module stores the received packet in an allocated space in the buffer memory. The switching module then processes the packet by referring to the filtering database. Processing involves examining the header of the packet to determine whether the packet is to be filtered (discarded) or forwarded. If the destination MAC is connected to the same port on which the packet arrived, then the packet is discarded. If not, the filtering database, which is a simplified routing table, contains information about the port number for the destination MAC. The packet is then placed in the transmit queue and subsequently forwarded by the MAC module to the destination LAN segment, after which its buffer space is deallocated.

10.7.3   Real-Time SLAN Protocols

The most popular protocol in the SLAN environment is the CSMA/CD-based Ethernet. However, this protocol suffers from some critical limitations that render it unsuitable for real-time traffic, as described earlier.

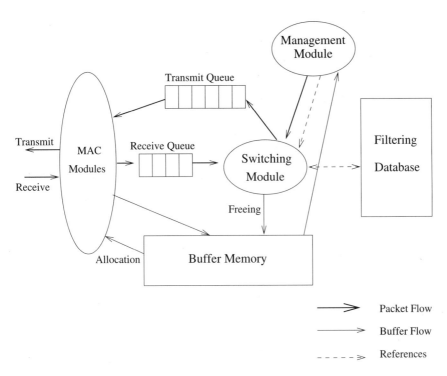

Figure 10.15
Internal working of the switch

When we consider the 100Base-T (IEEE 802.3u) (fast Ethernet) protocol [18] over existing 10Base-T networks, the problems involved in using CSMA/CD for real-time traffic once again arise. The 802.12 demand priority protocol [18] has a round-robin scheduling policy, which may ensure fairness at the expense of priority inversion, making it unsuitable for real-time traffic. The presence of just two priority levels in the protocol is another severe limitation. Also, once a node accesses the channel, it can transmit a single frame only. This restriction limits its use to fixed-length packets. This problem is worsened when different nodes generate frames of different lengths. The 802.12 protocol would be unfair to nodes generating shorter frames, which could be critical in the context of real-time applications. Another problem with the 802.12 standard is that since it does not reserve network resources according to the node requirements dynamically, it cannot be used in a network where the real-time traffic load of each node changes as new real-time messages are admitted.

We now describe a dynamic planning-based protocol for guaranteeing real-time communication in the SLAN environment [24]. This protocol is based on the LDCR-G protocol described earlier in the chapter. In this protocol, only a message that passes the admission test is guaranteed to be transmitted before its deadline. This predictability in message transmission allows support for both hard and soft real-time traffic.

10.7.3.1 Assumptions   The protocol makes the following assumptions:

- All nodes know the maximum number of nodes possible on any LAN segment.

- Centralized switch architecture is assumed. Centralized architecture is chosen because of the prohibitive overhead in distributed architectures. Since in a distributed approach, every processor has its own associated filtering database (FDB), the destination of an intersegment message cannot be resolved in a single lookup of the FDB, as in the centralized scheme.

- All nodes in each segment know the number of segments connected by the switch.

- Every pair of nodes has at most one switch between them; that is, a message needs to be transmitted through at most two hops.

- The SLAN switch design issues involve adopting either transparent or source routing-based switching. The use of transparent switching as an efficient method is assumed.

10.7.4 Dynamic Planning-Based SLAN Protocol

From the above discussion, it can be observed that there is a need to develop protocols that can ensure a guaranteed worst-case channel access delay and allocate bandwidth in an equitable manner for the SLAN environment. This would allow schedulability analysis to be performed while admitting messages into the system, which is crucial for transmitting messages with hard real-time requirements, and also prevent priority inversion.

The dynamic planning-based SLAN protocol called extended LDCR (ELDCR) guarantees message transmission using an admission test that is based on the admission test (AT) proposed for the LDCR-G protocol. The working of the ELDCR is as in LDCR-G. The admission test is verified later in this section for correctness.

The message admission semantics of the LDCR-G protocol apply to the ELDCR as well. Thus only if a message passes the admission test is it guaranteed to be transmitted. The key idea of the SLAN admission test is that it assumes worst-case channel access time (WCT) at the source LAN segment, the switch, and the destination LAN segment. Thus, the WCT computation must incorporate two aspects that are characteristic of the SLAN architecture:

- An intersegment message must access the channel at the source LAN segment to reach the switch.

- A message buffered at the switch must access the channel at the destination LAN segment to reach the destination node.

The manner in which the ELDCR protocol computes the WCT and the admission test it employs are given below. The admission test is split into two phases:

- Phase AT_1. The first phase of the admission test within the LAN segment for both intersegment and intrasegment messages is

$$WCT_{\text{segment}} + C_i \leq D_i - t.$$

- Phase AT_2. The second phase, intended for intersegment messages, is

$$WCT_{\text{max}} + C_i \leq D_i - t.$$

10.7.4.1 Explanation of the Admission Test The term WCT in the admission test represents the worst-case channel access time. For phase AT_1, the need and proof of correctness is as given earlier. This phase of the test has to be performed for all messages irrespective of whether they are intersegment or intrasegment messages, because for both kinds of messages, a node has to access the channel and transmit the message up to the centralized switch, where the message is either forwarded or discarded, depending on whether the destination is in a different LAN segment or in the same segment, respectively.

For phase AT_2, intended only for intersegment messages, WCT_{max} is computed as follows. The worst case collision resolution (WCCR) tree for the largest LAN segment is re-created at the sending node. We designate the largest LAN segment as the worst-case LAN segment since the channel access time would be maximum for this segment. The WCCR tree is actually the CR tree for the largest LAN segment, augmented with $(n-1)$ virtual nodes for an SLAN with n segments. The $(n-1)$ virtual nodes are assigned to all LAN segments other than the worst-case LAN segment. Intersegment messages from a node in a particular LAN segment always arrive at the virtual node to which they are assigned.

The concept of a virtual node is to abstract the switch and the source node into a single node that is virtually attached to the CR tree of the worst-case LAN segment. This allows us to model intersegment and intrasegment message transmission in the same way. If the worst-case LAN segment is the destination segment, then message transmission is successful when the virtual node accesses the channel on the destination LAN segment. Therefore, there is a logical reduction of the two hops necessary for intersegment message transmission into a single hop using the virtual node abstraction. This helps further simplify the computation of the worst-case channel access delay.

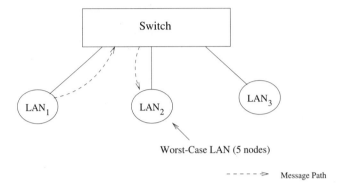

Worst-Case LAN (5 nodes)

- - - - ->   Message Path

Figure 10.16
SLAN topology

Two schemes for assigning the virtual nodes to the LAN segments can be adopted in order to compute the WCT:

• The worst-case time for the WCCR tree, WCT_{wccr}, is computed by the source node, by assuming that the LAN segment to which it belongs is assigned the last virtual node in the WCCR. By doing this, the source node can accurately compute the maximum (upper-bound) amount of time that it must wait before its message can access the channel.

• WCT_{wccr} can also be calculated based on static priorities assigned to different LAN segments, allowing a LAN segment to have a fixed position in the WCCR tree. This means that since every LAN segment is assigned a unique position, the WCT computed by nodes in different LAN segments will vary. It is also possible to give higher priority to the virtual nodes by positioning them at the beginning of the preorder traversal of the CR tree. This can be justified, since a relatively small number of virtual nodes are added, as generally there are fewer LAN segments compared to the number of nodes within a segment. Even though the slots assigned to the virtual nodes may be idle most of the time, they do not waste much bandwidth. This gives intersegment traffic a higher priority over intrasegment traffic.

The worst-case time WCT_{wccr} is added to the worst-case time $WCT_{segment}$ from phase AT_1 to generate the WCT_{max} value used in phase AT_2. Thus the equation for WCT_{max} is $WCT_{max} = WCT_{wccr} + WCT_{segment}$.

An example scenario is depicted in figure 10.16, in which a message is to be sent from LAN_1 to LAN_2, where LAN_2 is the largest LAN segment among the three segments. The CR tree of LAN_2 is shown in figure 10.17, and the WCCR tree of LAN_2 that is recreated

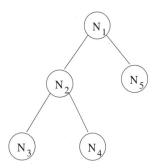

Figure 10.17
CR tree for worst-case LAN segment

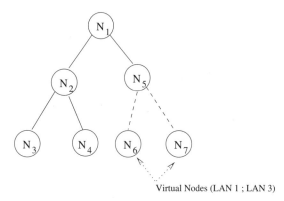

Virtual Nodes (LAN 1 ; LAN 3)

Figure 10.18
WCCR tree

at the source node is shown in figure 10.18. The WCCR tree depicted is the CR tree of the worst-case LAN segment (LAN_2), augmented by the addition of two virtual nodes for LAN_1 and LAN_3.

10.7.4.2 Proof of Correctness To prove the correctness of the message admission phase AT_2, we need to highlight the following issues involved in computing the worst-case channel access delay accurately in spite of a lack of knowledge on the global state of the system:

• For a message at some node in a LAN segment, there is no a priori knowledge of the destination; that is, the source does not know the destination LAN segment of the message.

• When several nodes in different LAN segments try to send messages to a node (of a LAN segment), there is no knowledge of the order in which the centralized switch will service these simultaneous messages.

The following claim is made about the correctness of phase AT_2.

Claim: If a message passes AT_2 and its service time is less than or equal to the worst-case service time estimate M_{est}, then the protocol guarantees the successful transmission of the message.

Proof: There are two cases:
Case (i). Source and destination nodes of a message belong to the same LAN segment. If AT_1 holds, guarantees for intrasegment LAN traffic are not violated, as proved in the LDCR-G protocol.
Case (ii). Source and destination nodes of a message belong to different LAN segments, and phase AT_2 is applied. The two problems that contribute to the lack of global knowledge are handled as follows:

• In case (ii), the worst-case situation occurs when the destination of a message is assumed to be a node in the largest LAN segment with the maximum number of nodes (worst-case LAN segment). The WCCR tree is then the tree representing the worst-case LAN segment. This tackles the first problem, since the WCT is computed using the WCCR tree.

• The worst-case delay a message can encounter at the switch would be at most the channel access time for a virtual node (LAN segment) assigned the last position in the WCCR tree. This worst-case scenario is assumed while computing WCT in admission phase AT_2. Hence, the order in which the messages are serviced by the switch does not violate the guarantees.

Thus the claim of guaranteed message transmission holds as the upper bound on channel access delay for admitting messages is used.

10.7.5   Performance Metrics

Figures 10.19 and 10.20 show the various real-time LAN protocols discussed in this chapter. The performance metrics that are used to evaluate and compare these protocols are given below:

• *Success ratio* (SR). This is defined as the ratio of the total number of messages successfully transmitted to the total number of messages that arrived in the system. The SR is an important metric that reflects the throughput of the network.

protocol name	message length	guarantee type
TDMA	fixed	deterministic (periodic message)
BRAM, MSAP	fixed	deterministic
FDDI	fixed	deterministic

Figure 10.19
Controlled access protocols

protocol name	message length	guarantee type
DCR, DCR-P, DOD-P	fixed	deterministic
Waiting Room	fixed	deterministic
VTCSMA	variable	best effort
PBCSMA	variable	best effort
MDCR	variable	best effort
LDCR	variable	best effort
LDCR-G	variable	deterministic
ELDCR	variable	deterministic

Figure 10.20
Contention-based protocols

• *Effective channel utilization* (ECU). This is the ratio of the time slots used for successful transmission of messages to the number of time slots that elapse until all messages are transmitted or dropped. A higher value of ECU would imply that the channel utilization due to successful message transmission is large compared to the total overhead due to collision and notifier transmission.

• *Normalized transmission length* (NTL). This is the ratio of the mean length of the transmitted messages to the mean length of the generated messages. The closer the value of NTL to one, the less the bias toward long or short messages. In other words, when a protocol offers an NTL of one, the protocol behaves independently of message service time and is therefore fair to messages of different lengths.

10.8   Summary

• Real-time messages have deadlines and are broadly classified into periodic messages and aperiodic messages.

• Three important issues distinguish the bus scheduling problem from the processor scheduling problem: task preemption, priority-level granularity, and buffering.

• A real-time protocol should ensure predictability and should have properties such as fairness, better utilization of resources, low run time overhead, and stability under transient overloads.

• Traditional 802.x MAC protocols are inadequate for real-time communication because they either resolve collision probabilistically or lead to priority inversion problems.

• Two types of guarantees can be provided to real-time messages, namely, a deterministic guarantee or a best-effort guarantee.

• Protocols can follow three approaches in an effort to guarantee aperiodic messages: periodic server, conservative estimation, and dynamic reservation.

• MAC protocols can be classified into two categories: controlled access protocols and contention-based protocols. In controlled access protocols, channel bandwidth is reserved for each node, whereas in contention-based protocols, nodes access the channel on a message-by-message basis.

• The switched LAN is proposed as a solution to increasing bandwidth requirements that cannot be supported by the real-time LAN. Traditional switched LAN protocols are unsuitable for real-time communication.

Exercises

1. Highlight the limitations of real-time LAN protocols with respect to the fundamental precepts of real-time communication, namely, guaranteed transmission, priority inversion avoidance, and low run time overhead.

2. Is it true that in the conservative estimation approach, guarantees of successful message transmission can be given independent of the system load? Justify your answer. Discuss the importance of choosing M_{est} correctly for the LDCR-G protocol in this context.

3. Explain the importance of the threshold value in the DOD-P and LDCR protocols.

4. Is it possible that the performance of the VTCSMA and PBCSMA protocols can fall as the message laxity is increased beyond a certain point? Explain.

5. Can the success ratio fall and effective channel utilization simultaneously increase? Explain why or why not.

6. Explain why best-effort protocols offer better performance than guarantee-based protocols.

7. Derive an admission test for the preorder DCR protocol along the lines of the one proposed for the LDCR-G protocol. Use terms from the LDCR-G admission test appropriately.

node index	N_1	N_2	N_3	N_4	N_5	N_6
(arrival,service,deadline)	(4,3,30)	(2,2,6)	(0,1,3)	(3,4,7)	(5,4,16)	(16,3,23)

Figure 10.21
Exercise 10.11 message set

node index	N_1	N_2	N_3	N_4	N_5	N_6	N_7
(service,deadline)	(5,27)	(7,34)	(3,10)	(2,11)	(4,17)	(3,21)	–

Figure 10.22
Exercise 10.13 message set

8. In the VTCSMA protocols, can the VC span an interval of virtual time more than once? Explain how this affects message transmission.

9. Can the ELDCR protocol be adapted for switched LANs having several hops/switches between LAN segments? What information is required for the admission test?

10. (a) Show an example having two messages in the message set whose deadlines can be met without pacing and cannot be met with pacing.

(b) Suggest a way to schedule the following message sets without pacing loss. Comment on the relationship between scheduling potential and the ratio p/n.

i. a three-packet message with a period of 10.

ii. a three-packet message with a period of 13.

11. Show the channel (bus) status during the working of the PBCSMA protocol for the message set in figure 10.21, given that the laxity threshold is 5 time slots. Compute the success ratio for the message set.

12. The following problem is to be worked out using the waiting room protocol. Consider a 10-node LAN. Given a message size of 5 time slots, with overhead for arbitration of 2 time slots, calculate the worst-case channel access time for

(a) a message inside the waiting room.

(b) a message in the front of the send queue.

(c) a message occupying (i) $k = 5$ and (ii) $k = 20$ positions in the send queue.

13. The following problem is to be worked out using the LDCR, MDCR, and LDCR-G protocols. Given the message set in figure 10.22, at some time instant t for a seven-node LAN, with the threshold value of 1:

(a) Draw the time axis and indicate the state of the channel as various events occur for the LDCR and MDCR protocols.

(b) Give the success ratio and channel utilization for each of the above protocols.

(c) Which protocol is better? Explain.

(d) Find an expression for N_{col} in the LDCR-G protocol.

(e) i. Calculate the worst-case channel access delay for a message (6,395) at node 7 with position 5 in the send queue. Assume $M_{est} = 10$, $Time\_for\_Not = 1$, and collision overhead $= 1$ slot.

ii. Will the above message be admitted?

14. This problem is to be worked out for the ELDCR switched LAN protocol, given the example LAN topology in figure 10.16, where LAN_1 and LAN_3 have five nodes, and LAN_2 has seven nodes. A message $(5, 552)$ is to be transmitted from node 4 in LAN_1, having rank 3, to node 3 in LAN_3, with the virtual node already containing two messages in its send queue. Assume that the worst-case method is adopted where every LAN segment is assigned the last virtual node in the WCCR tree.

(a) Compute the worst-case channel access delay WCT_{mesg} of the intersegment message. Will the message pass the admission test using the same parameters as in question 13?

(b) If so, compute a worst-case bound on the number of messages that will arrive at the centralized switch in the time interval $[t, t + WCT_{mesg}]$.

References

[1] M. Anita, G. Manimaran, and C. Siva Ram Murthy. "Dynamic real-time channel establishment in multiple access bus networks." In *Proc. Intl. Workshop on Parallel and Distributed Real-Time Systems,* Springer, Berlin, 1999 (Lecture Notes in Computer Science—1586, pp. 319–328).

[2] C. M. Aras, J. F. Kurose, D. S. Reeves, and H. Schulzrinne. "Real-time communication in packet-switched networks." *Proc. IEEE,* vol. 82, no. 1, pp. 122–139, Jan. 1994.

[3] K. Arvind, K. Ramamritham, and J. A. Stankovic. "A local area network architecture for communication in distributed real-time systems." *Real-Time Systems,* vol. 3, no. 2, pp. 115–147, Mar. 1991.

[4] K. Arvind, K. Ramamritham, and J. A. Stankovic. "Window MAC protocols for real-time communication services." Technical report, University of Massachusetts, Amherst, 1992.

[5] C. C. Chou and K. G. Shin. "Statistical real-time channels on multi-access bus networks." *IEEE Trans. Parallel and Distributed Systems,* vol. 8, no. 8, pp. 769–780, Aug. 1997.

[6] D. E. Comer and D. L. Stevens. *Internetworking with TCP/IP. Vol. 2.* Prentice-Hall International, Englewood Cliffs, NJ, 1994.

[7] FDDI Media Access Control (MAC), ANSI Standard X3T9.5, Rev. 4.0, 1990.

[8] N. Homayoun and P. Ramanathan. "Dynamic priority scheduling of periodic and aperiodic tasks in hard real-time systems." *Real-Time Systems,* vol. 6, pp. 207–232, June 1994.

[9] IEEE 802.1d. "IEEE Std-802.1d—1990. Standards for local and metropolitan area networks: Medium access control (MAC) bridges." IEEE, New York, 1990.

[10] R. Jain. "FDDI: Current issues and future plans." *IEEE Communications,* pp. 98–105, Sept. 1993.

[11] D. D. Kandlur, K. G. Shin, and D. Ferrari. "Real-time communication in multi-hop networks." *IEEE Trans. Parallel and Distributed Systems,* vol. 5, no. 10, pp. 1044–1055, Oct. 1994.

[12] S. H. Khayat and B. D. Bovopoulos. "A simple and efficient bus management scheme that supports continuous streams." *ACM Trans. Computer Systems,* vol. 13, no. 2, pp. 122–140, May 1995.

[13] J. F. Kurose, M. Schwartz, and Y. Yemini. "Multiple access protocols and time-constrained communication." *ACM Computing Surveys,* vol. 16, no. 1, pp. 43–70, Mar. 1984.

[14] J. P. Lehoczky and L. Sha. "Performance of real-time bus scheduling algorithms." In *Proc. Performance '86,* pp. 44–53, 1986.

[15] G. Le Lann and N. Rivierre. "Real-time communications over broadcast networks: The CSMA-DCR and the DOD-CSMA-CD protocols." Technical report, Institut National de Recherche en Informatique et en Automatique, France, Mar. 1993.

[16] C. L. Liu and J. W. Layland. "Scheduling algorithms for multiprogramming in a hard-real-time environment." *Journal of ACM,* vol. 20, no. 1, pp. 45–61, Jan. 1973.

[17] N. Malcom and W. Zhao. "Hard real-time communication in multiple-access networks." *Real-Time Systems,* vol. 8, no. 1, pp. 35–77, 1995.

[18] M. Molle and G. Watson. "100 Base-T/IEEE 802.12/packet switching." *IEEE Communications,* vol. 34, no. 8, pp. 64–73, Aug. 1996.

[19] S. K. Oh and G. H. Macewen. "Task behaviour monitoring for adaptive real-time communication." *Real-Time Systems,* vol. 11, no. 2, pp. 173–195, 1996.

[20] K. Ramamritham. "Channel characteristics in local-area hard real-time systems." *Computer Networks and ISDN Systems,* vol. 13, no. 1, pp. 3–13, 1987.

[21] K. Ramamritham and J. A. Stankovic. "Scheduling algorithms and operating systems support for real-time systems." *Proc. IEEE,* vol. 82, no. 1, Jan. 1994.

[22] F. B. Ross. "An overview of FDDI: The fiber distributed data interface." *IEEE JSAC,* vol. 7, no. 7, pp. 1043–1051, Sept. 1989.

[23] N. Samphel, S. Balaji, G. Manimaran, and C. Siva Ram Murthy. "Deterministic best effort and planning based protocols for real-time communication in multiple access networks." In *Proc. Intl. Workshop on Parallel and Distributed Real-Time Systems,* Orlando, FL, 1998.

[24] N. Samphel, G. Manimaran, and C. Siva Ram Murthy. "New protocols for hard real-time communication in the switched LAN environment." In *Proc. IEEE Conference on Local Computer Networks,* 1998.

[25] N. Samphel, S. Balaji, G. Manimaran, and C. Siva Ram Murthy. "Deterministic protocols for real-time communication in multiple access networks." *Computer Communications,* vol. 22, no. 2, pp. 128–136, Jan. 1999.

[26] K. G. Shin and P. Ramanathan. "Real-time computing: A new discipline of computer science and engineering." *Proc. IEEE,* vol. 82, no. 1, pp. 6–24, Jan. 1994.

[27] A. S. Tanenbaum. "Computer networks." Prentice-Hall Inc., Englewood Cliffs, NJ, 1989.

[28] M. Teener and R. Gvozdanovic. "FDDI-II operation and architecture." In *Proc. IEEE Conference on Local Computer Networks,* pp. 49–61, 1989.

[29] O. Ulusoy. "Network access protocol for hard real-time communication systems." *Computer Communications,* vol. 18, no. 12, pp. 943–948, Dec. 1995.

[30] V. Upadhya. "Design and analysis of real-time LAN protocols." M.S. thesis, Department of Computer Science and Engineering, Indian Institute of Technology, Madras, Jan. 1996.

[31] J. C. Valadier and D. R. Powell. "On CSMA protocols allowing bounded channel access times." In *Proc. Intl. Conference on Distributed Computing Systems,* 1984.

[32] D. Venkatesulu and T. A. Gonsalves. "Efficient fault-tolerant reliable broadcast in a multi-switch extended LAN." *Computer Communications,* vol. 22, no. 3, pp. 266–278, Feb. 1999.

[33] L. Yao and W. Zhao. "Performance of an extended IEEE 802.5 protocol in hard real-time systems." In *Proc. IEEE INFOCOM,* 1991.

[34] R. Yavatkar, P. Pai, and R. Finkel. "A reservation-based CSMA protocol for integrated manufacturing networks." *IEEE Trans. Systems, Man and Cybernetics,* vol. 24, no. 8, pp. 1247–1257, Aug. 1994.

[35] W. Zhao and K. Ramamritham. "Virtual time CSMA protocols for hard real-time communication." *IEEE Trans. Software Engg.,* vol. 13, no. 8, pp. 938–952, Aug. 1987.

[36] W. Zhao, J. A. Stankovic, and K. Ramamritham. "A window protocol for transmission of time constrained messages." *IEEE Trans. Computers,* vol. 39, no. 9, pp. 1186–1203, Sept. 1990.

11 Case Study: Distributed Air Defense System

Overview

In this chapter, we first present the problem of designing a distributed air defense system. This problem was posed as part of the call for papers for the Fifth IEEE International Workshop on Parallel and Distributed Real-Time Systems, held in Geneva April 1–3, 1997, for which outline solutions were requested [1]. Here, based on the various concepts presented in earlier chapters of this book, we present a solution for this problem.

11.1 Problem Specification

The problem under consideration is to design a distributed air defense system capable of simultaneously handling up to 10,000 *tracks* of possible *threats* (targets), up to 1,000 known threats (tracks that have been definitively identified as targets), and up to 100 *engagements* (in which a defensive weapon is being employed against a known target). Tracks of possible threats may include many things other than threats, like civilian aircraft in the area, friendly aircraft, decoys, and birds, as well as real threats.

This system is to consist of 10 *mobile nodes,* each of which can handle at least 1,000 tracks, 1,000 targets, and 10 engagements. These nodes will be deployed throughout the battlespace and will cooperate in providing the overall air defense. The nodes will be interconnected by a relatively low-bandwidth medium (500 KB/sec) because of the need to encrypt all transmissions. Each node can have a single processor or a multiple processor computer or can consist of a LAN of individual computers (e.g., workstations).

Each node will be deployed with a battery of defensive weapons (e.g., missiles) and 10 launchers for those weapons. Each defensive weapon requires guidance from its associated node to home in on its target. It must receive guidance update information at least once per second after it has been launched. If it receives no guidance update for longer than three seconds, then it can be assumed to be lost.

The differences in orders of magnitude from 100 to 1,000 to 10,000 are merely reflections of physical limitations of the problem. Since there are a total of 100 launchers in the system, this is the maximum number of engagements that can occur simultaneously. It is recognized that it is impossible to implement a single-node system that can handle the entire air defense problem. Furthermore, such a single-node system would represent a single point of failure, and the intent here is to field a survivable, reliable system. Reliance is placed on the mobility of the nodes and the fact that the enemy will not always know where all the nodes are prior to an enemy strike. It is under-stood that if the enemy were to direct all of its effort at a single node, it could over-whelm that node. Overloaded nodes should therefore be able to hand off processing of the most critical functions to nodes that have underutilized processing capacity at that time.

The nodes of the system get their information about tracks from three sources. First, each node has its own radar system; second, it gets track information from other nodes when those nodes are overloaded; and third, a satellite battlefield surveillance system downlinks encrypted track information to the nodes at up to 10 Mb/sec. To utilize the satellite down-link broadcast capability, a mobile node must communicate track information over the 500 KB medium described above to uplink it to the satellite. The only advantage of doing this is that the track information is then broadcast to all the mobile nodes simultaneously.

Track data (tracks) consist of 256 bytes of information that includes a unique identifier for the track plus all the relevant information about the track (e.g., coordinates, velocity, various attributes). There needs to be a method for ensuring that the target information is consistent among nodes in the event that the area of operation of one or more nodes overlaps. It is desirable that *all* track information be consistent among nodes, but as a minimum all target information must be consistent. This capability is needed to ensure that multiple batteries (nodes) will not engage the same target simultaneously and that all nodes can distinguish friendly tracks from targets.

Each local radar subsystem, because of its physical characteristics, produces information on tracks in its local region once a second, so this part of the problem is periodic in nature. However, tracks can appear aperiodically on the radar screen and also vanish aperiodically. Consequently, during any given one-second interval, the system does not know how many local tracks it is going to receive, and it is possible that it will receive more than the 1,000 tracks it is designed to handle. Also, overload tracks from other nodes are received aperiodically. Track information from the satellite surveillance system is also received periodically once a second. There is a requirement that once a track appears from any source, it must be tested within 2 seconds to determine whether it is in fact a target. The tests performed to make this determination may not be conclusive, in which case, within another second, the track may still be on the radar, and processing in that case will need to be continued to try to determine if the track is a target. These tests are based on certain attributes, like the radar cross-section of the track, its velocity, and its position. Each second, an as yet unidentified track may contain information that it did not contain during the last one-second interval that may allow for a successful classification. The classification process goes on until the track either disappears from the screen, is identified as a nontarget, or gets so close that it is automatically classified as a target.

When a track is classified as a target, it then has to be monitored once a second each time the radar illuminates the target. All targets get illuminated approximately once a second, but since the targets are moving with respect to the radar, the time interval between successive illuminations may not be constant, and therefore need not be strictly periodic for an individual target. During this monitoring of the target, additional tests are run to determine its lethality, which influences its significance. Finally, once a target is identified, it must be engaged within 2 seconds, provided there is a weapon system available to engage it, with priority being given to engaging the most significant threats first. For targets that are currently engaged, guidance update information has to be relayed to the defensive weapon that has been dispatched every second while it is homing in on the target.

Since track information is arriving from multiple sources simultaneously, it has to be correlated. Even track information from the local radar must be periodically correlated, which has to do with the fact that tracks frequently "cross" on the display, corresponding to points in time when the radar cannot distinguish two physically distinct tracks for two targets and therefore may not know, for instance, what direction applies to which track without doing a "correlation" calculation. Correlations between local tracks and those received from other nodes or the surveillance system must be conducted to ensure the consistency of track information among nodes. A track sent by a remote node may turn out to be identical to one of the tracks the local node already knows about.

Each requirement corresponding to the deadlines of 1 second and 2 seconds has an associated significance. If, for example, the calculation associated with one of the 1,000 tracks were to miss its deadline, this normally would not be as significant as if the processing associated with one of the 100 targets missed its deadline, which in turn would not be as significant as if one of the engaged weapons (in-flight missile) missed its guidance update deadline. It should be possible for the engagement controllers (users) to dynamically change these significances.

Not all threats have the same lethality (one attribute of a target). One incoming target may have the capability to wipe out the entire air defense system, whereas another may have the capability only to degrade its performance, thereby rendering the second target less significant than the first. The air defense system is also responsible for protecting other assets in the area as well as itself. Some identified targets may not be approaching the air defense system but moving toward one of these assets. The value of that asset then also affects the significance of the target. How close a target is to the asset(s) it is threatening is another factor that affects the significance of a target. The air defense system must be designed to defend against targets of highest significance first and the others in decreasing order of significance as resources permit.

To complicate the situation, the enemy may field thousands of decoys, or the system may have to be used in congested areas (e.g., the Persian Gulf) where friendly aircraft in the vicinity together with civilian traffic and enemy threats temporarily exceeds the capacity of a given node in one way or another, that is, more than 100 threats or more than 10 engageable targets. It is therefore impossible to design such a system so that it will never encounter overload.

11.2   Solution

We now present a solution, called DREAD (Distributed REal-time Air Defense system), to the problem of distributed air defense described above [2]. The system consists of a set of 10 mobile nodes communicating with each other through a 500 KB/sec low-bandwidth medium and via a surveillance satellite. These nodes are deployed on the battlespace and coordinate with each other to satisfy the system requirements. The system is able to handle up to 10,000 tracks, up to 1,000 tracks identified as targets, and up to 100 tracks engaged by missiles. This involves analyzing tracks and determining whether they are targets, analyzing targets to determine their lethality, and providing the signaling required for missile guidance. Thus, this real-time problem reduces to scheduling different types of real-time tasks before their respective deadlines. In addition, the number of tracks, targets, or to-be-engaged tasks can temporarily exceed the capacity of a given node. Also, different nodes must coordinate with each other to avoid redundant engagements and to ensure a consistent view of all tracks by all nodes of the system. This entails not only scheduling the extra aperiodic real-time tasks needed to support the above activities but also efficient location, transfer, and information policies for load balancing and consensus protocols for ensuring a consistent view of all the tracks.

The rest of this chapter is organized as follows. Section 11.3 presents the system model in terms of the different modules and tables maintained to carry out the functions described above. Section 11.4 describes the different design aspects, including scheduling, load balancing, and consistency maintenance. Finally, section 11.5 presents a summary of the chapter.

11.3   System Model

Every node in the distributed system receives input from radar, satellite, and the network in the form of track information and processes this information to determine targets, computes

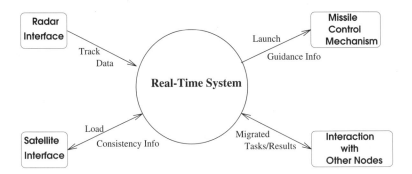

Figure 11.1
Overview of DREAD at each node

these targets' lethality, and finally, launches and guides missiles to hit these targets. In addition, the different nodes in the system coordinate among themselves to balance load and to ensure a consistent view of all the tracks among all nodes of the system. Figure 11.1 gives an overview of the real-time system at each node.

The system can be represented in the form of modules, each containing a few tasks, as shown in figure 11.2. Tasks belonging to each type carry out some of the above functions and trigger further tasks to be executed by other modules. The different modules and tables within each node are as follows:

1. *Input module.* Information is received by the input task (I) at every node from the following three sources:

(a) Radar—a continuous stream of tracks from objects within the area of operation

(b) Satellite—load balancing and consistency related information

(c) The network—migrated tasks and results of migrated computation

This information may be received by the input module synchronously or asynchronously. We assume that time is divided into slices of T seconds and that a correlation task (C) is created for the set of tracks arriving between kT and $(k + 1)T$, where $k \in I^+$.

2. *Correlation module.* The correlation task (C) in this module correlates newly arrived track information with old track information for the current node and checks if new information received corresponds to a known track. It triggers new tasks either to continue with the existing analysis, if the track included in the new information is identified as identical to an existing track, or to start analysis, if the track is identified as new. In addition, the correlation and arbitration (CA) task correlates tracks among different nodes to ensure a

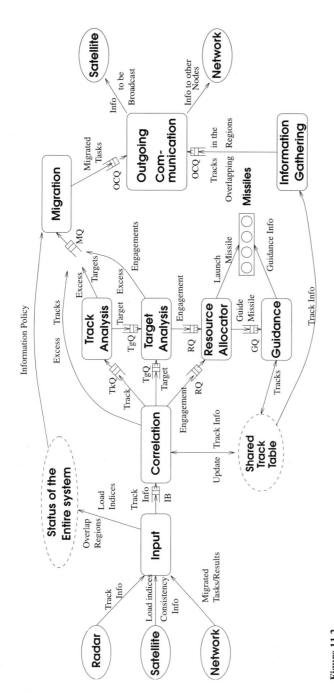

Figure 11.2
DREAD system diagram

consistent view of tracks that fall where neighboring areas of operation overlap and decides which node takes responsibility for such common tracks.

3. *Track analyzer.* This module is realized by two tasks, namely the track analysis task (Tk) and the migrated track analysis task (MTk). The task Tk analyzes new information received about tracks (possibly using the old information) and classifies them as a target, not a target, or a track (classification must wait until further information is available). When a target is identified, a target analyzer task (Tg) (see item 4) is created. The task MTk analyzes migrated tracks (see item 7) and passes on the results to the communication module to be sent back.

4. *Target analyzer.* This module is also realized by two tasks, namely, the target analysis task (Tg) and the migrated target analysis task (MTg). The task Tg analyzes both old and new information about targets and determines, if possible, the lethality of each target. It also determines the priority level for engagement of each target, depending on its lethality. Then it triggers a resource allocator task (R) (see item 5). The task MTg analyzes migrated target information (see item 7) and passes on the computed lethality to the communication module.

5. *Resource allocator.* The resource allocator task (R) in this module allocates targets to missile launchers, treating each launcher as a resource. Priority is given to each target based on its lethality. Whenever a target is assigned to a missile launcher, a launch task (L) is created (see item 6). The resource allocator may be able to calculate the expected time for the missile to hit the target and do a look-ahead scheduling of subsequent targets.

6. *Guidance module.* The launch task (L) launches the missile, performs a one-time precomputation of information necessary for guiding the missile to its target, and creates a guidance task (G). The guidance task is a self-triggering task that provides the guidance information required by a missile for a period of 1 second, then triggers another guidance task. This sequence continues until the missile either hits or misses the target. At that point, a resource allocator task is triggered, which checks if another target can be engaged.

7. *Migration module.* The migration task (Mg) in this module executes the location policy algorithm, which determines the destination for tasks to be migrated from an overloaded node, based on load and link information. The correlation and the track analysis modules transfer tracks to the migration module whenever the number of tracks or targets at a particular node goes beyond the specified limits.

8. *Outgoing communication module.* The communication task (Cm) schedules outgoing messages and communicates them to other nodes or to the satellite survelliance

system. The required scheduling and transmission functions can be implemented in hardware.

9. *Information module.* The information-gathering (IG) task in this module periodically computes the following data to be broadcast to all nodes in the system via the satellite:

(a) Load index: denotes the amount of processing capacity being used at the current node

(b) Link usage

(c) Area of operation: the region of influence over which the current node's radar can observe

(d) Information on the tracks that fall in the region where the node's area of operation intersects with that of another node.

10. *Maintenance module.* The maintenance task (Mt) in this module periodically executes certain maintenance tasks, such as purging old unused track information and validating the results of consensus protocols.

11. *Shared track table.* The above modules share a common data table called the shared track table (STT). This table stores the current information about each track as well as all the necessary older information for correlation, track analysis, target analysis, resource allocation, and guidance. It maintains the status of analysis for each track, which can be any one of the following:

• Track analysis not yet complete

• Friendly track

• Identified as a threat, target analysis yet to be done

• Identified as a target, resource allocation not yet done

• Resource allocation complete, guidance in progress

• Free entry

11.4   System Design Aspects

In this section, we discuss different aspects in the design of the system. We consider a number of different issues:

• *Real-time scheduling.* We present a scheme for scheduling both periodic and aperiodic tasks.

• *Load balancing.* We discuss how excess tracks are migrated to underutilized nodes.

	task type	period	resources	priority	module	deadline
	Periodic Tasks:					
1	Input Task (I)	T	IB	Medium	1	$a + d_1$
2	Guidance Task (G)	1	Launcher	High	6	1
3	Information Gathering (IG)	t_1	STT	Low	9	t_1
4	Maintenance Task (Mt)	t_2	STT,OCQ	Low	10	t_2
5	Correlation and	1	–	Low	2	1
	Arbitration Task (CA)					
	Aperiodic Tasks:					
6	Correlation Task (C)	–	IB,STT,TkQ	Medium	2	$a + d_2$
			TgQ,RQ,GQ,MQ			
7	Track Analysis (Tk)	–	TkQ,TgQ	Low	3	$a + 2$
8	Target Analysis (Tg)	–	TgQ,RQ	Medium	4	$f + d_3$
9	Resource Allocation (R)	–	RQ,GQ	High	5	$f + 2$
10	Launch Task (L)	–	Launcher	High	6	$f + 2 + d_4$
11	Migrated Track Analysis (MTk)	–	TkQ,TgQ	High	3	$a + 2 - c$
12	Migrated Target Analysis (MTg)	–	TgQ,RQ	High	4	$f + d_3 - c$
13	Migration Task (M)	–		High	7	k
14	Communication Task (Cm)	–	OCQ	Medium	8	–

Figure 11.3
Task types and their attributes

- *Coordination.* We discuss how different nodes coordinate with each other to provide a consistent view of the system.

11.4.1 Real-Time Scheduling

The operating system executing at each node schedules the different tasks generated at that node onto a set of processors. The scheduling scheme can schedule both periodic and aperiodic tasks and also incorporates resource reclaiming.

11.4.1.1 Task Model The system has both periodic and aperiodic tasks, as given in figure 11.3. Each task is a 7-tuple of the form

$\langle NodeId, TaskId, TaskType, Period, ResourcesRequired, Deadline, Priority \rangle.$

Tasks at each node are assigned a unique task-id, and hence, the $\langle NodeId, TaskId \rangle$ tuple is unique for each task. All periodic tasks are associated with a specified period. The periods T, t_1, and t_2 are tunable parameters that can trade off overhead against timeliness. Higher values of T, t_1, and t_2 are associated with lower overhead because the corresponding tasks are invoked less frequently; however, tracks can be correlated only at the end of T, t_1, and t_2 units of time, causing loss of timeliness. A balance between these two conflicting requirements must be achieved. Tasks may also use resources in shared or exclusive mode. In our case, all resource usage is in shared mode.

All tasks are associated with deadlines (d_i), which are defined with a constant offset from the task's arrival time. The values of d_1, d_2, d_3, and d_4 can be tuned so as to optimize the schedulability of the associated tasks. The deadlines ultimately result from the different basic *deadline constraints* in the system. The basic deadline constraints in the system are as follows:

1. All periodic tasks must complete execution before the completion of their period. This automatically ensures that guidance information is provided once a second.

2. Tasks I, C, and Tk together must be done within 2 seconds once an input track triggers this set of tasks.

3. Tasks Tg and R must be done within 2 seconds once a target has been identified.

In addition, each deadline requirement is associated with a significance. Hence, we associate each task with a priority, which may be low, medium, or high. When all tasks that have arrived cannot be scheduled, the scheduler picks the tasks with the highest priority for scheduling so that the most significant deadlines are met. a is the arrival time of a particular track, and f is the finish time of track analysis. c is a measure of the communication delay between the source and destination nodes in the case of migrated tasks.

Since a new track can trigger either a Tk, Tg, or R task, any of the three task triggerings can happen as shown in the precedence graph in figure 11.4.

11.4.1.2 System Model   The system model at each node is shown as part of the task-level diagram (upper portion) in figure 11.5. Each node has a set of processors communicating via shared memory. The processors are divided into two sets for executing periodic (*periodic processors*) and aperiodic (*aperiodic processors*) tasks. Each aperiodic processor is associated with a dispatch queue from which it continually picks up the next task and executes it, whereas the periodic processors dispatch the arriving periodic tasks using a precomputed schedule, which is stored in the form of a table. The scheduler runs in parallel with the processors, scheduling newly arriving aperiodic tasks. The schedule so formed is used to periodically update the dispatch queues. This is done to ensure that the processors will always find some tasks in the dispatch queues when they finish executing the current task. A resource reclaiming algorithm is invoked by a processor at the completion of each of its tasks. Resource reclaiming algorithms running at the aperiodic

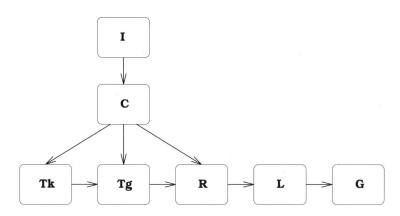

Figure 11.4
Task precedence graph

processors periodically inform the scheduler about the amount of time reclaimed, so that the scheduler uses this time in scheduling subsequent aperiodic tasks. At the periodic processors, if the resource reclaiming algorithm is not able to execute the next periodic task in its dispatch table, it picks up an aperiodic task whose worst-case execution time is less than the reclaimed time from the aperiodic task queue. In addition, the scheduler also coordinates with the information-gathering module to calculate a load index for the node. This load index can be a function of average processor queue length and queue length of the aperiodic processors.

11.4.1.3 Scheduling Strategy   We assume that it is possible to schedule all local tasks if there are less than 1,000 tracks, 100 targets, and 10 engagements. Hence, we first precompute a schedule (static table-driven approach) for the worst-case number of periodic tasks that could be generated for a specified level of input, using the minimum number of processors. The rest of the processors can then be used to schedule the aperiodic tasks (using a dynamic planning-based approach). When tasks in the static periodic schedule and the dynamic aperiodic schedule are executed, many holes may be created in the schedule through task deallocation and tasks executing at less than their worst-case computation time, which necessitates resource reclaiming. Thus, the scheduling strategy has the following three components:

1. *Scheduling periodic tasks.* We assume that enough resources are available so that each mobile node can solely handle the specified input limit: 1,000 tracks, 100 targets, and 10 engagements. We precompute a schedule S for all the periodic tasks for time $LCM(T, 1, t_1, t_2) = \tau$ assuming worst-case circumstances, that is, that the arriving input

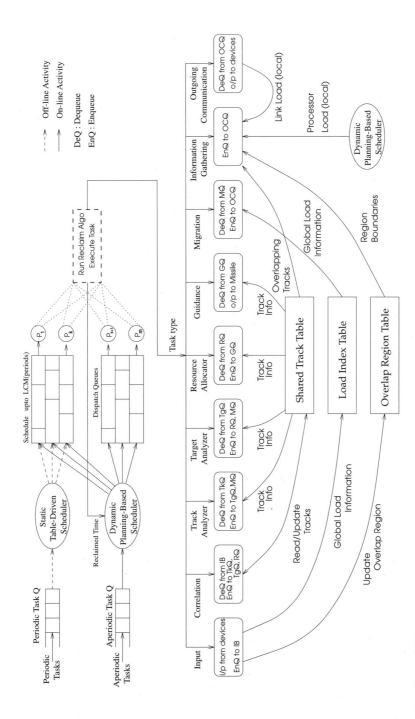

Figure 11.5
Task-level diagram of DREAD

is such that the total processor time required by the tasks it triggers is maximized. This would mean that

(a) $G_1, G_2, \ldots, G_{10}$: All 10 engagements are in progress.

(b) I, C, Tk, Tg, R, L: Each input track is a new track requiring track and target analysis, resource allocation, and launching.

(c) IG, Mt, G: All other modules execute for the worst-case amount of time.

An optimal schedule is precomputed once, using a search-based technique employing the minimum number of processors, and stored as a table. At run time, the processors execute tasks based on the table every τ units of time.

2. *Scheduling aperiodic tasks.* Aperiodic tasks are scheduled using a dynamic planning-based approach, which performs a schedulability check on-line for incoming tasks without violating the guarantees already given to existing tasks. If an incoming task fails the schedulability check, it is rejected. Otherwise, it is inserted into the schedule. We use the Spring (myopic) scheduling algorithm described in chapter 2. The aperiodic tasks to be scheduled are

• the MTk, MTg, Cm, and Mg tasks for internode load balancing and consistency.

• any extra I, C, Tk, Tg, R, and L tasks arriving due to excess input.

Whenever the backtracking limit is reached, one task is rejected. We must ensure that rejected tasks are less significant than the accepted ones. Hence, we base the choice of the rejected task on priority, with the least-priority task being rejected first (e.g., track analysis has lesser priority than target analysis). The recommended priorities for the task types are shown in figure 11.3.

3. *Resource reclaiming.* Resource reclaiming, discussed in chapter 3, is the problem of reclaiming resources when

(a) a task completes earlier than its worst-case time.

(b) some tasks do not get executed because of the nature of the input (task deallocation). Not every arriving track must undergo the entire sequence of track and target analysis, resource allocation, and launching. For example, a given track may trigger only a track analysis task.

However, the resource reclaiming algorithm must not lead to run time anomalies; that is, if real-time guarantees have been provided for a real-time task, then these guarantees should not be negated because of resource reclaiming. In addition to processor time, we can also reclaim missile launch facility time when a missile leaves one region, or it hits or misses its target.

The resource reclaiming algorithm executes on processors that would otherwise be idle. It seeks to execute the next task in the dispatch queue ahead of its scheduled start time. We use the RV algorithm described in chapter 3.

11.4.2   Load Balancing

To make use of processor capacity of any underutilized nodes, overloaded nodes should be able to hand off processing of critical functions, such as track and target analysis, and guidance computation to such nodes. We assume that although the computation required for missile guidance can be migrated, the signaling required for missile guidance must be sent from the node where the missile is launched. The three issues in load balancing are transfer policy, location policy, and information policy, as discussed in chapter 5:

1. *Transfer policy* (when to transfer). Tracks and targets are transferred when the input exceeds the specified limit of 1,000 tracks and 100 targets. Incoming tracks and identified targets are assigned unique identifiers starting from 1. When the number of tracks or targets goes beyond the limit, the correlation or track analysis modules detect this condition, and a certain number of tracks are passed on to the load balancing module for migration.

2. *Location policy* (where to transfer). The load balancing module uses global link usage and processor load index information to determine an appropriate destination node for each group of tracks it receives. It may choose randomly among a few of the lightest nodes to which a connection can be established, to avoid all nodes picking the lightest node as destination and overloading it.

3. *Information policy* (how to gather the necessary information). Processor load, link usage, and topology information are periodically gathered and broadcast via satellite by the information gathering module. This information is used by the location policy to choose a destination node for migrating the overload tasks.

11.4.3   Coordination

This subsection discusses how nodes coordinate with each other to maintain consistency of track information and to transfer the guidance task from one node to another in case a missile in air goes from one area of operation to another. Information gathering to support these tasks is done periodically, wherein the following parameters are calculated and communicated to the satellite:

1. Load index at the current node (computed based on a load estimation algorithm)

2. Area of operation information

3. Link information in terms of usage

4. Track information received from radar (in the overlapping areas of operation)

11.4.3.1 Consistency We must correlate tracks transmitted from different nodes to check if any of them match. Track data consists of 256 bytes of information that includes a unique identifier. We use a correlation algorithm to match this data and find identical tracks. This is undertaken to ensure that

1. all nodes distinguish friendly tracks from targets, and

2. no two nodes engage the same target.

If any matches among tracks are found, arbitration must be conducted to define a particular track either as a target or as a nontarget uniformly across nodes and to allow only one engagement per target identified.

Hence, we do the following. When a particular node has identified a given track as a target, then the other node(s) utilize this new information to modify their own tables. Then the track is assigned to the lighter (lightest) node, and the heavier (heaviest) node is asked to relinquish it unless that node has already engaged it. If one of the nodes has already engaged the target, the other node is asked to relinquish it. In case multiple engagements are found to be in progress, the node farther away from the target may be asked to abort its guidance of the missile it has sent. These activities can be conducted in either a centralized or a distributed manner. In a centralized scheme, the processing is done centrally and the results are broadcast via satellite to all the nodes. In a distributed scheme, which we use here, individual nodes carry out the above processing and engage a consensus protocol to ensure consistent arbitration. In our case, these functions are executed by the correlation and arbitration task.

11.4.3.2 Task Transfer If a track that is being monitored at the current node leaves the present area of operation and enters another, then all the information computed so far pertaining to the track is handed over to the neighboring node whose area the track has entered. If a missile is going out of range of guidance of one node, then the engagement task is handed over to the next node. These jobs are handled by the maintenance module, which passes on the information or the task to the communication task to be sent out.

11.5 Summary

In this chapter, we have outlined a solution for a distributed real-time air defense problem. In the solution, we have used a shared memory multiprocessor for each node. The solution addresses only the system's most crucial issues, such as scheduling, load balancing, and coordination among nodes. The solution has the following features:

• A schedule has been constructed statically at each node for the worst-case situation (i.e., maximum anticipated load on a node) using a static table-driven scheduling algorithm.

• To handle overloads due to an excess number of either tracks or targets, or to handle task migration from other nodes, a schedule has been constructed dynamically at each node using a dynamic planning-based scheduling algorithm.

• To utilize the system's resources efficiently, resource reclaiming is employed. Resources (processor time and missile launch facility time) are reclaimed when the actual computation time of a task is less than its worst-case computation time, and when a missile hits its target or goes out of a given node's region. The scheduler model allows resource reclamation from both periodic and aperiodic tasks.

• To balance any excess load that arises at a node, tracks are migrated to a suitable destination using transfer policy and location policy algorithms. The information about load at each node is collected using the satellite broadcast.

• To maintain a consistent view of track information among nodes, the nodes exchange their track information via satellite and correlate the information received.

References

[1] M. Boasson. "Report on the case-study session." In *Proc. IEEE Intl. Workshop on Parallel and Distributed Real-Time Systems,* pp. 105–107, Geneva, 1997.

[2] A. Manikutty, M. Shashidhar, G. Manimaran, and C. Siva Ram Murthy. "DREAD: Distributed REal-time Air Defense System." In *Proc. IEEE Intl. Workshop on Parallel and Distributed Real-Time Systems,* pp. 108–118, Geneva, 1997.

12 Case Study: Air Traffic Control System

Overview

In this chapter, we first present the problem of designing an air traffic control system. This problem was posed as part of the call for papers for the Sixth IEEE International Workshop on Parallel and Distributed Real-Time Systems, held in Florida March 30– April 3, 1998, for which outline solutions were requested. Here, based on the various concepts presented in earlier chapters of this book, we present a solution for this problem.

12.1 Problem Specification

Air traffic control presents many challenging problems in distributed real-time computing. The August 1997 issue of *IEEE Spectrum* [1] features an article that describes some of these challenges.

This problem statement has been developed in coordination with engineers who are involved with software upgrades to the U.S. air traffic control system (ATCS). Additionally, a U.S. air traffic controller was involved in producing the problem statement. Thus, the problem statement reflects characteristics of the U.S. ATCS. The United States is divided into 20 airspace regions called air route traffic control centers. Each center is further divided into sectors. An air traffic controller may control one or more air traffic sectors in a center. The airspace surrounding an airport is termed the TRACON (terminal radar approach control) area. The TRACON area is usually defined as a 40-mile radius around a major airport, up to an altitude of around 10,000 feet. Each TRACON receives control of aircraft that are landing at that TRACON's airport and passes control of aircraft that are leaving its airspace. The airport tower has final approach control of aircraft arriving at the airport and departure control of aircraft wanting to leave the airport.

The specific problem to be solved here is the design of an air traffic control system that is both fault-tolerant and scalable. The requirements of ATCSs include real-time aspects. Because of their criticality, ATCSs must continue to provide full functionality, even if some hardware processors or networks fail. The system must be able to handle varying loads. At a minimum, it must be capable of handling 2,600 flight plans and 700 active tracks in one center airspace region (these terms are defined in [1] and also in the following paragraphs). The ATCS also must be able to handle loads that exceed this minimum. Furthermore, there is no upper-bound (or worst-case) load, and the load varies significantly, so average load is a virtually useless characterization.

Functionally, the ATCS must be able to provide track prediction, conflict probe and alert, resolution advisories, and minimum safe altitude advisory warnings, as well as time-based arrival and departure metering. It must be able to display the available information (track, flight plan, metering lists, arrival lists, departure lists, flight strips, and weather data) up to 120 displays and allow various controller inputs to manipulate not only the display but also the track and flight plan information. The system must be able to send and receive data to and from surrounding centers, TRACONs, and towers. Finally, the system has to be able to provide recording of any data sent or received between processes and/or remote systems, as well as data while any process is running. The remainder of this section details these requirements.

This system must be able to acquire data and convert it into a format the controller can use. Data inputs include a maximum of 25 long- and short-range radars, with new radar or track information arriving every 5 seconds. Multiple radars may return radar hits on the same aircraft. From these multiple radar hits, a primary and secondary radar must be chosen for each aircraft. Radar data from all the different radars in the system must be mosaiced so that all the radar is projected onto a single plane of reference. Track information for an aircraft consists of its (x, y) coordinates, altitude, and beacon code. The beacon code is a unique numeric identifier that only one aircraft in a particular center airspace at a given instant can have. The system must be able to handle 2,600 flight plans that may be input from other centers, flight service stations, and bulk flight plan storage (tape storage). Flight plan data consists of aircraft identification, aircraft type and equipment, beacon code, filed airspeed, coordination fix, coordination time, requested altitude, and route of flight. Each time new track information is received, it must be correlated with flight plans stored in the system. Finally, weather information must be accepted, so that it can be used later for track prediction and can be displayed to the controller.

Several alert and advisory functions must be provided so that aircraft in the center airspace are safely separated. The system must provide a track prediction function as well as a conflict probe, alert, and advisory function that can provide an alert to the controller if two or more aircraft are too close to each other. The normal separation distances for aircraft over U.S. airspace are 5 miles horizontally and 1,000 to 2,000 feet vertically. The track prediction function must provide predicted future track positions of a given aircraft. The future track predictions of all aircraft must be examined to determine if the projected paths of any of the aircraft currently under control in the center airspace will put them in conflict with each other in the immediate future. The resolution advisor must provide the controller with a possible solution to current or future conflicts among aircraft. Finally, a minimum safe altitude warning function must be provided to alert the controller if an aircraft is flying in proximity to any type of natural or man-made obstructions in the airspace or is flying at an unsafe altitude, so that an action can be taken to avoid a possible collision.

A time-based metering function must be provided by the system to optimize arrival and departure aircraft flows and create a plan that satisfies the airport arrival rate restriction as well as increasing fuel efficiency and reducing delays. The time-based metering functionality must make use of performance models of all aircraft that fly in the center and TRACON regions and adapt to changes in the air traffic situation, controller imposed constraints, and pilot and airline preferences. Metering lists must be provided to the appropriate controllers, and the controllers must have the ability to manipulate these lists according to their aircraft sequence requirements.

The system must be able to handle up to 120 separate controller displays that will show center and sector boundaries, arrival and departure routes, aircraft positions, aircraft data (including aircraft ID, reported altitude, assigned altitude, and ground speed), metering arrival and departure lists, and weather information, as well as electronic flight strips. A flight strip consists of data the controller needs to know about an aircraft in order to control it. It contains at a minimum the following data: flight identification, aircraft data, true airspeed, estimated ground speed, sector number, computer identification number, strip number, previous posted fix, assigned altitude, coordination fix, coordination time, beacon code, and any remarks deemed appropriate. The controller must be able to update and modify the flight strip information, and these changes must be reflected on any other flight strips that may be displayed in the system. The displays must be able to accept controller inputs that modify flight plan information and track data as well as to provide the ability to hand off control of an aircraft from one sector to another sector.

Links for center-to-center and center-to-TRACON communications must be provided, so that flight plan data and track data can be passed on to other centers or TRACONs that may be receiving arrival flights or received from centers or TRACONs that are handing off departure flights. Links for this communication can also provide the TRACONs with the ability to talk to one another when flights are going from TRACON to TRACON and are not entering center airspace. These links can be also used to provide arrival and departure metering lists to adjacent centers as well as any flight plan or track information any center may want to request.

This system must offer a comprehensive data-recording facility that allows performance analysis of the system and data-recording reductions to provide specific information (flight, track, display, and controller input) about any and all aircraft, as well as information about internal process functionality, interprocess communication, and intercenter and inter-TRACON communications.

The required ATCS is a dynamic real-time system. As noted above, its load varies significantly over time and has no upper bound. Loading scenarios can vary significantly, hence the average loading of the ATCS is not a highly useful metric for schedulability and other analyses. Although an upper bound on load could possibly be imposed artificially, this may not be a cost-effective solution, since preallocation of computing resources for such a worst case would lead to very poor resource utilization. A dynamic resource management policy is thus preferred.

12.2   Solution

The ATCS is organized around three types of facilities (centers, TRACONs, and airport towers) along with the associated radar and weather-sensing equipment. The *centers* track aircraft flying at high altitudes between airports; the *TRACONs* handle aircraft ascending and descending to and from airports; and the *airport towers* monitor aircraft on the ground and provide landing and takeoff clearances. The various facilities in the system are also connected through communication links, which are used for exchanging flight plans and track data, and for coordination during handoffs. The ATCS must be capable of handling upwards of 2,600 flight plans and 700 active tracks per center airspace region with no upper bound on these parameters. It must support a variety of highly critical alert and advisory functions, provide for time-based arrival and departure metering at the airports, and coordinate the various facilities to ensure that all aircraft are continuously tracked from takeoff to landing. The system must display all relevant status information to up to 120 controller displays in addition to accepting inputs from the human controllers to manipulate system parameters and data. Finally, all system activities, including information about internal processes, interprocess communication, and interfacility communication, must be logged for the purpose of performance analysis. Such a specification requires that the system be dynamic, real-time, fault-tolerant, and scalable.

In this chapter, we present a solution to the air traffic control problem [2] using the dynamic path-based paradigm described in chapter 6. The rest of the chapter is organized as follows. In section 12.3, we present the system model and describe it in terms of the functional modules and the tables that have to be maintained to execute these functions. Section 12.4 then represents the system in terms of dynamic paths, identifying and classifying the paths based on the nature of their initiation, criticality, and timeliness properties. Section 12.5 discusses the various system design aspects, such as resource management, fault tolerance, interfacility communication, and coordination among the various facilities of the ATCS. Section 12.6 discusses in detail the path-scheduling mechanism and strategies for resource reclaiming. Finally, a summary of the chapter is presented in section 12.7.

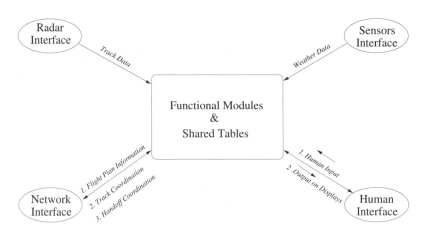

Figure 12.1
ATCS diagram: Node level

12.3   System Model

Each facility (center, TRACON, or airport tower) in the ATCS can be described in terms of the prescribed set of functions that it must perform. In the following discussion, we first describe a general node in the ATCS in terms of all the relevant functional modules and their interactions. Any facility in the actual ATCS can then be represented in terms of a subset of these modules, depending on the actual functions that the facility is expected to perform.

Every node in the system receives input from one or more of the following four sources: radar, weather-sensing equipment, other facilities (via the interfacility communication links), and air traffic controller personnel (figure 12.1). The functional modules at each node must coordinate with each other to ensure a consistent view of the system status using the data received from all these sources. The radar interface provides the track data, with new track information arriving every 5 seconds. The weather-sensing equipment provides data that goes into a weather information database for use during track prediction and for display. Information arriving via the communication links from other facilities includes flight plan information, track information, and coordination message exchanges during handoff (i.e., when flights pass from the airspace region under the control of one facility to that of another facility). Finally, inputs from air traffic controllers can include additions and/or deletions to system tables and flight strips as well as control instructions during sector-to-sector handoffs.

	table	read by	updated by
1	Track Table	TM, CM, DM, AAM, HM	TM, CM, HM
2	Flight Plan Table	TM, CM, DM, AAM, HM, LTMM	CM, HM
3	Topology Information Database	DM, HM	(static info)
4	Weather Information Database	DM, AAM	(from sensors)
5	Geographic Information Database	AAM	(static info)
6	Ground/Runway Status Table	LTMM, DM	LTMM

TM: Track Module   CM: Communication Module AAM: Alerts/Advisories Module
HM: Handoff Module DM: Display Module   LTMM: Landing/Takeoff Mgmt. Module

Figure 12.2
Access to shared information in ATCS

12.3.1 Tables and Databases

The system databases and tables (figure 12.2) used by the functional modules contain the following information:

1. *Track table.* This table contains the latest updated track information for every active track in the airspace region being handled by a given facility. The table includes, for every track, information such as the coordinates, altitude, beacon code, primary and secondary radar identification numbers, and last reported speed.

2. *Flight plan table.* This table is constructed using stored flight plans and is augmented by information received from other facilities via the interfacility communication links. It includes, for every registered flight plan, information such as aircraft ID, aircraft type and equipment, beacon code, filed airspeed, and route.

3. *Topology information database.* This database includes information regarding sector boundaries and TRACON/center airspace boundaries. This information is used for track coordination (in the track module) and for detecting handoffs. The information from this database is also displayed on the controllers' display screens.

4. *Weather information database.* The information received from the weather-sensing equipment or from other facilities is entered into this database and is used for track prediction.

5. *Geographic information database.* This database includes information about the presence of tall buildings and obstacles as well as restricted airspace regions and is used to detect altitude violations.

6. *Ground/runway status table.* This table contains all information regarding the nature and number of runways and ground facilities. It also indicates the allocation of aircraft to the runways and specifies the schedule of arrivals and departures. Current runway status information from the table is also output on controllers' display screens.

12.3.2   Functional Modules

As illustrated in figure 12.3, six basic functional modules can be identified in any node. These modules interact by sharing information present in the various system tables and databases. This interaction could also take the form of a task in one module initiating the creation of a task in another module. The different modules and their functions are described below.

12.3.2.1   Track Module   The track module receives track information from the radars associated with a particular facility and performs the following functions:

• *Track analysis* to identify whether the information corresponds to a fresh track or an existing track. In the case of a new track, the following actions are performed:

• *Track coordination* involves identifying whether the track occurs in a region of overlap with another facility. If it is, the two facilities involved coordinate to exchange their respective load indices (calculated based on the number of active tracks currently being handled by each). Based on this information, the two facilities independently make a consistent decision about which will assume responsibility for this common track (as discussed in section 12.5.3). The chosen facility then executes the rest of the functions outlined below.

• *Flight plan correlation* involves identifying the entry in the flight plan table that corresponds to the flight whose track has been spotted. This is accomplished by matching the beacon code present in the track information with an identical entry in the flight plan table. Suitable updates are made to both the track table and flight plan table to correlate any matching entries.

• *Radar selection* involves identifying a pair of primary and secondary radars for the new track and making entries in the track table to reflect this selection.

• *Track updating* enters the current (x, y) position and altitude of an aircraft specified in the track information into the track table. This must be done for both newly identified and existing tracks.

12.3.2.2   Alerts/Advisories Module   The alerts/advisories module is responsible for the following critical functions:

• *Conflict alert.* The coordinates and altitude information in the track table are continuously monitored to detect any violation of the specified minimum separation distances

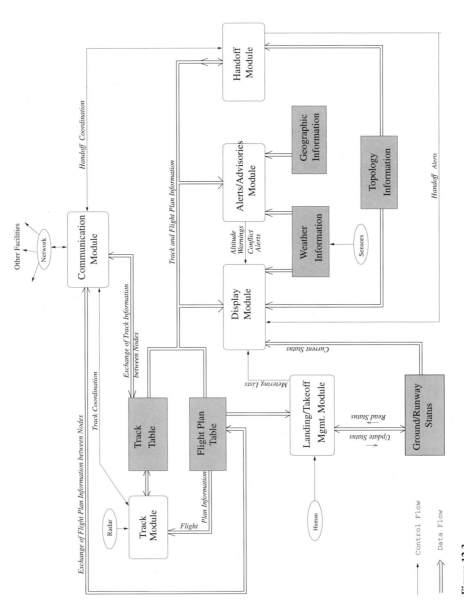

Figure 12.3
Module-level diagram of a node in ATCS

(5 miles horizontal and 1,000 to 2,000 miles vertical). If a violation is detected, two actions are initiated. The first action passes the relevant information about the conflict to the display module to be output on the display screens. Simultaneously, a conflict resolution task is initiated that is responsible for proposing a possible resolution to the detected conflict and passing the advisory information on to the display module.

• *Minimum altitude warnings.* The track table is continually scanned in conjunction with information present in the geographic information database to detect any minimum altitude violations and possible conflicts with obstacles and man-made structures. If a violation is detected, actions similar to those described above for flight path conflicts are initiated (i.e., alerting the human controller and also initiating the resolution advisory task).

• *Track and conflict prediction.* The information in the track table is used, along with data from the weather information database, to perform track prediction (which involves extrapolating the current route of the aircraft to project their positions at various times in the future). This enables detection of possible conflicts. If any such conflicts are detected, actions similar to those in the above two cases are initiated.

12.3.2.3   Handoff Module   The handoff module handles the situations when aircraft pass from the airspace region under control of one facility to the region under the control of another. From the point of view of any particular facility and its associated airspace, two cases are possible:

• *An aircraft is passing out of the airspace region.* Such handoff situations are detected by continuously monitoring the track table and interpreting the information contained in it in light of the data stored in the topology information database. Once the need for a handoff is detected, information about the handoff must be forwarded to the display module to alert the controller. The neighboring facility to which the control of the aircraft has to be passed is also identified based on the route specified in the flight plan table. The handoff module then interacts with the communication module to alert the neighboring facility and pass on the aircraft's track and, if necessary, its flight plan information. Communication between the handoff modules at the two facilities continues until the aircraft passes completely into the neighboring facility's airspace region.

• *An aircraft is entering the airspace region.* A facility's communication module forwards any handoff alerts received from adjacent facilities to the handoff module. The handoff module in turn forwards information about the impending handoff to the display module to alert the controller. It then examines the flight plan table to verify whether information about the incoming aircraft is already available. If not, it requests the required information from the facility that is handing off the aircraft and enters it into the track and flight plan tables.

12.3.2.4   Landing/Takeoff Management Module   The landing/takeoff management module applies only to airport towers or TRACONs that manage the arrival and departure of aircraft at nearby airports. It is equipped with information regarding ground and runway facilities at the airport, aircraft properties (regarding the nature and length of runway required), and other airline or pilot preferences. It also maintains and accesses the ground/runway status table. Using all the above information, the landing/takeoff management module generates arrival and departure metering lists and forwards the list to the landing and takeoff guidance systems. As aircraft arrive and depart, these systems make the necessary updates to the ground/runway status table.

12.3.2.5   Communication Module   The communication module uses the interfacility communication links to exchange flight plan and track information with other facilities and suitably updates the track and flight plan tables. It also interacts with the handoff module, both in communicating handoff alerts to neighboring facilities and in receiving handoff alerts from them. The track module uses the communication module for coordination when the tracks of in-flight aircraft take them into the region of overlap between two adjacent facilities. It is responsible for maintaining real-time communication channels and routing tables to execute its communication functions.

12.3.2.6   Display Module   The display module is responsible for managing up to 120 displays used for conveying information to the air traffic controller personnel. It has to perform the following functions:

• Format and display reasonably static information, such as sector and TRACON boundaries (from the topology information database) and current weather data and forecast (from the weather information database).

• Format and display continuously changing information from the track and flight plan tables and the ground/runway status table. This function includes generation of flight strips (using the track and flight plan information) and mapping various radar-generated coordinates into a single plane of reference.

• Respond to requests from other modules (such as the handoff module and alerts/advisories module) to display alerts and warnings.

The display module has the overall responsibility of ensuring that the information displayed on the various screens of the ATCS is consistent and that all updates to that information are simultaneously propagated to all the relevant screens.

12.4   System Representation Using Dynamic Paths

In this section, we describe a node in the ATCS in terms of dynamic paths, as defined in chapter 6. The dynamic path-based paradigm is convenient for specifying end-to-end system objectives and for analyzing the timeliness, dependability, and scalability of distributed real-time systems. The notion of a dynamic path is also useful for describing systems with dynamic variability, wherein the behavioral characteristics of the various tasks cannot be determined statically. The ATCS system, as modeled above, is quite suitable for applying the dynamic path paradigm for the following reasons:

• The system is a highly dynamic real-time system whose load can vary significantly over time with no upper bound. Therefore a system description that can accommodate this dynamic variability is required, and any static resource allocation scheme (based on an artificially imposed upper bound) will lead to poor resource utilization.

• Most of the system specifications directly translate into timeliness constraints (deadlines) only for higher-level execution paths. Therefore a task-based description of the system would require imposing artificial deadlines on individual tasks, whereas the problem specification imposes a timeliness constraint only on the execution of a sequence of tasks. For example, the fact that new radar input arrives once every 5 seconds requires only that the sequence of actions (track analysis, track coordination, flight plan correlation, radar selection, and track updation) be completed before the next radar input. The individual functions themselves have no deadlines.

• Finally, many of the situations in the ATCS are such that most of the tasks or functions have no prespecified deadlines. For example, when a conflict between aircraft paths is detected, the deadline before which a warning must be displayed to the controller and a resolution must be computed depends on when the conflict can be expected to occur, and so will vary from conflict to conflict. Similarly, upon receipt of a handoff alert from an adjacent facility, the handoff module at a given node must take the necessary actions to prepare for an incoming aircraft. The deadlines for these actions are, once again, dependent on the actual situation and the time difference between the receipt of the alert and the expected arrival of the aircraft in the receiving facility's airspace region. In such cases, the dynamic path-based paradigm is an appropriate mechanism for describing the system specifications.

A dynamic path is an abstraction of larger granularity than the traditional task abstraction. As mentioned in chapter 6, dynamic paths can be classified into the following categories (figure 12.4):

path no.	path type	characteristics
P1	Continuous	Data Source - Radar Data Streams - Tracks Data Consumer - Track Updation Task
P2	Continuous	Data Source - Track Table Data Streams - Table Entries Data Consumer - Conflict Detection Task
P3	Continuous	Data Source - Track Table Data Streams - Table Entries Data Consumer - Altitude Violation Detection Task
P4	Continuous	Data Source - Track & Flight Plan Tables Data Streams - Corresponding Entries from the (two) Tables Data Consumer - Track & Conflict Prediction Task
P5	Continuous	Data Source - Track and Flight Plan Tables Data Streams - Table Entries Data Consumer - Handoff Detection Task
P6	Continuous	Data Source - All the Relevant Tables and Databases Data Stream - Table Entries Data Consumer - Display Functions Task
P7	Continuous	Data Source - Ground/Runway Status Table Data Stream - Table Entries Data Consumer - Landing and Takeoff Systems
P8	Transient	Triggering Event - Detection of Conflict Ending Event - Display of Conflict Alert
P9	Transient	Triggering Event - Detection of Conflict Ending Event - Display of Computed Resolution
P10	Transient	Triggering Event - Detection of Altitude Violation Ending Event - Display of Alert
P11	Transient	Triggering Event - Detection of Future Conflict Ending Event - Display of Alert
P12	Transient	Triggering Event - Detection of Future Conflict Ending Event - Display of Computed Resolution
P13	Transient	Triggering Event - Detection of Handoff/Alert via Network Ending Event - Display of Handoff Alert
P14	Transient	Triggering Event - Detection of Handoff/Alert via Network Ending Event - Successful Handoff completion

Figure 12.4
Dynamic path characteristics in ATCS

- *Transient path (TP)*. This consists of an event source, an event stream, and an event consumer. A TP is activated by an event, which causes the consumer to initiate an action. The response to the event must occur within a specified amount of time, which is the *required latency* or *activation deadline* of this path. Usually, timeliness is very critical for TPs, and this deadline is hard. For example, path P9 in figure 12.5 is a TP that is activated upon conflict detection. The activation deadline for this path is the time within which the resolution must be computed and displayed on the relevant display screens. It is important to note that multiple conflicts can be detected in a short period of time, causing concurrent activations of this path.

- *Continuous path (CP)*. This consists of a data source, a data stream, and a data consumer. The data stream is a set of data elements with attributes. The data source cyclically produces updates about the attributes of the elements in the data stream that are then processed by the data consumer. The set of elements in the data stream can change with time. Such a CP can be characterized by its *cycle deadline,* which is the time by which all the elements in the data stream must have been processed once. *Tactical throughput* (the number of elements processed per unit time) and *data interprocessing time* (the time interval between successive updates to a data element) are measures that characterize the timeliness of a CP. Path P1 in figure 12.5 is an example of a CP. The data source is the radar sensors that produce tracks of aircraft in the facility's airspace region. The tracks of the various aircraft form the data elements, and the set of tracks constitutes the data stream. The track updation step, which processes new track information, acts as the data consumer. There is no upper bound on the number of data elements (tracks) that constitute the data stream. The data interprocessing time should ideally be less than 5 seconds, though this deadline is not hard.

- *Quasi-continuous path (QCP)*. This is activated and deactivated by events. However, between the activation and deactivation events, a QCP behaves like a CP, cyclically processing the items in a data stream. Each QCP has a *deactivation deadline,* which is the time by which it must be deactivated. In most applications, this deadline is determined upon activation. The landing and takeoff guidance systems typically contain QCPs that control the arrival and departure of aircrafts.

12.4.1   Example

In this section, we describe the object-level implementation of the flight plan correlation and radar selection element in path P1 of figure 12.5. As shown in figure 12.6, this software element is implemented in terms of three objects:

- *The correlation object (CO)*. This object exports a method Input, which is called by the track analysis software element to pass on track information. The function of this object

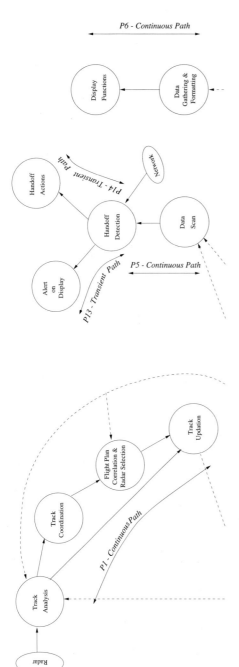

Figure 12.5
Dynamic path-level diagram of a node in ATCS

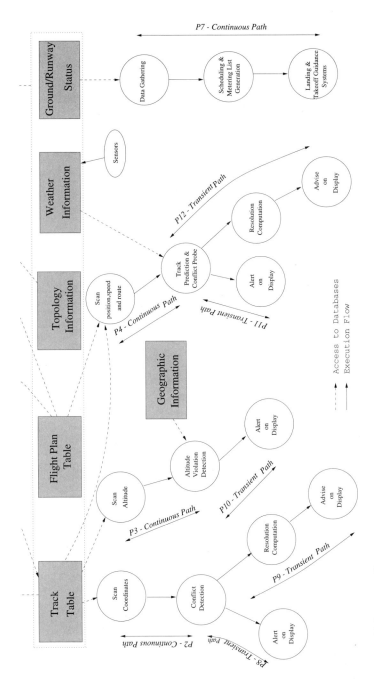

Figure 12.5 *(continued)*

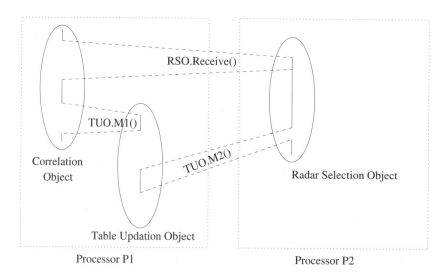

(a) Object interaction without cloning and ARPC

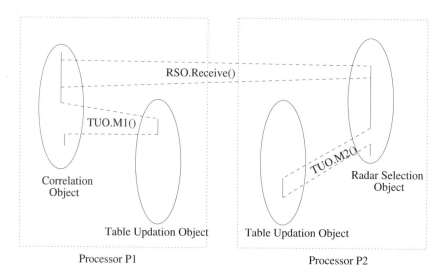

(b) Object interaction with cloning and ARPC

Figure 12.6
Cloning and ARPC

is to scan the stored flight plan table and identify the flight plan corresponding to a newly identified track. It then sends a message to the *table updation object* to create a new entry in the track table using the relevant information extracted from the flight plan table.

• *The radar selection object (RSO).* This object is responsible for identifying a primary and secondary radar for every newly identified track. It receives the track information from the CO (via the Receive method that this object exports), selects the primary and secondary radars, and passes on the selected radar IDs to the table updation object.

• *The table updation object (TUO).* This object exports two updation methods, *M1* and *M2,* which are called by CO and RSO respectively. Its function is to create a new track table entry using the information provided by the CO and update the radar IDs for this entry based on the information provided by RSO.

Figure 12.6(a) illustrates the interaction between the three objects when no asynchronous remote procedure call (ARPC) or cloning techniques are employed. CO and TUO are assumed to have been scheduled on a processor P1, whereas RSO is scheduled on a different processor P2. Figure 12.6(b) presents the same scenario, except that the method call *RSO.Receive* is implemented as an ARPC (wherein the calling object CO continues its processing without blocking for the method to return from RSO) and TUO is cloned on processor P2 (to reduce the communication overhead associated with method call *M2*).

12.5   System Design Aspects

This section presents some of the important aspects in the design of the air traffic control system. The following issues are considered here:

• *Interfacility communication.* We classify the information exchanged between adjacent nodes based on periodicity and criticality and identify mechanisms for meeting these communication requirements.

• *Fault tolerance.* We identify the most critical tasks among those that constitute the dynamic paths in the system and specify the techniques to be employed to make these critical tasks fault-tolerant.

• *Coordination.* When tracks fall in a region common to the airspace controlled by two adjacent nodes, we present a mechanism by which to decide which of the two nodes will take control of the common track.

• *Resource management.* We identify the need for scheduling at the path level and present a mechanism that combines off-line and on-line scheduling strategies. We also present techniques for reclaiming resources based on the run time scenario.

12.5.1   Interfacility Communication

The information exchanged between the various facilities in the ATCS falls into two major categories:

• Critical information exchanges between adjacent nodes take place during handoff and track coordination. This communication must be designed to be fault-tolerant and must satisfy timeliness constraints. We propose that real-time channels with deterministic guarantees (that is, absolute guarantees on available bandwidth, delay bound, packet loss rate, etc.) be established between each pair of adjacent nodes (nodes whose respective airspace regions either overlap or have a common border). To handle failures of interfacility links, we propose that every pair of adjacent nodes establish two such real-time channels connecting them. The primary channel is established via one of the shortest (based on hop count) paths connecting the two nodes. The secondary (backup) path is established so as to be link disjoint with the primary channel. Since the topology of the interfacility communication network in the ATCS is relatively static, the selection of routes for the primary and secondary channels between each pair of nodes can be determined a priori and stored in the routing tables of the communication modules at each node.

• Noncritical information exchanges between various nodes may include weather information, registered flight plans, and other information at a similar level of criticality. Since this communication is not expected to be as frequent as that conveying critical information, we propose that for such communication, real-time channels (with statistical guarantees) between the relevant nodes be created as and when required and then be released once the information transfer is over. To avoid excessive overhead due to channel establishment, information to be transmitted from one source node to another destination node is buffered until enough information has been collected to make it worthwhile to establish a channel. Piggybacking techniques can also be employed to reduce this overhead further.

12.5.2   Fault Tolerance

Figure 12.7 lists the most critical tasks in the system and the proposed approach for making each of these tasks fault-tolerant. Since the resolution computation task could conceivably have an acceptance test that verifies that the computed resolution does not generate any other flight path conflicts, the primary-backup (PB) approach (chapter 4) has been chosen for this task. Similarly, since it may need to be verified whether a given alert has actually been displayed on the controller's screen successfully, the PB approach has also been adopted for the alert on display task.

	critical task	approach to fault tolerance
1	Conflict Detection	TMR
2	Altitude Violation	TMR
3	Track Prediction & Conflict Probe	TMR
4	Resolution Computation	PB
5	Alert on Display	PB

Figure 12.7
Approach for ensuring fault tolerance of critical tasks in ATCS

12.5.3   Coordination

The airspace regions under the control of adjacent nodes in the ATCS may overlap. Tracks that fall within such an overlap region will be detected by both nodes. Coordination involves ensuring that the two nodes arrive at a consistent decision about which of them is to take control of the common track. We first define the *load index* at any given node as the number of active tracks being handled by that node. The following actions take place during coordination:

• Each node transmits to the other node its load index and proximity to the common track.

• The two nodes independently perform the following comparisons:

– If the two load indices are unequal, then the node with lower load index takes control of the track.

– In the case of matching load indices, the node that is closer to the track takes control.

12.5.4   Resource Management

Resource management in a dynamic real-time system involves both scheduling and reclaiming of resources. In the following sections, we identify the need for scheduling at the path level and present the system model to be employed at each node in the ATCS.

12.5.4.1   Scheduling at the Path Level   In a traditional task-level description of a distributed real-time system, the entities used for scheduling purposes are tasks. However, when the system is described in terms of the path-based paradigm, a scheduling strategy based on paths is more appropriate for the following reasons:

• The paths have well-defined deadlines and resource requirements directly implied by the specification of the system. The same is not true when extended to the task-level abstraction.

• Scheduling paths as a whole rather than scheduling individual tasks (that constitute these paths) makes more sense especially in the context of failures. For example, consider a path consisting of a sequence of four tasks (such as the path P1 in figure 12.5). Suppose the first two tasks execute successfully but the third task is not schedulable. In this case, the execution of tasks 1 and 2 results in a wastage of resources. A much better strategy would have been to initiate executions of tasks 1 and 2 only when it is guaranteed that the entire path is schedulable.

• Paths being an abstraction of larger granularity than tasks, the number of scheduling entities to be handled by the scheduling algorithm is smaller in the case of a path-based scheduler. This results in lower scheduling cost.

12.5.4.2 System Model   The computing platform at each node in the ATCS consists of a distributed system of processing nodes (PNs), each of which could either be a uniprocessor or a multiprocessor system. These processing nodes are connected via a multiple access local area network (such as a high-speed Ethernet or token ring network) with software support for handling real-time communication with deterministic guarantees. Each processing node is conceptually composed of the following types of processors sharing a common memory:

• *Computational processors* that execute the actual tasks

• A *scheduling processor* that executes the scheduler and the associated routines at run-time

• A *communication processor* to handle real-time communication between the processing nodes

The paths to be scheduled can be created at any PN in the system. For example, if five processing nodes are interfaced with the radar equipment, then path P1 in figure 12.5, which performs track analysis and updation, could be created at any of these five processing nodes. A path P_i is characterized by its arrival time, worst-case execution time, and deadline. Once a particular path is created, its execution time and deadline are known. Each processing node uses both static table-driven and dynamic planning-based schedulers, as illustrated in figure 12.8. In the case of multiprocessor PNs, these schedulers run on separately allocated processors, whereas they run as tasks on uniprocessor PNs. The static scheduler dispatches paths based on the precomputed schedule stored in the form of a table. The processors invoke resource reclaiming algorithms at the completion of each of their tasks. The resource reclaiming algorithm running in conjunction with the dynamic scheduler informs that scheduler of the total amount of time reclaimed. The resource reclaiming algorithm running in conjunction with the static scheduler identifies holes in the schedule

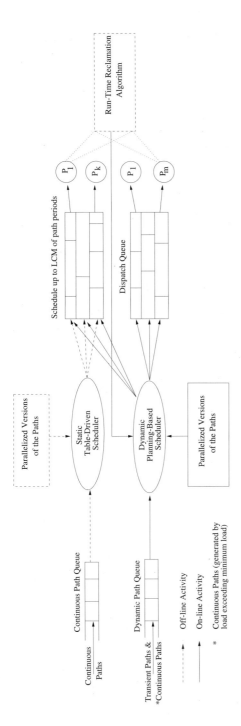

Figure 12.8
Scheduling mechanism at a processing node in ATCS

stored in the dispatch table and picks up dynamically arriving paths to be executed in these holes.

12.6   Resource Management

In this section, we briefly present techniques for effective scheduling of dynamic paths and present strategies for enhancing system performance through resource reclaiming.

12.6.1   Scheduling

The first step in the description of the scheduling strategy is the classification of paths based on their arrival characteristics. All the transient paths in the system are triggered by events and therefore have unpredictable arrival characteristics. The rate of occurrence of these triggering events is also unknown in advance. Therefore it is possible to have any number of concurrent executions of these transient paths. A dynamic planning-based scheduling approach is employed to schedule such paths. We assume that there is enough computational power in the system to schedule all the paths generated when there are fewer than 2,600 flight plans and 700 active tracks per center airspace region. For this particular load, the cycle deadline and periodicity of the continuous paths can be computed. Therefore, a static table-driven scheduling approach can be employed to precompute a schedule for these paths. The actual potential load is unbounded, however, and any load in excess of the above specifications can generate continuous paths in excess of those required to carry the minimum load. These additional paths are treated as dynamically arriving paths and scheduled by the dynamic planning-based scheduler.

12.6.2   Resource Reclaiming

In the scheduler depicted in figure 12.8, the restriction vector (RV) algorithms described in chapter 3 are used for resource reclaiming in conjunction with the dynamic planning-based scheduler mentioned above. This scheduler provides the necessary restriction vectors for use by the RV algorithm.

12.7   Summary

In this chapter, we have outlined a solution to the air traffic control system problem. In our solution, we have adopted the notion of a node that represents the functional abstraction of any facility (center, TRACON, or airport tower) in the actual air traffic control system. Our first-level abstraction of the system has been represented as a collection of interacting functional modules and shared information stores. Our solution has addressed the crucial issues of scheduling, coordination, interfacility communication, and fault tolerance. It has the following important features:

• The need for representing the system in terms of the dynamic path-based paradigm has been discussed. The system has been completely specified in terms of dynamic paths, and the characteristics of these paths have been identified based on the problem specification.

• A scheduling strategy that combines both off-line and on-line scheduling techniques has been described and the need to use paths as scheduling entities has been discussed. Resource reclaiming algorithms have also been identified to improve system performance.

• For efficient interfacility communication, message traffic has been classified based on criticality and periodicity, and separate techniques have been presented for managing the two types of traffic. We have also addressed the problem of system tolerance of link failures.

• The most critical tasks in the system have been identified, and based on their characteristics, techniques have been identified to address their fault tolerance requirements individually.

References

[1] T. S. Perry. "In search of the future of air traffic control." *IEEE Spectrum,* vol. 34, no. 8, pp. 18–35, Aug. 1997.

[2] R. Sriram, G. Manimaran, and C. Siva Ram Murthy. "Air traffic control system." Technical report, Department of Computer Science and Engineering, Indian Institute of Technology, Madras, Jan. 1998. Presented at the IEEE Intl. Workshop on Parallel and Distributed Real-Time Systems, Orlando, FL, 1998.

Acronyms

CBR	Constant Bit Rate
CSMA	Carrier Sense Multiple Access
DCR	Deterministic Collision Resolution
DOD-P	Preorder Deadline-based Protocol
DVRMP	Distance Vector Multicast Routing Protocol
EDF	Earliest Deadline First
FDDI	Fiber Distributed Data Interface
IGMP	Internet Group Management Protocol
IP	Internet Protocol
LAN	Local Area Network
LLF	Least Laxity First
LVDF	Least Value Density First
MAC	Medium Access Control
MBone	Multicast Backbone
MIN	Multistage Interconnection Network
OSPF	Open Shortest Path First
PBCSMA	Preemption Based CSMA
PIM	Protocol Independent Multicast
QoS	Quality of Service
RMS	Rate Monotonic Scheduling
RSVP	Reservation Protocol
RV	Restriction Vector
SDP	Session Directory Protocol
TCP	Transmission Control Protocol
TDMA	Time Division Multiple Access
TTL	Time-To-Live
UDP	User Datagram Protocol
VBR	Variable Bit Rate
VTCSMA	Virtual Time CSMA

Index